Environmental Law in Development

NEW HORIZONS IN ENVIRONMENTAL LAW

Series Editors: Kurt Deketelaere, *Professor of Law and Director, Institute of Environmental and Energy Law, University of Leuven, Belgium* and Zen Makuch, *Department of Environmental Science and Technology, Imperial College, London, UK*

Environmental law is an increasingly important area of legal research. Given the increasingly interdependent web of global society and the significant steps being made towards environmental democracy in decision-making processes, there are few people that are untouched by environmental lawmaking processes.

At the same time, environmental law is at a crossroads. The command and control methodology that evolved in the 1960s and 1970s for air, land and water protection may have reached the limit of its environmental protection achievements. New life needs to be injected into our environmental protection regimes. This new series seeks to press forward the boundaries of environmental law through innovative research into environmental protection standards, procedures, alternative instruments and case law. Adopting a wide interpretation of environmental law, it will include contributions from both leading and emerging European and international scholars.

Titles in the series include:

Whaling Diplomacy
Defining Issues in International Environmental Law
Alexander Gillespie

EU Climate Change Policy
The Challenge of New Regulatory Initiatives
Edited by Marjan Peeters and Kurt Deketelaere

Environmental Law in Development
Lessons from the Indonesian Experience
Edited by Michael Faure and Nicole Niessen

Environmental Law in Development

Lessons from the Indonesian Experience

Edited by

Michael Faure

Professor of Comparative and International Environmental Law, University of Maastricht, The Netherlands

and

Nicole Niessen

Lecturer of Comparative Administrative Law, University of Maastricht, The Netherlands

NEW HORIZONS IN ENVIRONMENTAL LAW

Edward Elgar

Cheltenham, UK • Northampton, MA, USA

Published by
Edward Elgar Publishing Limited
Glensanda House
Montpellier Parade
Cheltenham
Glos GL50 1UA
UK

Edward Elgar Publishing, Inc.
136 West Street
Suite 202
Northampton
Massachusetts 01060
USA

A catalogue record for this book
is available from the British Library

Library of Congress Cataloguing in Publication Data

Environmental law in development : lessons from the Indonesian experience
edited by Michael G. Faure and Nicole Niessen.
p. cm—(New horizons in environmental law series)
Includes bibliographical references and index.
1. Environmental law—Indonesia. 2. Environmental law—Developing countries. I. Faure, Michael (Michael G.) II. Niessen, Nicole, III. Series
KNW3127.E58 2006
344.59804′6—dc22

2006040149

ISBN-13: 978 1 84542 519 7
ISBN-10: 1 84542 519 7

Typeset by Cambrian Typesetters, Camberley, Surrey
Printed and bound in Great Britain by MPG Books Ltd, Bodmin, Cornwall

Contents

Contributors

Michael Faure, Maastricht University, The Netherlands

Aalt Willem Heringa, Maastricht University, The Netherlands

Nicole Niessen, Maastricht University, The Netherlands

Marjan Peeters, Maastricht University, The Netherlands

Takdir Rahmadi, Andalas University, Padang, Indonesia

Daud Silalahi, Padjadjaran University, Bandung, Indonesia

Frits Stroink, Maastricht University, The Netherlands

Andri G. Wibisana, Maastricht University, The Netherlands

Abbreviations

ABDL	Leadership for Environment and Development
AWB	Algemene Wet Bestuursrecht
BACT	Best Available Control Technology
BAPEDAL	National Environmental Impact Management Agency (Indonesia)
BAT	Best Available Technology
BATNEEC	Best Available Technology Not Entailing Excessive Costs
BOD	Biological/Biochemical Oxygen Demand
BREF	BAT Reference Document
CBA	Cost Benefit Analysis
CBD	Convention on Biological Diversity
CEA	Cost Effective Analysis
CEMS	Continuous Emissions Monitoring System
CLC	Civil Liability for Oil Pollution Damage
CO_2	Carbon dioxide
EAP	Environmental Action Plan
EC	European Communities
ECHR	European Convention on Human Rights
ECtHR	European Court of Human Rights
EIA	Environmental Impact Assessment
ELR	European Law Review
EMA 1997	Environmental Management Act
EMAS	Environmental Management and Audit Scheme
EPA	Environmental Protection Agency
EQS	Environmental Quality Standard
ERA	Environmental Risk Assessment
ERC	Emission Reduction Credit
EU	European Union
FAQ	Frequently Asked Questions
GALA	General Administrative Law Act in the Netherlands (AWB)
GR	Government Regulation
ICEL	Indonesian Centre for Environmental Law
ICJ	International Court of Justice
IMF	International Monetary Fund
IMO	International Maritime Organization

IPPC	Integrated Pollution Prevention and Control
KISS	Koordinoni, Integrari, Simplifikan, Sinteronisari
KKN	Korupsi, Kolusi, Nepotisme
LAER	Lowest Available Emission Reduction
MB	Marginal Benefit
MC	Marginal Costs
MCA	Marginal Costs of (pollution) Abatement
MEC	Marginal External Costs
METRO	Maastricht European Institute for Transnational Legal Research
MSC	Marginal Social Costs
NAAQS	National Ambient Air Quality Standards (US)
NBER	National Bureau for Economic Research
NGO	Non Governmental Organization
No	Number
OECD	Organization for Economic Cooperation and Development
P	Price
POP	Persistent Organic Pollutants
RAAC	Regional Autonomy Advisory Council (Indonesia)
RACT	Reasonable Available Control Technology
RGA	Regional Government Act
RHOC	Regional House of Representatives (in Indonesia)
s.	Section
SB	Social Benefit
SMS	Safe Minimum Standard
TEV	Total Economic Value
UK	United Kingdom
UN	United Nations
UNCLOS	United Nations Convention on the Law of the Sea
US	United States
VROM	Het ministerie van Volkshuisvesting, Ruimtelijke Ordening en Milieubeheer (Netherlands Ministry of the Environment)
WM	Wet Milieubeheer (Environmental Management Act – The Netherlands)
WRI	World Resources Institute
WTP	Willingness to Pay

1. Introduction

Michael Faure and Nicole Niessen

1. PROBLEM DEFINITION: REASONS FOR THIS BOOK

Many legal systems, both in the north and in the south have for decades been struggling with the question what the optimal legal and policy instruments are to implement environmental policy. In the north, stimulated by international conventions and (especially in the EU) by European directives one could discern a tendency to refine the use of legal instruments. On the one hand environmental policy today in the north is no longer merely based on the command and control type instruments of regulation, but is moving increasingly to the more market-oriented instruments such as environmental taxes and emission trading. Also environmental liability gains increasing importance. A second trend is undoubtedly that environmental law has moved away from the mere sectoral approach towards a more integrated approach. This integration can on the one hand be seen in the legal process where, for instance, the licensing procedure needs increasingly to take into account the effects of an activity on various components of the environment; on the other hand integration in some cases also means a tendency towards changing the form of legislation. Hence one can see many consolidated environmental acts and in some cases even environmental codes.

The question which is rarely addressed in the literature is to what extent these tendencies in environmental law and policy in the north are also typical of the development of environmental law in the south and more particularly in developing countries. Of course a lot of attention has been paid to the way in which environmental law can be developed in an efficient manner, but it apparently remains difficult to put that theoretical knowledge into practice. Moreover, the question also arises whether developing countries are ready to implement the new developments from the north like integration of environmental law and the use of market-oriented instruments. In addition the question arises, especially within larger developing countries to what extent environmental policy (standard setting and enforcement) should be regulated at the central level or rather at decentralized levels.

It is our aim to address some of these issues with respect to environmental law in development by looking on the one hand at theoretical issues and on the other hand at one specific case, namely Indonesia. It seems indeed interesting to test why some of the lessons concerning the development of environmental law have apparently not resulted in an efficient environmental policy yet. Indonesia provides in that respect a highly interesting case study since it has had an Environmental Management Act since 1982. However, this Environmental Management Act, which was not considered satisfactory, was revised in 1997 when a new Environmental Management Act no. 23 of 1997 was promulgated. However, both acts have as a characteristic that many provisions refer to implementing regulations which should provide further details. To a large extent the regulatory authorities apparently failed to promulgate these implementing regulations as a result of which a debate arose on a complete revision of the Act no. 23 of 1997, even before it had effectively been implemented.

A key issue in a country as large as Indonesia is obviously how administrative tasks in environmental law and policy, for example, for standard setting but also for inspection, monitoring and enforcement should be divided. Hence, a major question is whether a revision of the Environmental Management Act can be well-attuned to the Act on decentralization of government. A difficulty in that respect is, moreover, that apparently the latest Regional Autonomy Act (Act no. 22 of 1999) will be subject to revision as well. However, at a general level one can examine how specific powers and competencies can be best divided between on the one hand the central authorities and on the other hand decentralized authorities within the framework of a unitary state (presuming that Indonesia is to remain a unitary state which, however, allows for various degrees of regional autonomy).

Moreover, a traditional problem with countries as large as Indonesia where environmental law is still at an early stage of development, is how adequate monitoring and enforcement can be guaranteed. This calls for an adequate inspection system, whereby the question arises what kind of authorities should be competent to inspect, control and monitor compliance with environmental legislation. As of 1986, Indonesia has emphasized the role of its Environmental Inspection Agency (BAPEDAL) in this matter. Starting as a unit that operates from Jakarta, in recent years it has grown into an agency with several (decentralized) branches throughout the Indonesian archipelago. These efforts notwithstanding, effective monitoring and enforcement are still remote objectives. Obviously, a new Environmental Management Act will further strengthen the technical and administrative capacities of an environmental inspection agency (whether this be named BAPEDAL in the future or not). On the other hand, the question also arises whether alternatives to traditional enforcement (command and control) by public authorities can be implemented as well.

In addition to the public enforcement schemes which will remain necessary in any system of environmental law, the question arises whether one could use more flexible, often called 'modern' instruments of environmental law and policy, that rely more on the personal responsibility of the actors in environmental law. Typical instruments in that respect are the environmental and management audit schemes (EMAS), but also environmental covenants (also referred to as environmental agreements) between public authorities and industry. It has often been held that these kinds of agreement, whereby the regulated parties/activities are, even at an early stage, involved in standard setting, will make them more involved with environmental law and therefore lead to a higher degree of compliance. Again, the Environmental Management Act of 1997 contained possibilities of environmental audits and environmental dispute resolution, but apparently these provisions have hardly been enforced in Indonesia so far.

It is therefore the aim of this book to provide on the one hand some general insights on issues that arise at the moment of constructing environmental legislation in developing countries, and on the other hand to examine in a very specific way what type of environmental legislation might be suitable for Indonesia. We believe that this approach may lead to interesting insights also with respect to the question of whether specific legal and policy tools that are appropriate for the north are appropriate for developing countries as well. This book therefore aims at gaining new theoretical insights which may indicate how environmental law should be shaped in an optimal way to remedy pollution problems in developing countries. At the same time the book is also policy oriented since the discussion of the revision of the Environmental Management Act of 1997 in Indonesia can show at a very concrete level what type of legislation is particularly suited as an environmental policy tool in a developing country.

2. HISTORY AND ORIGINS OF THIS BOOK

This book originates from the long-standing cooperation between various Indonesian and European institutions that led to the realization of the research project which was the origin of this book. The editors of this book (Michael Faure and Nicole Niessen) have cooperated with the Indonesian Ministry for the Environment and with the Indonesian Centre for Environmental Law (ICEL).

The background for this book was the specific desire of the Indonesian Ministry of the Environment to revise the Environmental Management Act no. 23 of 1997 and to receive some input from European scholars in that respect. To that end, in 2001 a project proposal emerged which was submitted to the Netherlands Ministry of the Environment (VROM). It was decided that Dutch scholars from the Maastricht European Institute for Transnational Legal Research (METRO) would provide assistance in the revision process of the Environmental Management Act of 1997. Within the framework of this project our Indonesian counterparts (mostly legal scholars and staff employees of the Ministry engaged in the revision of the Environmental Management Act in Indonesia) visited METRO in January 2004. On that occasion a workshop was prepared to be held in Indonesia (Bogor) in August 2004 where both Indonesian and European academics presented specific proposals for the reform of the Indonesian Environmental Management Act no. 23 of 1997. More than fifteen papers were presented by various academics. For the most part, the European participants presented ideas on which reactions were formulated by the Indonesian participants with respect to the usefulness of the proposals in the reform process in Indonesia. As a result of an editorial review process, the papers were rewritten after the conference and a selection was made of the chapters presented in this book.

3. METHODOLOGY

As we have already indicated various approaches were followed in the different chapters presented in this book.

3.1 Legal Multidisciplinary

A legal multidisciplinary approach has been followed by many authors since the problem of developing environmental law is so important that various legal disciplines should be used to provide a full picture. Environmental law has always been known as a discipline which covers various areas of law. The following legal disciplines have therefore been used and combined:

- Constitutional law and human rights: it seems important that the literature on the relationship between environmental law and human rights is taken into account in the revision of the Environmental Management Act. In the north (especially in Europe, but also in the US) environmental protection is increasingly formulated as an actionable human right, also subject to judicial review. Hence the question arises whether this tendency to address environmental pollution in terms of human rights protection is also useful in the context of a developing country.
- Environmental principles: in the north increasingly attention is paid to – internationally agreed upon – principles of environmental law, such as the polluter pays principle, the principle of prevention and the precautionary principle. Again the question arises to what extent these impor-

tant but still rather vague principles can be considered as important tools in the development of environmental law and policy in a developing country like Indonesia. Does it make any sense to incorporate principles like these when revising an Environmental Management Act?

- As has already been indicated, in the north attention has been paid to issues of integration, coordination and harmonization of environmental law. Thereby attention is on the one hand paid to the contents of the integration (internal and external integration), but also to issues of form, like codification. The question again arises whether this tendency towards integration of environmental law is also a realistic perspective for a developing country like Indonesia.
- International law: clearly the reform process in a developing country like Indonesia should take into account international developments. Indeed, developing countries like Indonesia are also partners in international conventions and hence have the obligation to implement them. Thus a reform process may lead to increasing compliance with international environmental agreements and on the other hand this compliance may increase the quality of national environmental legislation in developing countries.
- Administrative law: clearly an important part of environmental law still is (as a result of the use of licences under command and control regulation) administrative law. Hence the question arises what the specific competences of administrative authorities are in the area of standard setting, whether rather general rules or specific conditions in licences should be used and whether the enforcement is to be of an administrative nature.
- Criminal law: it may be clear that effective prevention of environmental pollution will only be possible if an adequate system of enforcement can also be organized and if the criminal law can be structured in such a way that it addresses the various pollution problems in a balanced manner through adequate criminal provisions. In this respect attention also has to be paid to the interdependencies between administrative and criminal law enforcement.
- Liability law: a crucial issue undoubtedly is how environmental pollution damage can be compensated; what type of liability (negligence/strict liability) rule needs to be used? How can victims bring a suit and should compulsory insurance be introduced?
- Decentralization: all of the previous issues have in common that the question can be asked whether administrative regulation or enforcement should take place at the central level or at the regional or even local level. These issues of decentralization play an important role in any state, regardless of whether it has a federal or a unified structure.

Indonesia, a unitary state, has as a result of various laws on decentralization (also under consideration) moved increasingly in the direction of decentralization. The question, however, arises how the political wish to grant more autonomy to regional and local authorities can be reconciled with the demands of effective environmental policy.

3.2. Comparative Approach

This book clearly places much emphasis on legal comparison. We have already indicated that relevant international conventions will be examined, but also all of the above-mentioned aspects will be approached from a comparative perspective. This comparative perspective entails that in formulating suggestions for this revision process lessons/experiences from various legal systems will be taken into account.

3.3. Multidisciplinary

Obviously, the development of environmental law depends upon many factors, some of which are not necessarily legal. Still, the central subject of this book being environmental law in development, the main focus will be on how the law should be shaped in order to provide optimal protection against environmental pollution in the context of a developing country like Indonesia. However, various other disciplines can also be useful in providing answers to that question. Regarding the integration of environmental law or decentralization issues, for instance, the literature on public administration is relevant. And as far as the functioning, for example, of liability rules or various other environmental tools and instruments is concerned, much research has been conducted within the so-called 'law and economics' tradition. Indeed, economists see the role of environmental law mainly as an instrument to remedy the 'externality' (external effects) caused by environmental pollution. Economic analysis has also indicated what types of legal and policy instruments are most suitable in specific circumstances to provide this optimal remedy. Economic analysis has, for instance, developed criteria indicating under which circumstances regulation will provide more efficient results than liability rules. Therefore, economic analysis of law has also been used by various contributors to this book.

4. FRAMEWORK OF THE PROJECT

As indicated above, the project which inspired this book was performed by the Maastricht European Institute for Transnational Legal Research (METRO) in collaboration with the Indonesian Ministry for the Environment (Jakarta,

Indonesia). The project was financed and supported by the Netherlands Ministry for the Environment (VROM). The European researchers engaged in the project all participate within the Ius Commune Research School and have conducted their research within the framework of that school. The Ius Commune Research School is a collaboration between the Universities of Amsterdam, Leuven, Maastricht and Utrecht and focuses on the role of law in integration processes.

5. STRUCTURE OF THIS BOOK

After this introduction by the editors, the relationship between human rights and environmental legislation is discussed by Aalt Willem Heringa (Chapter 2). Then Andri Wibisana discusses the way in which environmental principles can be incorporated into environmental legislation, by focusing specifically on the polluter pays principles, the principle of prevention and the precautionary principle (Chapter 3). The implications of international conventions for domestic environmental law are analysed by Daud Silalahi (Chapter 4). The important issue of integration of environmental law is addressed at a general level by Marjan Peeters (Chapter 5) and with respect to the Indonesian experience by Takdir Rahmadi (Chapter 6). The relationship between decentralization issues and environmental policy is analysed in the contribution by Nicole Niessen, especially with reference to the case of Indonesia (Chapter 7). The following chapters deal with enforcement issues. Administrative supervision and enforcement of environmental law is discussed by Frits Stroink (Chapter 8), whereas Michael Faure presents a new model for the criminalization of environmental harm and discusses the implications of that model for a developing country like Indonesia (Chapter 9). Michael Faure, Marjan Peeters and Andri Wibisana provide a general overview of economic instruments like environmental taxes and emission trading. In particular they discuss to what extent these market-based instruments can be considered as useful policy tools within the context of a developing country like Indonesia (Chapter 10). Concluding remarks and an outlook that attempts to formulate some lessons from the chapters presented in this book are formulated by the editors Michael Faure and Nicole Niessen (Chapter 11). The text of the Indonesian Environmental Management Act (Act no. 23 of 1997) is provided in an Appendix.

6. CONTRIBUTORS

The contributors to this book originate on the one hand from Europe (Michael Faure, Aalt Willem Heringa, Nicole Niessen, Marjan Peeters, Frits Stroink) and on the other hand from Indonesia (Takdir Rahmadi, Daud Silalahi and Andri Wibisana). The European contributors – and also Andri Wibisana – are all connected to the Faculty of Law at Maastricht University and most of them more particularly to the Maastricht European Institute for Transnational Legal Research (METRO). A complete list of contributors and their affiliation is provided after the table of contents.

7. WORDS OF THANKS

As editors of this book we are grateful to all those who made both the project which constituted the origin of this book and also the book itself possible. First of all we would like to thank the Netherlands Ministry for the Environment (VROM) for generous support for the project and more particularly Mr Hubert Menalda van Schouwenburg for stimulating cooperation. Without his continuing efforts to make this project a success it would have been impossible to achieve this result. We are also grateful to all those who supported this project on the Indonesian side, either financially or with practical help. We refer particularly to Mr Hoetomo and Mrs Vivien Rosa of the Indonesian Ministry of the Environment and to Professor Koesnadi Hardjasoemantri, the leader of the Indonesian delegation. We are also grateful to all those who contacted our Indonesian counterparts even when (as a result of political instability) direct contacts between Europe and Indonesia were sometimes difficult. In this respect we are especially grateful to Dr Sebastiaan Pompe of the IMF in Jakarta and to Mrs Barbara van Hellemond of the Netherlands Embassy in Jakarta (Indonesia).

In addition we are grateful to all those who made both the conference in Bogor and the publication of the book possible. We owe special thanks to our research assistant Anita Jolink who reviewed the footnotes and the referencing. Finally we also owe thanks to Marina Jodogne and Yleen Simonis of the secretariat of the Maastricht European Institute for Transnational Legal Research (METRO) for editorial assistance and the preparation of this book for publication.

The texts were finalized in January 2005, so developments after that date could not be taken into account.

Michael Faure
Nicole Niessen
Maastricht, January 2005

2. Human rights and general principles and their importance as a legislative technique. Do they matter in legislation? An analysis with specific reference to environmental protection

Aalt Willem Heringa

1. INTRODUCTION

The purpose of this chapter is to show the usefulness of inserting general principles or even fundamental rights in legislation in a variety of areas. The assumption is that it can be considered appropriate in legislation to follow a pattern of general clauses, more specific clauses and subsequently more detailed clauses which need to be capable of regular amendment and adaptation to new circumstances.

The general idea I will put forward is that a general clause (or general clauses) can be helpful in various ways. Such an approach indicates to the courts and the executive how, and in what vein, the detailed provisions in the primary and subordinate legislation must be applied and interpreted. Executors and courts always meet unforeseen circumstances and possible lacunae in legislation; it seems therefore wise to give them guidance in how to resolve these when they occur.

My proposals therefore do not simply or only reflect the idea that legislation set up in this manner, descending from a level of generality to very specific and detailed clauses, is the best way of making legislation, but I start primarily from the assumption that general clauses allow the legislature better to steer and control action by the executive and application and interpretation by the courts.

Added to this argument, and derived from the idea of the primacy of the legislature, which is therefore under an obligation to provide as much guidance as possible to the executive and the courts, is the assumption that the formulation of basic general principles can aid legal certainty. Because they can help in the interpretive process, legal certainty is certainly promoted when the application process is founded upon coherent general principles. Even when we accept that legal principles may point to conflicting applications, it seems better to reconcile conflicts also at the level of applicable principles instead of solely at the level of day to day application. Reconciliation through general principles will prove essential to the quality of the debate and will provide more clarity for future cases and might add to greater acceptance.

The formulation of relevant 'directive' rights or principles does not necessarily have to take place in all legislative acts regulating a specific economic or social field. They might be found or formulated in a constitutional document, or in a preamble to the constitution, or in legislative acts laying down general principles common to more specific primary or secondary legislation.

The idea of promoting a legislative activity to identify and draft underlying general principles is not solely based upon separation of powers arguments: namely that the legislature should direct and be the foundation of further executive subordinate rule making and executive application. It is also linked to the finding that in well-developed constitutional systems the courts, in the absence of explicitly formulated general principles, occasionally need fundamental principles to lead the way to solutions and to be the coordinating factor in order to harmonize solutions and identify common bases and common solutions, without the risk of arbitrarily picking solutions and having insufficient respect for the coherence of the law. And general principles help us in detecting coherency and leading the way in new areas of conflict.

This is nothing new and nothing very revolutionary: what might differ from one country to another is the intensity with which courts will search for underlying fundamental principles. That has been the subject of much research: here I will make the point that legal practice has shown that without leaving it simply to the courts, we should endeavour to include fundamental principles in legislation.

2. INTERPRETATION

We know from studying the case law of constitutional courts, and of international courts such as the European Court of Justice and the European Court of Human Rights, that courts generally tend to found judgments in difficult cases upon general underlying assumptions, theories and principles. This is particularly true when no hard fixed specific rule seems to exist and a case must still be decided. What has also become apparent from constitutional and European courts' case law is that in the absence of general open-ended clauses containing the fundamental principles underlying the legislation, the courts will also try to deduce them from the text. For that reason it might seem wise to anticipate this attitude which is natural to many courts and to assist them in finding and interpreting general underlying principles.

Allow me to give an example from the Dutch and German courts: put before the courts were claims of children, born out of wedlock, who wanted to know the identity of their biological fathers: they invoked a right to be informed of their biological origins. The Dutch Court of Cassation honoured their requests.[1] The interpretation method it employed was that they noted that the Constitution protected various specific rights with respect to private life and privacy. From these rights the Court derived a general underlying principle, of which these rights were the expression. The general principle was the right to personhood: a general principle as to the protection and development of one's personality. From this general underlying principle it seems evident that other sub-principles or rights can be derived. If we take it that the legislature intended to guarantee and build a coherent model, this seems to be a logical interpretation method. And in the case of these illegitimate children the Court accepted that they had a constitutional right to have access to data with respect to their biological identity: this right flowed from the general unwritten constitutional principle.

This principle was an unwritten general principle; in Germany the Constitutional Court accepted a similar right, but was able to found it upon a constitutional provision which contained the general principle: the dignity of man.[2] In that respect the Court was given guidance by the constitutional lawmaker which had taken care to formulate a general principle underlying the Constitution and steering the process of constitutional interpretation.

In my opinion resorting to this technique whenever appropriate certainly deserves our consideration; and I believe that in the area of environmental law general principles can be detected and can also be formulated with sufficient precision so as to allow for guidance and interpretative help.

3. LEGISLATIVE TECHNIQUE

Using this technique of descending generality, or put differently of resorting to explicitly formulated goals and principles, is not only a question of legislative beauty of design, but also an approach that captures eventualities and improves upon lawmaking. It will help to determine what to regulate on what level with what degree of specificity. It is also an incentive for the legislature

---

1 Hoge Raad, 15 April 1994, *Nederlands Juristenblad*, 1994, 608.

2 Bundesverfassungs Gericht (BVerfG; German Constitutional Court), 31 January 1989, 79 BVerfGE 256.

to gradually and steadily improve upon the level of protection. The general principles can be taken as the beacon by which to orient oneself about where to go and what to do; they might also serve as starting points of societal and legislative discussion about how to proceed and what to do next. They can enlighten society about its ambitions and goals and about the general elements that keep the body of law together and ensure coherence and continued improvement.

Therefore apart from the purpose of allowing the executive and the courts to come up with enlightened applications and interpretations within the spirit and purpose of specific provisions, there is also an argument in the context of the quality of legislation and legislative debate and legislative coherence. They are being served by also paying attention to the formulation of general underlying principles.

4. APPLICATION IN ENVIRONMENTAL LAW: LEARNING FROM THE EUROPEAN COURT OF HUMAN RIGHTS

In essence, my inspiration for promoting this legislative method is based upon examples of constitutional interpretation by constitutional courts, but also derives from witnessing the European Court of Human Rights' reliance upon this 'general principles-based approach' as well as developing general principles requirements in the area of environmental law. This is also the case in other areas, but for the purposes of this chapter I will specifically and in greater detail focus upon the environmentally relevant issues and judgments.

4.1. General Principles Approach by the European Court of Human Rights

The European Court of Human Rights was established under the European Convention of Human Rights; this Convention was drafted in the context of the Council of Europe. This organization encompasses 46 European states (including the 25 member states of the European Union). Individuals have the right to petition this Court whenever they can claim to be the victim of a human rights violation by any of the Contracting States. Judgments of the Court are binding: whenever the Court rules that a state has committed a violation, the state is under a duty to afford the compensation which the Court might order it to pay and to undo the negative effects for the petitioner.

In the 50 years of its existence, the Court has gradually developed an immense case law in which it has also had to decide many issues for which it had to thoroughly interpret the Treaty. For this the Court developed several maxims of interpretation; also in the process of interpretation coherence and continuity must be carefully guarded, which the Court has been doing.

First of all the Court has noted that the rights should be interpreted extensively and that the Convention is a dynamic treaty which needs to be adapted to changing circumstances.[3]

Secondly, the rights guaranteed in the Convention must be effective and not illusory rights.[4] This also means that the Contracting States must do everything possible to effectively ensure that rights can be enjoyed in practice. This rule therefore can also imply that positive obligations can be imposed upon states to actively interfere and protect. An illustrative example is that states can be compelled to provide for legal aid if an individual is hindered because of a lack of resources to fully and effectively enjoy the right to go to court and to have a fair trial.

Thirdly, the Court, when interpreting the Convention, takes into account the consensus among the Contracting States.[5] Recently this led the Court to extend the protection of transsexuals, because it had become clear that an increasing number of states was doing the same thing. This approach can therefore mean that gradually the scope of the Treaty will be widened, in areas like environmental law, if and when the Contracting States also seem to accept environmental protection as being part of a human rights approach.

Most clauses of the Convention contain specific and detailed provisions. However, the Court has, from the beginning, researched the underlying general principles. An example: Article 6 is about a variety of guarantees in the context of court proceedings. The Court has understood this to mean a general article protecting an access to courts as well as the notion of fair trial and equality of arms. Through this approach the Court was able to resolve many issues which might not have been covered by the letter of Article 6!

This also holds true of Article 8: Article 8 is solely about private life, family life, the home and correspondence. There is no reference to physical integrity, no mention of the environment, no reference to human autonomy or anything like it. However, the Court has interpreted Article 8 as also giving expression

---

3 An early example: the Tyrer case, ECtHR, 25 April 1978, A. vol. 26: 'the Convention is a living instrument which must be interpreted in the light of present day conditions. In the case now before it, the Court cannot but be influenced by the developments and commonly accept the standards in the penal policy of the Member States of the Council of Europe.' Further on this subject: Prebensen (2000, pp. 1123–37).

4 For example, ECtHR, 9 October 1979, A. vol. 32, Airey; 26 March 1985 A. vol. 91, *X and Y* v. *the Netherlands*.

5 On this method of interpretation, see Heringa (1996, pp. 108–45).

to a general principle of human autonomy and personhood. Please allow me a long quotation from a recent judgment. The case was about a severely ill and dying woman who claimed the right to be able to determine her own end and death. The Court denied her claim but at the same time adopted, based upon a long line of precedents, the following general principle interpretation of Article 8.

4.2. Applicability of Article 8 § 1 of the Convention

As the Court has had previous occasion to remark, the concept of 'private life' is a broad term not susceptible to exhaustive definition. It covers the physical and psychological integrity of a person.[6] It can sometimes embrace aspects of an individual's physical and social identity.[7] Elements such as, for example, gender identification, name and sexual orientation and sexual life fall within the personal sphere protected by Article 8.[8] Article 8 also protects a right to personal development, and the right to establish and develop relationships with other human beings and the outside world.[9] Although no previous case has established any right to self-determination as such as being contained in Article 8 of the Convention, the Court considers that the notion of personal autonomy is an important principle underlying the interpretation of its guarantees.

This judgment provides a good example of how the Court proceeds in a step by step way, but also ultimately looks for and finds a general principle which can lay the foundations for specific rights and is the ultimate rationale for the interpretation by the Court. That is, the Court tries to tie together all aspects of Article 8 and combines them in one general principle: in the context of Article 8, the right of self-determination and the notion of personal autonomy. In other future cases this general principle may give rise to further specific rights in concrete cases.

---

6 See *X and Y* v. *the Netherlands*, judgment of 26 March 1985, Series A no. 91, p. 11, § 22.

7 See *Mikulić* v. *Croatia*, no. 53176/99, § 53, ECHR 2002-I.

8 See, for example, *B.* v. *France*, judgment of 25 March 1992, Series A no. 232-C, pp. 53–4, § 63; *Burghartz* v. *Switzerland*, judgment of 22 February 1994, Series A no. 280-B, p. 28, § 24; *Dudgeon* v. *the United Kingdom*, judgment of 22 October 1981, Series A no. 45, pp. 18–19, § 41; and Laskey, Jaggard and Brown, judgment of 19 February 1997, Reports 1997–I, p. 131, § 36.

9 See, for example, Burghartz, cited above, opinion of the Commission, p. 37, § 47, and *Friedl* v. *Austria*, judgment of 31 January 1995, Series A no. 305-B, opinion of the Commission, p. 20, § 45.

4.3. The General Principles and their Role in Environment Cases

One of the first cases relevant and noteworthy in this area was the López Ostra case:[10] According to the facts of this case, the applicant lived in the vicinity of a heavily polluting chemical waste plant. The plant did not fully live up to the conditions imposed by permit and the local government had failed to take adequate measures. The Court opened by saying that:

> 51. Naturally, severe environmental pollution may affect individuals' well-being and prevent them from enjoying their homes in such a way as to affect their private and family life adversely, without, however, seriously endangering their health.
>
> At all events, the Court considers that in the present case, even supposing that the municipality did fulfil the functions assigned to it by domestic law (see paragraphs 27 and 28 above), it need only establish whether the national authorities took the measures necessary for protecting the applicant's right to respect for her home and for her private and family life under Article 8 (Art. 8) (see, among other authorities and mutatis mutandis, the X and Y v. the Netherlands judgment of 26 March 1985, Series A no. 91, p. 11, para. 23). Subsequently the Court investigated whether the State had failed to meet its positive obligations:
>
> 56. It has to be noted that the municipality not only failed to take steps to that end after 9 September 1988 but also resisted judicial decisions to that effect. In the ordinary administrative proceedings instituted by Mrs López Ostra's sisters-in-law it appealed against the Murcia High Court's decision of 18 September 1991 ordering temporary closure of the plant, and that measure was suspended as a result (see paragraph 16 above).
>
> Other State authorities also contributed to prolonging the situation. On 19 November 1991 Crown Counsel appealed against the Lorca investigating judge's decision of 15 November temporarily to close the plant in the prosecution for an environmental health offence (see paragraph 17 above), with the result that the order was not enforced until 27 October 1993 (see paragraph 22 above).
>
> 57. The Government drew attention to the fact that the town had borne the expense of renting a flat in the centre of Lorca, in which the applicant and her family lived from 1 February 1992 to February 1993 (see paragraph 21 above).
>
> The Court notes, however, that the family had to bear the nuisance caused by the plant for over three years before moving house with all the attendant inconveniences. They moved only when it became apparent that the situation could continue indefinitely and when Mrs López Ostra's daughter's paediatrician recommended that they do so (see paragraphs 16, 17 and 19 above). Under these circumstances, the municipality's offer could not afford complete redress for the nuisance and inconveniences to which they had been subjected.
>
> 58. Having regard to the foregoing, and despite the margin of appreciation left to the respondent State, the Court considers that the State did not succeed in striking a fair balance between the interest of the town's economic well-being – that of having a waste-treatment plant – and the applicant's effective enjoyment of her right to respect for her home and her private and family life. There has accordingly been a violation of Article 8 (art. 8).

---

[10] ECtHR, 9 December 1998, *López Ostra* v. *Spain*, A 303-C.

That is, the nuisance for the applicant and her family and the dangers to their health, combined with the failure of the state to adopt reasonable steps to protect these individual interests, led the Court to conclude that a violation had occurred. For the first time, an environmental issue was resolved under Article 8, giving rise to a violation of that same article.

A subsequent case in which the environmental issue was addressed by the Court was the Guerra case:[11] the complainants lived in the vicinity of a factory which they suspected of being involved in potentially dangerous activities. The problem was, however, that the government did not respond to questions for information and clarification with respect to the potentially hazardous impact.

The Court approached this issue from the perspective of Article 8 and reasoned that information of this kind is relevant in order for people to be able to take reasoned decisions with respect to their private life.

The Court said:

> 1. The Court considers that Italy cannot be said to have 'interfered' with the applicants' private or family life; they complained not of an act by the State but of its failure to act. However, although the object of Article 8 is essentially that of protecting the individual against arbitrary interference by the public authorities, it does not merely compel the State to abstain from such interference: in addition to this primarily negative undertaking, there may be positive obligations inherent in effective respect for private or family life (see the Airey v. Ireland judgment of 9 October 1979, Series A no. 32, p. 17, § 32).
>
> In the present case it need only be ascertained whether the national authorities took the necessary steps to ensure effective protection of the applicants' right to respect for their private and family life as guaranteed by Article 8 (see the López Ostra v. Spain judgment of 9 December 1994, Series A no. 303-C, p. 55, § 55).

That is also the issue of positive obligations.

Subsequently the Court took from the López Ostra case its principled statement about the applicability of Article 8.

> 2. The Court reiterates that severe environmental pollution may affect individuals' well-being and prevent them from enjoying their homes in such a way as to affect their private and family life adversely (see, *mutatis mutandis*, the López Ostra judgment cited above, p. 54, § 51). In the instant case the applicants waited, right up until the production of fertilisers ceased in 1994, for essential information that would have enabled them to assess the risks they and their families might run if they continued to live at Manfredonia, a town particularly exposed to danger in the event of an accident at the factory. The Court holds, therefore, that the respondent State did not fulfil its obligation to secure the applicants' right to respect for their private and family life, in breach of Article 8 of the Convention.

---

[11] ECtHR, 19 February 1998, *Guerra* v. *Italy*, Reports 1998-I.

There has consequently been a violation of that provision. Now it was not so much the direct environmental infringement of a private life, but a closely related procedural aspect that was at stake: the right to be informed.

This latter right is not used exclusively in the area of environmental issues but has been resorted to by the Court in other Article 8 cases as well: it is identical to the right to be informed about the identity of one's father, because it concerns information essential to making reasoned decisions about one's life. Another example in which the Court relied upon this right to be informed was in a case in which a former British soldier sought information about the level of radiation to which he had been exposed whilst in military service in the vicinity of nuclear tests.[12]

In a more recent judgment the Court had to decide about the noise generated by landing and departing planes at Heathrow Airport: the petitioners claimed that Article 8 had been violated by the extreme noise, especially during the night, and by the ensuing decreasing value of their homes (the Hatton case). In fact there were two judgments: one by a chamber of the Court, which found that Article 8 had been violated[13] and the second, in appeal by the Grand Chamber, and overruling the Chamber, concluding that no violation had occurred.[14] In an older case the Court had previously already decided with respect to the same airport that Article 8 was applicable in relation to noise and decreasing value of property, but it had also decided that the airport noise was not incompatible with the applicable treaties in that respect and that the UK had not exceeded its large margin of appreciation taking into account the economic interests that were at stake.[15]

Now to return to the Hatton case: a happy ending for the United Kingdom, because of the overruling by the Grand Chamber of the Chamber judgment that a violation had occurred. But still significant, because the Court actually did impose important requirements upon the UK government about how to operate in major environmental questions.

Why had the Chamber achieved a negative judgment? The reason for it was twofold: the level of noise during the night had increased, the government had failed to carry out research detailing the importance of night flights for the economy of the UK as well as assessing the effects of night flights on local residents' health and well-being. That is, the Chamber in fact introduced two major requirements in the context of environmental situations: first of all it looked into the seriousness of the infringement for which it is also important

---

[12] ECtHR, 9 June 1998, *McGinley and Egan* v. *the United Kingdom*, 1998-III.

[13] ECtHR, 2 October 2001, Hatton and others v. the United Kingdom (Hatton 1).

[14] ECtHR, 8 July 2003, Hatton and others v. the United Kingdom (Hatton 2).

[15] ECtHR, 21 February 1990, *Powell and Rayner* v. *the United Kingdom*; series A, vol. 172.

to note that, as the Chamber had noted, a deterioration had taken place in the level of noise. This is the substantive aspect.

The second requirement relates to procedure: if a serious infringement occurs and a deterioration has taken place, it is incumbent upon the government to carefully research all interests that are at stake. Because of the absence of such careful procedural effort the Chamber found a violation of Article 8!

However, the UK government appealed this decision and the Grand Chamber overruled. The Grand Chamber found that the applicants' private life was adversely affected and so was the scope for their enjoyment of the amenities of their respective homes. Since the noise was created by planes belonging to private companies and not by the state itself, the question is whether the state's responsibility in this environmental case arose from a failure to regulate private industry in a manner securing proper respect for the rights enshrined in Article 8. The question therefore is whether a fair balance was struck between the competing interests of the individuals affected by the night noise and the community as a whole.

Subsequently the Court distinguished between the López Ostra and Guerra cases on the one hand and the Hatton case on the other. The main distinction was that in the former two cases there had also been a failure by the domestic authorities to comply with domestic law. In López Ostra the waste treatment plant operated without a licence; and in Guerra the state was under an obligation under domestic law to provide the applicants with the requested information.

In the opinion of the Court this element of domestic irregularity is missing in the Hatton case: the number of night flights was fully in accordance with domestic law! In justification of the night flights the Court notes the arguments of the government: the economic interests of the operators of airlines and other enterprises as well as the economic interests of the country.

The Court then asks the question whether it should apply a strict scrutiny test or whether it should allow the state a larger margin of appreciation. Strict scrutiny had been applied before in the case of intrusions into private life (for example, the Dudgeon case with respect to criminal measures); however the Court finds that the normal rule should be applied, meaning that a state must give due consideration to particular interests, with the choice between the different ways and means of meeting this obligation left up to the state. The Court's supervisory function being of a subsidiary nature, it is limited to reviewing whether or not the particular solution adopted can be regarded as striking a fair balance.

Overall, the Court judges that the UK government had not overstepped their margin of appreciation, either substantially or procedurally. Although the Court showed leniency to the state in its overall assessment, the Hatton judgment clarified many issues and approaches by the Court, which will be useful for future issues and environmental matters.

Despite the prior examples of case law under Article 8 pertinent to environmental issues, it must be pointed out that the Court has also ruled that the European Convention of Human Rights does not include a specific right to environmental protection as such. Whenever a complaint is filed under Article 8 relating to an infringement of environmental protection, the Court requires a sufficient objective individual interest, tracing back to Article 8 issues. In every case the Court will investigate whether and to what extent the circumstances complained about affect or threaten the personal situation (home, health, etc.) of the applicant and for which the government can be held responsible.[16]

4.4. General Lessons

What is it that can be learned from the cases of the European Court?

First of all it is to be noted that environmental issues, affecting an individual's private life (physical integrity), health or home, or relating to autonomy or self-development, have to be interpreted and evaluated under Article 8 of the European Convention of Human Rights.

Secondly, such environmental issues can also entail that a state is under a positive obligation to afford protection or to undertake other appropriate action. This also means that a state cannot duck its responsibility by arguing that the infringement of one's private life is actually the consequence of the activities of private persons. What is relevant then is to find out whether the state can be expected to have undertaken appropriate protection and to have given sufficient protection.

Thirdly, the absence of state activities aimed at protecting a citizen is the more relevant when such absence is also due or related to non-compliance with domestic law. In these cases the Court is inclined to adopt a strict scrutiny test.

In the fourth place it is essential what exactly is the impact upon one's private life: does the interference actually intrude on the core of Article 8? Is the interference directly related to intrusive state measures? If such is the case, the Court seems inclined also to adopt a small margin of appreciation. This aspect probably implies that environmental cases do lead to the application of less strict scrutiny and the application of a larger margin of appreciation.

Fifthly, whatever the scrutiny applied, in cases in which a state is under a positive obligation, it must have addressed the relevant issues and given them under serious consideration. This means that at the very least a state must show that the particular individual interests have been the subject of review,

---

16 ECtHR, 22 May 2003, *Kyrtatos* v. *Greece*.

study and attention and have been balanced with the general interest that might have been at stake. Subsequently, the state must have shown that it has allowed for proper procedural steps: involvement of the enterprises and individuals concerned, appeal procedures, compensation procedures etc.

Finally, a state must be open and informative with respect to relevant data and in providing them to the citizens involved, so as to allow them to make reasoned and well-founded choices pertinent to their private lives. This Guerra criterion was also apparent in the Hatton case, in which the Court also took into account that those who lived in the vicinity of the airport and felt very much aggrieved by the noise and the disturbance of their sleep, could ask for compensation and sell their houses and move.

5. LESSONS FOR CODIFICATION PROJECTS

Evidently, I am aware of the fact that Article 8 is a provision in a treaty, which also explains the focus upon state responsibility and therefore upon developing the notion of positive obligations. However, the experiences under Article 8, in combination with my general remarks pertinent to constitutional interpretation and lawmaking, show in my opinion the wisdom of enriching substantive environmental laws with general clauses which can allow for general guidance and coherence. They also do justice to the primacy of the legislature, in showing the courts and the executive how to implement the legislative intentions in application and in interpretation.

It is self-evident that general clauses can never take the place of detailed and precise lawmaking and subordinate rule making. However, it is the combination that seems to work and be effective. The general clauses can be forward looking: can be relied upon to address unforeseen problems, to resolve gaps and maintain coherence and legislative intent. In combination with detailed clauses, a systematic system is constructed with an open mind as to the general model as well as the detailed intricacies.

In the area of human rights, from which I have drawn the inspiration for this approach, we can also witness some examples of codifications along the lines of this model.

I have already referred to the German Constitution, which contains some very basic notions which assist and allow the Constitutional Court to build a coherent interpretative model and to resolve hard cases which at first sight seem difficult to tackle, but can be dealt with on the basis of a careful analysis, taking into account these general basic values and principles. Which are they? The most prominent are: the dignity of man, the free democratic order, the separation of powers, democracy and the combative nature of the German democratic order. These principles lead the German courts in many instances in their interpretation. Maybe the Constitutional Court could also have come up with them in the absence of such clauses in the Constitution; however, I submit that a Court's legitimacy is greatly enhanced by general clauses to this effect. They also provide guidance to the other branches of government and thereby contribute to a coherent and legitimate constitutional and legislative model.

A second example is the Bill of Rights chapter in the future European Constitution: that is, the Charter adopted in Nice in 2000. Careful study of this Bill of Rights shows that its various chapters have indeed been based upon the general-specific model. Most of the parts start with a general clause which seems to contain the general principle: the section on equality and non-discrimination opens with a generally formulated open equality clause, after which follow various specific non-discrimination guarantees.

The Bill of Rights also opens, in a similar way to the German Constitution, with a general right to dignity clause; and the section on due process of law opens with a general clause about fair trial. In all instances: first, there is a general article containing the leading, underlying general principle, followed by more specific and detailed guarantees.

In that respect the EU Bill of Rights is a good example of modern constitutional lawmaking: taking into account the necessities of precise drafting as well as meeting the need for open clauses which articulate the underlying general principles and give direction to the overall interpretation of specific clauses and allow gaps to be filled and hard cases resolved.

6. HOW TO PROCEED IN ENVIRONMENTAL LAWMAKING?

Either in a constitutional document or in the general provisions of an environmental act one could consider taking up general principles. These could go further and should encompass more than what I have indicated has been discovered and achieved under the European Convention. The lessons to be learnt from the European Convention and its Article 8 are limited in that respect in that they are derived from Article 8, the individual right to private life. In the area of environmental law, however, there is more at stake than a simple direct relationship with this right.

Environmental law relates to the quality of life as such, to a healthy planet habitable also for future generations, and the survival of life on earth. Apart from legal principles directly related to individual rights, environmental law is also concerned with environmental legal principles, which also merit codification because they should be considered important directives for the application and interpretation of environmental law.

Article 8 of the European Convention, however important it might be, has at the same time a narrow focus on environmental issues. It focuses only on questions with a direct impact upon an individual's private life. This narrow focus showed itself in the Botta case. In this judgment the applicant complained that his private life and personal autonomy were at stake since in Italy insufficient facilities existed for disabled people to have access to beaches and holiday resorts because the Italian government had failed to provide facilities allowing access. The Court dismissed this complaint by declaring that Article 8 did not apply to his complaint because of the insufficient link between his private life and the omissions complained about.

This judgment will definitely also hold true for a variety of environmental issues: Article 8 requires a direct link between the environmental issue and personal consequences for private life. For that reason, the articulation in constitutions or documents of further underlying legal principles seems essential. In that respect, Article 8 of the European Convention is an example of how this approach might be fruitful, however limited its scope and however few the judgments.[17]

The general principles guiding the interpretation of the constitution and statutory laws can evidently be derived from a variety of sources: the constitution, treaties, legislation and unwritten law. To what extent this is permissible and legitimate depends on the domestic legal order. In France, for instance, the Constitution explicitly stipulates that the general principles which may be derived from legislation have constitutional status. Under this rule the courts can and indeed do derive basic principles from legislation and elevate them to constitutional principles. Subsequently these constitutional principles prevail over conflicting legislation and serve as a means of legislative interpretation and application.[18]

General principles guiding environmental law therefore do already exist in some constitutional models; however the existing principles seem to be mainly legal principles along the lines of generally recognized individual rights:

---

[17] See also the Kyrtatos case, *supra*, footnote 16.

[18] See: preamble of the 1946 Constitution (which is still valid under the present 1958 Constitution through the preamble to the latter constitution): 'the fundamental principles recognized by the laws of the Republic'. In Conseil Constitutionnel decision no. 71-44 DC of 16 July 1971 the Conseil ruled that among the fundamental principles recognized by the laws of the Republic and solemnly reaffirmed by the Constitution was the freedom of association, for this principle underlied the general provisions of a statute of 1901. Another example is CC Decision no. 77-87 DC of 23 November 1977 about the freedom of education as a principle, already to be found in the Finance Law of 1931, and a fundamental principle recognized by the laws of the Republic and therefore a principle of constitutional value.

human dignity, private autonomy, private life, physical integrity and similar principles.

Without detracting from that use it might be useful to go one step further and to articulate general environmental principles as well, even if they do not seem to have a direct impact upon an individual. In that context prominent examples are: a principle seeking a higher level of protection so that at least a guarantee can be built in against a worsening of environmental protection; and a principle that general environmental interests can be promoted and defended by non-governmental organizations. Or the principle that environmentally damaging measures deserve the highest scrutiny and careful analysis and a careful balancing with the relevant economic interests with the appropriate involvement of the individuals and organizations concerned.

General principles along the lines of Article 8 protect individual rights and interests; we do, also however, need to defend our common interests in terms less of the direct impact upon a particular individual and more in terms of the creeping and general impact upon society and mankind. It is for that reason that I submit that applicable general principles in the area of environmental protection also aim at protecting general common interests.

On the constitutional level as well as on the level of legislation efforts to do so are not very widespread: certainly it is not easy to distil the general principles and to articulate them with sufficient precision. However, it seems to be worth the effort. The Article 8 of the European Convention focus shows that courts can truly rely upon them and are able to undertake the effort themselves. Legislatures should have the primary task of assisting the courts so that the courts can seek further refinements, however: based upon constitutional or legislative principles.

REFERENCES

Heringa, A.W. (1996), 'The "Consensus Principle", the Role of "Common Law" in the ECHR Case Law', Maastricht Journal of European and Comparative Law, **3**, 108–45.

Prebensen, J. (2000), 'Evolutive Interpretation of the European Convention of Human Rights', in: P. Mahoney, F. Matsher, H. Petrzold and L. Wildhaber (eds), *Protecting Human Rights: The European Perspective*, Köln/Berlin/Bonn/München: Heymanns, pp. 1123–37.

3. Three principles of environmental law: the polluter-pays principle, the principle of prevention, and the precautionary principle

Andri G. Wibisana

1. INTRODUCTION

This chapter attempts to discuss three principles in environmental law, namely the polluter-pays principle, the preventive principle, and the precautionary principle. The discussion is intended to answer the question whether the existing Indonesian Environmental Management Act (Act No. 23 of 1997) has recognized those principles and how this Act interprets those principles. To answer the question, we need to discuss first what the principles mean exactly. In this case, several objectives of the principles will be put forward for discussion. After discussing those principles, we will analyse how the current act recognizes or interprets the principles. Several consequences of incorporating the principles into national legislation will also be discussed.

This chapter will discuss environmental policies from a law and economics perspective. In this regard, this chapter analyses the interpretations of the above-mentioned principles not only from a legal perspective, but also from an environmental economics perspective. Furthermore, this chapter will also address a crucial question as to why and how the principles should be incorporated into the environmental legislation of a developing country such as Indonesia. By answering this question, I try to show whether the principles have an important function in developing countries as well, although they have mainly been developed within the context of countries with a rather well-elaborated legal system.

After this introduction I will first discuss the polluter pays principle (Section 2); then I will discuss the preventive principle (Section 3) and the precautionary principle (Section 4). A few final observations conclude the chapter (Section 5). The reader should, however, be aware that within the context of this chapter I merely discuss environmental economics in as far as it is necessary to analyse and understand the polluter pays, preventive and precautionary principles. Economics is of course far more important for other domains of environmental law. To some extent environmental economics is also discussed in the chapter on economic instruments.[1]

2. THE POLLUTER-PAYS PRINCIPLE

2.1. The Origin of the Principle

One area of microeconomics, referred to as welfare economics, has paid a great deal of attention in exploring how the market can coordinate the decisions of utility-maximizing consumers and profit-maximizing producers so as to spontaneously generate an efficient allocation of resources. This efficiency is known as Pareto optimality, a situation where it is no longer possible to reallocate resources in such a way that we can make one person better off, without at the same time making someone else worse off.[2] This condition is to be reached under a competitive market without any sort of government intervention. However, most economists would agree that there are several factors contributing to the existence of market failures, among which are externalities.

An externality occurs when the decisions of an economic agent affect the decisions made by others directly rather than through market prices. In this case, the consumption of a consumer or the production of a producer has a direct effect on the consumption or production of others that is not reflected in the market price.[3] Costs borne by the agent conducting an economic activity are called private costs, while all costs imposed on other people by a consumption or production activity of that agent are called external costs. The sum of private costs and external costs is called social costs, reflecting all costs borne by society. An efficient level of output occurs when the price of a product is equal to the marginal social cost of production, that is, the marginal cost of private production plus the marginal social external cost. Inefficiency in the presence of externality is shown by the difference between private costs and social costs.[4]

Environmental problems are considered as a typical example of externality. Environmental pollution and other environmental externalities are generally negative. They reflect the absence of markets (no exchange through supply and demand) and of market prices for (some) environmental resources or

---

1 See Chapter 10 in this volume.

2 Griffiths and Wall (2000, p. 431).

3 Pindyck and Rubenfield (2001, p. 592). However, effects on other people that directly result from market price are not considered as externality.

4 Solberg (1982, p. 540).

services.[5] Moreover, the prices of many resources often do not reflect the full costs involved in their use. In this regard, the use of environmental resources and its impacts have not been appropriately considered by the firm's decision-makers. As a result, the firm will produce output that maximizes its private profit, regardless of the large external costs it potentially imposes on society. Obviously, the case of externalities exhibits a situation where competitive unregulated markets lead to inefficiency.

The internalization of environmental externalities is the main objective of the polluter-pays principle.[6] Economists believe that only when external costs have been fully considered will firms act so as to prevent market failures and move to a socially optimal level of output.[7] Consequently, from an economic point of view, the existence of environmental law or policy should be primarily directed at remedying the externality, namely by forcing the firm to internalize external costs in order to eliminate the difference between marginal social costs and marginal private costs.[8] The fact that in the absence of law there will be no adequate incentive for the firm to internalize the externality indicates that the goal of environmental law seems to be a simple one: to

---

5 Groosman (2001, p. 539).

6 One should bear in mind, however, that there could be cases where the existence of environmental externalities cannot be traced back only to the polluter, but also to the victims. This issue has been raised by Ronald Coase, a Nobel Prize winner, who states that the traditional approach of striving to ameliorate externalities – referring to the Pigouvian approach – has tended to obscure the nature of choice by focusing on the reduction or avoidance of harm only on the side of potential polluter. This actually constitutes a mistake, since in reality we are dealing with a problem of a reciprocal nature, where we face various harms and thus we have to choose one solution where harm is the least. Hence, the main questions are whether or not pollution abatement will harm the firm, and whether or not such a reduction has a greater value than the value of what has been sacrificed to obtain it (the cost of pollution reduction). In his conclusion, referred to as the 'Coase theorem', Coase states that when parties can bargain together and settle their disagreements by cooperation, their behaviour will be efficient regardless of the underlying rule of law (Coase, 1960). Unfortunately, we do not have enough space to discuss this theorem more deeply.

7 Turner et al. (1994, p. 77).

8 In a competitive market, price (P) will be set equal to marginal private cost (MC). With the presence of externalities, MC will not reflect the true costs, since there are some costs that are externalized. Here, the true marginal costs (or marginal social costs – MSC) are the sum of MC and marginal external costs (MEC). Having taken into account the external costs, the new price should be set equal to MSC. Hence, with the internalization of the externality the price will be:

$$P = MSC = MC + MEC$$

(Hunter et al. 1998, p. 108).

induce the potential polluter to take into account the pollution it might cause in its decision-making process.[9]

The polluter-pays principle has been adopted in several international conventions, among them:[10] the 1980 Athens Protocol for the Protection of the Mediterranean Sea against Pollution from Land-based Sources and Activities, the 1992 Helsinki Convention on the Transboundary Effects of Industrial Accidents, the 1993 Lugano Convention on Civil Liability for Damage resulting from Activities Dangerous to the Environment, the 1992 Helsinki Convention on the Protection and Use of Transboundary Watercourses and International Lakes, the 1996 London Protocol to the Convention on the Prevention of Marine Pollution by Dumping of Wastes and Other Matter.

The principle has also been included in Principle 16 of the Rio Declaration, which reads as follows:

> National authorities should endeavour to promote the internalization of environmental costs and the use of economic instruments, taking into account the approach that the polluter should, in principle, bear the cost of pollution, with due regard to the public interest and without distorting international trade and investment.

Although it has been quite widely recognized, there are several problems with the principle itself related to the clarity of certain terms. Clarity is of importance, particularly when we need to make the principle applicable. This issue will be discussed in the following subsection.

---

9 Faure (2001, p. 10). However, when invoking environmental policy to overcome the externality, one should also bear in mind the possibility that this kind of government intervention might yield another form of inefficiency, or might even aggravate environmental degradation. Kerry Turner et al. conclude that, in some cases, it is the government that fails the environment, and not the market. This conclusion is based on the following reasons: first, at one extreme, governments may be interested only in pursuing their own interests, or at least favouring the interests of some section of the community rather than the whole. This means that governments may well not act to protect the environment, especially if they think that environmental protection will impose costs on the members of powerful pressure groups; secondly, governments may not be very good at getting the right information which enables them to trace the full consequences of a particular action; thirdly, even though government, in the form of politicians, may have good intentions and frame a good environmental law in principle, their intentions still have to be translated into practice, involving experts as part of government bureaucracy. Since bureaucrats are very often not elected officials and tend not to be paid by results, they often have little incentive to behave in the best interests of the community unless they are closely controlled by the politicians. See Turner et al. (1994, pp. 80–1). These arguments demonstrate that government intervention may be inefficient either because it is based on incomplete information or because it is carried out to pursue private, rather than public, interests.

10 De Sadeleer (2002, pp. 23–4).

2.2. Application of the Principle

In this subsection, we discuss briefly some instruments that can be used to remedy environmental externalities. This is to show that theoretically the objective of the polluter-pays principle could be achieved through the use of various instruments, such as economics instruments, standards or liability rules. In addition, the effectiveness of the instruments is also important in answering the questions of what constitutes the pollution and the polluter and how much the polluter should pay for the pollution it causes.

2.2.1. Instruments to implement the principle

2.2.1.1. Liability rules: negligence versus strict liability

Liability rules may be called for to overcome the problems of externalities. From an economic perspective, the goal of tort law is not only to protect the interest of the people in their property and persons from damage by others, but also to minimize the sum of precaution, accident and administration costs (referred to as total accident costs).[11] In this sense, the starting point for economists is that tort law should be able to give incentives to potential parties to undertake careful behaviour.[12]

To begin our analysis regarding the choice of liability rules, it is worth noting that damage may be either unilateral or bilateral in nature. Unilateral damage occurs when there is only one party to whom the damage can be attributed. On the other hand, in many cases the damage is caused not only by the injurer, but also by the victim. Here, we are facing a bilateral accident, where both parties can influence the damage.[13] For simplicity, our discussion will focus on unilateral cases, since in most cases of environmental pollution it is usually assumed that only the injurer's activity will determine the existence of environmental pollution.[14]

Under a negligence rule, the injurer will be held liable for the damage only if he has taken precautions below the optimal level. The injurer will not take precaution below the optimal level, since if he does so and the accident occurs, he will be liable for the damage. Therefore, below the optimal level of precau-

---

11 Cooter and Ulen (1988, pp. 327 and 347).

12 Faure (2001, p. 73). The author also makes a comparison between the economist's and lawyer's points of view. While economists tend to focus on the deterrent effect for the potential polluters, lawyers usually tend to focus primarily on compensation for the potential victims.

13 This is consistent with the classification as discussed by many prominent law and economic writers. See Shavell (1980, p. 1).

14 See Faure (2001, p. 86).

tion, the injurer has to bear the cost of precaution and the cost of expected damage. It can also be said that the injurer will satisfy the optimal level of precaution, since the cost of non-negligence is much higher for him compared to that of negligence. On the other hand, it is also worth mentioning that he will not take precaution above the optimal level, since to avoid liability it is enough for the injurer to attain the optimal level. When the injurer takes precaution above the optimal level, he will no longer bear the cost of expected damage (because he is no longer liable to pay for the damage). At this level, the cost that the injurer has to bear is the cost of precaution. More importantly, since a negligence rule will give an incentive to the injurer to take the optimal level of precaution, it can be said that up to this point the negligence rule is efficient.

Under a strict liability rule, the injurer will be held liable to compensate the damage whenever an accident occurs. Under strict liability, social costs, represented by total accident costs, will become private costs, because the injurer will be liable for the social costs he causes. Here, to reduce the possibility of being held liable, the injurer will take as many precautions as possible, since the higher the precaution level he takes, the more the probability of accident will be reduced. However, a rational injurer will take an optimal level of precaution, since, at this level, total accident costs (social costs) are reaching the minimum point, namely the point where the cost of precaution per unit equals the reduction of probability from taking an additional unit of precaution times the damage cost. This is exactly the same precaution level that the injurer will take under a negligence rule. Therefore, it can be said that strict liability is also efficient with respect to the incentive of taking optimum precautions.

Although negligence and strict liability will both have the same result with regard to the incentive of taking precautions, they will have different results in terms of expected liability costs for the injurer at the point of the optimal precaution level. Under the negligence rule, the injurer will not be held liable whenever he takes the optimal level of precaution. Hence, at this point he has to bear the cost equal only to the cost of precaution at the optimal level of precaution. Under strict liability, the injurer is still liable for the damage, although he has taken the optimal level of precaution. Therefore, at this point, the injurer will have to bear the cost equal to the cost of precaution at the optimal level of precaution plus the cost of damage. At the optimal level of precaution, the injurer bears more costs under strict liability than under a negligence rule. Hence, given the condition of optimal precaution level, under strict liability the victim is still compensated, whereas under a negligence rule he is not.

The result will also be different if the level of activity is introduced.[15] In

[15] The following explanation is adapted from Kaplow and Shavell (1999, pp. 4–5).

this case, the social benefit is the benefit of the activity minus the total social costs (total accident costs) of engaging in the activity. Under a negligence rule, at the optimal level of precaution the injurer will only bear the cost of precaution up to the cost of the optimal level of precaution. As long as the precaution level is kept at the optimal level, increasing the injurer's activity level will cost him only part of the total social costs, since the cost of damage is excluded from his liability. Hence, it can be interpreted that since the injurer will escape the liability as long as he takes the optimal level of precaution, the injurer will not take the optimal level of activity. As a result, the amount of activity may be excessively inefficient.

The result will be different under strict liability. Since the injurer will be liable whenever the accident occurs, at the optimal level of precaution, he will bear costs equal to the total social costs. Considering the activity level, the benefit for the injurer will be as much as the social benefit (SB). It can be said that under strict liability, the injurer will pay adequate attention not only to the optimal level of precaution, but also to the optimal level of activity.

Theoretically, the risk of an accident taking place depends not only on the level of precaution, but also on the number of activities one has been involved in.[16] Hence, since strict liability will induce the injurer to take into account both optimal precaution and activity level, we could argue that strict liability is superior to the negligence rule.

2.2.1.2. Liability and regulation

Shavell has discussed several factors that determine the desirability of liability and of regulation. The first determinant is the possibility of different knowledge about risky activities possessed by private parties and by a regulatory agency. Differences in knowledge might embrace information about the value of parties' activities, the costs of reducing risks, or the probability or magnitude of risks. Shavell concludes that if private parties possess information that is superior to that of the regulatory authority, it would be more desirable if the private parties decide how to control risks without intervention of the authority. Hence, if private parties have better information about controlling risks than the authority does, then it is better to apply liability than regulation. Conversely, if the authority possesses better information, the social advantage would seem to lie in the direction of favouring the use of regulation. Shavell also states that, in terms of information, liability is generally prefer-

---

16 Faure and Skogh have given an example about the risk of having a traffic accident, which depends not only on the care that the driver takes but also on the number of kilometres driven in a certain period of time. Here the authors also conclude that in terms of providing incentives to engage in the optimal activity level, only strict liability will be efficient. See Faure and Skogh (2003, pp. 252–3).

able because private parties are those who are engaged in and derive benefits from their activities. Therefore, they know quite a lot about the nature of the risks of their activities, about the changes of the risks, and the costs of reducing the risks. However, information sometimes requires efforts to develop or special expertise to evaluate. In this case, the regulatory authority might possess superior information, and thus regulation would be more desirable.[17]

The second determinant concerns the issue of capability to pay for liability. It is often argued that private parties might be incapable of paying the full magnitude of harm done. The problem of judgment proof will significantly undermine liability rules because it inefficiently reduces the injurer's incentive to take the optimal level of precaution.[18] This especially holds in cases under strict liability, because if the injurer's assets are less than the harm, the injurer will bear liability that is less than the actual harm, hence he will take less than the optimal precaution.[19]

Under a regulatory approach, the question about a party's capability to pay damage is irrelevant, since the parties could be required to take precaution as a precondition for engaging in their activities.

If the potential injurer decides to purchase liability insurance against liability that significantly exceeds his assets, the question remains as to whether the insurer can easily determine the risk-reducing behaviour of the potential injurer and correlate such behaviour with the premium charged. If the insurers are not able to fully control the behaviour of the insured parties, it might be expected that the insured party (the injurer) would take less precaution that he would do if he was not covered by insurance. In this case, regulation is still more desirable than liability.[20]

The third determinant that might cause liability to be preferred less than regulation is the possibility of not being sued under a liability system.[21] If the

---

17 Shavell (1983, pp. 4–7).

18 In addition, the injurer's activity level will also tend to be socially excessive and contribute too much to risk. See Shavell (2003, p. 5).

19 Under a negligence rule, the injurer may continue to take optimal precaution, as long as his assets are greater than the costs of precaution. Hence, we could conclude that, in this case, the negligence rule is superior to the strict liability rule. See Polinsky and Shavell (1992, pp. 7–8).

20 Shavell (1983, pp. 7–9).

21 Lawsuits will not materialize for several factors. First, the harm might be dispersed over many victims, so that there will be no victim that will find it beneficial to bring a case to court. Secondly, the harm might occur after a long time period, so that it would be very difficult for the victims to adduce evidence of their damage. Thirdly, it could also be the case that the victims will have difficulties in attributing the harm to the responsible party (to prove the causal link between the harm and the injurer). Fourthly, even if harms can be linked to the actions of firms and suits successfully brought, the effect of suits on the behaviour of decision-makers within firms may be

injurer realizes that he does not face the threat of suit for harm done, he will take less precaution than he would do if he faced such threat. Such a possibility, however, will be irrelevant in the case of regulation.

The fourth determinant is related to the administrative costs incurred by private parties and by the public. Under a liability system, the administrative cost is borne only if harm occurs. Hence, if harm is unlikely, the administrative cost will be low. In addition, if an accident occurs, the administrative cost is still low because sometimes there will be no suit against such an accident. Under regulation, however, the administrative cost will be incurred whether or not the harm occurs. It is also often argued that under regulation, all parties are equally subject to verification procedures in the absence of specific information about their category of risk. Conversely, the administrative cost from a liability rule could be focused on controlling the group of parties that are most likely to cause harm, since under a liability rule the administrative cost is incurred by parties who cause the harm.[22]

2.2.1.3. Liability and insurance

As mentioned in the preceding subsection, the judgment proof problem has impacts that could significantly undermine the effectiveness of liability. In this regard insurance could be considered as an efficient tool to deal with the judgment proof problem. Some economists argue that insurance has proved to be an effective tool for providing victims with compensation and for modifying behaviour related to environmental risks.

In order to make an activity insurable, two conditions should be met from the perspective of insurance company.[23] First, the insurer should be able *ex ante* to identify and quantify the risk. The insurer should have enough information to enable it to estimate what losses the insurer is likely to incur when providing different levels of coverage. Secondly, the insurer should also have knowledge about the risk of a particular injurer in relation to other injurers' risks when setting the premium for each potential injurer or class of injurers. If the insurer is able to meet such conditions, we could say that an activity in question is insurable.

The first condition is concerned with the predictability of probability and the magnitude of damage. Some authors consider it as a crucial element in making the activity insurable. However, the insurer's knowledge depends on the availability of statistical data concerning the probability and the magnitude

slight, because with the passage of time, it would also be difficult to identify which among the employees of the firms were the responsible parties. See Shavell (1983, p. 10).

22 Shavell (1983, pp. 11–13).

23 Kunreuther and Freeman (2001, pp. 305–6).

of damage. This creates difficulties for the insurer in insuring environmental risks, since *ex ante* information on the predictability of environmental risks and its magnitude of damage is often very limited. In addition, the generally accepted techniques to quantify environmental damage may also be absent.[24]

The second condition deals with the issue of moral hazard and adverse selection. The insurer's ability to control the behaviour of injurers after they buy insurance determines the effectiveness of insurance. If the insurer does not possess enough control and information about injurers' behaviour, it might be the case that injurers will no longer have an incentive to take the optimal level of precaution as they would do without insurance. They would do so because with the availability of insurance coverage, the injurers will no longer have to bear the burden of paying full compensation. Since it is assumed that the likelihood of damage occurring depends heavily on the injurer's level of care, we could predict that the number of accidents will rise with the availability of insurance. In literature, this problem is referred to as moral hazard.

On the other hand, the insurer's failure to meet the second condition will create the problem of adverse selection. Since insurance premiums are related to expected losses, the insurer must be able to differentiate some of the injurers who are more likely to have losses from those who are less likely. If the insurer is unable to make such differentiation, he will assume the worst scenario and charge a high premium equally for all injurers within the same group. Hence, insurance will no longer be attractive for those who are comparatively good risks, because the premium becomes too expensive for them. If they leave the insurance, only those with comparatively bad risks will stay. Finding that only bad risks are left, insurer will further increase the premium, inducing those who have better risks to leave the insurance. At the end, insurance will no longer be beneficial for the insurer, and, in the most extreme situation, the insurance market will no longer be available.[25]

2.2.2. Regulation or liability: defining the polluter

Another important issue of environmental standards concerns the joint use of liability and standards. This is aimed at answering two important questions, namely whether adherence to a standard would constitute a legitimate defence in order to avoid liability; and whether the violation of a standard would automatically cause liability to the polluter. Using this analysis, we could then reach a definition of pollution and polluter.

Shavell argues that the answer to both questions above is 'No'. He argues that if a failure to satisfy a standard will automatically lead to liability, then

---

24 Faure (2003, pp. 125–7).
25 Shavell (1983, pp. 152–5).

some parties, particularly those who face higher than usual costs of care or who pose less than the usual potential harm, would also be inappropriately induced to satisfy the standard.[26] Here Shavell divides the injurers into two groups, namely the majority of typical injurers, who should undertake the standard level of care to reduce the expected accident costs; and the minority of atypical injurers of which precaution level will not lower the risk of an accident. It is also assumed that the authority cannot identify the two groups *ex ante*, so that they will set the standard equally for them; and that the authority cannot fully enforce the regulatory standard so that some injurers may escape the authority's attention. Obviously, if there were no threats of being held liable, the atypical would be the precaution level that is less than the level required by the regulatory standard, and this is a desirable result.

A different opinion, however, has been put forward by Burrows. He states that the answer to the question of whether or not the non-compliance with a regulatory standard should automatically lead to the imposition of negligence liability will apparently depend on the configuration of the regulatory standard, the negligence standard, and the optimal level of care. If it is assumed that for all injurers the optimal level of care is stricter than the regulatory standard and the regulatory standard is stricter than the negligence standard, imposing a negligence liability for those who fail to meet the regulatory standard could still be beneficial. In this case, the existence of liability could induce the injurers' level of care to get closer to the optimal level. Yet, if the optimal level of care is stricter than the negligence standard but more lenient than the regulatory standard, imposing liability could pull the negligence standard above the optimal level, namely when the regulatory standard is under-enforced. If, however, the regulatory standard is fully enforced, the additional liability will not alter the injurer's behaviour, since the injurers are already compelled to take precautions by the regulatory standard. In this case, it is the regulatory standard itself that is responsible for over-precaution, and not the joint use of regulation and liability. Therefore, Shavell's rejection of using negligence liability for non-compliance with regulatory standard does not seem to be suitable for all situations.[27]

As to the question of whether compliance with a regulatory standard can be used as a defence to avoid the liability, authors mostly concur with Shavell's

---

26 Shavell (1983, pp. 14–15).

27 Burrows also argues that Shavell does not reveal two assumptions that he has probably employed when rejecting the joint use of regulatory standard and liability for those who fail to meet the regulatory standard. The first assumption is that regulation is stricter than the optimal level of care, and this regulation is under-enforced. The second is that the marginal liability is excessive (greater than the marginal of damage). See Burrows (1999, p. 237).

argument. In relation to this question, Shavell argues that if injurers' satisfaction of the regulatory standard could enable them to avoid liability, then no one would do more than merely satisfying regulatory requirements. Yet, there would be atypical parties who ought to do more than what has been imposed by the regulatory standard, since these parties bear lower costs of taking care or are more likely to generate harms. Again, it is assumed that the authority cannot differentiate the population, so that he sets the standard equally for all injurers. Obviously, without the threat of being held negligent, a typical party would not be induced to take the optimal level of care that in his case is higher than the regulatory standard.[28]

Faure and Ruegg have added to this point two other reasons for rejecting the use of compliance as a legitimate defence to avoid liability.[29] First, the addition of negligence liability to a regulatory standard could function as an effective tool to correct the captured regulatory standard. In this case, liability may serve not only to guarantee that the victims will be compensated for the damage arising from the captured standard, but also to induce the injurers to take the optimal level of care, namely the level that should have been set in the standard. Secondly, assuming that an *ex ante* regulatory standard is not able to consider all possible precautions, since it only expresses minimum requirements, exposure to liability would induce the potential injurers to carry out such precautions to avoid harm to other parties.

The conclusions I have mentioned above are based on the assumption that an *ex ante* regulatory standard has been in place before an *ex post* liability rule. Although the results might be somewhat similar, the underlying arguments could be quite different if we envisage introducing a regulatory standard into the incumbent liability system. In this regard, we could refer to Kolstad et al.'s paper concerning the impact of introducing a regulatory standard into the liability system. They conclude that such an introduction could enhance efficiency, by driving the potential injurers' level of care closer to the optimal level, if it satisfies several conditions.[30] First, the introduction is justified if uncertainty concerning the legal standard (that is, the negligence standard) is large. Here, Kolstad et al. argue that the more uncertain the negligence standard is, the more likely the injurers are to take less than the optimal level of care. Hence, an *ex ante* regulatory standard could improve efficiency by reducing uncertainty.

Uncertainty concerning the exact level of the negligence standard could

---

28 For an atypical party, following a regulatory standard has already been a sufficient relief to avoid the sanction of non-compliance with the standard as well as of negligence liability (Shavell, 1983). See also footnote 16.

29 Faure and Ruegg (1994, pp. 55–6).

30 Kolstad et al. (1990, pp. 888–901).

also increase the marginal costs of precaution at the optimal level of care. When it occurs, injurers will undertake too little care to prevent an accident, due to the fact that by under-compliance, the injurers can greatly reduce their costs of precaution while increasing the expected liability costs relatively slightly. This situation justifies the addition of an *ex ante* regulatory standard into the liability rule under the second condition, namely if the marginal costs of precaution at the optimal level of care are large.

Thirdly, an *ex ante* regulation could also be employed if potential injurers perceive the negligence standard to be less than the optimal level. Thus, *ex ante* regulations could be invoked to ameliorate the injurers' perception towards negligence standards.

Of importance is that when liability rules are in place, a regulatory standard can be introduced so long as it is set at a point lower than the optimal level. To put it differently, a regulatory standard should prevail and be set at the optimal level when there is no liability in place, or when the probability of a successful suit against the injurer is zero. This is an important finding of Kolstad et al.'s work, which favours the use of *ex ante* regulation. Such a finding holds particularly in case of uncertainty concerning a new harm which is unclear but suspected of being catastrophic or when it is predicted that there will be no (successful) legal suit against the potential injurer.

From the discussion above, we could conclude that the definition of polluter cannot be limited to unlawful activities. It is important to note that although an activity does not constitute any infringement to standards or threshold previously set forth, it can still be considered as pollution if its impacts could lead or have given rise to damage for the environment or victims. This conclusion can be justified for several reasons. First, from the fairness perspective, limiting the financial compensation only to unlawful impairment could burden society with the cost of clean-up from authorized emissions. Secondly, from the appropriateness perspective, limiting compensation only to unlawful harms could undermine the incentive for the polluter to reduce its emission level even further.[31]

2.3. The Polluter-Pays Principle According to Act No. 23 of 1997

Recognition of the polluter-pays principle appears in the elucidation of Article 34 of Act no. 23 of 1997. The elucidation of this article states that the article 'constitutes the realisation of the environmental law principle that the polluter pays'. Article 34 is actually a provision concerning compensation according to liability based on fault rule. In this case, fault is interpreted as an unlawful act.

---

31 De Sadeleer (2002, pp. 39–40).

Accordingly, liability will only come into play if the action infringes the law and at the same time gives rise to adverse impacts on other people or the environment.

Based on our previous discussion, we could argue that Article 34 has reduced the function of the polluter-pays principle only as a part of the liability system. Instead of placing the principle as an overarching principle that underlies the need to internalize the externalized environmental costs, Article 34 interprets the principle as a basis for the negligence rule. Moreover, Article 34 also requires unlawfulness in order to apply the polluter-pays principle.

We could argue that this interpretation is inconsistent with the aim of the polluter pays principle, since there are several methods that can be employed to internalize the environmental externality; and these methods are not limited only to the negligence rule. Hence, we could propose a new article that could interpret the polluter-pays principle more appropriately. Such an article should place the principle as the basis of any proposed instruments to remedy environmental externality and should interpret pollution in a broader sense that is not limited only to damage resulting from unlawful acts.

3. THE PREVENTIVE PRINCIPLE

3.1 Introduction

Many commentators consider the Trial Smelter arbitration as the first manifestation of the principle of prevention. The arbitration has created an obligation that every state should protect other states against damages caused by activities within its jurisdiction.[32] In 1972, the principle was included in the Principle 21 of Stockholm Declaration, which reads as follows:[33]

> States have, in accordance with the Charter of the United Nations and the principles of international law, the sovereign right to exploit their own resources pursuant to their own environmental policies, and the responsibility to ensure that activities within their jurisdiction or control do not cause damage to the environment of other States or of areas beyond the limits of national jurisdiction.

It is worth noting here that although both principles mandate the preventive measures to be taken, Principle 21 could be distinguished from the principle of prevention for several reasons. First, Principle 21 stems from the recognition of

---

32 De Sadeleer (2002, p. 62).

33 Principle 2 of the Rio Declaration has also stated a somewhat similar formulation to that of Principle 21 of the Stockholm Declaration.

state sovereignty to exploit resources available within its jurisdiction, while the principle of prevention stems from the need to protect the environment as a goal in itself.[34] Secondly, the principle of prevention is not confined to the issue of transboundary impacts of certain activities. Rather, it is directed at minimizing the risk of environmental pollution.[35]

The preventive principle thus relates to the anticipatory measures aimed at avoiding environmental pollution before it occurs. Hunter and others argue that the principle of preventive action may reflect a view which considers that environmental protection is 'best achieved by preventing environmental harm in the first place rather than by attempting to remedy or compensate for such harm after it has occurred'.[36]

The recognition of the principle of prevention is illustrated by the adoption of the principle in several conventions, ranging from the marine environmental protection regime to biodiversity.[37] The principle has even gained acceptance in the ICJ's ruling on the Gabcikovo-Nagymaros case, which states that prevention is required due to the irreversible character of damage to the environment and of the limitations inherent in the mechanism of reparation once damage occurs.[38]

However, one should bear in mind that the obligation to take preventive measures requires the states only to exert due care in order to avoid damage. A state cannot be held liable for the transboundary damage if it has carried out measures to prevent the damage from occurring. The question thus remains as to what kinds of measures can be considered as due care or due diligence. In this regard, several conventions have also set forth some types of due care, such as the obligation to carry out environmental impact assessment (EIA), monitoring, and consultations, as part of states' obligation to prevent environmental damage.[39]

It is important also to note that in undertaking a preventive action against environmental harms from a particular technology or activity, one needs to consider that the available alternatives for such a technology or activity would create less harm to the environment. This is particularly the case when the preventive action is taken by banning a certain substance, technology or activity. For this reason, Sunstein argues that the principle of prevention can only

---

34 Trouwborst (2002, pp. 35–6).

35 In this regard, Sands argues that under the principle of preventive action, 'a state may be under an obligation to prevent damage to the environment *within its own jurisdiction*, including the obligation to take appropriate regulatory, administrative and other measures' (emphasis in original). See Sands (1995, p. 195).

36 Hunter et al. (1998, p. 364).

37 De Sadeleer (2002, pp. 65–6).

38 De Sadeleer (2002, p. 67).

39 Hunter et al. (1998, pp. 364–5).

be justified if, all things considered, it is better than the alternatives, which means that the benefits of the prevention exceed the costs incurred.[40] Hence, pollution prevention, so Sunstein argues, should be 'what is recommended by cost–benefit analysis'.[41]

3.2. The Relationship between the Preventive Principle and Other Principles

As we discussed earlier, the polluter-pays principle is primarily aimed at internalizing the externality, thus avoiding the costs of repairing the damage being borne by society and not by those who have caused the damage. However, theoretically, the effective instrument would impose high costs on the potential polluter. In this case, the polluter-pays principle may have a deterrent effect, so that it could finally prevent the repetition of similar damages from occurring. On the other hand, the preventive principle is mainly aimed at avoiding the reparation of damages: to prevent is better than to cure. In contrast to the polluter-pays principle, prevention thus applies when damage has not yet materialized, but there are reasonable grounds to suspect that the damage would occur if prevention had not been undertaken.

The preventive principle is also closely related to the precautionary principle. If the former aims to tackle risks under certainty, the latter obliges preventive measures to be taken even when the risks have not yet been established with full scientific certainty. Moreover, the precautionary principle is directed only at risks or threats that are irreversible or serious in nature. The difference between the two principles will be discussed in the following section.

Finally, it is also important to note the relationship between the preventive principle and the rectification principle.[42] De Sadeleer has discussed the difference between the two principles in relation to their scope. While the preventive principle has a wide scope of application, the rectification principle is focused on the prevention at source of environmental pollution, by obliging the potential polluter or polluting activity to make use of the best available techniques (BAT) in order to prevent the pollution in the first place.[43] Thus, the principle

---

40 Sunstein (2002, p. 101).

41 Sunstein (2002, p. 102).

42 The principle of rectification obliges states to tackle environmental pollution at the source of the pollution. We could refer this principle to Article 174 (2) EC Treaty, which states that the Community's environmental policy 'shall be based on . . . the principles that . . . environmental damage should as a priority be rectified at source . . .'.

43 Ibid., p. 75. According to the Council Directive 96/61/EC of 24 September 1996 concerning integrated pollution prevention and control, the Best Available Technology is 'the most effective and advanced stage in the development of activities and their methods of operation which indicate the practical suitability of particular

of rectification constitutes a shift from the end-of-pipe approach. On the other hand, the rectification principle also expresses the need to rely more on quality standards rather than on emissions standards.[44]

3.3. The Preventive Principle According to Act No. 23 of 1997

The preventive principle has been included in Act No. 23 of 1997. Article 10 of the Act stipulates that the government has an obligation to develop and apply instruments of a pre-emptive, preventive and proactive nature in an effort to prevent decreases in environmental supportive and carrying capacity. Moreover, Article 14 states that stipulations on environmental quality standards, prevention of and coping with pollution and restoration of its carrying capacity are regulated by government regulation.

In addition to the two articles above, several articles related to the obligation to carry out environmental impact assessment can also be considered as an interpretation of the preventive principle. In this case, the proponent of an activity should submit the assessment of possible impacts arising from its activity. EIA thus constitutes an important procedure for the authorization of an activity, which is expected to be able to inform the authorities, the proponent of a project, and third parties about the potential impacts that could result from the proposed project. This information could also be regarded as a requirement for a fuller integration of environmental concerns into the decision-making process.[45]

A final remark on the interpretation of Act No. 23 on the preventive principle deals with the issue of best available techniques or technology. In the previous subsection, it was argued that the preventive principle is closely related to the notion of BAT, as required under various environmental conventions. Unfortunately, the Act has not incorporated the BAT obligation into the formulation of the preventive principle.

---

techniques for providing in principle the basis for emission limit values designed to prevent and, where that is not practicable, generally to reduce emissions and the impact on the environment'. In addition, the use of BAT should take into account the costs of providing such techniques/technology. Economically, it is not desirable to force the potential polluter to undertake or purchase the best techniques to prevent environmental pollution, if they can only be purchased at an excessive price. For this reason, the BAT could also be interpreted as the BAT not entailing excessive costs (BATNEEC).

44 Krämer observes that the first use of rectification principle appeared during the debate between the Commission and the UK government over the question whether discharges into water should be tackled on the basis of emission standards or quality standards. One reason to apply emission standards was that of the rectification principle, obliging states to rectify as many environmental impairments at source as possible. See Krämer (2003, p. 12).

45 Ibid., p. 87.

4. THE PRECAUTIONARY PRINCIPLE

4.1. The Development of the Principle

Policy measures to deal with environmental damage have undergone several stages of modification over time. The first stage focused on remedial action, which materialized in the form of government intervention to remedy the damage after an accident occurred. In the second stage, the policy measure had to include the preventive approach, in the sense that it allowed the authorities to intervene prior to the occurrence of damage. This stage comes to the fore because the threats of environmental damages are considered tangible, hence timely preventive measures should be taken to avoid damaging consequences.

The latest development in environmental policy is marked by the need for anticipation. It differs from the second stage in that it is primarily aimed at dealing with threats of damages that are considered serious or irreversible, and hence it requires preventive measures to be taken, although there is still scientific uncertainty as to whether the threats will materialize.[46]

The existence of uncertainty and irreversibility has policy implications that require decision-makers to take preventive measures and to recognize our lack of knowledge, which is always part of the scientific analysis. Consequently, the lack, or even absence, of scientific certainty should not be a valid reason for postponing the preventive measure. The potential harm to society from a proposed activity should not be disregarded simply because there is uncertainty as to the exact nature of the risks involved from the activity.[47]

This new approach in the decision-making process, the precautionary principle, has marked the development of a legal instrument, especially in relation to human health and environmental protection. The emergence of this principle has arisen particularly from the recognition that most processes of environmental degradation are irreversible. There is thus a concern that activities carrying a significant risk of irreversible environmental harm should be regulated in order to prevent the harm, even if scientific uncertainty remains as to the nature of damage that is likely to result from them.

In short, the precautionary principle stems from growing concern for environmental protection, which in turn urges states to take measures to prevent environmental degradation even if the deleterious effects of this degradation remain unproven. Certainly, a careful implementation of such an approach suggests that the risks of the foregone benefits should be balanced against the risks of incurred costs arising from imposing unnecessary protection.

---

46 Ibid., pp. 91–2.
47 Geistfeld (2001, p. 11328).

This section will be devoted to a discussion of the emergence and development of the precautionary principle in international environmental law. The discussion will embrace not only the issue of formulations of the precautionary principle in some selected international documents and the elements derived from such formulations, but also the issue of whether or not there should be a common interpretation of the precautionary principle. At the end of this section, a debate on the choice as to whether we need to make a sharp distinction between risk assessment and risk management in applying the precautionary principle will be presented.

4.2. The Development of the Precautionary Principle at International Level

The precautionary principle has its root in German environmental policies concerning the *Vorsorgeprinzip* in the early 1970s. Harald Hohmann states that the purpose of the *Vorsorgeprinzip* is to prevent potential pollution by foresight and to sustain the ecological basis for future generations by careful use of available resources.[48]

Since the 1980s, the precautionary principle has become the subject of much international discourse and has begun to gain acceptance. In 1982, UN General Assembly adopted 'The World Charter of Nature', which recognizes the precautionary principle as stated in Principle 11. The charter has defined three important elements of the precautionary principle. First, it emphasizes the avoidance of irreversible effects. Secondly, it also states the reversal of the burden of proof on the proponents of which activities are likely to create such irreversible effects. Finally, the charter has indirectly recognized the uncertainty (of potential adverse effects) as a reason to err on the side of avoiding irreversible effects.[49]

In spite of its legal effect being declaratory rather than conventional, the World Charter of Nature has paved the way for more acceptance of the precautionary principle at international level. In the early 1980s, the precautionary principle emerged in the international North Sea ministerial conferences on the protection of the North Sea, through the German proposals made to these conferences. Freestone and Hey argue that through these conferences the principle

---

48 See Hohmann (1994, pp. 10–11).

49 The notion of uncertainty is somewhat confusing, since it could be interpreted that it is uncertainty, not the irreversible effects, which constitutes a reason not to allow an activity to proceed. Hence, the expression of '. . . where potential adverse effects are not fully understood, the activities should not proceed . . .' should be interpreted in conjunction with the concept of irreversibility effects and the reversal of the burden of proof.

found its way into the work of the Oslo and Paris Commissions, into global marine environmental regimes, and into global environmental regimes.[50]

The precautionary principle has also developed outside the regime of marine protection. In this regard, the 1985 Vienna Convention on the Protection of the Ozone Layer is considered as the first international convention that explicitly refers to precaution.[51] In the fifth paragraph of its preamble, the Convention states that the Parties are 'mindful also of the precautionary measures for the protection of the ozone layer which have already been taken at the national and international levels'.

The year 1992 marked a significant development for the precautionary principle, shown by the adoption of the principle in at least four international conventions, one treaty and one international declaration. Such a development indicates that the precautionary principle has been increasingly adopted and accepted in many international conventions, especially after the adoption of Rio Declaration.[52]

In May 1992, the UN Framework Convention on Climate Change was adopted. The Convention has articulated international recognition of the application of the precautionary principle in dealing with climate change. It states:

> The Parties should take precautionary measures to anticipate, prevent or minimize the causes of climate change and mitigate its adverse effects. Where there are threats of serious or irreversible damage, lack of full scientific certainty should not be used as a reason for postponing such measures, taking into account that policies and measures to deal with climate change should be cost-effective so as to ensure global benefits at the lowest possible cost. To achieve this, such policies and measures should take into account different socio-economic contexts, be comprehensive, cover all relevant sources, sinks and reservoirs of greenhouse gases and adaptation, and comprise all economic sectors . . .[53]

In June 1992, the United Nations Conference on Environment and Development was held in Rio de Janeiro. The conference has concluded a declaration on Environment and Development (Rio Declaration), which reaffirms the recognition of the precautionary principle, by stating in Principle 15 that:

---

[50] Freestone and Hey (1996, p. 4). It should also be noted that the development of the precautionary principle in national legislation and in various decisions of international judiciary bodies has also significantly sharpened the interpretation of the principle. However, this issue will not be discussed in this chapter.

[51] Cameron (2001, p. 114).

[52] In this respect, Freestone and Hey write that the precautionary principle has become intrinsic to international environmental policy, especially with the adoption of the Rio Declaration in 1992. Since then, the precautionary principle has been included 'in virtually every recent treaty and policy document related to the protection and preservation of the environment' (Freestone and Hey, 1996, p. 3).

[53] Article 3 (3).

> In order to protect the environment, the precautionary approach shall be widely applied by states according to their capabilities. Where there are threats of serious or irreversible damage, lack of full scientific certainty shall not be used as a reason for postponing cost-effective measures to prevent environmental degradation.

The same conference has also adopted the Convention on Biological Diversity (hereinafter called CBD). The ninth paragraph of the CBD considers that '. . . where there is a threat of significant reduction or loss of biological diversity, lack of scientific certainty should not be used as a reason for postponing measures to avoid or minimise such a threat'. Although it does not explicitly mention the precautionary principle, the phrase above obviously refers to this principle. Similarly, the protocol to CBD, namely the 2000 Cartagena Protocol on Biosafety, has also adopted the precautionary principle, as shown in Article 11.8 of the protocol:

> Lack of scientific certainty due to insufficient relevant scientific information and knowledge regarding the extent of the potential adverse effects of a living modified organism on the conservation and sustainable use of biological diversity in the Party of import, taking also into account risks to human health, shall not prevent that Party from taking a decision, as appropriate, with regard to the import of that living modified organism intended for direct use as food or feed, or for processing, in order to avoid or minimise such potential adverse effects.

4.3. Interpretations of the Precautionary Principle

4.3.1. Different formulations on the precautionary principle

The presentation of the preceding subsection has demonstrated that many conventions or declarations have different formulations concerning the precautionary principle. Secondly, we have also seen that some documents have used the term 'precautionary principle', while others have used 'precautionary approach' or 'precaution measures'. Others, such as CBD, do not even explicitly mention one of those terms. Thirdly, although most of the documents explicitly specify the definition of the precautionary principle, other documents, such as the Maastricht Treaty or Energy Charter Treaty, do not. Those facts have given rise to a question of whether the principle has been recognized as a legal principle at international level. In this respect, many writers have argued that the principle lacks clarity and is too vague to serve as a legal principle.[54]

---

[54] Bodansky, as quoted by Boehmer-Christiansen, states that the precautionary principle is too vague to serve as a regulatory standard because it does not specify how much caution should be taken. See Boehmer-Christiansen (1994, p. 52). Marchant states that the principle gives no guidance on any of the fundamental questions that are faced in making any risk decision. He also considers the principle as ambiguous, for

However, many international documents have used somewhat similar formulations, namely by referring to the precautionary principle as set forth in the Rio Declaration. Therefore, the documents, to a certain degree, have shown commonalities, which should not have been ignored by those questioning the lack of clarity and consensus concerning the principle. For this reason, this subsection will discuss some leading formulations of the principle.[55]

Sandin has expounded a comprehensive classification of the precautionary principle. The author discusses some versions of the precautionary principle, based on four constructing elements of the principle.[56]

The first element is the threshold.[57] Before undertaking a preventive measure, the precautionary principle requires a threshold to be set in accordance with the harmful potential of an activity. Once this threshold has been crossed, the preventive actions are required or suggested. Nollkaemper states that in principle determination of the threshold level excludes the considerations of costs. However, in practice, the threshold leaves so much room for discretion that it is difficult to assess whether the decision that a threshold has been crossed is a decision based purely on scientific considerations.[58]

Various formulations of the precautionary principle reveal that there are several expressions to address the threshold level. The most common terminology is 'serious or irreversible damage', which I consider as a high level of

---

example, as to what level of risk is acceptable, what role costs should play in risk decisions, what quantum of scientific evidence is sufficient for making decisions, and how potential risk–risk trade-offs should be addressed. See Marchant (2002). For the same reason, Birnie and Boyle sceptically state: 'Despite its attraction, the great variety of interpretations given to the precautionary principle, and the novel and far-reaching effects of some applications suggest that it is not yet a principle of international law. Difficult questions concerning the point at which it becomes applicable to any given activity *remain unanswered and seriously undermine its normative character and practical utility*, although support for it does indicate a policy of greater prudence on the part of those states willing to accept it' (Birnie and Boyle, 1995, p. 98; emphasis added); (Tickner and Reffensperger, 2004, pp. 3–4).

55 Here, I assume that different formulations will lead to greater differences in interpretation. Conversely, a more similar formulation, to a certain degree, could generate a more common understanding on the principle.

56 Based on the terminology used to express these elements, referred to as 'dimensions', Sandin then discusses the precision and the strength of various formulations. By 'strength', he means the 'degree of cautiousness, i.e. the number of cases in which precautions were to be taken'. See Sandin (1999, p. 890).

57 Sandin uses the term 'threat' to refer to threshold. However, I prefer to use the word 'threshold' because it is related to the minimum limit that should have existed before precautionary measures are invoked.

58 Nollkaemper (1996, pp. 81–2). In this regard, we could refer to a strict division between risk assessment and risk management. This issue will be discussed later.

threshold, compared to other phrases such as 'possible or potentially damaging effects' or 'harm or hazards to humans or the environment'.[59] We can see that threshold levels are determined in a very broad as well as in quite a specific terminology. In this regard, the easier the threshold to be crossed, the stronger (more cautious) the principle will be. In addition, the threshold can also explain that the precautionary principle is intended as an exceptional principle which holds only for certain risks considered to have extraordinary magnitude. Hence, a very broad definition of the threshold may inevitably undermine the intention of applying the precautionary principle.

The second element is 'uncertainty'. Sandin observes that the less precise the definition of uncertainty, that is, the less plausible the threat has to be, the stronger the principle is.[60] In general, most of the documents interpret uncertainty in terms of scientific uncertainty as a 'lack of scientific certainty'. However, some documents have attributed such scientific uncertainty to the evidence concerning the causal link between the inputs and the effects, that is, the proof about the threshold.

The third element concerns the measures to be taken. Such measures are mostly expressed in the need to 'avoid' or 'prevent' the threat from occurring. They will be taken whether or not the threat is scientifically certain. This implies that under uncertainty preventive measures will be taken as if the threat is certainly known. Therefore, the precautionary principle is closely related to the principle of prevention. The only difference between the two principles is that the former applies for some uncertain threats, while the latter is for some certain threats. The precautionary principle is nothing more than an extension of the prevention principle, which will be implemented because some threats are considered so irreversible and serious that we need to prevent them even if they are not known with scientific certainty.[61]

---

59 Usually authors categorize 'irreversible', 'serious', and 'catastrophic' damages in one group, as contrasted to 'reversible', 'non-catastrophic', and 'well-behaved' damage. See Flemming (1996, pp. 157–8).

60 Sandin (1999, pp. 892–3).

61 Marr and Schwemer have discussed the precautionary principle under German environmental law. According to the authors, the German origin of the precautionary principle 'implies the adverse effects to the environment or human health on the basis of potential risks (*Risikovorsorge*), rather than classical hazard prevention (*Gefahrenabwehr*) under the preventive principle'. The essential difference between risk avoidance (the prevention principle) and precaution lies in the possibility of identifying a given risk, where the latter corresponds to the pervasiveness of uncertainty. See Marr and Schwemer (2004, p. 134). See also von Moltke (1996, p. 102). Cameron and Abouchar have also expressed a similar opinion by stating that the precautionary principle is the extension of Principle 21 of the Stockholm Declaration (obligation not to cause harm) to situations of scientific uncertainty. See Cameron and Abouchar (1996, p. 46).

It is also important to note that some documents have set out certain limitations to the implementation of preventive measures. In general, considerations other than safety should also be taken into account as a part of the precautionary principle. The Rio Declaration's version of the precautionary principle, for example, has integrated measures with cost-effectiveness. Other documents have explicitly required that cost–benefit analysis (CBA) be undertaken in determining whether or not to take a measure.[62] This limitation constitutes an important part of the precautionary principle, which will determine the strength of the principle.[63] However, one should be careful with the distinction between the concept of CEA (cost-effective analysis) and CBA.[64] Apparently, there is only one document, the 2002 Stockholm Convention on POPs, which has explicitly required that the precautionary principle be employed in accordance with CBA.

The fourth element is the command dimension of the precautionary principle. In this regard, the strength of the precautionary principle will be determined by the status of the measures.[65] A mandatory status of the precautionary principle is typically expressed in phrases such as 'shall strive to adopt', or 'must not wait'. However, most of the status is expressed in a vague formulation, namely that uncertainty 'shall not be used as a reason for postponing' preventive measures. It is unclear whether the measures are mandatory or not, because its only stated that uncertainty does not justify inaction.[66]

Although there is only one document, namely the 1982 World Charter of Nature, which has explicitly formulated the shifting in the burden of proof, we

---

62 Other limitations to the precautionary principle are expressed in terms of 'the Best Available Technology' (BAT), 'the developments in scientific knowledge' or 'technical and economic considerations'.

63 Sandin, however, does not consider such limitations in his classification. On the other hand, the importance of such limitations has been addressed by several articles in order to avoid a strictly absolutist construction of the precautionary principle. See Nollkaemper (1996, pp. 87–93), who addresses the need for a balance between benefits and risks, and between risks and risks. See also Christoforou (2003, pp. 249–50) on the need to weigh the costs and benefits of the precautionary measures.

64 In CBA, both costs and benefits should be measured in monetary units. A project will pass the CBA test if the monetized benefits are greater than the costs. In contrast, CEA enables us to make a clear separation between the costs and benefits of a project. In this regard, since the measurement of future benefits is the most problematic part of the economic appraisal of a project, the use of CEA will allow the analyst not to measure the benefits in monetary units. An alternative proposal or a project is considered as cost-effective, hence it passes the CEA test, if it can give the most benefits at a given cost (budget constraint) or it can achieve a given level of benefit at the least cost. Sugden and Williams (1978, p. 190).

65 Sandin (1999, p. 895).

66 Wiener, however, interprets the precautionary principle as non-mandatory, because it only permits preventive action to be taken.

cannot ignore the importance of this issue in implementing the precautionary principle. Many authors, however, have criticized the shifting in the burden of proof on the basis that the shifting places an impossible burden on the proponents of activities, because they have to prove that their activities will not generate harms (zero-risk proof).[67] This argument, however, has confounded the difference between the standard of proof and the burden of proof. The former corresponds to the question of legitimate threat, such as 'how safe is safe enough', which will continue to exist whether or not the burden of proof is shifted. On the other hand, a shifting of the burden of proof deals particularly with the question of which parties are in a better position to acquire the information.

A summary of the various expressions of the precautionary principle at international level is listed in Table 3.1, at the end of this chapter. The table has employed the four elements discussed above to make it easier to understand the differences and similarities of the formulations.

4.3.2. The need for a common interpretation of the precautionary principle?

As I have mentioned earlier, the precautionary principle has been subject to criticism because of its lack of clarity. The question is, however, whether we ought to reach a (global) consensus concerning the implementation of the precautionary principle.

Cameron and Abouchar conclude that the precautionary principle is no less vague than most principles of international law; hence, the differences in the precautionary principle do not necessarily mean that the principle is meaningless. Instead, such differences indicate room for further refinement.[68] Similarly, Jordan and O'Riordan argue that the precautionary principle is 'a culturally framed concept that has evolved along different pathways and at different rates in different countries. Searching for a single, all-encompassing

---

67 See for example Bergkamp (2002, p. 27).

68 Cameron and Abouchar (1996). Along these lines, as mentioned by Patrick van Zwanenberg and Andrew Stirling, many commentators have criticized the precautionary principle because conventional enunciations of the principle do not specify the circumstances under which it should be applied, nor what types of precautionary actions are warranted and at what cost. See van Zwanenberg and Stirling. As regards the issue of measures to be taken, we could state that the precautionary principle is as vague as the prevention principle. However, many authors have demanded the precautionary principle be clear on this issue, whilst they do not demand the same clarity of the prevention principle. Per Sandin, for example, has criticized the Rio Declaration's version of the precautionary principle by arguing that the Declaration is unclear on what kind of actions should be carried out in relation to the precautionary principle. See Per Sandin (1999, p. 895).

definition is, therefore, likely to be a fruitless endeavour because individuals will never agree upon what is or is not precautionary in a given situation'. A precautionary approach in one cultural context may not be regarded as precautionary in another. In this respect, value positions are of importance in determining the precautionary measures, as Jordan and O'Riordan have also written that those who regard the environment as inherently robust and capable of withstanding human impact are inclined to be less precautionary than those who regard human impact on nature as unpredictable and potentially calamitous.[69]

Fisher also shares that view. Fisher has made a sharp distinction between a principle and a rule. The precaution, she writes, should be viewed as a principle rather than a rule. According to this distinction, critiques concerning the clarity of the precautionary principle have assumed that the principle is a rule. Therefore, such critiques have proceeded on the wrong basis and ignored the basic feature of the precautionary principle. As a principle, the precautionary principle will vary depending on its jurisprudential and jurisdictional context. Instead of functioning as an 'explicitly formulated' rule that is unchanging in its application, the precautionary principle should be flexible, depending on specific circumstances.[70] Furthermore, Fisher goes on to state that how the precautionary principle will be formulated, interpreted, and implemented will depend largely on the legal culture surrounding it. In this context, because the precautionary principle operates within a specific risk regulation regime, it will in turn be shaped by the surrounding public law framework, the types of risk that are being regulated, and the broader socio-political culture. On the other hand, the legal culture will also make the implementation of the precautionary principle vary, depending on how the principle is included in legislation, who is interpreting it, why they are interpreting it, as well as on the factual and prevailing socio-political context.

Therefore, as the precautionary principle is a legal principle produced and shaped by legal culture, Fisher believes that variations in its formulation, interpretation, and implementation demonstrate how deeply the principle is included in different legal cultures. Accordingly, variation is not a proof of the failure of the precautionary principle, but a proof of its success.[71] Indeed, what constitutes a precautionary measure will depend on various factors such as culture, politics, and economic considerations. In this sense, one could argue

---

69 Jordan and O'Riordan (1999, p. 18).

70 Fisher (2002, p. 9).

71 Similarly, Boehmer-Christiansen, in challenging Bodansky's criticism on the precautionary principle, states that it is not necessary for a principle also to function as a standard. As a result, in contrast to a standard, the precautionary principle does not have to be precisely formulated and detailed. See Boehmer-Christiansen (1994, p. 53).

that there is no need to achieve a common interpretation of the precautionary principle.

However, there are some concerns that the precautionary principle's lack of clarity will make it very likely to be abused as a 'guise of a trade protectionist measure'.[72] More importantly, a lack of clarity is also responsible for an abuse of the precautionary principle that could be as devastating as initiating a war.[73] In this regard, Sandin has rightly pointed out that although the implementation of the precautionary principle does not necessarily require a clear and unambiguous formulation, doubtless, a clear formulation will greatly facilitate such an implementation.[74] Inevitably, if we are willing to implement the precautionary principle appropriately, conditions set up for this implementation are of great importance. Hence, incorporating the precautionary principle with cost-benefit analysis (CBA) might be very helpful.

4.4. The Precautionary Principle and CBA

A reference to economic considerations when applying the precautionary principle has been provided in Principle 15 of the Rio Declaration. However, some advocates of the precautionary principle argue that such a reference is not an integral part of the precautionary principle. We could refer this argument to Bernstein, for example, who states, 'caveat about cost-effectiveness is foreign to the principle and originates from sources that are hostile to it, notably the U.S. government'.[75]

On the other hand, critics of the precautionary principle have also been triggered partly by the assumption that the precautionary principle has ignored the possible large costs that society could incur when applying the principle. Indeed, several critiques of the precautionary principle have plausible reasons to argue that the principle might lead to inefficient outcomes.[76] In this case, Brombacher, as quoted by Resnik, argues that the precautionary principle could lead to a highly conservative measure, which in turn might impede

---

72 Vogel (2003, p. 40).

73 Wiener argues that when the US government tried to justify the doctrine of pre-emptive strike, they employed a reason similar to that of the precautionary principle. In criticizing the advocates of the precautionary principle, Wiener has argued: '. . . the terrorism example illustrates that the new U.S. doctrine of preemptive self-defense is based on the same logic as the precautionary principle. In advocating precaution, European leaders – especially Greens – make the same point that President Bush has made about terrorism: if we wait to confirm that the threat is real, it will be too late' See Wiener, 2003, p. 240.

74 Sandin (1999, p. 898).

75 Bernstein (1999, p. 153).

76 Sunstein (2002, p. 103).

scientific and technological progress as well as economic growth.[77] Thus, failing to consider the costs of taking precautionary measures may create a worse situation than the initial risks that the principle wishes to prevent.[78]

For this reason, some economists have argued that the implementation of the precautionary principle should be accompanied by an economic evaluation, namely cost–benefit analysis. David Pearce, for example, has hypothetically drawn a conclusion regarding various regulatory standards resulting from different combinations in implementing the precautionary principle. The author argues that the strictest implementation of the precautionary principle will result in the highest regulatory standards. This is the case when the implementation of the precautionary principle disregards the costs of taking precautionary measure relative to the benefits of doing so. Subsequently, the reference to the best available technology (BAT) will render lower regulatory standards compared to the strictest version of the precautionary principle. However, the reference to BAT could also be insufficient to reduce the absolutism of the precautionary principle, because what constitutes the best available technology could be economically prohibitive. In this case, the obligation to apply BAT could be construed in a less rigid manner, namely by taking into account the economic capability to provide such technology. Therefore, the implementation of the precautionary principle can be accomplished with reference to the concept of BATNEEC (Best Available Technology Not Entailing Excessive Cost).[79] In addition, Pearce concludes that these three regulatory standards, which result from the application of various versions of the precautionary principle, remain stricter than those resulting from the application of CBA alone.[80]

Although Pearce does not provide any empirical proof to support his thesis, he provides an important insight, namely that by referring to cost-effectiveness, the precautionary principle would create standards that are economically more feasible. On the other hand, reference to the precautionary principle would contribute to a more thorough evaluation of CBA. In this regard, Jordan and O'Riordan argue that the cost-effectiveness of an action is similar to the application of proportionality of response designed to show that there should be a regular examination to identify the social and environmental gains arising from an action to justify the costs.

---

[77] Resnik (2003, p. 330).

[78] Goklany concludes that errors resulting from the implementation of the precautionary principle could forego benefits, and therefore would increase the overall risks. See Indur (2000, p. 24).

[79] The concepts of BAT and BATNEEC are discussed in Section 3.2.

[80] Pearce (1994, p. 147). See also Ramchandani and Pearce (1992, pp. 16–21). See also Nollkaemper (1996, p. 92).

Thus, there are two possibilities that should be taken into account by the decision-maker. On the one hand, the net social cost of adopting precautionary measures might be extremely large, especially if the adverse environmental impacts turn out to be less important than previously predicted. On the other hand, ignoring irreversible consequences simply because they are uncertain might also result in an inefficient outcome, namely where consequences that have not been prevented finally occur. Given these two possibilities, some environmental economists believe that a realistic CBA would be one that incorporates the wider social and environmental costs of development.[81] In this respect, Jordan and O'Riordan argue that the decision-maker should make a presumption in favour of high environmental quality, namely that a project should only be allowed if its benefits are much greater than (rather than simply greater than or equal to) the associated costs.[82] The arguments above confirm the need to incorporate the precautionary principle with CBA, indicating that one should seriously take into account the costs side of applying the principle.

However, one might wonder how CBA would calculate the benefits and costs of a proposed project when the decision-maker is faced with uncertainty. In this case, the so-called quantitative CBA[83] might be subject to serious limi-

---

81 Some economists argue that environmental impacts and other non-market goods or services are relevant in both analysis and decision-making, hence, they deserve equal considerations with those for goods or services that can be priced through market mechanisms. See Hanley and Spash (1993, p. 10). Consequently, CBA needs to consider the total economic value (TEV) to embrace a more comprehensive evaluation. This value comprises several values, as put forward by Pearce, namely:

direct use value, for instance value that can be measured from market and survey data;
indirect use value, which correspond to the concept of ecological functions;
option value, expressing individuals' willingness to pay (WTP) to undertake conservation for future use. It is thus a value for keeping open the possibility of enjoying benefits of some goods or services in the future. It is a very significant value for CBA, given the fact that some developments could forego the benefits forever;
existence value, which reveals people's preference for environmental assets unrelated to either current or future use of those assets.

In addition to these values, another important value should also be considered by the decision-maker when faced with uncertainty and irreversibility. This is the *quasi-option value* developed by Arrow and Fisher in 1974.

82 Jordan and O'Riordan (1999, p. 26). In comparing a developmental project and preservation, for example, the presence of risks of irreversible damage which could probably result from development implies that the decision-maker needs high benefits of development to reject preservation. See Crowards (1998, pp. 308–10).

83 This approach links up quantitative risk assessment and the decision-making process. Once risks associated with an activity or technology have been assessed, the decision-maker should decide whether the activity or technology will be regulated. Thus each option will be valued on the basis of each risk. The term risk indicates that

tations. First of all, one might recall all the debates on the value of life and the environment and on the discount rates that are inevitable when carrying out CBA.[84]

Secondly, one might also doubt whether CBA will seriously take into account the issue of uncertainty.[85] Thirdly, risk assessment, on which the quantitative CBA will be based, often does not reflect people's perception of risk. This raises the question of whether the decision-maker should solely follow the results of scientific risk assessment.[86]

Finally, associating costs and benefits with quantitative risks, which means that the decision-maker places too much emphasis on the expected value of outcomes, might fail to reflect people's attitude towards risk. This is because people's attitudes towards risks are sometimes motivated by the level of utility associated with uncertain outcomes.[87] In this case, the decision-maker can no longer rely on the assumption of risk-neutrality. Instead, risk aversion should be used as an assumption.

Consequently, if CBA is to be applied alongside the precautionary principle, it should seriously take into account the issues of uncertainty and irreversibility. It should give value to precautionary measures. This could be done by applying the quasi-option value, while assuming risk-neutrality.[88] In addition,

---

the magnitude of damage should be multiplied by its probability. See Fraiberg and Trebilcock (1998, p. 857).

[84] Many commentators consider CBA as ethically problematic, since it is accused of 'monetizing' human life, health, safety, and the environment, calculating these assets as commodities. See for example Asford (1999, p. 200). For a more optimistic view towards CBA, see for example Kornhauser (2000, pp. 1037–57). Also Posner (2000, pp. 1153–77). Added to these debates, there are also difficulties as to how to measure the value of life. Fraiberg and Trebilcock argue that individuals may value their lives differently. Such differences may contribute to the problem of uncertainty surrounding quantitative CBA. See Fraiberg and Trebilcock (1998, pp. 858–64).

[85] Van den Bergh criticizes the use of quantitative CBA applied to climate change policy, where uncertainty is pervasive. Van den Bergh (2004, pp. 386–7).

[86] This issue will be discussed in the next section.

[87] Neo-classical economic theory argues that a rational decision-maker will chose an option that maximizes its utility. Frank (1999, p. 201).

[88] The theory of 'quasi-option value', first developed by Arrow and Fisher, uses the assumption of risk neutrality, namely by focusing on the expected value of possible outcomes. However, it is assumed that some valuable information will be acquired in the future. In this case, the authors conclude that if a proposed development involves irreversible changes to the environment, and if there is uncertainty about the payoff to the investment in the development, the decision-maker should err on the side of under-investment, namely conservation, rather than over-investment, namely development. This is because the development is irreversible, and hence the mistake of over-investment cannot easily be remedied. In addition, the possibility of obtaining information in the future means that the expected benefit of development under uncertainty is less than that under certainty. Arrow and Fisher (1974, pp. 312–9).

CBA could also assume a certain type of risk aversion, and apply the theory of precautionary effect.[89] Alternatively, if one considers that there is a pure uncertainty, indicated by inability to assign probabilities to each outcome, one could apply the maximin rule[90] or the minimax-regret rule,[91] in order to compare the benefits and opportunity costs of implementing the precautionary principle.

Certainly, the best decision is one based on full information about all possible outcomes. The best thing a decision-maker can do is to strive to resolve the uncertainty. However, it will take some time until the decision-maker resolves

---

89 According to the precautionary effect theory developed by Gollier et al., more uncertainty should induce a prudent decision-maker to take more precautionary decisions today in order to reduce exposure to risk in the future. According to the authors, the precautionary principle is justified if the prospect of improving knowledge induces the decision-maker to increase its current level of prevention. This situation will be achieved when 'the precautionary effect', measured by the level of prudence (P), is greater than twice the 'wealth effect', measured by the level of absolute risk aversion (A). In short, the precautionary principle is justified when $P \geq 2A$. In defining absolute risk aversion, the authors refer to the so-called Arrow–Pratt coefficient of absolute risk aversion, namely $-U''(.)/U'(.)$, and in defining the absolute prudence, the authors refer to the so-called Kimball coefficient of absolute prudence, namely $-U'''(.)/U''(.)$, where $U(.)$ indicates the utility function of the decision-maker. Gollier et al. (2000, pp. 229–53). Quite similarly, Kuntz-Duriseti also interprets the precautionary principle as the precautionary premium which is measured by the level of absolute prudence (P). However, in this case, the author argues that the precautionary principle is justified when $P \geq A$. See Kuntz-Duriseti (2004, pp. 291–301).

90 The maximin rule, in which the decision-maker focuses only on possible losses and choses an alternative that offers the lowest possible losses, is used by Bishop to explain the concept of Safe Minimum Standard (SMS), first developed by Ciriacy-Wantrup in 1968. The SMS is a decision rule which suggests that the decision-maker should avoid the use of resources in a zone where the depletion of resources becomes irreversible. By using the maximin rule, Bishop argues that in the presence of uncertainty and irreversibility, the SMS should be implemented unless the costs of doing so are 'unacceptably large'. Bishop (1978, pp. 10–18). See also Ciriacy-Wantrup (1952, pp. 252–7) and Ready and Bishop (1991, pp. 309–12).

91 Palmini revises Bishop's maximin model by employing a minimax-regret rule. In this regard, the decision-maker should choose an alternative that offers the lowest regret, namely the reduction of welfare resulting from making a wrong decision. Here, the author uses not only the possible direct costs, but also the possible opportunity costs of each alternative. Similar to the conclusion of Bishop, Palmini argues that one needs large social costs of preservation (the SMS) or large benefits of development to reject the preservation. This conclusion confirms a shift of the basic assumption proposed by Ciriacy-Wantrup, namely that preservation is assumed to be highly beneficial unless it is proven that the preservation will require 'immoderate' social costs. Palmini (1999, pp. 463–72). The shift of basic assumption regarding the benefits of preservation will result in a shift in the burden of proof. It is the proponents of development who bear the burden of showing that preservation involves an unacceptably high social cost. See Tisdell (1990, p. 84).

the lack of scientific certainty. Implementing the precautionary principle and CBA will recognize the issue of uncertainty and irreversibility in the decision-making process. This will create a decision that is flexible enough to allow a revision to be made, once necessary information has been acquired sometime in the future.

4.5. Risk Analysis and the Precautionary Principle

Some documents, such as the 2001 EC Communication on the Precautionary Principle, treat the precautionary principle as a means of risk management. The Communication sharply distinguishes risk assessment from risk management. However, the subjective element is pervasive in decision-making, including that of experts. Hence, one could argue that it becomes more difficult to see whether an assessment results from a purely scientific evaluation. Obviously, the question of whether we should maintain the sharp distinction between risk assessment and risk management is still subject to disagreements among commentators. Accordingly, it is also unclear whether the precautionary principle should be considered as a part of risk management, as is proposed by the Communication, or if it should have been applied since the beginning of risk analysis. If the precautionary principle were to be applied from the risk assessment stage, we might find difficulties in designating the economic consideration to the principle, because it seems uncomfortable to employ economic considerations in risk assessment. On the other hand, if we use the precautionary principle merely at the risk management stage, it becomes implausible to carry out an economic analysis of preventive measures relating to an activity when risk assessment has concluded that the activity poses no risk. Unfortunately, it is likely that uncertainty will be ignored in risk assessment.

To some extent, the call to apply the precautionary principle has been triggered by disenchantment towards risk analysis, particularly because it is considered that analysis fails to address public concerns over some environmental risks. For this reason, James Cameron, Will Wade-Gerry and Juli Abouchar argue that the precautionary principle, instead of being treated as a means of risk management, should replace the conventional risk assessment.[92]

---

[92] Cameron et al. (1998, pp. 105–7). Similarly, Tickner and Raffensperger have criticized risk assessment by arguing that it contains several shortcomings, *inter alia* that it is fundamentally undemocratic. They argue that risk assessment traditionally does not include public perceptions, priorities, or needs, and that the process in risk assessment is most often confined to agency and industry scientists, consultants, and sometimes a high-tech environmental group. See Tickner and Raffensperger (2004, pp. 14–15). However, despite its failures, it is very difficult to deny the importance of

Accordingly, the link between the democratization of risk analysis, in the sense of opening up the decision-making process to broader public involvement, and the implementation of the precautionary principle seems to be quite clear. By allowing greater public participation, with respect to as many opinions as possible, including those from contending scientists and lay people, the outcomes resulting from risk analysis would be more diverse compared to the outcomes when the analysis only involves the limited parties of appointed experts.[93]

However, it could still be argued that the task of decision-makers is to follow the evidence, presented by scientists, and not popular opinion. In contrast to the populist approach discussed above, this approach, referred to as the technocratic approach, has based its opinion on some empirical studies demonstrating that the public most of the time has been ill-informed about the risks and hence has perceived the risk mistakenly and irrationally.[94] In this regard, the question of whether ordinary people's perception of risk deserves respect as if it resulted from a rational basis has overarched the debate over technocratic and populist approaches to risk analysis, and this will also influence the debates over the validity of the precautionary principle.

5. CONCLUSION

The three principles, the polluter-pays, prevention, and precautionary principles, are getting more important in environmental policy. This chapter has discussed the possibility of adopting the principles in the Environmental Management Act in Indonesia.

The chapter showed that the three principles are of crucial importance for environmental law and for environmental policy in general. If interpreted correctly, the principles can assist in providing guidance on how policy instru-

---

risk assessment. Risk assessment is useful to form a better understanding about the hazards of an activity and to compare options for prevention, as well as to prioritize activities such as restoration activities and hazardous waste site cleanups. See Tickner and Raffensperger (2004). See also Chapman (1999, pp. 944–7). The latter article shows that neither risk assessment nor the precautionary principle are perfect tools, and that not all tools are appropriate for all situations.

93 In this regard, Vos argues that public participation in the decision-making process could lead not only to public trust in risk analysis, and would thus be capable of fostering a legitimate policy on risks and public acceptance of technologies or activities whose risks are being considered, but could also improve information for policy-making. This is because, so the author states, input from the public might be capable of providing relevant information, values, or questions, which might have been neglected by scientists. See Vos (2004, pp. 18–19).

94 Sunstein (2001, pp. 2–3).

ments should reach an optimal internalization of the externality caused by environmental harm. Thus, the principles certainly have an important role in the development of environmental law and policy for any developing country, whether Indonesia or other country. Of course it is not sufficient merely to incorporate the principles in legislation; this needs to be accompanied by the appropriate (economic) interpretation, as was suggested in this chapter. Moreover, a consequence of the economic analysis presented here might be that more use should be made of economic instruments which are more market oriented. That, however, could not be discussed within the framework of this chapter, which focused on the economic ideas behind environmental principles.[95] Several conclusions may be reached concerning the economic interpretation of the principles we discussed.

The polluter-pays principle, which is aimed primarily at internalizing the so-called environmental costs, argues that the polluter should bear any social costs resulting from its activity, so that the price of its product will reflect the true marginal social costs, namely the costs of marginal private plus marginal environmental costs. An important message from this principle is that one does not need to pursue zero pollution, since this principle assumes that any activity could generate not only costs but also benefit for the society.

The polluter-pays principle may be implemented through various instruments, ranging from environmental taxes to a liability system. Unfortunately – at least this is what has happened in Indonesia – the principle has been misunderstood as merely a part of a liability system, namely a negligence rule. This chapter, on the other hand, suggests that the principle should function as an overarching principle, constituting a goal for environmental policy and law: internalizing the externality.

Some activities pose certain risks that induce decision-makers to take action before the risks materialize because to prevent is better than to cure. This is the idea of the prevention principle. In several conventions, the prevention principle is usually accompanied by an obligation to undertake environmental impact assessment, monitoring, and consultations.

The prevention principle is closely related to the polluter-pays principle and the precautionary principle. Applied effectively, the polluter-pays principle may have a deterrent effect, so that it could ultimately prevent the repetition of similar damage from occurring in the future. Thus, the deterrent effect resulting from the precautionary principle may also have preventive implication. However, in contrast to the polluter-pays principle, prevention applies when damages have not yet materialized, but where there is sound reason to suspect that damages would occur if prevention had not been taken.

---

95 The economic instruments are separately discussed in Chapter 10 of this volume.

Table 3.1 Elements of the precautionary principle in various documents

Document/year	Terminology referring to 'threshold'	Terminology referring to 'uncertainty'	Precautionary measures		
			Type of actions/ explanation	Considerations other than safety reasons before/ when taking actions	The nature of actions
The 1982 World Charter of Nature	Might have an impact on nature; likely to cause irreversible damage to nature; likely to pose a significant risk to nature	Potential adverse effects are not fully understood	Exhaustive examination activities should not proceed		Mandatory ('activities should not proceed')
The 1984 Bremen Declaration, adopted at the First International Conference on the Protection of the North Sea	Damage, which is irreversible or remediable only at considerable expense and over long periods	Proof of harmful effects	Action and precautionary measures	With respect to atmospheric pollution, precautionary measures should be applied based on the BAT	Mandatory ('must not wait')

The 1985 Vienna Convention on the Protection of the Ozone Layer	–	–	Precautionary measures	Measures which have been taken at national and international level	–
The 1987 London Declaration, adopted at the Second International Conference on the Protection of the North Sea	Possible damaging effects of the most dangerous substances	Before a causal link has been established by absolutely clear scientific evidence, the state of knowledge is insufficient	Action to control inputs of such substances; Establishing environmental quality standards and emission standards that provide a strict limitation on emissions of pollutants at source based on safety reasons		Non-mandatory ('maybe required')

Table 3.1 Continued

Document/year	Terminology referring to 'threshold'	Terminology referring to 'uncertainty'	Precautionary measures		
			Type of actions/ explanation	Considerations other than safety reasons before/ when taking actions	The nature of actions
The 1990 The Hague Declaration, adopted at the Third International Conference on the Protection of the North Sea	Potentially damaging impacts	There is no scientific evidence to prove a causal link between emissions and effects	To take action to avoid potential impacts of substances that are persistent, toxic and liable to bioaccumulate		
The 1990 London Protocol to the Vienna Convention			To take precautionary measures to control equitably total global emissions of substances that	The developments in scientific knowledge; Technical and economic considerations;	

			deplete the ozone layer	the developmental needs of developing countries	
The 1990 UN/ECE Ministerial Declaration on Sustainable Development (The 1990 Bergen Declaration)	Serious or irreversible damage	Lack of full scientific certainty	Measures to anticipate, prevent, and attack the causes of environmental degradation		Vague (uncertainty is not a reason for postponing precautionary measures)
Bamako Convention on the Ban of the Import into Africa and the Control of Transboundary Movement and Management of Hazardous Wastes within Africa, signed on 30 January 1991	Cause harm to humans or the environment	Scientific proof regarding harm	Preventing the release of substances into the environment, specifically through the application of clean production methods	–	Mandatory ('shall strive to adopt the preventive and precautionary approach')

Table 3.1 Continued

Document/year	Terminology referring to 'threshold'	Terminology referring to 'uncertainty'	Precautionary measures		
			Type of actions/ explanation	Considerations other than safety reasons before/ when taking actions	The nature of actions
The 1992 Maastricht Treaty[1]	–	–	–	–	–
The 1992 Helsinki Convention on the Protection and Use of Transboundary Watercourses and International Lakes	Potential transboundary impact	Scientific research has not fully proved a causal link between hazardous substances, on the one hand, and their potential transboundary impacts, on the other hand	Action to avoid such potential impact		Vague (uncertainty is not a reason for postponing precautionary measures)

The 1992 Helsinki Convention on the Protection of the Marine Environment of the Baltic Sea Area	Hazards to human health, harm living resources and marine ecosystems, damage amenities or interfere with other legitimate uses of the sea	There is no conclusive evidence of a causal relationship between inputs and their alleged effects	Preventive measures		Mandatory ('shall apply the precautionary principle, i.e. to take . . .')
The 1992 UN Framework Convention on Climate Change	Threats of serious or irreversible damage	Lack of full scientific certainty	To take measures to anticipate, prevent or minimize the causes of climate change and mitigate its adverse effects	Cost-effective to ensure global benefits at the lowest possible cost, particularly the measures should take into account different socio-economic contexts, be comprehensive, cover all relevant sources, sinks and reservoirs of	Vague (uncertainty is not a reason for postponing precautionary measures)

Table 3.1 Continued

Document/year	Terminology referring to 'threshold'	Terminology referring to 'uncertainty'	Precautionary measures		
			Type of actions/ explanation	Considerations other than safety reasons before/ when taking actions	The nature of actions
				greenhouse gases and adaptation, and comprise all economic sectors	
The 1992 Rio Declaration	Threats of serious or irreversible damage	Lack of full scientific certainty	Measures to prevent environmental degradation	Cost-effective	Vague (uncertainty is not a reason for postponing precautionary measures)
The 1992 Convention on Biological Diversity (CBD)	Threat of significant reduction or loss of biological diversity	Lack of scientific certainty	Measures to avoid or minimize such a threat	–	Vague (uncertainty is not a reason for postponing precautionary measures)

The 1992 Convention for the Protection of the Marine Environment of the North-East Atlantic (OSPAR Convention)	Hazards to human health, harm living resources and marine ecosystems, damage amenities or interfere with other legitimate uses of the sea	There is no conclusive evidence of a causal relationship between the inputs and the effects	Preventive measures	–	Mandatory ('to be taken')
The 1993 Odessa Declaration on the Protection of the Black Sea[1]					
The 1994 Oslo Protocol on Further Reduction of Sulphur Emissions[1]					

Table 3.1 Continued

Document/year	Terminology referring to 'threshold'	Terminology referring to 'uncertainty'	Precautionary measures		
			Type of actions/ explanation	Considerations other than safety reasons before/ when taking actions	The nature of actions
The 1994 Convention on the Cooperation for the Protection and Sustainable Development of the Danube River (Danube River Protection Convention)[1]					
The 1994 Energy Charter Treaty[1]					

The 1995 Convention for the Protection of the Marine Environment and the Coastal Region of the Mediterranean (The 1995 Barcelona Convention)	Threats of serious or irreversible damage	Lack of full scientific certainty	Measures to prevent environmental degradation	Cost-effective	Vague (uncertainty is not a reason for postponing precautionary measures)
The 1995 Esjberg Declaration adopted at the Fourth International Conference on the Protection of the North Sea[2]					
The 1996 Izmir Protocol on the Prevention of Pollution of the Mediterranean					

Table 3.1 Continued

Document/year	Terminology referring to 'threshold'	Terminology referring to 'uncertainty'	Precautionary measures		
			Type of actions/ explanation	Considerations other than safety reasons before/ when taking actions	The nature of actions
Sea by Transboundary Movements of Hazardous Wastes and their Disposal (Protocol to the 1995 Barcelona Convention)[1]					
The 1998 Aarhus Protocol (Protocol to the 1979 LRTAP Convention)[3]			Measures to anticipate, prevent or minimize emissions	Consider available information	

The 1998 Aarhus Protocol on Persistent Organic Pollutants (Protocol to the 1979 LRTAP Convention)[3]					
The 1999 Gothenburg Protocol to Abate Acidification, Eutrophication and Ground-Level Ozone (Protocol to the 1979 LRTAP Convention)[3]					
The 2000 Cartagena Protocol on Biosafety	The potential adverse effects and risks to human health	Lack of scientific certainty due to insufficient relevant scientific information and knowledge regarding the	Taking a decision in order to avoid or minimize such potential adverse effects		Mandatory ('shall not prevent')

Table 3.1 Continued

Document/year	Terminology referring to 'threshold'	Terminology referring to 'uncertainty'	Precautionary measures		
			Type of actions/ explanation	Considerations other than safety reasons before/ when taking actions	The nature of actions
		extent of the potential adverse effects of a living modified organism on the conservation and sustainable use of biological diversity			
The 2002 Stockholm Convention on Persistent Organic Pollutants (POPs Convention)[3]	Likely, as a result of its long-range environmental transport, to lead to significant adverse human health and/or environmental effects	Lack of full scientific certainty	To proceed with the proposal in accordance with annex A, B, or C	Socio-economic considerations, particularly costs-benefits analysis, before taking measures	Mandatory ('shall not prevent')

The 2002 Valetta Protocol concerning Cooperation in Preventing Pollution from Ships and, in cases of Emergency, Combating Pollution of the Mediterranean Sea[1]	
The 2002 Bergen Declaration adopted at the Fifth International Conference on the Protection of the North Sea[1]	

Notes:

1 only mentioning the precaution without specifying it or referring to other formulations;
2 referring to the formulation in the 1992 OSPAR Convention;
3 referring also to the fifteenth principle of the Rio Declaration.

One usually refers to the prevention principle to tackle risks under certainty. However, sometimes the probability and magnitude of an event cannot be predicted with full certainty. Nevertheless, if those events are expected to be catastrophic, decision-makers still have an obligation to take action to prevent such catastrophic events, regardless of whether they have full scientific evidence at hand. In this case, one refers to the precautionary principle.

Unfortunately, the importance of the precautionary principle seems to be eroded by the difficulties of determining the level of precaution one should take under uncertainty. In this case, the principle seems to be impracticable and could lead to unnecessary, if not arbitrary, measures. Therefore, if one wishes to implement the principle effectively, economic evaluation is in order. This is the idea of incorporating the principle with cost-effective analysis (or cost–benefit analysis) as formulated for instance in Principle 15 of the Rio Declaration.

REFERENCES

Arrow, K.J. and A.C. Fisher (1974), 'Environmental Preservation, Uncertainty, and Irreversibility', *The Quarterly Journal of Economics,* **88** (2), 312–19.

Asford, Nicholas A. (1999), 'A Conceptual Framework for the Use of the Precautionary Principle in Law', in Carolyn Raffensperger and Joel Tickner (eds), *Protection Public Health and the Environment*, Washington, DC: Island Press, pp. 198–206.

Bergkamp, L. (2002), 'Understanding the Precautionary Principle (Part I)', *Environmental Liability,* **1**, 27.

Bernstein, A. (1999), 'Precaution and Respect', in Carolyn Raffensperger and Joel Tickner (eds), *Protection, Public Health and the Environment,* Washington, DC: Island Press, pp. 148–58.

Birnie, P. and A. Boyle (1995), *International Law and the Environment*, Oxford: Clarendon Press.

Bishop, R.C. (1978), 'Endangered Species and Uncertainty: The Economics of a Safe Minimum Standard', *American Journal of Agricultural Economics*, **57**, 10–18.

Boehmer-Christiansen, S. (1994), 'The Precautionary Principle in Germany – Enabling Government', in T. O'Riordan and J. Cameron (eds), *Interpreting Precautionary Principle*, London: Earthscan Publications, pp. 31–60.

Burrows, P. (1999), 'Combining Regulation and Legal Liability for the Control of External Costs', *International Review of Law and Economics*, **24**, 227–44.

Cameron, J. (2001), 'The Precautionary Principle in International Law', in T. O'Riordan., J Cameron and A. Jordan (eds), *Reinterpreting the Precautionary Principle*, London: Cameron May, pp. 113–42.

Cameron, J. and J. Abouchar (1996), 'The Status of the Precautionary Principle in International Law', in D. Freestone and E. Hey (eds), *The Precautionary Principle and International Law: The Challenge of Implementation*, The Hague: Kluwer International, pp. 29–52.

Cameron, J., W. Wade-Gerry and J. Abouchar (1998), 'Precautionary Principle and Future Generation', in E. Agius, S. Busuttil, T. Kim and K. Yazaki (eds), *Future Generation and International Law*, London: Earthscan Publications, pp. 93–116.

Chapman, P.M. (1999), 'Risk Assessment and the Precautionary Principle: A Time and a Place', *Marine Pollution Bulletin*, **38** (10), 944–7.

Christoforou, T. (2003), 'The Precautionary Principle in European Community Law and Science', in J.A. Tickner (ed.), *Precaution, Environmental Science, and Preventive Public Policy*, Washington, DC: Island Press, 241–62.

Ciriacy-Wantrup, S.V. (1952), *Resource Conservation: Economics and Policies*, Berkeley: University of California Press.

Coase, R.H. (1960), 'The Problem of Social Cost', *The Journal of Law and Economics*, **3**, 1–44.

Cooter, R. and T. Ulen (1988), *Law and Economics*, first edition, London: Scott Foresman

Crowards, T.M. (1998), 'Safe Minimum Standards: Costs and Opportunities', *Ecological Economics*, **25**, 308–10.

De Sadeleer, N. (2002), *Environmental Principles: From Political Slogans to Legal Rules*, Oxford: Oxford University Press.

Faure, Michael (2001), *Environmental Law and Economics,* Maastricht: METRO.

Faure, Michael (ed.) (2003), *Deterrence, Insurability, and Compensation in Environmental Liability: Future Developments in the European Union*, Vienna: Springer-Verlag.

Faure, M. and M.H.S. Ruegg (1994), 'Environmental Standards Setting through General Principles of Environmental Law', in M. Faure, J. Vervaele and A. Weale (eds), *Environmental Standards in the European Union in an Interdisciplinary Framework*, Antwerpen: Maklu, pp. 39–60.

Faure, M. and G. Skogh (2003), *The Economic Analysis of Environmental Policy and Law. An Introduction*, Cheltenham: Edward Elgar.

Fisher, E. (2002), 'Precaution, Precaution Everywhere: Developing a "Common Understanding" of the Precautionary Principle in the European Community', *Maastricht Journal of European and Comparative Law*, **9** (1), pp. 7–28.

Flemming, D. (1996), 'The Economics of Taking Care: An Evaluation of the Precautionary Principle', in D. Freestone and E. Hey (eds), *The Precautionary Principle and International Law: the Challenge of Implementation*, The Hague: Kluwer International, pp. 147–70.

Fraiberg, J.D. and M.J. Trebilcock (1998), 'Risk Regulation: Technocratic and Democratic Tools for Regulatory Reform', *McGill Law Journal*, **43**, 836–88.

Frank, Robert H. (1999), *Microeconomics and Behavior*, Boston: McGraw-Hill, fourth edition.

Freestone, David and Ellen Hey (1996), 'Origin and Development of the Precautionary Principle', in David Freestone and Ellen Hey (eds), *The Precautionary Principle and International Law: The Challenge of Implementation*, The Hague: Kluwer Law International, pp. 4–15.

Geistfeld, M. (2001), 'Implementing the Precautionary Principle', *The Environmental Law Reporter*, **31**, 11326–33.

Gollier, C., B. Jullien and N. Treich (2000), 'Scientific Progress and Irreversibility: An Economic Interpretation of the "Precautionary Principle" ', *Journal of Public Economics*, **75**, 229–53.

Griffiths, A. and S. Wall (2000), *Intermediate Microeconomics: Theory and Applications*, Harlow: Prentice Hall, 2nd edition.

Groosman, B. (2001), 'Pollution Tax', in B. Bouckaert and G. de Geest (eds), *Encyclopedia of Law and Economics Volume II: Civil Law and Economics*, Cheltenham: Edward Elgar, pp. 538–68.

Hanley, Nick and Clive L. Spash (1993), *Cost–Benefit Analysis and the Environment*, Aldershot: Edward Elgar.

Hohmann, H. (1994), *Precautionary Legal Duties and Principles of Modern International Environmental Law: The Precautionary Principle: International Environmental Law between Exploitation and Protection*, London: Graham & Trotman.

Hunter, D., J. Salzman and D. Zaelke (1998), *International Environmental Law and Policy*, New York: Foundation Press.

Indur, M. Goklany (2000), 'Applying the Precautionary Principle to Global Warming', *Weidenbaum Center Working Paper*, 158, November 2000, Murray Weidenbaum Center on the Economy, Government, and Public Policy, Washington University in St Louis, 24.

Jordan, A. and T. O'Riordan (1999), 'The Precautionary Principle in Contemporary Environmental Policy and Politics', in C. Raffensperger and J. Tickner (eds), *Protection Public Health and the Environment*, Washington, DC: Island Press, pp. 13–36.

Kaplow, L. and S. Shavell (1999), 'Economic Analysis of Law', *NBER Working Paper*, 6960 (February).

Kolstad, C.D., T.S. Ulen and G.V. Johnson (1990), 'Ex Post Liability for Harm vs. Ex Ante Safety Regulation: Substitutes of Complements?', *The American Economic Review*, **80** (4), 888–901.

Kornhauser, Lewis A. (2000), 'On Justifying Cost–Benefit Analysis', in: *The Journal of Legal Studies*, **24**, 1037–57.

Krämer, L. (2003), 'The Genesis of EC Environmental Principles', *Research Paper in Law No. 7, European Legal Studies*, 12.

Kunreuther, H.C. and P.K. Freeman (2001), 'Insurability, Environmental Risks and the Law', in A. Heyes (ed.), *The Law and Economics of the Environment,* Cheltenham: Edward Elgar, pp. 304–5

Kuntz-Duriseti, K. (2004) 'Evaluating the Economic Value of the Precautionary Principle Using Cost Benefit Analysis to Place a Value on Precaution', *Environmental Science and Policy*, **7**, 291–301.

Marchant, G.E. (2002), 'Two Problems with the Precautionary Principle', <www.life-sciencesnetwork.com/repository/education/defining_pp.pdf>, 30 May.

Marr, S. and A. Schwemer (2004), 'The Precautionary Principle in German Environmental Law', in the Yearbook on European Environmental Law, Oxford: Oxford University Press, pp. 125–48.

Nollkaemper, A. (1996), ' "What You Risk Reveals What You Value" and Other Dilemmas Encountered in the Legal Assault on Risks', in D. Freestone and E. Hey (eds), *The Precautionary Principle and International Law: The Challenge of Implementation*, The Hague: Kluwer International, pp. 81–92.

Palmini, D. (1999), 'Uncertainty, Risk Aversion, and the Game Theoretic Foundations of the Safe Minimum Standard: A Reassessment', *Ecological Economics*, **29**, 463–72.

Pearce, David W. (1994), 'The Precautionary Principle and Economic Analysis', in Tim O'Riordan and James Cameron (eds), *Interpreting the Precautionary Principle*, London: Earthscan, pp. 132–51.

Pindyck, R.S. and D.L. Rubenfield (2001), *Microeconomics,* New Jersey: Prentice Hall.

Polinsky, A.M. and S. Shavell (1992), 'Optimal Cleanup and Liability after Environmentally Harmful Discharges', *NBER Working Paper No. 4176.*

Posner, Richard (2000), 'Cost–Benefit Analysis: Definition, Justification, and Comment on Conference Papers', *The Journal of Legal Studies*, **24**, 1153–77.

Ramchandani, R. and David W. Pearce (1992), 'Alternative Approaches to Setting Effluent Quality Standards: Precautionary, Critical Load, and Cost–Benefit Approaches', *CSERGE Working Paper*, WM 92-04.

Ready, R.C. and R.C. Bishop (1991), 'Endangered Species and the Safe Minimum Standard', *American Journal of Agricultural Economics*, **73**, 309–12.

Resnik, D.B. (2003), 'Is the Precautionary Principle Unscientific?', *Studies in History and Philosophy of Biological and Biomedical Science*, **34**, 330.

Sandin, P. (1999), 'Dimensions of the Precautionary Principle', *Human and Ecological Risk Assessment,* **5** (5), 889–907.

Sands, P. (1995), *Principles of International Environmental Law, Volume I, Frameworks, Standards and Implementation*, Manchester: Manchester University Press.

Shavell, S. (1980), 'Strict Liability versus Negligence', *The Journal of Legal Studies*, **9**, pp. 1–10.

Shavell, S. (1983), 'Liability for Harm versus Regulation of Safety', *NBER Working Paper*, No. 1218.

Shavell, S. (2003), 'Economic Analysis of Accident Law', *NBER Working Paper*, No. 9694, chapters 4, 5.

Solberg, E.J. (1982), *Intermediate Microeconomics,* Texas: Business Publications.

Sugden, R. and A. Williams (1978), *The Principles of Practical Cost–Benefit Analysis*, Oxford: Oxford University Press.

Sunstein, C.R. (2001), 'The Laws of Fear', *Chicago John M. Olin Law and Economic Working Paper*, No. 128.

Sunstein, C.R. (2002), *Risk and Reason: Safety, Law, and the Environment*, Cambridge: Cambridge University Press.

Tickner, J. and C. Raffensperger (2004), 'The Precautionary Principle in Action: A Handbook', *Science and Environmental Health Network (SEHN)*, <www.biotech_info.net/handbook.pdf>, 26 March, 3–4.

Tisdell, C.A. (1990), 'Economics and the Debate about Preservation of Species, Crop Varieties and Genetic Diversity', *Ecological Economics*, **2**, pp. 77–90.

Trouwborst, A. (2002), *Evolution and Status of the Precautionary Principle in International Law*, The Hague: Kluwer Law International.

Turner, R.K, D. Pearce and I. Bateman (1994), *Environmental Economics: An Elementary Introduction,* New York: Harvester Wheatsheaf.

Van den Bergh, J.C.J.M. (2004), 'Optimal Climate Change Policy is a Utopia: From Quantitative to Qualitative Cost–Benefit Analysis', *Ecological Economics*, **48**, 386–7.

Van Zwanenberg, Patrick and A. Stirling (2003), 'Risk and Precaution in the US and Europe: A Response to Vogel', in H. Somsen (ed), *Yearbook of European Environmental Law*. Vol. 3, Oxford: Oxford University Press, pp. 43–56.

Vogel, D. (2003), 'The Politics of Risk Regulation in Europe and the United States', in H. Somsen (ed.), *Yearbook of European Environmental Law, Vol. 3,* 2003, available at <http://faculty.haas.berkeley.edu/vogel/uk%20oct.pdf>.

Von Moltke, K. (1996), 'The Relationship between Policy, Science, Technology, Economics and Law in the Implementation of the Precautionary Principle', in D. Freestone and E. Hey (eds), *The Precautionary Principle and International Law: The Challenge of Implementation*, The Hague: Kluwer International, pp. 97–108.

Vos, Ellen (2004), 'Overcoming the Crisis of Confidence: Risk Regulation in an Enlarged European Union', inaugural speech, University of Maastricht.
Wiener, J.B. (2003), 'Whose Precaution after All? A Comment on the Comparison and Evolution of Risk Regulatory Systems', *Duke Journal of Comparative and International Law,* **13**, 207–62.

4. The implications of international conventions for the development of the Environmental Management Act

Daud Silalahi

1. INTRODUCTION

This chapter deals with a particular aspect of the revision process of the Indonesian Environmental Management Act, namely the relationship between international law and more particularly international environmental agreements and national environmental law, especially the Environmental Management Act of 1997. It is my strong belief that within this reform process of the Environmental Management Act the dispositions contained in international environmental agreements will have to play an important role. Of course I will examine this relationship more particularly with respect to the case of Indonesia, although it will be clear that it bears importance for many other countries as well. My general message is therefore that incorporating international environmental obligations in national law can on the one hand lead to a furthering and strengthening of international environmental legal obligations but on the other hand also increase the quality of national environmental law.

Indeed, pollution appears at local, regional or global level. For example, the use of an environmentally unfriendly technology can become a threat for biosafety. There is also significant use of dangerous chemical toxics which are used in industrial activities. These may harm not only the environment and human health, but also the global climate, including the ozone layer. Environmental impacts, therefore, often go beyond national boundaries. Consequently, there is an urgent need to create environmental standards and legal mechanisms, including international cooperation for a better environment. Through international conventions, progress on international law has influenced the development of national law. It has encouraged national law to meet minimum international standards.[1] The contribution of international

1 On the way in which international environmental law influences environmental legal regimes in national states generally, see Birnie and Boyle (2002) and Sands (2003).

principles, requirements and standards to the establishment of new national legislation can be described as follows.

The improvement of principles of international law has affected the development of national law, either through the improvement of existing laws, through the creation of new law, or through case law. Principles of international environmental law will soon also influence local environmental regulations. Indonesian local communities have developed an increased environmental awareness due to local environmental disasters caused by cross-boundary pollution, such as forest fires caused by illegal logging in Indonesia and seashore pollution caused by (foreign) ships passing through the Indonesian seas. Hence, even at the local level in Indonesia, there is a growing interest in the value and importance of international environmental law.

Indonesia is an archipelagic state. Therefore, the transnational legal aspects of sea and shore law management will be associated with the legal concept of an archipelagic state. Based on the new international Law of the Sea 1982,[2] Indonesia was internationally recognized as an archipelagic state, and is now known for its archipelagic (nusantara) legal principles. They were applied with respect to several cases of sea pollution such as the Showa Maru (1975) and Nagasaki Spirit (1993) cases. After those events, there were later incidents such as the case of a Greek ship at Balikpapan, the sinking of a storage tank at Karimun and the case of Tanjung Balai in August 2004. In all of those cases local authorities had been requested to take action. There is an urgent need for a new law amending the current Indonesian Environmental Management Act since these aspects are insufficiently taken into account in the current act. Another indication of the need for a new law is the government's effort to ratify the Biodiversity Convention, the Climate Change Convention, including the Kyoto Protocol and the Cartagena Protocol.

The importance of including transnational legal aspects of environmental issues in the amendment of the EMA of 1997 can be seen in the elucidation of Article 17 of the previous Environmental Management Act of 1982.[3] This stated that restoration of the environment that has been damaged and polluted by activity from abroad is based on the memo of understanding between countries.[4] The 1982 Environmental Management Act thus took into account

---

[2] We refer here to the well-known United Nations Convention on the Law of the Sea (also referred to as UNCLOS).

[3] Article 17 of the Act no. 4 of 1982 concerning basic provisions for the management of the living environment provided: 'Provisions on the overall and sectoral prevention and abatement of damage and pollution of the living environment and its control shall be established by legislation'.

[4] Indeed, the elucidation of the Environmental Management Act of 1982

transnational-environmental issues, but this interest is not shown in the 1997 Environmental Management Act. Nevertheless, it should be emphasized that as an archipelagic state, Indonesia is seriously at risk of becoming a victim of transboundary pollution that may damage its ecosystem. Therefore, it is important to incorporate transnational legal aspects with respect to environmental issues once again in a new version of the Environmental Management Act, as was the case with the Environmental Management Act of 1982.

Hence, it will be clear that during the reform process of the Environmental Management Act of 1997 international environmental law will have to be taken into account. After this introduction (Section 1) I will give an overview of transnational environmental legal issues that in my view will have to be included in the new Environmental Management Act (Section 2). In this respect special attention will be paid to conventions dealing with marine pollution, given their importance for Indonesia as an archipelagic state. However, other conventions, especially those dealing with international legal principles, will be mentioned as well. Then I will take a brief look at the situation in a few other countries, to indicate in what way international conventions play a role in national law in Australia, the Philippines, Canada and the USA (Section 3). Finally, I will comment on several specific rules in the current Environmental Management Act of 1997 and indicate in what respect they will have to be adapted, taking into account the obligations under international environmental law (Section 4). Hence, this study is a contribution to showing the relationship between international environmental law and the reform process of environmental legislation in a developing country like Indonesia. Hence, I wish to show with this essay that principles contained in international environmental agreements may further the development of environmental regulation in developing countries. The chapter ends with a few concluding remarks (Section 5).

2. TRANSNATIONAL-ENVIRONMENTAL ISSUES TO BE INCLUDED IN THE NEW ENVIRONMENTAL MANAGEMENT ACT

As an archipelagic state whereby three quarters of its territory consists of sea, Indonesia is in a risky position as a potential victim of sea pollution. The substance of marine pollution is addressed through the IMO (International

---

provided as far as Article 17 is concerned: 'the abatement of environmental damage and pollution caused by activities outside the state territory is carried out through agreements between countries'.

Maritime Organization) conventions. Indonesia is located on a sea-transportation route that connects industrial countries and developing countries. This route is used to link oil-producer countries (in the Middle East) with oil-buyer countries (Japan, Australia and other Asian countries). It is relevant to discuss conventions relating to the control of transnational marine pollution issues in the amendment of the 1997 Environmental Management Act, considering the high incidence of marine pollution in this area, for example in the Malaka Straits, the Makasar Straits and the location of oil terminals in the ports of Balikpapan, Dumai, Cilacap, etc. In my opinion, the adoption of conventions that deal with the prevention and restoration of marine pollution was stated in the 1982 Environmental Management Act by a law statement 'to prevent, reduce, and control sea pollution, including environment restoration'. Indonesia, home to and coast of the world's largest tropical forests, rich in biodiversity and other natural resources, faces natural-resources exploitation levels that damage environmental conservation and sustainable environmental management. The new Environmental Management Act should determine the scope of the state's responsibility at local, regional and global, as imposed by the biodiversity and climate change conventions of 1992. The implications of those conventions for the revision of the Environmental Management Act are discussed below.

The United Nations Convention on the Law of the Sea 1982, especially part XII concerning Protection and Preservation of Marine Environment, is highly important in the reform process.

2.1. Article 211 Law of the Sea 1982 concerning Sea Pollution from Vessels

This article regulates the states' obligation to establish international rules and standards for the prevention, reduction and control of pollution of the marine environment from vessels. Therefore, the possibility of incidents that may cause sea pollution, including seashore and other pollution that endangers the archipelagic state, can be reduced. States shall establish laws and regulations for the prevention, reduction and control of pollution of the marine environment from vessels flying their flag or vessels of their registry. Such laws and regulations shall at least have the same effect as that of generally accepted international rules and standards established through a competent international organization or general diplomatic conferences. Coastal states may, in exercising of their sovereignty within their territorial sea, establish national laws and regulations for the prevention, reduction and control of marine pollution from vessels. Such laws and regulations however shall not hamper the innocent passage of foreign vessels.

2.2. Article 220 Law of the Sea 1982 concerning Enforcement by Coastal States[5]

This provision states that when a vessel is voluntarily within a port or at an offshore terminal of a state, that state may bring proceedings against any violation of national laws and regulations established in accordance with the present convention or applicable international rules and standards for the prevention, reduction and control of pollution from vessels when the violation has occurred within the territorial sea or the exclusive economic zone of that state. If there is clear evidence that a vessel navigating in the territorial sea has violated national laws and regulations established in accordance with the present convention or applicable international rules and standards for the prevention, reduction and control of pollution from vessels, that state may undertake physical inspection of the vessels relating to the violation and may, when it is warranted by the evidence of the case, cause proceedings, including arrest of the vessel, to be taken in accordance with its law.

2.3. Article 227 concerning Investigation of Foreign Vessels

States shall not delay a foreign vessel longer than is essential for the purposes of investigation provided for in Articles 217, 219 and 221 of this convention. If the investigation indicates a violation of applicable laws and regulations or international rules and standards for the preservation of the marine environment, release shall be made subject to reasonable procedures such as bonding or other appropriate financial security. Without prejudice to applicable international rules and standards relating to the seaworthiness of ships, the release of a vessel may, whenever it would present an unreasonable threat of damage to the marine environment, be refused or made conditional upon proceeding to the nearest appropriate repair yard.

2.4. Article 228 concerning Suspension and Restrictions on Institution of Proceedings

Proceedings to impose penalties in respect of any violation of applicable laws

---

5 Article 220 (1) concerning the enforcement by coastal states provides: 'When a vessel is voluntarily within a port or at an off-shore terminal of a State, that State may, subject to section 7, institute proceedings in respect of any violation of its laws and regulations adopted in accordance with this Convention of applicable international rules and standards for the prevention, reduction and control of pollution from vessels when the violation has occurred within the territorial sea or the exclusive economic zone of that State'.

and regulations or international rules and standards relating to the prevention, reduction and control of pollution from vessels committed by a foreign vessel beyond the territorial sea of the state instituting proceedings shall be suspended upon the taking of proceedings to impose penalties under corresponding charges by the flag state within six months of the first institution of proceedings, unless those proceedings relate to a case of major damage to the coastal state or the flag state in question has repeatedly disregarded its obligations to enforce effectively the applicable international rules and standards in respect of violations committed by its vessels.

2.5. Article 229 and 235 concerning Institution of Civil Proceedings and Responsibility and Liability

These articles state that nothing in the present convention shall affect the institution of civil proceedings in respect of any claim for loss or damage resulting from pollution of the marine environment (Article 229) and that states are responsible and shall ensure that resources are available in accordance with their legal systems for prompt and adequate compensation or other relief. Article 237 regulates the obligations under other conventions on the protection and preservation of the marine environment such as the IMO conventions on the marine environment.[6]

2.6. Article 292 concerning Prompt Release of Vessels

This article stated that, where the authorities of a state party have detained a vessel flying the flag of another state party and it is alleged that the coastal state has failed, neglected or refused to comply with the relevant provisions of the present convention for the prompt release of the vessel or its crew upon the posting of a reasonable bond or other financial security, the question of release from detention may be brought before any court or tribunal agreed upon by the parties. Failing such agreement within 10 days from the time of detention, the question of release may be brought before any court or tribunal accepted by the detaining state under Article 287, unless the parties otherwise agree.

In order to understand the implications of such international rules and standards, based on the convention, for national laws and regulations, I have

---

6 Article 237 (1) of UNCLOS concerning the obligations under other conventions on the protection and preservation of the marine environment provides: 'the provisions of this part are without prejudice to the specific obligations assumed by states under special conventions and agreements concluded previously which relate to the protection and preservation of the marine environment and to agreements which may be concluded in furtherance of the general principles set forth in this convention'.

identified several regulations in Indonesia that contain provisions related to this convention, such as:

2.7. Act No. 6/1996 concerning Indonesian Waters

This Act deals with, for example, foreign vessels which carry hazardous and toxic waste and with the management, protection and preservation of the Indonesian marine environment (Article 23). Article 24 deals with the execution of state jurisdiction and with law enforcement in Indonesian waters.

2.8. Act No. 21/1992 concerning Navigation

This Act deals with salvage activities to help vessels in case of an accident (Article 19). The Act equally deals with issues like compensation (Articles 20, 33), seaworthiness (Articles 35–43), responsibility of the captain and master of the ship (Articles 55–64), prevention and restoration of ships (Articles 65–8), investigation (Article 99) and with the crime of marine pollution from ships (Articles 119, 120).

2.9. Act No. 5/1990 concerning Conservation and Ecosystem

This has developed from Article 9 (3) of the 1997 Environmental Management Act as a part of the law on the environmental management system.[7] The provisions in this article regulate biodiversity related to the Biodiversity Convention and the Cartagena Protocol of 2000, including the UN Framework Convention about Climate Change as ratified by the Government of Indonesia.

2.10. Action Programmes

Action programmes that are promulgated regionally or globally are often the driving forces behind change and foster the development of national environment legislation. In this respect we can refer *inter alia* to:

- The basic provisions concerning the Management of the Sea and the seashore as laid down in Chapter 17 of Agenda 21 concerning Integrated Coastal Zone Management. These international rules became

---

[7] Article 9 (3) of the current Environmental Management Act of 1997 provides that: 'environmental management must be performed in an integrated manner with special management protection of non-biological natural resources, protection of artificial resources, conservation of biological natural resources and their ecosystems, cultural preservation, bio-diversity and climate change'.

guidelines for the making of the Indonesian Act on Coastal Zone Management which is, at this moment, being publicly consulted.

- Development of a concept of protected areas and restricted areas for coastal zone and marine space, taken from part XII Law of the Sea 1982.[8] This document is also the basis for a regional cooperation programme called Reversing Environmental Degradation Trends in the South China Sea and Gulf of Thailand Project that relate to marine and seashore pollution controls with respect to marine and seashore resources such as mangrove, sea grass, coral reef, fisheries, and wetlands.
- Rules from the Convention on Biodiversity and its protocols that need to be taken into account during the change of the Environmental Management Act are *inter alia*:

  - the precautionary principle and the common but differentiated responsibility principle;
  - the need for institutional strengthening of community capacity building and the need for the development of an information management system based on recognized standards;
  - efforts to attain the optimal benefits from modern uses of biotechnology in a way which is safe for humans and does not affect biodiversity.

- Rules from the UN Framework Convention on Climate Change and the Kyoto Protocol on Climate Change that need to be taken into account during the revision of the Environmental Management Act are:

  - enforce rules relating to national activities and businesses that potentially create air pollution in order to allow them to receive funds from industrial countries to develop low-emission industry and transportation. Even though developing countries don't have the obligation to reduce greenhouse gases under the convention, they can voluntarily participate;
  - open new investment opportunities for industrial countries in Indonesia through the so-called Clean Development Mechanism;
  - enforce cooperation with industrial countries through the Clean Development Mechanism to resolve and strengthen the capacity, law, institutions and technology to reduce the emissions of greenhouse gases;

---

8 As I mentioned above, part XII of UNCLOS deals with the protection and preservation of the marine environment.

- foster the development of industry and transportation with lower emissions through clean and efficient technology and through the use of sustainable energy;
- improve forest and land capacity to absorb greenhouse gases.

– Rules from the Vienna Convention (1985) and Montreal Protocol (1992) for the protection of the ozone layer which need to be considered during the change of the Environmental Management Act. If these rules are taken into account in the new Environmental Management Act, the existing general and sectoral rules will have to be re-formulated as national and sectoral basic laws.
– Rules from other national acts that are relevant for the change of the Environmental Management Act are:

- Act No. 41/1999 with respect to Forestry
- Act No. 7/2004 with respect to Water
- Act No. 9/1985 with respect to Fisheries
- Act No. 5/1983 with respect to Economic Exclusive Zone
- Act No. 5/1990 with respect to Conservation and Ecosystem
- Act No. 5/1984 with respect to Industry
- Act No. 21/1992 with respect to Navigation
- Act No. 6/1996 with respect to Indonesian Waters

Other rules that are relevant for this discussion concern land conversion and land-used contract. These laws are of importance in order to guarantee that the reform will not reduce national food production. In addition, funding of mechanisms financed by the industrial countries to reduce greenhouse gas emissions through voluntary participation will have to be developed.

3. COMPARATIVE STUDIES

As a comparative study we can mention that many other countries' environmental regulations have already taken into account international conventions in their environmental laws. In particular:

3.1. Australia

Australian national legislation adopted international conventions, but they included further adjustments with respect to issues such as biological diversity, protected areas, wildlife protection, wetlands, forests, trade in endangered species, the Convention on the Control of Transboundary Movement and

Disposal of Hazardous Wastes adopted in Basel 1989 and the London Dumping Convention for the prevention of hazardous waste dumping at sea. The Australian law has also integrated OECD principles into its environmental policy because of the use of hazardous toxic substances and waste in their industrial activities.

3.2. The Philippines

In the Philippines, most of the rules incorporated in the conventions were directly adopted as a source of law by the decision-maker and judges, without an obligation to provide additional implementing legislation as is the case in Indonesia. A case concerning a permit for forest cutting was decided by the Supreme Court in the Philippines in 1994 by using the international conventions and more particularly the Rio Declaration 1992. Hence in the Philippines treaty provisions can be applied directly by national courts without the need to have implementing legislation.

3.3. Canada and USA

Both countries are using their national environment legal system to implement the convention's rules in their national acts. Take the example of the Oil Pollution Act of 1990 in the US. With this Act the US has integrated international oil pollution prevention and removal into its national acts. The integration of a convention's rule into a national act, especially for marine pollution, can also be a reference for the development of a new Environmental Management Act.

4. COMMENTS ON SEVERAL RULES OF THE ENVIRONMENTAL MANAGEMENT ACT OF 1997

From the explanation of the dispositions contained in the various conventions discussed above, the subsequent identification of related rules and acts in Indonesia and Indonesian experience with transboundary pollution cases, including other countries' experiences, several comments can be formulated with respect to the need to revise the Environmental Management Act in Indonesia:

4.1. The Improvement of Several General Provisions

The general provisions, especially the definitions and the terms adopted from international conventions, should be formulated in a simple and interpretable manner. Among terms that still need a definition and more precision are: ecological damages, environmental threats, danger to human health, sustainable development law, and certainty related to the legal regime.

4.2. Improvement of Basic Principles

An assessment and implementation of international conventions should lead to further improvement in the new laws that relate to the field of environmental law. Some of those new principles are the precautionary principle, common but differentiated responsibilities, the principle of prior notification, the strict liability principle in compensation, etc.[9]

4.3. Institutional Arrangements

Several measures have to be taken to improve the institutional arrangements with respect to environmental law and policy. These institutional arrangements then have to function as policy formulation, they have to set national goals and objectives, promote and facilitate coordination, cooperation and designate institutional responsibilities, including delegated authority of regional agencies. Because of decentralization in Indonesia, the definition and scope of responsible authorities and the relationship between them as well as the distribution of powers are seen in this light. The decentralization idea equally has its importance for other issues, like relations with other countries, the availability of experts and of community and institutional capacity.[10] Also the relationship with international organizations or institutions, either as a focal point of international and regional programmes or as project executor of national, regional and institutional programmes that are funded by international organizations or institutions needs to be clarified in institutional arrangements.

4.4. Legal Instruments

There is another issue to be taken into account in the revision of the Environmental Management Act: the relationship between Environmental Impact Assessment (EIA) and Environmental Risk Assessment (ERA). The EIA needs to be simplified. The new Environmental Management Act should provide a stronger and clearer legal base for EIA and should also include the development of an ERA policy and procedure. A clear relationship between

---

9 See on the importance of incorporating general principles into the Indonesian Environmental Management Act also the contribution by Wibisana to this volume.

10 On the importance of the decentralization issue for the revision of the Environmental Management Act in Indonesia, see Chapter 7 of this volume.

the EIA, environmental audit and the ERA needs to be elaborated in the new EMA. A clear legal concept of EIA, ERA and environmental audit could improve the development of substance, procedures and institutions through acts, government regulations, regional regulations, ministrial decrees as well as technical guidance. Moreover, guidelines and lists of activity that should have an EIA or an ERA, and guidelines for environmental audit should be developed.

A further point for consideration is the assessment and adjustment of environment quality standards, including standards relating to the marine environment as an adjustment to international conventions (conservation, protection area, application of *if clauses* such as an 'escape clause or review clause' on mining based on available technology assessment, and transnational aspect of hazardous waste and toxic activities, reception facilities regulation, seashore management).

Also important is the formulation of certification and licences (integrated with the environmental audit system including the drafting of a Master Plan of Development of Seashore and Special, Strategic Areas) and simple procedures applicable at the regional level, including the possibility of cancelling a certification or a licence when the holders failed to meet the professional requirements.

There need to be improvements to technical advisory committees and peer-groups, with qualifications of expert with special expertise; the criteria for lists of expert groups witness as a base for expert appointment.

Attention should also be paid to aspects of legal procedure. Indeed a specific procedure for environmental disputes may have to be developed as *lex specialis* for environmental cases. This is felt to be needed due to the controversial debate concerning Article 35 (*strict liability*) and Article 39 of the current Environmental Management Act related to the existing law of procedure for the application of strict liability in Indonesia.[11] Strict liability for environmental harm should be implemented as a requirement of the international conventions, specifically in environmental cases.

Also instruments of environmental funding have to be installed. When

---

[11] Currently Article 35 of the Environmental Management Act of 1997 provides for a strict liability role: 'The party responsible for a business and/or activity which gives rise to a large impact on the environment, which uses hazardous and toxic materials, and/or produces hazardous and toxic waste, is strictly liable for losses which are given rise to, with the obligation to pay compensation directly and immediately upon occurrence of environmental pollution and/or damage'. (See on this strict liability regime in Indonesian environmental law). Article 39 of the Environmental Management Act, however, stipulates: 'Procedures for the submission of legal actions in environmental problems by individuals, the community, and/or environmental organizations refers to the applicable civil procedures law in CPNL'.

installing these instruments, international conventions on the environment, particularly those related to the protection of the marine environment, need to be taken into account. In this respect we refer more particularly to the obligation contained in many international conventions (as for instance the convention on civil liability for oil pollution damage, the so-called CLC Convention) to impose insurance or other financial guarantees to make sure that compensation to victims will be awarded. Since Indonesia is, as we stated clearly above, an archipelagic state, the guarantee of such funding for damages is especially important in marine environmental cases. Therefore, when redrafting the Indonesian Environmental Management Act, it seems important that the funding mechanisms provided for in international conventions and in international standards are also incorporated in Indonesian law.

Finally, an environmental tribunal should also be installed to take responsibility for the administrative review of administrative decisions.[12] Moreover, one might equally consider the setting-up of ad hoc tribunals to deal with environmental cases.

5. CONCLUSIONS

The analysis above can be summarized as follows.

The contribution of the principles of sustainable development embedded in various conventions and protocols to the amendment of the Environmental Management Act of 1997 should be recognized as the new development of environmental law in Indonesia. The implications of those provisions to the progressive development of environmental law in Indonesia will be discussed through legislation (and environmental cases). As an archipelagic state, Indonesia should consider that some transnational legal aspects exist in marine and coastal areas. Some cases related to marine and coastal areas in Indonesia should be learned to be used as significant evidence for the development of the Environmental Management Act of 1997. Some principles and provisions within the international conventions and its protocols ratified by the government of Indonesia should be learned and discussed in order to consider their implications for the amendment of EMA 1997. This evaluation should be considered, first, as the implementation of international obligations contained in the ratified conventions and protocols, and secondly, as the updating of the existing legislation with respect to the progressive development of law in general. Comparative study of environmental acts of other states should be used to support and encourage the harmonization of provisions of similar acts

12 On administrative review, see also Chapter 8 of this volume.

and standards, specifically of transnational aspects of the Environmental Management Act. Moreover, several specific conclusions can be based on the observations formulated above.

From the general provisions of the ratified conventions, which of course also have their importance for Indonesia, we can learn that environmental legislation has to be formulated, in simple terms in its legal terminology, in a way in which the terminology can be made operational as well. Therefore I believe that general principles of environmental law, as incorporated in the international conventions, can have an importance for Indonesian environmental law as well and more particularly for the revision of the Environmental Management Act. In this respect I more particularly refer to the precautionary principle, the principle of prior notification, the importance of creating scientific certainty where possible, the necessity to have reliable authority and scientific competence, the principle of common and differentiated responsibility, just to mention a few.

In addition I believe that as a result of international conventions, the concepts and principles in a new Indonesian Environmental Law can substantially be improved. In this respect I refer for instance to a principle such as sustainable development. This could be incorporated specifically in environmental legislation applicable to a specific activity. In this respect one can refer to the legislation applicable to the use and management of natural resources (like forests, energy, mining, water and land), the goal of which is often to reduce conflicts between the users of the natural resources. That is indeed often the goal of natural resources and environmental legislation.

In addition, as a result of international conventions, specific legal instruments such as environmental impact assessment, environmental audits and environmental risk assessment can be either improved or formulated. For instance the notion of environmental risk assessment will still have to be developed. Moreover, environmental quality standards will have to be developed for Indonesia as well. For instance, a role can be played in that respect by the Basle Convention on Transboundary Movement and Disposal of Hazardous Waste. Moreover, measures will have to be taken in national Indonesian law concerning toxic monitoring in order to improve the regulation of hazardous waste and toxic substances. In addition, legal instruments also have to be installed in order to promote the conservation and sustainable use of natural resources based on the Cartagena and Kyoto Protocols.

The legal procedures and more particularly the environmental legal procedures need to be clarified in order to promote integrated law enforcement. This is particularly important as far as dispute settlement with respect to environmental issues in Indonesian waters is concerned.

Environmental funding mechanisms will have to be developed, including insurance and other financial guarantees. Moreover one can think about private legal dispute settlement mechanisms and the use of fines, such as are regulated in international maritime law conventions and the IMO conventions concerning marine pollution. The relationship between different legal instruments, such as the permit, the licence and the certification system, has to be clarified. Also a guarantee and insurance system has to be installed that takes into consideration the dispositions of international conventions with respect to investment processes.

New legal concepts and doctrines need to be adopted concerning the scientific verification of environmental cases. In this respect Indonesian national environmental law can also learn from international environmental cases. The final goal is, as we have argued in this chapter, to use international environmental law to improve the quality of Indonesian environmental law as much as possible. Hence, as a general issue, I believe that international legal rules need as much as possible to be taken into account in the revision process of the Environmental Management Act. Thus Indonesia may on the one hand implement its obligations under international environmental conventions and on the other hand such implementation may lead to an improvement in the quality of the Environmental Management Act.

REFERENCES

Birnie, P. and A. Boyle (2002), *International Law & the Environment*, Oxford: Oxford University Press, second edition.

Kantaatmadja, K. (1981), *Gantirugi Internasional Pencemaran Minyak Di Laut* (*International Compensation on Oil Pollution on Sea*), Bandung: Alumni.

Kantaatmadja, K. (1982), *Bunga Rampai Hukum Lingkungan Laut Internasional*, Bandung: Alumni.

Reicher, H. (1995), *Australian International Law, Cases and Materials*, North Ryde, NSW: Lawbook.

Sands, P. (2003), *Principles of International Environmental Law I*, Cambridge: Cambridge University Press, second edition.

Silalahi, D. (1982), *Hukum Lingkungan Dalam Sistem Penegakan Hukum Lingkungan Indonesia* (*Environmental Law in Enforcement System of Environmental Law in Indonesia*), Bandung: Alumni.

Sunkin, M., David M. Ong and Robert Wight (2002), *Sourcebook on Environmental Law*, London: Cavendish Publishing Limited.

5. Elaborating on integration of environmental legislation: the case of Indonesia

Marjan Peeters[1]

1. TO DISTINGUISH THE CONCEPTS OF EXTERNAL AND INTERNAL INTEGRATION

1.1. Sustainable Development and External Integration

The Environmental Management Act of 1997 marked an important evolution in Indonesian environmental law: a step was made in the process of building an adequate environmental legislative framework, aiming at the holistic concept of sustainable development and – in that respect – recognizing the importance of having integrated policies for protecting the environment. Of course, the real effectiveness of this Act only becomes clear after an examination of its concrete provisions and their implementation in practice.[2] But, to start with, the basic goal of the EMA 1997 is clearly to improve the environmental situation, in order to ultimately reach the challenging goal of a sustainable society. This is confirmed in the considerations of the EMA 1997, where it is stated that:

> In utilising natural resources . . . , it is necessary to implement environmentally sustainable development guided by an integrated and comprehensive national policy which takes into account the needs of present as well as future generations.[3]

---

[1] The author wishes to thank Michael Faure and Anthony Ogus for their comments. The text was concluded on 1 December 2004.

[2] Nicole Niessen has already argued that the EMA 1997 lacks sufficiently detailed provisions for immediate application. She has noted that a few years after its entry into force, only a few implementing regulations of the EMA 1997 had been produced, which often made it necessary to revert to those based on the former EMA. Niessen (2003, pp. 66–93).

[3] Preamble of the Law Concerning Environmental Management, Law No. 23 of 1997 (as posted on http://sunsite.nus.edu.sg/apcel/dbase/indonesia/primary/inaem .html).

In addition, it is recognized that

> There is a need to implement environmental management to preserve and develop environmental capacity in a harmonious, coordinated and balanced manner to support the implementation of environmentally sustainable development.

The concept of 'sustainable development' basically aims at upgrading the quality of both society and environment to a satisfactory level. What the optimal level of an environmentally sustainable society would be is hard to determine exactly. However, the concept of sustainable development urges that environmental concerns will be considered within other policy areas that might affect the environment.[4] For instance the Rio Declaration on Environment and Development has emphasized already the integration of environmental concerns within development processes.[5] This principle of (external) integration, aiming at taking environmental concerns into other policy areas, has been laid down as well in the European law order.[6] The basic message is that environmental protection should be integrated into other EC policies, like agriculture, transport, energy, and so on.[7] Integration in this sense has a clear external function: it aims at integrating economic and social development with environmental protection.

The concept of sustainable development, including the principle of external integration, is not only applicable at the international level of standard setting and decision-making: it is widely seen as a fundamental goal for domestic policies. Both supranational and national law systems need to implement this holistic goal. The external integration of environmental policies is in this respect widely seen as an important method, although the real application in practice is a challenging task.

---

4 Sands (2003, pp. 252–66).

5 UN Rio Declaration on Environment and Development, 16 June 1992, Principle 4: 'In order to achieve sustainable development, environmental protection shall constitute an integral part of the development process and cannot be considered in isolation from it'.

6 European Community Treaty, Art. 5; see also The European Convention (not yet into force, but as agreed on by the Heads of State or Government on 18 June 2004), Part II: The Charter of Fundamental rights of the Union, Art. II-37: 'A high level of environmental protection and the improvement of the quality of the environment must be integrated into the policies of the Union and ensured in accordance with the principle of sustainable development'.

7 Dhondt (2003).

1.2. Internal Integration: The Focus of this Contribution

Besides the important idea of external integration of environmental concerns, the integration of environmental law as such deserves attention as well. The basic aim of internal integration would be that environmental law would be coherent and consistent, taking fully into account the different ecological aspects of an activity. This internal integration would lead or attribute to an effective and efficient environmental policy (to be considered in Section 2). A well-functioning environmental law system can of course be seen as a precondition for reaching the overall goal of sustainable development. In this respect, not only the external integration of environmental concerns, but also the possibilities, design options, and limits of internal integration of environmental law should be closely examined. To this end, this contribution will discuss the more narrow approach of integration, which is the concept of internal integration, being one of the starting points for designing domestic environmental legislation.

We will start from a theoretical point of view in order to provide some main insights about the internal integration of environmental law. On this basis we will examine what options might be suggested to the Indonesian legislator in the process of improving its environmental legislation. The contribution is structured as follows: Section 2 will discuss theoretical considerations on the integration of environmental law. The focus will be on polluting activities.[8] After integration, two other challenging topics of environmental policy will be discussed, which are (1) the choice and mix of instruments and (2) the design and functioning of the administrative organization. It will be argued that these two topics should be related to the concept of integration of environmental law, and therefore these three basic concepts must be approached in a balanced way in designing environmental legislation. Section 3 will discuss some instruments for internal integration in greater depth, with close attention to the integrated permit and the alternative approach by general rules. Section 4 will examine the command and control provisions of the EMA 1997, in order to investigate what suggestions may be made in respect of the theoretical considerations in the previous sections. Section 5 will provide a conclusion and final recommendations.

---

8 In addition, it is worth examining the integrated approach towards the protection of natural resources like forests and species.

2. INTEGRATION OF ENVIRONMENTAL LEGISLATION

2.1. Some Strong Arguments for Integration of Environmental Legislation

2.1.1. Ecological unity as a justification for integration

The motive for integration is not primarily a legal one: an integrative approach ought to be suitable to the ecological unity of the environment. A sectional or fragmented approach would deny the ecological concept, and could result in undesirable cross-media transfers of pollution, for example from air to soil.[9] And, with a fragmented pollutant-specific approach undesirable, synergetic effects between substances could occur.[10] For a real integrative approach, the assessment of, for example, industrial activities should concern not only pollution towards several environmental media, but also efficient use of raw materials, or even the environmental effects of collecting the raw materials.[11] An extensive integrative assessment would also include the environmental and human health effects of the product itself.[12]

The basic ecological argument for having an integrated environmental law in assessing polluting activities stresses that the concept of integration is a universal goal for environmental law. In this respect, the specific legal culture of a country is basically not relevant for the acceptance of this concept. However, the concept of integration as such must be examined carefully; we cannot rule out that in certain situations there may be strong justification for regulating some activities in a more isolated way.

2.1.2. Integration as an economic sound approach

An integrative approach can also be recommended from an economic point of view: the environmental costs would then be fully internalized within the decision-making process.[13] When integration is fully applied in this way, every aspect of environmental pollution is connected to a regulatory cost, which would mean that no form of environmental pollution would still be an externality. An additional interesting economic point of view is that an optimally

---

9 An elaborated discussion of integration of environmental law has been given by Guruswamy (1991, pp. 41–56).

10 Guruswamy (1991, p. 51). Complication results from the fact that there can be uncertainty about these synergetic effects.

11 Guruswamy (1991, p. 47). In this sense also the protection of natural resources will be part of the integrated assessment of activities.

12 Guruswamy (1991, p. 50). Guruswamy indicates several ranges of integration, from narrow to broad.

13 Faure and Lefevre (1996, pp. 112–22, esp. pp. 113–14).

efficient integrated approach should be based on the assimilative capacity of the environment:

> A more efficient and cost-effective way to control pollution would be to distribute the wastes among water, air, and land in a manner that optimizes the total environment and any special or particular assimilative capacity each medium might possess. This policy would lead to a balanced approach to pollution control, avoiding the problems associated with standards that are overstringent in some areas and unduly lax in others.[14]

Although a full application of this idea in practice seems to be rather complicated, it would, however, be challenging to find ways and methods to approach this basic idea.

There is also another economic reason for integrating environmental rules. In contrast with a sectoral approach, in the case of integration the total of administrative costs are supposed to be lower, both for government and for industry. For example, it can easily be seen that administrative costs will be lower when just one integrated permit is needed for an activity, instead of the situation where for several media specific permits are in force (such as separate permit schemes for soil, water, air, noise, waste, etc.). The 'one stop shop' seems in this respect an attractive option. However, the concept of an integrated permit leads to the subsequent question whether administrative authorities, firms and so-called third parties have indeed adequate knowledge and other capacities in order to be able to assess the environmental effects of an activity in an integrated way. Will the integration as predicted by law indeed be followed by an integrated (and efficient) assessment in practice?

2.1.3. Integration, centralization and decentralization

The wish to pursue an integrative approach to the environmental problem includes the idea that industry would also be happy to consider its activities in an integrated way. Industry would be in the position to examine – with a complete assessment of their activities – which measures fit best and lead to the most efficient way of preventing environmental damage. In this sense, integration would start with a decentralized regulatory approach, meaning that private entities would make an integrative environmental assessment of their activities. In this respect, the integrative approach aims at maximizing the (specific) knowledge of industry itself. Subsequently, the integrative assessments by industry must be reviewed and approved by the government. It should be considered carefully at what governmental level the administrative authorities would be capable of executing these integrative assessments. The

---

14 Guruswamy (1991, p. 45).

fact that every environmental effect will be considered in one decision, or several coordinated decisions, requires the government to be capable of testing the integrated proposals of the industry. It can be assumed that the specific knowledge, capacities and skills (that is, of qualified civil servants) are more difficult to provide at the lowest decentralized governmental level.

2.2. Harmonization and Coordination as Methods for Coherency

It can be assumed that practical arguments or even political restraints might hinder the full application of the ideal of an integrative assessment of environmental concerns.[15] A full integrative assessment for each activity in one governmental decision could be difficult to implement within the existing administrative structure – as it would often mean a reshuffling of competences. It may even be inadequate to integrate every environmental aspect into one governmental decision. Moreover, there exists a specific legal reason why integration might be hindered: the international lawmaking process is very fragmented, which could cause problems in executing international legal obligations in the national (integrated) order.

When full integration is not (yet) possible, the prospects for coordination and harmonization could be examined. The coherency in environmental law thus might increase by harmonization and coordination.[16, 17] The fact that permit schemes for several media are established does not necessarily exclude internal integrative assessment of the environmental effects. Here precisely lies the power of harmonization and coordination: it can be legally required that (1) the specific procedures will be the same, and (2) that the administrative authorities competent for several licence decisions must procedurally and – more importantly – substantially coordinate their respective decisions, in order to reach an effective integrated approach. In this way, harmonization of procedures will facilitate coordination. The progress of environmental law towards harmonization and coordination can be seen perfectly in the history of Dutch environmental law. First, a media-oriented approach was taken, based on different sectoral environmental acts. From 1980, harmonized decision-making procedures were prescribed through a general act containing predominantly procedural rules for environmental law, the 'Wet algemene bepalingen milieuhygiëne' (some of these rules, like the procedural rules for decision-making, were transposed to

---

15 Drupsteen (1990, p. 199).

16 Faure (2000, pp. 174–82). Another conceptual approach has been taken by Otto (2003, p. 127).

17 An important impetus for harmonizing national laws comes from a business perspective: Lewis describes the call from the Transatlantic Business Dialogue (TABD) for the convergence of laws and regulations: Lewis (2002, p. 227).

the General Administrative Law Act, in 1994). The 'Wet algemene bepalingen milieuhygiëne' was replaced by a more advanced environmental framework act. This Environmental Management Act came into force in 1993, and introduced a rather integrated permit scheme. Due to reasons of administrative organization, the permit scheme for water pollution was left outside this permit scheme. In other words, the legislator did not want to deprive the established water boards of their competence to issue water pollution permits. However, the integrated permit and the water pollution permit, based on the Water Pollution Act, are procedurally harmonized, and the competent administrative bodies are required to coordinate both procedures.[18] The duty to coordinate (and the duty to follow the prescribed procedure) can be enforced in the courts.

Integration through coordination is also present in European secondary environmental legislation. This has occurred in a number of environmental directives.[19] The European Directive 96/61 concerning integrated pollution prevention and control clearly introduces the integrated environmental permit, but it has nevertheless been explicitly accepted that integrated assessment should be executed through a coordinated approach when more than one competent authority is involved. However, this coordination should be done very carefully: Article 7 of the IPPC Directive prescribes that the conditions of, and procedure for, the granting of the permit need to be *fully* coordinated in order to guarantee an effective integrated approach.[20] Subsequently, a new obligation to coordinate has already been prescribed by Directive 2003/87. This Directive introduces a greenhouse gas emissions trading scheme in the European Union, in which a so-called greenhouse gas permit is included as well. It is prescribed that the conditions of, and procedure for, the issue of a greenhouse gas permit should be coordinated with those for the IPPC permit.[21]

An environmental law system that uses coordination instead of integration is not necessarily to be judged as less adequate. It is true that the administra-

---

[18] Freriks and Peeters (1994, pp. 194–204). On the integration in the Dutch Environmental Management Act, see also Chapter 7 of this volume.

[19] A directive is a legal act of the European legislating institutions, and is addressed to the Member States of the European Union. The Member States are obliged to implement these directives in time in their national legislation. European Community Treaty, Art. 249, states: 'a Directive shall be binding, as to the result to be achieved, upon each Member State to which it is addressed, but shall leave to the national authorities the choice of form of methods'.

[20] Directive 96/61/EC of 24 September 1996 concerning integrated pollution prevention and control, *Official Journal* L 257, 10.10.1996, pp. 26–40.

[21] Directive 2003/87/EC of 13 October 2003 establishing a scheme for greenhouse gas emission allowance trading within the Community and amending Council Directive 96/61/EC, *Official Journal* L 275, 25.10.2003, pp. 32–46.

tive costs seem to be higher when coordinated actions have to be taken instead of an integrative approach by one competent body. But, on the other hand, an integrative assessment will not necessarily lead to a better environmental decision. With a separation of responsibilities among different authorities which are obliged to coordinate their decisions, the respective environmental concerns will have a better chance of being defended when compared to the situation where these environmental interests are integrated into one environmental decision.

2.3. Ultimate Goal: One Environmental Code

2.3.1. Indeed an ultimate goal

In the Netherlands the idea of integration has resulted in a framework act, the Environmental Management Act of 1993. This Act forms so-called build-on legislation, meaning that it can be extended with new topics and chapters. Since 1993, several extensions have indeed occurred. Apart from the Environmental Management Act, important specific environmental laws still exist, like a Water Pollution Act, a Soil Protection Act, and a Hazardous Substances Act. The strong idea of integration in the Netherlands has been causing discussions about improving (the structure of) the environmental legislation, in which respect one integrated Environmental Code is more than once seen as an ultimate goal. In the literature it has also been stated that the concept of codification – meaning the enactment of one Environmental Code – is to be seen as the ultimate form of harmonization.[22] However, a recent comparative survey towards the integration of environmental legislation in six EU Member States has shown how different the process towards integrated environmental legislation, and towards the appreciation and enactment of one Environmental Code has been in several national systems.[23] In fact, every country (all of them Member States of the European Union) that was examined had its own, specific development in environmental legislation, with sometimes very specific culture-related aspects. In several countries, discussion on further integration of national environmental legislation has scarcely begun (Denmark, United Kingdom). In Sweden, there have been impressive developments in the direction of an Environmental Code, but when the extent of real substantive integration is examined, it must be concluded that the result is not overly convincing. Germany developed an impressive proposal for an

[22] Faure discusses several views of different authors on the codification of environmental law (2000, pp. 176–7). There is an impressive academic proposal for restructuring Dutch environmental legislation, in order to install one Environmental Code, serving the concept of sustainable environmental legislation: Biezeveld (2002).

[23] Deketelaere et al. (2003).

Environmental Code (*Umweltgesetzbuch*) as well, but – surprisingly – for political reasons and reasons of public law, this Code has not yet been adopted, and there are no clear signs that it will be adopted in the near future.

2.3.2. A scheme for one Environmental Code

It is nevertheless an interesting exercise to consider the optimal structure for an Environmental Code. The German *Umweltgesetzbuch* for instance is an attractive proposal from which legislators could take inspiration. It consists of a part with general provisions for environmental law, followed by a part with specific (for instance medium-oriented) provisions. In the Flemish region there have been rather similar interesting developments towards the enactment of an Environmental Code as well.[24]

The scheme shown in Table 5.1 is inspired mainly by legislative developments in Sweden, Belgium and Germany. It could also be used as an inspiring example for setting up an Environmental Code in developing countries:[25, 26]

In the *General provisions* rows, the common provisions relevant for the whole environmental policy field, like environmental principles, environmental quality standards, environmental planning, and environmental impact assessment could be regulated. Under the *Specific provisions*, the necessary (medium-specific) regulations, like soil-sanitation obligations could be included.

At first glance, the schematic approach seems to be very attractive as it is clearly structured, and looks rather simple. Nevertheless, when filling in the scheme serious dogmatic questions could arise. Some main questions are:

- What exact policy area will be covered by the Environmental Code? To what extent will the Act also include or relate to spatial planning decisions, waterflow or water drought measures, or decisions on traffic and transport? This in fact concerns the problem of filling in a sound external integration of environmental concerns. Also the question whether

---

24 Deketelaere et al. (2003).

25 This scheme is based on an idea of Kurt Deketelaere, Catholic University of Leuven, Belgium, as presented in a workshop held for the comparative research project. In the literature, Gustaf Biezenveld has presented another model for an Environmental Code. Another author has considered a further going idea, namely integrating all the legislation concerning spatial planning and the environment (like spatial planning law, water management law, environmental law, and nature conservation law), but he also thinks that with coordination coherency can be reached: Michiels (2002).

26 For a conceptual approach towards the establishment of a coherent legal framework for decision-making, see also Anker (2002, pp. 199–209).

Table 5.1

<table>
<tr><td rowspan="8">General provisions</td><td colspan="6">principles, duties of care</td></tr>
<tr><td colspan="6">environmental quality standards</td></tr>
<tr><td colspan="6">environmental planning</td></tr>
<tr><td colspan="6">environmental impact assessment</td></tr>
<tr><td colspan="6">environmental permit</td></tr>
<tr><td colspan="6">enforcement</td></tr>
<tr><td colspan="6">procedures for environmental information
procedures for public participation
procedures for access to court in environmental matters</td></tr>
<tr><td colspan="6">. . .</td></tr>
<tr><td>Specific provisions</td><td>air</td><td>soil</td><td>water</td><td>nature</td><td>waste</td><td>. . .</td></tr>
</table>

specific nature conservation rules should be incorporated into the Environmental Code needs to be addressed.

- How will the provisions of environmental law be tuned with the provisions in the general codes, like the Constitution, and respectively the Civil, Administrative, and Penal Code? For example, do the procedural rules for public participation in (environmental) decision-making need to be laid down in an Administrative Code, or in the Environmental Code, or in both, supplementing each other?[27]
- To what extent will a variety of regulatory instruments be used, and how can the use of different types of instruments be fitted into the structure presented? Should one integrated permit – such as a horizontal provision – indeed be preferred as the best regulatory option? Do other types of regulatory interventions – like market-based instruments – fit into the comprehensive or integrated structure of the Environmental Code (see also the next paragraph)?
- Will it be possible to keep the content of the Environmental Code simple and easy to understand? Is it not the case that due to the complexity and broadness of the environmental policy field the content of the Environmental Code will be difficult to design, and that as a result internal inconsistencies between the rules might still occur?[28]

---

[27] The latter option is current practice in the Netherlands, meaning that the main procedural rules are included in the General Administrative Law Act, and specific procedural rules are included in the Environmental Management Act, and/or specific environmental acts.

[28] For instance, the proposal of G. Biezeveld, aiming at addressing the different types of problems to be addressed by one Environmental Code, is also rather complicated.

The fundamental question that has to be kept in mind when altering the existing legislative system by incorporating environmental rules in one Environmental Code would be to what extent this would contribute to the transparency, effectiveness and efficiency of environmental law. In the literature it has already been noted that although an environmental legal system where all legislation is brought together may appear attractive at first sight, decision-making in fact takes place in a disintegrated or even uncoordinated matter. Not the form, but the substance, of environmental law should be examined primarily.[29] Therefore, a general practical suggestion would be to first examine closely whether a stepwise approach might contribute significantly to the protection of the environment, before deciding on radically changing its legislative structure. It might often be more profitable to invest also and primarily in the execution of the law in practice, instead of starting expensive and often long-lasting legislative projects. In this respect, a scheme as presented above might be an interesting concept to be developed in the longer term.

2.4. The Concept of Integration Balanced with the Choice of Instruments and the Structure of the Administrative Organization

As stated above, the substance of environmental law should be taken as a number one priority, instead of focusing on the form of the legislative model. In this respect, two other topics need attention besides the need for having an integrated assessment of environmental effects. These are first, the choice of an optimal instrument mix, and secondly, the need to fit environmental competences into the typical administrative organization of a country.

2.4.1. An optimal instrument mix

Originally, so-called command and control instruments were predominantly included in environmental legislation. Voluntary approaches and market-based instruments are recommended as significant alternatives or additional approaches to the command and control rules. Not only the choice between, but especially the combination of several types of instruments is something to be looked at. But then the question arises how the idea of having an environmental policy toolbox fits with the concept of internal integration. This question deserves still further exploration by research and practical experience, to be evaluated in order to gain new, more mature insights.

---

[29] Faure (2000, p. 165). See also Anker (2002, p. 208), arguing that the legal framework does not need to have a specific form. See starts from the concepts of cross-media integration, cross-agency integration, and instrumental integration. She assumes that the biggest challenge is probably instrumental integration.

In particular, the basic idea that one governmental decision should assess all the environmental effects of one activity does not seem to fit smoothly with ideas about improving regulatory effectiveness and efficiency. There are, for instance, strong arguments for using market-based instruments to regulate polluting behaviour, such as taxes, liability regimes, and marketable permits (emissions trading).[30] Especially for long-distance pollution problems, like acid rain, the concept of tradable permits seems to be an attractive policy option. Emissions trading is one of the new, upcoming instruments of European environmental law, and even of international environmental law, aimed at combating the climate change problem and protecting the ozone layer.[31] Domestic experience with this regulatory approach in the US has led other countries to consider this regulatory option.[32] Subsequently, and after a period of doubt,[33] Europe has made a strong commitment to this market-based approach, as it is introduced as one of the main regulatory tools for combating the climate change problem.[34] In fact, the European Commission felt that it was necessary to propose an EU-wide system, in order to prevent a patchwork of several domestic emissions trading schemes occurring, as there were initiatives by individual Member States to introduce domestic emissions trading schemes for greenhouse gases (for example in Denmark and in the United Kingdom).

Broad acceptance of emissions trading leads also in the case of Indonesia to the challenging question of whether this type of regulation would be a sound option for especially non-local pollution problems. A careful examination of whether the institutional and enforcement provisions would be sufficient in order to introduce this system is recommended. This should be done with respect to a range of other regulatory options, like environmental taxes.

2.4.2. The administrative organization

The basic characteristics of the administrative organization in a country are to be taken into account when regulatory instruments for environmental policy are considered. For example, in the Netherlands the regional water boards are part of the historical administrative culture. Those water boards are competent to issue the water pollution permit. Despite the strong desire for an integrated

---

30 For a more detailed discussion of these 'economic' instruments see the contribution of Michael Faure and Andri Wibisana to this volume (Chapter 10).

31 Peeters (2003b, pp. 147–70).

32 Tietenberg (2002, pp. 197–231); Environmental Law Institute Research Report, Implementing an Emissions Cap and Allowance Trading System for Greenhouse Gases: Lessons from the Acid Rain Program, September 1997.

33 Christiansen (2004, pp. 27–46).

34 Peeters (2003a, p. 87).

environmental law, these water boards are still kept competent to issue permits, and there has been no political support for transferring these competences to the provinces and municipalities. Instead, there is an obligation to coordinate the decision-making procedures of the permit based on the Environmental Management Act and the Water Pollution Act (see section 2.2). On the other hand, also from the viewpoint of integrated policy making, but in this case of integrated water management, it may be argued that transferring competence for issuing water pollution permits from the professional water boards to the general decentralized authorities – without having built up specific knowledge – would not be a good idea. Here, two policy fields (and two administrative organizational structures) meet, and in this respect, the option of coordination is a practical approach. As far as the activities falling under the IPPC Directive are concerned, the Netherlands has to be very careful in executing this coordination in order to meet the obligation for integrated decision-making. Nevertheless, as said before, the IPPC Directive accepts the fact that different competent bodies are in charge, meaning that full coordination should take place.

In Indonesia, the Regional Governance Act has confirmed the strong wish and need for decentralization. It is clear that Indonesia wants as far as possible to have a decentralized regulatory approach. The question arises as to how fundamental considerations about and developments towards a basic public law structure for a country (in this case: Indonesia) is also the preferred structure for implementing and executing environmental regulatory interventions. The basic question here is whether environmental competences should indeed be attributed to decentralized governmental bodies, or whether one or more of these competences would fit better at a higher level. In the (specific) case of environmental policy, it has to be reviewed closely at what level governmental actions can be executed best – taking into account the knowledge and costs needed for administrative decision-making. This relationship between decentralization and environmental legislation will mainly be addressed in the contribution of Nicole Niessen to this book. It is clear, however, that at the very least relationships exist between (1) the concept and design of internal integration; (2) the choice and design of regulatory options and (3) fundamental arguments for a decentralized structure of a state. And, of course, (4) the typical characteristics of the (specific) environmental problems are also decisive in the design of the preferred environmental regulatory intervention. For instance, for regional (not local) or even transnational environmental topics, a higher level seems more appropriate. Here, the possibilities and attractiveness of vertical coordination between centralized and decentralized governments is something to be looked at as well.

2.5. Conclusion: The Challenging Task to Design Environmental Legislation

The short overview given above of the concepts that are relevant for the design of environmental legislation illustrates that it is a challenging task to design effective, efficient, and coherent environmental legislation. In this respect, comparative research towards the design and substance of domestic environmental legislation can provide inspiring thoughts. In particular, developing countries can learn from the mistakes, faults, and also successful approaches of countries where a history of environmental legislation has already evolved. In this respect, it is important that developing countries should not start where the developed countries started some decades ago, but try to learn from experiences and – in this respect – try to introduce a more modern concept of environmental legislation, to be fitted to the specific environmental problems, characteristics and capacities of the country concerned. Even the use of market-based instruments should not be excluded from these considerations.

The overview however did not cover every fundamental characteristic of designing environmental legislation. One other significant circumstance is that legislative activity clearly happens in a political context. The economic costs of environmental legislation could decrease the ambition of the legislator to enact environmental legislation with real teeth. In this respect, multidisciplinary studies looking at the effects of environmental legislation on the economy (of developing countries) are extremely important.

Not only must the costs for industry and society be taken into account, but also the regulatory costs for the government: this raises basic questions like how many civil servants are needed to execute for instance an integrated permit system, what technical monitoring provisions are needed for the inspectors (and what do they cost), and what kind of permanent education should be provided. Besides drawing up an effective and efficient working administrative organization, the integrity of this organization – and the courts – also needs to be addressed closely. In this respect, the design of regulatory structures that reduce the opportunities for corruption also needs to be addressed.[35]

All these factors – and others – influence the real substance and practical results of environmental legislation. Moreover, non-legal initiatives like communication and education can be important to look at as well, in order to improve the environmental behaviour of firms and consumers.[36]

---

35 Ogus has argued that it may, especially in the case of developing countries, be preferable to concentrate on reducing the opportunities for corruption – and thus in that respect to choose for regulatory instruments that give less scope for corruption. One could for instance think of 'rules instead of discretion'. Ogus (2004, pp. 229–46).

36 Faure (1995, pp. 5–6).

Besides studies on the theoretical design of environmental legislation – aimed at developing effective and efficient rules – evaluations of the results of legislative provisions are very much recommended as well. In the Netherlands, for instance, the administrative authorities are obliged to report on the execution of several chapters of the Environmental Management Act, such as the permit system. In addition, the national government, especially the Minister responsible for the environment, is required to report to parliament on the outcome of the Dutch Environmental Management Act every five years. Those evaluations are an important source of information about (different) regulatory provisions.[37]

3. TWO CLASSICAL WAYS FOR REGULATORY INTERVENTIONS AND THEIR ABILITY TO FACILITATE AN INTEGRATIVE APPROACH

3.1. Introduction

In this section some headlines will be presented that belong to the concept of an integrated permit system and to integrated general rules. Both instruments are in fact command and control instruments. Although a lot of alternative regulatory approaches should also be considered in designing environmental legislation, it is still necessary to explore the characteristics of these classical regulatory provisions. The first reason is that it does not seem realistic to assume that these instruments would no longer be important in the field of environmental law. The second reason is that progress will or must be made towards optimizing this regulatory approach also within the concept of command and control. The third reason is that in principle both the permit and the general rules seem to make an integrative approach very much possible. In fact, an integrative approach may well be easier to realize in a command and control setting than with market-based instruments like tradable permits. The fourth reason is that before being able to balance different regulatory options, adequate insights must exist into each specific regulatory option – among which are the command and control options. The description of the characteristics of both instruments is strongly inspired by the way they are designed in

---

[37] The national government (the Minister for the Environment) installed independent commissions to evaluate the outcome of the Environmental Management Act. For instance the Evaluatie Commissie Wet Milieubeheer (1999–2003) produced (having a budget to do so) an impressive number of reports (these reports are posted on www.ecwm.nl). The mandate of this commission terminated at the end of 2003; the research however will be continued in another organizational context.

the Dutch Environmental Management Act, and, in addition and as far as the permit is concerned, by the IPPC Directive.

3.2. The Integrated Permit

Much can be said about the alternative options to design a permit system. This section will only discuss the fundamental characteristics of a permit system (see Appendix for summary). This regulatory instrument should clearly be regulated in the primary legislation.

The basic idea of a permit system is that the law explicitly forbids a certain activity, and subsequently rules that this activity is only allowed when a competent authority has issued a permit. Within the primary law it must be prescribed exactly which authority is competent to issue the licence (characteristics (1) a permit obligation for (2) certain well-described activities, and (3) attribution of the administrative competence to issue a permit, to include permit conditions and to adjust or revoke the permit). The enumeration of the activities covered by the permit system can eventually be done in secondary legislation, or in an annex to the primary law.

The substantive core of the permit system is the focus of protection: what will be the scope of environmental protection (characteristic 4: description of the scope of protection)? Within this scope, the extent of integration (or isolated approach) will become clear.[38] In order to guarantee legal certainty it is recommended that the scope of the permit system is rather precisely defined.[39] From the viewpoint of dynamic decision-making it can however be argued that this scope should be flexible, in order for the permit system to adapt to new insights into environmental policy. From a legal point of view, however, legal certainty will be preferred. This legal certainty will facilitate the administrative authorities in taking responsibility for protecting the environment through permit decisions. If they are not sure whether they are indeed allowed to take account of certain specific environmental concerns within the permit, they might be reluctant to do so – fearing court proceedings by the applicant for the permit.

---

[38] From 1993, the scope of the permit system of the Dutch Environmental Management Act (which replaced and extended the Hinderwet) was intentionally broadened, for instance in the use of raw materials, and towards energy efficiency. An evaluative study showed that it is crucial that the central government provides the decentralized competent bodies with information on the application of the new elements in the permit decisions: Evaluatiecommissie Wet Milieubeheer, *De verruimde reikwijdte van de Wet milieubeheer,* ECWM 2001/3 (postbus 30945, 25000 GX Den Haag, the Netherlands).

[39] In the Netherlands, the scope of the permit scheme of the Environmental Management Act is not precisely described. Different opinions exist as to whether this is necessary: Boeve et al. (2004, pp. 153–4).

Where the scope does not include a fully integrative approach, the legislator should take into consideration what kind of harmonizing or coordinating provisions need to be provided (characteristic 5: attention to harmonizing and coordinative provisions). As already pointed out in Section 2.2, coordination is for instance prescribed in Dutch environmental law between the permit based on the Environmental Management Act, and the permit based on the Water Pollution Act.

Once the scope of the permit system has been designed, it must subsequently be clear on what criterion or criteria the decision is to be based. This is a very sensitive topic, as it will specifically determine the level of protection that will be given to the environment, and – vice versa – will also make clear what kind of activities will or will not be allowed for society (especially industry). Within the criteria (we can imagine that not just one criterion, but a set of criteria, will be necessary in order to give direction to the substantive decision-making), the challenging tension between economic abilities and environmental protection will be present. This is for instance expressed by the economic/technological criterion as used in the IPPC Directive. This Directive prescribes that the emission limit values, or equivalent parameters and technical measures, which are to be part of the integrated permit, shall be based on the 'best available technology' (BAT). In addition to this economic-technological criterion, geographical location and local environmental conditions should also be taken into account by the permitting body[40] (characteristic 6: description of the economic-technological criterion and other criteria for decision-making). However, in practice it is often not immediately clear what BAT really means. The definition of 'best available technology' in the IPPC Directive is rather vague and confusing.[41] However, it clearly cannot be assumed that a legislator will be able to prescribe in its primary or secondary legislation all the techniques that have to be applied by installations. It is predominantly for this reason that a permit system, in other words, a system of tailor-made decision-making, is needed.[42] In order to make clear what is meant by best available techniques (or other economic-technical criteria), guidelines are crucial; these guidelines provide the permitting (decentralized) bodies with relevant information. The guidelines may be provided by the central government, or by expert commissions. The legal status of guidelines may differ, depending on the specific legal context. As it is necessary to facilitate technological innovations, it may be argued that the guidelines should not

---

40 IPPC Directive, Art. 9.

41 IPPC Directive, Art. 2, section 11.

42 It is not strictly necessary for this tailor-made decision-making to be done by a command and control permit system. Market-based mechanisms, like emissions trading and taxes, may also be applied to certain environmental problems.

be strictly binding, but should function as clear recommendations to the permitting bodies. This would enable the permitting bodies to deviate from the guidelines where guidelines have become outdated.[43] The IPPC Directive for instance urges the Member States to ensure that the competent authorities follow or are informed of developments in best available techniques. Subsequently, these developments need to be applied in the permits. The Commission has installed a bureau that aims to provide the Member States with information on best available techniques.[44] This European IPPC Bureau regularly publishes so-called 'BREFs' (BAT reference documents), holding information on the best available techniques. This information is to be taken into account by the permitting bodies of the Member States.[45]

In addition to the economic-technical criterion for decision-making, the relationship with so-called environmental quality standards (EQS) should be made clear. Those EQS (when set) may differ in their legal status (such as being strictly binding, or, alternatively, only to be taken account of, meaning that with convincing arguments – like unreasonably expensive investments – deviations may occur). Depending on the legal status of the EQS, they may overrule the BAT criterion. For example, when an activity for which a permit is requested, and which intends to apply BAT, nevertheless causes an EQS to be crossed by its emissions, extra measures will be needed, or even refusal of the application for a permit.[46] In addition, when present, the relationship with environmental plans should also be made clear (characteristics 7a and 7b: relationship with environmental quality standards, and environmental plans).

As already mentioned about characteristic 3, the legislator should fine-tune the specific competences of the permitting body. These are not only about issuing a permit (or denying the request for a permit). Specifically the inclusion of permit conditions and the competence to update the permit and its conditions are extremely relevant. Through the specific permit conditions, the real (individual) standard setting will take place. Legislation should make clear what kinds of conditions might be included in the permit – in which respect a whole set of possibilities may be indicated.[47] In this respect, the

---

43 IPPC Directive, Art. 11.

44 The reports on best available techniques are published on the web: http://eippcb.jrc.es.

45 As regards BAT, it seems to be necessary to establish (additional) provisions which encourage the process of technological innovations.

46 The IPPC Directive Art. 10. rules: 'Where an environmental quality standard requires stricter conditions than those achievable by the use of the best available techniques, additional measures shall in particular be required in the permit, without prejudice to other measures which might be taken to comply with environmental quality standards'.

47 See for example Art. 8.13 Dutch Environmental Management Act.

consideration of goal-oriented or method-oriented conditions must take place. Goal-oriented conditions are often preferred as they give discretion to industry as to how to meet these limits. The IPPC Directive illustrates this strong preference for goal-oriented permit conditions (emission limit values), as it rules that the use of any technique or specific technology should not be included in the permit conditions.[48] Another important aspect of permit conditions are the monitoring provisions. To some extent, it can be prescribed within the permit conditions that the operator of an activity should measure its emissions and report them to the authority. Other necessary elements of the competence to issue or update the permit are:

- the duration of the permit; will it be temporary or not?
- clear rules on the competences of the administrative authorities to adjust the permit to new circumstances, or even to revoke the permit when this might be necessary in the interests of the environment;
- clear procedural rules on updating the permit in the event of changes in the activity.

In addition to the substantive characteristics mentioned above, procedural provisions are also extremely important in order to provide decisions that fit into the concept of democratic and transparent regulatory interventions. Provisions that aim at carefully preparing the ultimate decision are very important in this respect. In the first place, it should be clear what kind of impacts the activity might have on the environment. Environmental impact assessments, which are usually prescribed for activities that could significantly affect the environment, are a well-known instrument in this respect. For less significant activities, it may be prescribed that within the application of the permit the possible effects on the environment should be pointed out (this is in fact a 'mini-EIA') (characteristic 8: collection of relevant information on the environmental effects of a specific activity, for instance through environmental impact assessments or through requirements concerning the application of the permit).

In addition, it is commonly accepted that the decision-making process in environmental matters should be transparent, for both third parties and NGOs (characteristic 9: access to information), and that it should be open to comment (characteristic 10: access to environmental decision-making). On the latter, there could be discussion about who precisely may have access to environmental decision-making, for instance only the people concerned, that is, NGOs, or everyone (*actio popularis*).

48 IPPC Directive, Art. 9 section 4.

A permit system will be completed by the possibility of going to court, in order to challenge the administrative decision on a permit request (or other relevant administrative decisions, such as the decision to revoke or to adjust a permit (characteristic 11: access to court)). Here it may also be considered who will be given access to court: only the people concerned, that is, NGOs, or for example everyone (*actio popularis*).

Last but not least, it is clearly indispensable to provide clear and adequate enforcement competences (characteristic 12: monitoring and enforcement provisions).[49]

3.3. General Rules

The main reason for the introduction in the Netherlands of general rules to regulate polluting activities was that the permit system was found to be too expensive and too cumbersome to execute. The decentralized authorities did not really succeed in realizing an adequate, updated permit practice. In fact, a lot of activities were in operation without a permit. Hence, the legislator decided to introduce an alternative to the permit system, and provided a new competence for central government meaning that central government could establish common, directly binding rules for polluting activities (characteristic 1: competence established in primary law, to prescribe general rules in secondary legislation). These general rules were intended for categories of homogeneous activities, like bakeries, butchers, agricultural activities, and so on (characteristic 2: well-described categories of homogeneous activities). It was assumed that general rules would allow the decentralized authorities to direct their energy towards monitoring and enforcement actions. The idea was that decentralized authorities saved time by no longer being obliged to do individual standard setting through permit decisions. The general rules would relieve the decentralized authorities of its permit task, and would enhance attention to monitoring and enforcing activities. The operator of an activity is no longer obliged to follow a permit procedure. Instead, a system of announcements is introduced; an operator of a covered activity is obliged to announce its activity to the decentralized competent body (of the municipality). This announcement needs to be published and is transparent for the public. And, seemingly very relevant for developing countries, general rules create fewer opportunities for corruption, in contrast to permit competences which grant much discretion to permitting bodies.[50]

---

49 The administrative and criminal enforcement of environmental law will be addressed in other contributions to this book.

50 Ogus mentions for instance 'rules instead of discretion' (2004, p. 20).

The first general environmental rules in the Netherlands entered into force in 1988.[51] After that, a lot of new sets of general rules were established, now covering a significant proportion of industrial activities in the Netherlands (75 per cent).[52] It is clearly the case that general rules can only be applied for homogeneous activities, as standard setting is no longer tailored. However, within the general rules it may be indicated to what extent some room for discretion is left to the decentralized authorities to deviate from the general rules (characteristic 3: limited competences for decentralized authorities to deviate from the general rules). The instrument of general binding rules is mostly (or profoundly) applicable for smaller activities. Complex activities should probably still be regulated by a permit, which facilitates an individual assessment and tailor-made permit conditions.

The scope of protection of the general binding rules should be considered as well. The general rules in the Netherlands aim at an integrated approach towards the environmental effects of the activities covered, and have in fact the same scope of protection as is the case with the permit based on the Environmental Management Act[53] (characteristic 4: integrated (or isolated) scope). With respect to general rules, some harmonizing and coordinating provisions may indeed be necessary and do exist in Dutch environmental law – as the EMA does not contain a full integration of environmental law (characteristic 5: attention to harmonizing and coordinating provisions).[54] For instance, under both the Environmental Management Act and the Water Pollution Act, general binding rules can be prescribed.[55] The legislative provisions enabling these general rules are harmonized to a large extent, which facilitates the establishment of integrated general rules based on both the Environmental Management Act and the Water Pollution Act. For instance, the coordinating provisions also become important when the legislator allows some combinations between on the one hand the general rules, and, on the other hand, the permit system. According to Dutch law, in certain cases both instruments may be applicable to one activity – and in that case coordination must take place in order to prevent a conflict of rules. It may be the case that, for instance, general rules based on the Soil Protection Act apply, together with the integrated permit based on the Environmental Management Act. If so, the competent permit authority must ensure that no substantive conflict may arise between these general rules and the specific permit. The general rules prevail

---

51 Cleij and Neuerburg (1988).

52 Kamerstukken II, 2001.2, 24 036, No. 258, pp. 28–9.

53 Art. 8.40 juncto Art. 11 Dutch Environmental Management Act.

54 Art. 8.9 and Art. 8.10 section 2, of the Dutch Environmental Management Act.

55 Dutch Environmental Management Act, Art. 8.40–Art. 8.46; Water Pollution Act Art. 2a–2e. Some slight deviations exist between these two provisions.

(unless a specific administrative competence has been provided to deviate from these rules can be used).[56]

The general rules may be based on economic-technical considerations. The Environmental Management Act includes for instance such a criterion, meaning that environmental measures will be prescribed as far as can be reasonably urged by the operators. This provision is often called the alara criterion (meaning that authorities are obliged to prescribe measures '*a*s *l*ow (though) *a*s *r*easonably *a*chievable'). This economic-technological criterion applies to the competence to decide on general rules as well (characteristic 6: economic-technological considerations as a legislative direction for the general rules).[57] Due to the European environmental law, and more specifically the IPPC Directive, the 'Dutch' alara criterion will be replaced by the criterion called 'best available technique'.[58]

The relationship between the design of general rules with especially binding environmental quality standards is also taken into account in the Dutch Environmental Management Act, although it seems easier with permitting to take account of environmental plans and environmental quality standards (characteristic 7: relationship with EQS and planning to be considered).

General rules are in fact legislative acts, in which no individual standard setting takes place. This means that compared with permitting, the procedural elements for general rules differ a great deal. The collection of information – necessary for careful standard setting – takes place on a general, more abstract level, taking into account the homogeneous outcome of the specific category of activities (characteristic 8: collection of relevant homogeneous information, on a general scale). The draft texts for general rules are open to comments and advice. In this respect an open public decision-making process also takes place and access to general information is provided (characteristic 9: access to general information and characteristic 10: access to decision-making on the general rules.). In addition, access to environmental information about the specific activities, and access to possible fine-tuning decisions need to be addressed as well.

According to Dutch law the general rules cannot be challenged before the administrative court (the General Administrative Law Act does not (yet) provide for access to the administrative court for general binding rules).[59]

---

[56] Art. 8.9 juncto Art. 8.10 section 2 Dutch Environmental Management Act; Soil Protection Act, Art. 19.

[57] Dutch Environmental Management Act, Art. 8.11(3) juncto Art. 8.40(3).

[58] See the legislative proposal that was presented to the Second Chamber of the Dutch Parliament on 9 August 2004 (Wijziging van de Wet Milieubeheer en de Wet Verontreiniging Oppervlaktewateren), No. 29 711 (the text can be found at www.overheid.nl).

[59] GALA Art. 8.2.

However, there are ways in which it is possible to address the civil court. To some extent it is explicitly made possible within the general rules to fine-tune these rules through administrative decision-making on specific cases. Such a tailored decision can be brought to the administrative court (characteristic 11: access to court in order to fight the general rules, or particular individual decisions). And, as is the case with respect to permitting, for the general rules adequate monitoring and enforcement provisions need to be established as well (characteristic 12: monitoring and enforcement provisions).

Experience has showed that there are some compliance problems with the general rules.[60] In addition, to some extent the absence of flexibility is criticized. In an evaluative study of a selected set of general rules it was concluded that in order to protect the environment effectively it would be necessary to adjust the general rules to the specificities of the activities, and their local situation.[61] In recent sets of general rules, the central government has adopted more flexible standards, like a duty of care, and goal-oriented conditions. This more flexible approach is chosen in order to prevent statistical standard setting. As a consequence, more responsibility is given to the operators themselves, and their control over decentralized administrative bodies. In the end, one might wonder whether the general rules are indeed always the best option for large groups of activities. One might also examine whether a simple permit scheme, to be executed by decentralized bodies, together with general rules and/or guidelines from central government, would also be an attractive instrument. In choosing between these regulatory options, the restriction of opportunities for corruption should be addressed as well. In this respect, especially for developing countries where corruption often occurs, clear general rules seem to be preferred above competences with a lot of room for discretion and non-binding guidelines.

4. THE INDONESIAN ENVIRONMENTAL MANAGEMENT ACT 1997

This section will review what recommendations might be given to the Indonesian legislator on improving its EMA 1997 on the basis of the main insights presented in Sections 2 and 3. Section 2 discussed the need to achieve coherency in environmental law, by means of harmonization, coordination,

---

60 Evaluatiecommissie Wet Milieubeheer, *De nieuwe algemene regels ingevolge artikel 8.40 Wet milieubeheer,* ECWM 2002/10, Postbus 30945, 2500 GX Den Haag.

61 Evaluatiecommissie Wet Milieubeheer, *De nieuwe algemene regels ingevolge artikel 8.40 Wet milieubeheer,* ECWM 2002/10, Postbus 30945, 2500 GX Den Haag, p. 4.

and integration. This fundamental point of attention must be combined with a balanced choice of instruments, taking account of how the administration is or should be organized. Section 3 gave an overview of the fundamental characteristics of two command and control options: the integrated permit, and the general rules.

4.1. One Indonesian Environmental Code?

In the elucidation on the EMA 1997 it is stated that the EMA contains the norms of environmental law. However, the EMA 1997 can clearly not be qualified as an Environmental Code that contains all the necessary provisions (and basis for secondary legislation) for the whole environmental field. For instance, the codification of environmental principles, procedures for decision-making, access to information, provisions for integrated standard setting such as a permit scheme, and sectoral provisions (the vertical layers) are not or are not precisely enough codified in this Act. The EMA indeed mentions some of these topics, but then fails to provide additional rules. This concerns for instance the following provision of the EMA: 'Every person has the right to environmental information which is related to environmental management rules'.[62] Such a provision needs additional rules in order to clarify how this right can be effectuated.

The idea – or, to say, the ideal – of one Environmental Code with horizontal and vertical layers as presented in Section 2.3 is an ultimate goal which it is not easy to realize. As shown above, within such an exercise many dogmatic and even practical questions need to be answered. The Indonesian legislator should carefully consider whether it is profitable and realistic to start such a challenging project – aiming at integrating all the relevant environmental legislation in just one Code. In fact, the idea of having one Environmental Code seems to run counter to the method on which the EMA 1997 is based: this Act predominantly contains environmental norms that must form a basis for evaluating and adapting other laws that are related to environmental aspects.[63, 64]

---

62 EMA 1997, Art. 5(2).

63 The elucidation on the EMA 1997 states that the EMA will be a foundation for evaluating and adapting all laws and regulations which contain stipulations on the environment, that is laws and regulations regarding integration, mining and energy, forestry, biological and ecosystem resource conservation, industry, human settlement, spatial ordering, land use, and others.

64 Bedner argues with respect to the EMA 1997: 'However, it is still based on the idea that environmental management can be integrated by simply stipulating principles that must then be incorporated in sectoral legislation'. Bedner (2003, p. 4).

The option of radically transforming and adjusting the environmental law system in order to implement all the rules in just one Code should be balanced against the more pragmatic option of following a step-by-step approach in building and improving the legislative framework.[65] Within this process of building legislative capacity the idea of one Code might be an inspiring thought, but we should keep in mind that the substance is more important than the form. For the pragmatic option, one of the first steps would be to choose which major environmental problems would be given priority. Then, the type of regulatory intervention that would be best suited should be considered, to be followed by its legislative design in the EMA, and subsequently, its implementation. Within a process of priorities, the need to reach as much coherency as possible among the regulatory provisions should of course be the guiding principle. However, when choosing priorities, there can even be arguments to combat some pollution problems in a rather isolated way (this is for example the basic approach taken in Europe, in combating the climate change problem, as an EU-wide emissions trading system is installed for just one pollutant, CO_2). And, as already addressed in Section 2, the Indonesian legislator should not only think of the classical way of regulatory interventions, but should also be considering whether alternative types of regulations might perhaps be established.

A step-by-step approach based on a policy of priorities would probably inspire more public confidence in the government's ability to guide society to a more sustainable economy. When the most serious polluting problems are being addressed, further steps to enhance the coherency of legislative provisions and the adoption of additional regulatory interventions – addressing minor pollution problems – could be taken.

4.2. The EMA as a Basis for Integrated Regulatory Interventions

The EMA 1997 emphasizes the need to implement sustainable development. In this respect it also recognizes that an integrated approach is needed. For instance, environmental management is defined as: 'An integrated effort to reserve environmental functions which covers planning policy, exploitation, development, maintenance, reparation, supervisions and control of the environment'.[66]

---

[65] To be compared with the report of the EAP Task Force (Task Force for the Implementation of the Environmental Action Plan for Eastern Europe, established at the 1993 Ministerial Conference 'Environment for Europe') (2003), *Review of Environmental Permitting Systems in Eastern Europe, Caucasus and Central Asia*, final report, April 2003, p. 72: most practical way is a gradual adjustment of existing systems over a longer period.

[66] EMA 1997, Art. 1(2).

In general, the term 'integration' should be concretized with additional clarifications. Integration could mean external integration, internal integration, or even both. Subsequently, both the concepts of external and internal integration are rather vague, and different options exist to implement these concepts in practice. In other words, whether or not integration will be realized depends on the existence of instruments intended to implement these goals.

As a central environmental management act, and given the integrated effort to protect environmental functions, it would be logical for the EMA 1997 to contain the main regulatory instruments that would concretize the important but still vague concept of environmental management. As in most countries, command and control interventions are the main type of regulation; one might expect the EMA to include such options. However, the Environmental Management Act 1997 does not contain a clear and precisely defined framework for permit schemes and general rules, explicitly providing a coherent approach. There are indeed some basic references to permits and general rules, but unfortunately the EMA fails to regulate the main characteristics of these regulatory interventions. This will be illustrated below shortly.

4.2.1. Licensing

Chapter VI, part I, of the EMA, entitled 'Licensing' does not provide a well-designed permit scheme aiming at an integrated approach. It is not sufficiently clear which permit schemes (with what scope) actually exist, and how they relate to each other. There are some promising starting points included in the chapter, but the text as it stands is poorly drafted. It only consists of four articles, of which the first three will be commented on briefly below. The fourth, Article 21, does not focus on licensing, but rules that every person is prohibited from importing hazardous and toxic waste.

At first glance, one can see that a rather integrated approach is chosen, as Article 18 prescribes that 'Every business and/or activity which gives rise to a large and important impact on the environment must possess an environmental impact analysis to obtain the license to conduct a business and/or activity'. It is not clear which permit is being referred to, and what its legal base is. Moreover, it is not clear what role the EIA should play in issuing the licence. Article 18 indeed requires an environmental impact assessment as a condition for obtaining 'the license to conduct a business and/or activity'. It does not spell out what level of environmental protection should be given, taking into account the results of an EIA. It only says that in the licence to conduct a business and/or activity, conditions and obligations to carry out environmental impact efforts need to be included. It is exactly this topic, the scope of environmental protection, and the criteria for decision-making, that should be well defined.

Article 19 gives some procedural provisions for the 'license to carry out a business and/or activity'. Here the wording is rather poor and vague as well, which means that no clear idea can be formed about the precise scope and meaning of the procedural provisions. For instance, it is prescribed that in issuing a licence it is compulsory to take into account 'public opinion'. This main obligation is not supported by additional rules explaining how the administrative bodies should facilitate the public in expressing their opinion. A more elaborated procedure is missing here. It is to be noted that these procedural provisions might (to some extent) be part of other legislation (like an Administrative Code), but then it might be assumed that the Environmental Management Act would have made references to those provisions.

It seems to be the case that within Article 18 of the EMA the environmental impact analysis has been prescribed for (already) existing licences. In this respect, one could argue that an instrument of external integration has been introduced. The question is, however, whether a specific environmental permit should be established as well. At the moment, for instance, it is not clear how (and where) the characteristics of environmental protection through permitting are established. Moreover, Article 18 does not give any direction on how the environmental impact analysis should play a determining role in accepting or refusing the application for a permit. Article 19 gives some directions on the (procedural and) substantive aspects that need to be taken into account in issuing 'a license to carry out a business and/or activity', but this substantive framework is very poor. For instance, an economic-technical criterion is lacking here.

One would expect that an Environmental Management Act would provide for an integrated permit scheme, or alternatively, would provide for the coordination of several environmental permit schemes. Article 20 is in this respect an interesting point of consideration. It installs a specific licence concerning the disposal of waste in any environmental medium. Waste disposal may only be carried out at a disposal site that is determined by the Minister.[67] Article 1(16) EMA gives the following definition of waste:

> Waste is the residue of a business and/or activity.

This is a broad definition that supports a rather wide scope of a waste permit scheme. The elucidation on the EMA indeed seems to encourage a wide interpretation of the permit scheme:

> In principle disposal of waste to an environmental medium is prohibited. . . .

---

[67] The adjustment of the EMA to the RGA will be discussed in Chapter 7 of this volume.

This sentence is continued with:

> ... with the exception of certain environmental media which have been allocated by the Government.

Here the reader gets somehow confused, as it is not exactly clear what the real scope and meaning of the permit system is. Is it indeed also meant to apply to air pollution emissions? What does 'media that have been allocated' mean exactly? In other words, does Article 20 really intend to establish an *integrated waste permit scheme*, wherein all the emissions of all kind of residues are to be assessed? In principle, the article can be interpreted as meaning that an integrative approach is indeed to be taken in issuing this waste permit. However, here also the EMA is poorly designed, as it is not made sufficiently clear to what extent environmental protection should be given, what the economic-technical criterion is, what the relationship is with emissions quality standards, which procedure should be followed, and what kind of specific permit conditions might be included into the permit. Moreover, in practice, separate environmental licences still exist, based on separate secondary acts. It has not been made clear how the permit scheme of Article 20 relates to the licence to conduct a business and/or activity to which Article 18 refers. And one can also wonder why the duty to take account of public opinion has only been prescribed for the licence to carry out a business and/or activity, and not for the waste licence as established in Article 20.

Article 20 can be seen as a starting point for the further development of an integrated permit scheme. Such a scheme should not be restricted to 'waste' problems. It should be considered whether it would also include energy efficiency, the use of raw materials, noise, smell, and so on. In sum, it is a basic starting point for the further development of an integrated (or coordinated) permit scheme. However, the provisions in the EMA are poorly drafted, and need to be improved. In this process, there needs to be fundamental consideration about what kind of integrated or coordinated permit scheme should be established. In addition, it should be carefully considered to what governmental scale this competence should be attributed. In improving the section on licensing, the legislator should be aware of the characteristics that need to be made clear in the primary legislation.

4.2.2. General rules

Chapter VI of the EMA, entitled Environmental Compliance Requirements, addresses only the regulatory intervention known as licensing, but does not facilitate the adoption of general rules as discussed in Section 3. However, a kind of general standard setting can be found in Article 14, which rules:

1. To guarantee the preservation of environmental functions, every business and/or activity is prohibited from breaching quality standards and standard criteria of environmental damage.
2. Stipulations on environmental quality standards, prevention of and coping with pollution and restoration of its carrying capacity are regulated by Government Regulation.
3. Stipulations on standard criteria of environmental damage, prevention and coping with damage along with restoration of its supportive capacity are regulated by Government Regulation.

According to Article 1 (13) EMA, 'standard environmental damage criteria' are threshold limits of physical and/or biological changes in the environment which can be measured. This kind of general standard setting differs from the type of general rules as described in Section 3 that aim at integrated standard setting in relation to homogeneous activities. Article 14 starts from an effect-oriented approach, from which standards will be adopted in order to protect environmental functions.[68] Business and/or activities are prohibited from breaching the quality standards and the (effect-oriented) standard criteria of environmental damage. The fundamental question with an effect-oriented approach is how the established 'room for pollution' can be divided among the possible polluters. Normally the effect-oriented approach is therefore translated into a permit scheme. The possible relationship between on the one hand quality standards and on the other hand permit schemes is, however, not explained in the EMA 1997.

Surprisingly, Article 14 (2) is in practice obviously interpreted as a base for establishing permit schemes in secondary legislation. For instance, Government Regulation No. 82 of 2001 concerning water quality management and water pollution control (based on Article 14(2)) establishes several permit schemes (which might even include an emissions trading scheme).[69] This construction of problem-specific permit schemes in secondary legislation contributes to the fragmented character of the legislative framework. Also the transparency of the EMA is troubled by this construction, as Chapter VI contains a part called 'licensing' but surprisingly, the basis for licensing is found in provisions included in Chapter V: Preservation of environmental functions.

68 For instance, Government Regulation No. 82 of 2001 concerning water quality management and water pollution control establishes provisions as meant in Art. 14(2) EM (stipulations on environmental quality standards, prevention of and coping with pollution and restoration of its carrying capacity).

69 Art. 35 ('Every business and/or activity that intends to use wastewater for land application is required to obtain permission in writing from the Regent/Major'); Art. 40 ('Every business and activity intending to dispose of wastewater in water or water sources is required to obtain permission in writing from the Regent/Major').

4.3. A Balanced Approach

The literature has already recommended that the next step in developing Indonesian environmental legislation would be to integrate the different licences. A step towards integrating permit schemes might be feasible, given the fact that permit competences in most fields are being delegated to the districts. Formerly the permit competences were vertically divided among the governmental layers, meaning that central government provided the so-called business permit through decentralized branch offices, provinces issued the wastewater permits, and districts issued the nuisance licence. Bedner has already stated that consideration might be given to merging existing permits into one integrated permit scheme. As a second-best option, the coordination of the provisions of these permit schemes could be established.[70]

A recommendation in favour of a clearly designed integrated permit scheme can be supported, in so far as the negative and positive effects of establishing such a scheme are considered in detail. The characteristics as described in Section 3 should then at least be included in the EMA. As stressed before, full integration of the environmental assessment in just one permit scheme needs to be balanced against the possible attractiveness of other regulatory interventions, like general rules for a homogeneous group of activities. The big question is indeed whether Indonesia is not only ready for an integrated permit, but is even ready to adopt additional or alternative regulatory instruments. In other words, the process towards 'Koordinasi, Integrasi, Simplifikasi and Sinkronisasi' (with the acronym KISS)[71] should be balanced against choosing an optimal instrument to address the most serious environmental problems – to be fitted into the administrative structure.

5. CONCLUSION

The coherent design of effective and efficient environmental legislation is a challenging task. In this respect, it needs to be said that the opportunities and limits of integrated environmental law are still not fully clear. Hence, this is an area in which more research must be done in order to gain convincing and applicable insights. Developing countries, which are often still in the process of designing or improving their environmental legislation, could already learn from the successful ideas and also the mistakes of developed countries. But, even developed countries are themselves still in a learning phase as far as

70 Bedner (2003, p. 8).
71 Otto (2003, p. 13).

building an adequate environmental legal framework is concerned. In this respect there is the challenging idea of one Environmental Code. However, at the moment there does not seem to be an overarching blueprint for an Environmental Code that could smoothly be adopted by developing countries like Indonesia. The idea of horizontal and vertical layers in environmental legislation is in this respect encouraging, and could inspire further improvements in Indonesian legislation. Indeed, building a national adequate environmental legislative framework is to be seen more as a process, rather than as a sole and unique activity. In this respect, a closer look has been given to some of the regulatory provisions included in the EMA – especially the ones that seem to be suited to integrative standard setting. It has been suggested that the main characteristics of these approaches should be regulated within the EMA.

In sum, the following directions of thoughts can be recommended.

In the long term one might think of building towards an Indonesian Environmental Code that would contain coherent, effective and efficient regulatory provisions for the whole environmental field. It is recommended that there should be a research project to design in more detail how such a Code would look – also in relation to existing codes and regulations. The Code as such should not be the ultimate goal, but obviously the aim should be to choose regulatory methods, including related procedural, monitoring and enforcement provisions that best fit Indonesian financial and other capacities and culture. Maybe it will be concluded that (to some extent) specific acts and regulations need to stay on their own, and that – when necessary – in that case some harmonizing and coordinating provisions need to be established.

The ideal of the Environmental Code could be implemented, in a pragmatic way, in phases, by revising and expanding the existing EMA. It should be determined what topics would have first priority, and one might think in this respect of starting with a regulatory approach towards serious polluting activities through permits, general rules, or a combination of these instruments. In general, the already existing provisions in the EMA are rather poorly described, so these should be enhanced by subsequent legislative projects. So, in the short and mid term, well-designed horizontal and vertical layers could be adopted.

One of the short-term goals would be to optimize the legislative provisions with respect to permitting. In this respect, it should be considered whether it is yet feasible to introduce an integrated permit scheme for serious polluting, non-homogeneous activities, or instead, to consider harmonizing and coordinating provisions between several permit schemes.[72] With respect to permit-

[72] One of the practical but important legal questions to define what a 'serious polluting activity' might be.

ting, at least the characteristics as described in Section 3 should all be well drafted. In addition to the design of the substantive framework for the permit scheme, such as the scope of the permit scheme and the criteria for the decision-making process, including the relationship towards environmental quality standards and environmental management plans, it seems extremely important to address the question of procedural provisions as well. They help to make the administrative decision-making process transparent and open for control. Here one must think of access to environmental information, access to the decision-making process, and access to court for (at least) the people concerned. Those procedural provisions need to be applicable not only to the execution of the permitting competences, but also to the monitoring and enforcement competences.

For homogeneous polluting activities the instrument of general rules seems to be a reasonable option. When some fine-tuning of those general rules is considered to be necessary, some room for discretion then needs to be given to administrative decision-making for specific situations, and then of course attention should be paid to procedural provisions in order to control that administrative decision-making. It may even be the case that for certain polluting activities a simple permit scheme would be considered an attractive alternative to the general rules, as it is a more flexible approach. Such a simple permit scheme might even be combined with some general rules, or less binding guidance notes, to be taken into account by the permitting bodies. In sum, it is clear that a careful examination needs to be done to see what regulatory instrument best fits specific categories of polluting activities.

It should be considered as well under what circumstances it would be attractive to introduce alternative regulatory approaches – knowing that the command and control options might be costly and not fully effective. Therefore it needs to be examined whether alternative options like market-based instruments might indeed be introduced as part of the desirable instrument mix in a developing country like Indonesia.

However, none of these regulatory options would automatically have effect. The real teeth of environmental regulatory provisions will depend on their application in practice. This is the biggest challenge in letting environmental law work. In this respect, in the short term a medium-oriented regulatory approach aiming at combating a serious problem via a rather classical command and control permit scheme might even be preferable. Much attention should anyway be paid to the question of whether and how established regulatory provisions are executed in practice, and what specific practical problems – like a lack of knowledge and financial resources – really hinder the satisfactory outcome of legislative provisions. In the long term, however, the quality of the whole body of domestic Indonesian environmental legislation might be enhanced by a structured, phased process, based on the idea of internal integration but taking into account the optimal choice of instruments and the administrative structure, including the financial and other capacities of the administrative bodies.

REFERENCES

Anker, H.T. (2002), 'Integrated Resource Management – Lessons for Europe?', *European Environmental Law Review*, 199–209.

Bedner, A. (2003), 'Introduction', in A. Bedner and N. Niessen, *Towards Integrated Environmental Law in Indonesia?*, Leiden University, the Netherlands: CNWS Publications, CNWS Series 127, pp. 1–20.

Biezeveld, G.A. (2002), *Duurzame milieuwetgeving*, Den Haag: Boom Juridische Uitgevers.

Boeve, M.N., F.M. Fleurke and M.A Wiering (2004), 'Het begrip "milieu" in de Wet Milieubeheer', *Tijdschrift voor Milieu en Recht,* 221–6.

Christiansen, A.C. (2004), 'The Role of Flexibility Mechanisms in EU Climate Strategy: Lessons Learned and Future Challenges?', *International Environmental Agreements: Politics, Law and Economics*, **4**, 27–46.

Cleij, J. and E.N. Neuerburg (1988), *AMvB's op grond van artikel 2a van de Hinderwet, Vereniging voor Milieurecht 1988-1*, Zwolle: Tjeenk Willink.

Deketelaere K., R.A.J. van Gestel, P.C. Gilhuis, M. Peeters and M. Hertoghs (2003), *Integratie vergeleken: Buitenlandse milieuwetgeving als mogelijke inspiratie voor de verdere ontwikkeling van de Wet milieubeheer*, *rapport voor de Evaluatiecommissie Wet milieubeheer*, Tilburg: Schoordijk Instituut.

Dhondt, N. (2003), *Integration of Environmental Protection into other EC Policies. Legal Theory and Practice*, Groningen: Europa Law Publishing.

Drupsteen, T.G. (1990), 'Twintig jaar milieuwetgeving: tijd voor bezinning', *Tijdschrift voor Milieu en Recht*, *Themanummer: De toekomst van de milieuwetgeving*, 199.

Faure, M.G. (1995), *Enforcement Issues for Environmental Legislation in Developing Countries,* The United Nations University, INTECH (Institute for New Technologies), Working Paper No. 19.

Faure, M.G. (2000), 'The Harmonization, Codification and Integration of Environmental Law: A Search for Definitions', *European Environmental Law Review*, 174–82.

Faure, M.G. and J. Lefevre (1996), 'The Draft Directive on Integrated Pollution Prevention and Control: an Economic Perspective', *European Environmental Law Review,* 112–22.

Freriks, A. and M. Peeters (1994), 'De afstemmingsregeling inzake de Wm-vergunning en de Wvo-vergunning. Een twee-eenheid of van tweeën een?', *Tijdschrift voor Milieu en Recht*, 194–204.

Guruswamy, L. (1991), 'The Case for Integrated Pollution Control', *Law and Contemporary Problems*, **54** (4), 41–56.

Lewis, D. (2002), 'Law and Globalization: An Opportunity for Europe and its Partners and their Legal Scholars', *European Public Law,* **8** (2), 219–303.

Michiels, F.C.M.A. (2002), 'De toekomst van de Omgevingswet', in M. Lurks, W. Den Ouden, J.E.M. Polak and A.E. Schilder (eds), *De grootste gemene deler*, Deventer: Kluwer, pp. 307–20.

Niessen, N. (2003), 'The Environmental Management Act of 1997: Comprehensive and Integrated?', in A. Bedner and N. Niessen, *Towards Integrated Environmental*

Law in Indonesia?, Leiden University, The Netherlands: CNWS Publications, CNWS Series 127, pp. 66–79.

Ogus, A. (2004), 'Corruption and Regulatory Structures', *Law and Policy,* **26,** 229–46.

Otto, J.M. (2003), 'Incoherence in Environmental Law and the Solutions of Co-ordination, Harmonisation, and Integration', in A. Bedner and N. Niessen, *Towards Integrated Environmental Law in Indonesia?*, Leiden University, The Netherlands: CNWS Publications, CNWS Series 127, pp. 11–20.

Peeters, M. (2003a), 'Emissions Trading as a New Dimension to European Environmental Law: The Political Agreement of the European Council on Greenhouse Gas Allowance Trading', *European Environmental Law Review*, **12** (3), 87.

Peeters, M. (2003b), 'Legal Feasibility of Emissions Trading: Learning Points from Emissions Trading for Ozone-depleting Substances', in M. Faure, J. Gupta and A. Nentjes (eds), *Climate Change and the Kyoto Protocol. The Role of Institutions and Instruments to Control Global Change*, Cheltenham, UK and Northampton, MA, USA: Edward Elgar, pp. 147–70.

Sands, P. (2003), *Principles of International Environmental Law*, Cambridge: Cambridge University Press, second edition.

Tietenberg, T. (2002), 'The Tradable Permits Approach to Protecting the Commons: What Have We Learned?', in E. Ostrom, T. Dietz, N. Dolšak, P.C. Stern, S. Stonich and E.U. Weber (eds), *The Drama of the Commons,* Washington, DC: National Academy Press, pp. 197–231.

APPENDIX

Main Characteristics of an Environmental Permit Scheme

Characteristic 1: a permit obligation for
Characteristic 2: certain well-described activities, and
Characteristic 3: attribution of the administrative competence to issue a permit, to include permit conditions and to adjust or revoke the permit
Characteristic 4: description of the scope of protection of the permit scheme
Characteristic 5: when necessary: attention to harmonizing and coordinative provisions
Characteristic 6: description of the economic-technological criterion and other possible criteria for decision-making
Characteristics 7a and 7b: relationship with environmental quality standards, and environmental management plans
Characteristic 8: collection of relevant information on the environmental effects of a specific activity, for instance through environmental impact assessments or through requirements concerning the application of the permit
Characteristic 9: provisions for access to information
Characteristic 10: provisions for access to decision-making
Characteristic 11: provisions for access to court
Characteristic 12: monitoring and enforcement provisions (and related procedural rights)

Main Characteristics of General Environmental Rules

Characteristic 1: competence established in primary law, to prescribe general rules in secondary legislation
Characteristic 2: well-described categories of homogeneous activities
Characteristic 3: limited competences for decentralized authorities to deviate from the general rules
Characteristic 4: description of the scope of protection of the general rules
Characteristic 5: (when necessary) attention to harmonizing and coordinating provisions between general rules
Characteristic 6: economic-technological criterion, and possibly other criteria, to be taken into account when issuing the general rules
Characteristic 7: to consider the relationship with environmental quality standards and environmental management plans
Characteristic 8: collection of relevant homogeneous information, on a general scale, when designing the general rules
Characteristic 9: access to general and specific information

Characteristic 10: access to decision-making on general and specific standard setting
Characteristic 11: access to court in order to challenge the general rules, or in particular the fine-tuning of administrative decisions
Characteristic 12: monitoring and enforcement provisions (and related procedural rights)

6. Toward integrated environmental law: Indonesian experiences so far and expectations of a future Environmental Management Act

Takdir Rahmadi*

1. THE IDEA OF INTEGRATED ENVIRONMENTAL MANAGEMENT

The idea of integrated environmental management has entered the legal and political discourses in Indonesia not only in the era of the Environmental Management Act of 1997 (the EMA of 1997) that is still in force now, but also already in the period of its predecessor, the Environmental Management Act of 1982 (the EMA of 1982). Environmental issues have entered the political agenda in Indonesia since the mid-1970s and in particular after the participation of Indonesia in the Stockholm Conference of 1972.[1] Together with the concepts of coordination and harmonization, the idea of integration in environmental management has become subject to legal and political discourse since then.[2] We can use the definitions of these terms developed by Otto who also based his definitions upon those of other scholars. Otto suggests that the term coordination refers to 'a certain adjustment between separate parts to bring them into a proper, suitable and correct relationship'.[3] The term harmonization refers to 'when separate parts are brought into conformity with one another'.[4] The term integration refers to the merger or fusion in which two or more parts become one unity'.[5] However, in the context of Indonesia, I would

* I would like to thank Professor Michael Faure for his comments and suggestions on this chapter.

1 Cribb (2003, p. 38); also Koesnadi (1986, pp. 6–7).
2 Otto (2003, pp. 13–15).
3 Ibid.
4 Ibid.
5 Ibid.

say that the concept of integration ('*keterpaduan*') is broad enough to embrace the terms: coordination, harmonization and merger or fusion that can be defined as integration in a narrow sense.

Many Indonesian environmental scientists, non-governmental organization (NGO) activists as well as government officials have been involved in debating how an integrated approach to environmental management should be made a reality. This awareness, of course, results from echos of the Stockholm Declaration of 1972, in particular Article 13 that provides *inter alia*:

> States should adopt an integrated and coordinated approach to their development planning as to insure that development is compatible with the need to protect and improve the environment for the benefit of their population.

In order to guarantee that the idea of an integrated approach to environmental management obtains legal force, it has to be incorporated into policy and legal instruments. Therefore, Indonesia's participation in the Stockholm Conference stimulated Indonesia to promulgate an Act concerning environmental management in 1982 (hereafter referred to as the EMA of 1982). The EMA of 1982 adopts the idea of external integration as it is formulated in Article 18 that states *inter alia*:

> The management of the living environment on the national level shall be carried out in the integrated manner [*pengelolaan lingkungan hidup dilaksanakan secara terpadu*].

The idea of an integrated approach to environmental management in relation to development was once again reinforced by the Rio Declaration of 1992. Principle 4 of the Rio Declaration states: 'In order to achieve sustainable development, environmental protection shall constitute an integral part of the development process and cannot be considered in isolation from it'.[6] When the EMA of 1982 was replaced by the EMA of 1997, the idea of integrated environmental management was again incorporated. In the EMA 1997, it is formulated in three different places: in Consideration B, Article 9 concerning the policy on environmental management, and Article 11 concerning institutional arrangements. The words 'integrated' and 'holistic' are close to the meaning of the Indonesian words: *'terpadu'* (integrated) and *'menyeluruh'* (holistic) that are used in both acts to describe the basic idea of Indonesian environmental policy.

---

6 On the legal implications of the notion of sustainable development, see Birnie and Boyle (2002, pp. 84–96).

In fact, the term integration is not only related to the EMA of 1982 or the EMA of 1997. Many NGO activists have also used the concept of integration as the basis for their demand to the government to carry out legal reforms in the area of natural resource management because the current statutory regimes related to natural resources in Indonesia are fragmented and rely on a sector-based approach. Therefore, a number of Indonesian environmental NGOs have strongly lobbied the People's Assembly (MPR) in order to promulgate a Decree that provides competencies to the executive branch of government to bring about legal reform in the area of natural resource management in pursuance of the concept of integrated natural resource management in Indonesia. The result is that the People's Assembly has promulgated Decree No. IX/MPR/2001 concerning Agricultural Reform and Natural Resource Management that directs the government of the Republic of Indonesia to carry out reform of the existing Act on agriculture and to prepare an Act concerning natural resource management. Thus, the idea of integration in environmental law is not only specifically related to the EMA, but also to natural resources law. In addition, it is not a new issue to Indonesia or to other countries, since it has become part of the international discourse. The idea of integration of environmental law and policy can, as indicated, indeed be found in international documents, such as the Stockholm Declaration and the Rio Declaration.

2. HOW TO IMPLEMENT INTEGRATED ENVIRONMENTAL MANAGEMENT INTO REALITY: THE INDONESIAN EXPERIENCE SO FAR

The experience of Indonesia in the implementation of the concept of integrated environmental management can mainly be seen in two areas: institutional arrangements and environmental and natural resource law.

2.1. Institutional Arrangements

The idea of an integrated and holistic approach to environmental management in Indonesia is reflected in many necessary institutional arrangements. Environmental management cannot be assigned to a single ministry only, but has to become the responsibility of all ministries and non-departmental state agencies. The position of the Ministry of the Environment in Indonesia today is that of a ministry without department. Initially the functions of the Ministry of the Environment were mainly to coordinate the activities of other ministries and governmental agencies in environmental management, and to issue environmental quality standards and guidelines. On the other hand, the other ministries, usually referred to as sector ministries, for example, the Ministry of Forestry, the Ministry of Mining and Energy, the Ministry of Industry and Trade, and the Ministry of Transmigration as well as other governmental agencies, such as the National Atomic Agency, and the provincial governments hold administrative powers or regulatory powers. They have the responsibility to require every activity under their mandates or jurisdictions to carry out environmental management. They hold the power to enforce administrative environmental law and its own sector laws against any activity or any body in order to prevent environmental degradation and certainly can undertake clean-up activities or restore the environment when environmental disaster occurs. Under this kind of institutional pattern, the Ministry of the Environment could be viewed as having been successful in encouraging the rise of environmental awareness and public discourses in the 1980s as environmental issues have often been discussed in either academic fora or mass media since that decade. The public, however, later found there to be a large gap between their own environmental awareness on the one hand and the environmental performance of the business community and of the sector ministries or other governmental agencies on the other hand. The public and environmentalists in particular realize that many environmental cases are not adequately resolved and environmental regulations are not enforced against perpetrators by sector ministries or provincial governments. One example where sector ministries and provincial governments have not enforced administrative environmental law adequately, concerns the procedure of environmental impact assessment (EIA). Many activities that are subject to an EIA procedure have been carried out although their EIA documents have not yet been approved by the EIA Commission.

Most environmental scholars and officials at the Ministry of the Environment regard the existing institutional pattern in Indonesia as being a major source of the weaknesses of environmental management. Therefore, they would like to see a Ministry of the Environment with strong powers in administrative environmental law, since they believe that only a Ministry with a strong environmental mandate would be likely to enforce environmental regulations consistently. This can be seen in the promulgation of Government Regulation No. 20 of 1990 concerning water pollution, which was initiated and prepared by the office of the Ministry of the Environment. This regulation provides the Ministry of the Environment with the power to issue a licence to discharge liquid water into the soil. Under Government Regulation No. 82 of 2001 concerning Water Quality and Pollution Control which replaces Government Regulation No. 20 of 1990, the power to issue the licence to discharge liquid waste to water and land has been transferred to district or city governments in order to make it consistent with the idea of regional autonomy under Act No. 22 of 1999 concerning Regional Autonomy.[7] Another example of efforts by the Minister of the Environment to gain regulatory power is the establishment of a licence for dumping under Article 20 of the EMA of 1997.

However, since the Ministry of the Environment is a ministry without department, the Ministry of the Environment faces institutional limits. It cannot establish de-concentrated offices at the provincial and local level; moreover it lacks human resources. In practice, it is not able to do monitoring or surveillance to make sure that an activity, such as dumping waste, is not taking place. The problem is that the Ministry is based in Jakarta while Indonesia is geographically such a large country. Thus, it is not realistic to expect the Ministry of the Environment to be the holder of administrative environmental enforcement power as long as its status is still that of a ministry without department. Therefore, there has been some consideration given to changing the status of the Ministry of the Environment from a state ministry to a ministry with department. This idea has been challenged, however, by the argument that a ministry of the environment with department would create 'a super ministry'. It is feared that it would take over the power of most sectoral ministries. Hence, this idea meets some resistance.

Furthermore, environmentalists in the early 1990s demanded an institution with an environmental mandate and strong administrative powers. This culminated in the establishment of BAPEDAL, an Environmental Impact Agency. The idea of the establishment of BAPEDAL was actually inspired by the model of the USA Environmental Protection Agency. However, the high expectations that were held of BAPEDAL in the early years of its establishment turned to disappointment for many non-governmental environmentalists, since they found that BAPEDAL had very limited administrative law enforcement power. In fact, BAPEDAL only has the power to issue licences for the operation of hazardous waste treatment facilities, while industries generating hazardous wastes are still subject to the power of the Ministry of Industry and Trade, and transportation of hazardous wastes falls under the competency of the Ministry of Transportation. BAPEDAL only has power in the field that was previously not under the competency of any other ministry as introduced by Governmental Regulation No. 19 of 1994, and amended by Government Regulation No. 12 of 1995, in order to prevent environmental disasters caused by hazardous waste. In sum, the establishment of BAPEDAL has not basically changed the institutional competence in environmental management.

7 Act No. 22 of 1999 concerning Regional Autonomy has been replaced by Act No. 32 of 2004 concerning Regional Autonomy since November 2004. On the relation between environmental management and the decentralization act, see Chapter 7 of this volume.

However, under Presidential Decree No. 2 of 2002 BAPEDAL has been liquidated and integrated with the Minister of the Environment. Thus, under the present institutional arrangements, the Minister of the Environment still holds the power to coordinate but also has the power to issue licences in two fields: licence to dump and licence to operate a hazardous waste facility.

2.2. Struggling for the Creation of an Integrated Environmental Law

The concept of integrated environmental law in Indonesia is related to two issues. The first concerns the relationship between the EMA and sectoral legislation or statutes. The second relates to the scope of the EMA.

2.2.1. The relationship of the EMA with sectoral legislation

The relationship between a general environmental statute and sectoral legislation has been described in the elucidation of the EMA of 1982 that is the predecessor of the EMA of 1997. The elucidation of the EMA of 1982 *inter alia* provides:

> This act contains environmental norms. This act be a basis for evaluating and adjusting all legislation related to environmental management such as legislation on water, mining, and energy, forestry and conservation of natural resources, industry, human settlement, spatial planning and land use.

The same wording as stated in the EMA of 1982 has been adopted in the elucidation of the EMA of 1997. Thus, from the elucidation of the EMA of 1982 and the EMA of 1997 we may conclude that the makers of the EMA of 1982 and the EMA of 1997 wish to establish a legislative system in which all sectoral legislation and other environmental legislation should refer to the EMA as their basis or reference. Such a function of the EMA in relation to sector acts as well as environmental regulations has been labelled by the academics as 'an umbrella provision or act'.[8] The elucidation of the EMA of 1982 and the EMA of 1997 also suggests that other legislation be reformed and harmonized pursuant to the ideas or basic principles of the EMA. The adjustment of sectoral statutes to the EMA may be closely related to the concept of external integration under the Dutch approach as mentioned by Peeters.[9]

However, until the present time not all sectoral statutes have been reformed in order to be harmonized with the basic principles of the EMA. The reform of sectoral statutes occurs sluggishly. A new forestry act to replace the old one

---

[8] See Danusaputro (1982, p. 25); Koesnadi (1986, p. 91); Rangkuti (1986, p. 117).

[9] See Chapter 5 of this volume.

(the Forestry Act of 1967), was promulgated in 1999, that is, Act No. 41 of 1999 concerning Forestry. A new water act to replace the old one (the Water Act of 1974), was promulgated in 2004, that is, Act No. 7 of 2004 concerning Water Resource. This means that new acts are being promulgated after the EMA of 1982 has itself been repealed by the EMA of 1997. Even the Mining Act of 1967 concerning mining has still been in force until now and has not been revised or amended to adjust to the ideas of the EMA.

It is also important to look at how sectoral legislation has been adjusted to the EMA. Three acts enacted after the enactment of the EMA of 1982 can be analysed. These are the Industrial Act No. 5 of 1984, the Conservation Act No. 5 of 1990 and the Act concerning Spatial Planning No. 23 of 1992. The Industrial Act of 1984 has explicitly mentioned the EMA of 1982 in its considerations. Articles of the Industrial Act of 1984 are also related to 'the environment' or 'environmental management'.[10] In addition, the EIA process is also applied to industrial activities with significant impacts on the environment. Moreover, the Industrial Act adopts fully criminal sanctions under the EMA of 1982. The Industrial Act, however, does not always use the terms in environmental management as they are used in the EMA of 1982. For example, the EMA of 1982 uses the term 'preservation of environmental capacity', while, for the same idea, the Industrial Act uses 'preservation of the environment'. From a normative point of view, these two terms cannot be interchangeable and the difference cannot be considered as trivial, since both have a different conceptual meaning. An academic who was involved in the preparation of the EMA argues that the term 'preservation of environmental capacity' has a conceptual meaning and that it is not the environment per se that is preserved, but its capacity.[11] If the environment per se is preserved, then there is a connotation that the environment cannot be changed. If the latter term is used, it is in contradiction with the notion of development since development has the meaning that some changes, for instance, physical environmental changes, are acceptable or tolerable.

The EMA of 1982 is also mentioned in the considerations of the Conservation Act which is concerned with the protection of living natural resources and their ecosystem. Although the substance of the Conservation Act is directly related to environmental management, surprisingly it is not necessarily harmonized with the EMA of 1982. For example, the term 'ecosystem' is found in both acts, but it is defined differently.[12] Like both the Industrial Act

---

10 It contains articles such as Article 2, Article 3 paragraph 1, Article 9 paragraph 4, Article 21 paragraph 1, 2 and 3.

11 Koesnadi (1986, p. 115).

12 See Article 1 paragraph 3 of the EMA of 1982 and compare with Article 1 paragraph 3 of the Conservation Act.

and the Conservation Act, the Spatial Planning Act also adopts elements of environmental management.[13] Compared with the drafters of the two previous acts, the drafters of the Spatial Planning Act are more willing to adopt terms used in the EMA such as 'preservation of environmental capacity' and 'sustainability development'.

From the analysis of these three acts enacted after the promulgation of the EMA of 1982, we find that the three appear to contain some elements of environmental management, but in two of them there are apparent terminological inconsistencies with the EMA. Of the three acts, only the drafters of the Spatial Planning Act were apparently more willing to adopt the terms used in the EMA, at least compared with those of the other two acts. In conclusion, the idea of harmonization between sector and environmentally related legislation with the EMA as the umbrella act has not been made a reality.

3. THE FUTURE EMA

3.1. Environmental Code as an Ultimate Goal

Marjan Peeters states that an ultimate goal of integrated environmental law is to have one environmental code.[14] The concept of an Environmental Code needs to be considered here since in Indonesia there have been discourses to assess the scope of the EMA. Some people argue that the EMA is more concerned with pollution issues so that Indonesia needs another act that is concerned with natural resource management.[15] However, if we talk about environmental management, we refer not only to prevention and control of environmental pollution, but also to conservation of natural resources. Thus, the scope of the EMA should not only cover pollution issues as some people see the EMA of 1997. In the long term, Indonesia should have an Environmental Code that integrates spatial planning, conservation of natural resources, air, water and marine pollution control, as well as environmental impact assessment procedures.

Under the current approach, spatial planning and conservation of nature are established under statutory regimes, while air, water and marine pollution

---

13 The notion of environmental management is mentioned in the considerations and also in Article 3, Article 10 paragraph 2 and Article 11.

14 Chapter 5, this volume.

15 See the statement by the National Consortium for Preservation of Forest and Natural Resources (KONPHALINDO), an Indonesian NGO, in *Buletin Informasi* No. 09/August 1997 published by ICEL, p. 16; see also the Draft Academic Paper of the Act concerning Management of Natural Resource.

control as well as environmental impact assessment procedures are established in government regulations. The position of a government regulation is of course lower than a statute. However, the idea for Indonesia to have an environmental code that integrates environmental areas that are currently established in different statutory regimes and government regulations may face some objections. Some Indonesian lawyers may see a statute with hundreds of articles as an unusual legal document, except for the criminal and private codes that were adopted from the Dutch era. After the era of independence, perhaps almost all statutes consisted of less than a hundred articles. The Indonesian lawmakers apparently prefer to promulgate statutes with less than a hundred articles. Such a preference is influenced by the argument that an act should contain basic or general rules only, while detailed ones have to be incorporated into government regulations. The EMA of 1997, for example, contains 52 articles only. The EMA of 1982 is even shorter, consisting of only 24 articles. The Forestry Act of 1999 consists of 84 articles. The Act No. 7 of 2004 concerning Water Resource with 100 articles and the Human Rights Act of 1999 with 105 articles can be considered as acts with many articles. Of course, a conventional paradigm can be changed if strong arguments can be made in favour of an environmental code. Rather than having two acts: one dealing with pollution issues and the other concerning the conservation of natural resources, it may be better to have one environmental code that covers broad areas that are at the same time integrated.

3.2. Integrated Licences

The concept of integrated licence or in Indonesian terminology often called *'izin terpadu'* has been discussed as a ramification of integrated environmental management. Many environmental lawyers are attracted to discussing the concept of an integrated licence because existing licences are fragmented and overlapping.[16] Under different regulatory regimes, there are currently several licences that are directly or indirectly related to environmental management and particularly relevant to pollution control. They are (1) the licence to engage in business, for example, industrial licences, mining concessions, logging concessions; (2) nuisance licence; (3) site licences; (4) building licences; (5) licences to discharge waste water; (6) licences to dump waste in an environmental medium; (7) licences to operate hazardous waste facilities. The power to issue these licences is today assigned to different governmental agencies. Table 6.1 describes the current licences, their functions and the authorities who have the power to issue them.

---

16 See, for example, Rangkuti (1992); also Santosa (2001, pp. 250–2).

Table 6.1 Types of existing licences, their functions and authorities responsible for issuing the licences

No.	Type of licence	Main function	Authorities
1	Licence to engage in business/to operate an activity, e.g. industrial licences, mining concessions, logging concessions, licence to transport hazardous wastes	Legality for operating an activity and also used for environmental protection	Sectoral ministers, e.g. Ministers of Industry, Mining, Forestry, and Transportation
2	Nuisance licence	Protecting people from smell and noise	Heads of District or Mayor
3	Site licences	Insuring consistency with spatial planning	Heads of District or Mayors
4	Building licences	Insuring consistency with spatial planning	Heads of District and Mayors
5	Licences to discharge waste water	Water and soil pollution control	Heads of District or Mayors
6	Licence to dump	Environmental protection and pollution control	The Minister of the Environment
7	Licence to operate hazardous waste facilities	Pollution control	The Minister of the Environment

Among these licences is the licence to engage in a business or to operate an activity that is connected to the environmental impact assessment procedure. Under current environmental regulations, in order to get a licence to engage in a business or activity that has a significant impact on the environment, a proponent of the activity has to conduct an environmental impact assessment. The current licence system not only involves an unnecessarily high cost to investors because they need to get several licences for an activity, but also creates difficulties and inconsistencies in law enforcement.

Therefore, the Indonesian environmental lawyers have proposed the concept of an integrated licence. The discourses on an integrated licence actually rose when the government of the Republic of Indonesia decided to replace the EMA of 1982 with the new EMA that is promulgated as the EMA of 1997. The fact that the EMA of 1997 has not brought about any change in the licence regime proves that the idea of an integrated licence system has never received support from the bureaucrats in the sectoral departments. In addition, the district and municipal governments would also like to maintain the current regulatory regime because they tend to treat these licences as sources of local revenue. Every licence is usually accompanied by a fee. Although the national and regional governmental decision-makers are reluctant to adopt the idea of an integrated licence system, discourses concerning this issue have never ended after the enactment of the EMA of 1997 and are still flourishing today.

Although the Indonesian environmental lawyers recognize the need for an integrated licence, they have different concepts of what they mean by an integrated licence. One argues that merging existing licences to become one licence is not necessary, but an integrated procedure is needed.[17] The proponent of this idea has not discussed further what he means by an integrated procedure. This idea still holds some weaknesses. First, it keeps the already existing licences so that the idea is unable to overcome unnecessary high cost regulation and is also inconsistent with the notion of an efficient regulatory regime. As a developing country, Indonesia needs to develop an efficient regulatory regime so that many investors will be attracted to invest their money in Indonesia. Efficiency as a criterion to judge the adequacy of a law or a policy has been proposed by some scholars under the banner of the economic approach to law.[18] Secondly, the idea ignores the fact that the nuisance licence is inadequate at protecting environmental interests in the modern era. The nuisance licence is based upon the *Hinder Ordonnantie* of 1926 that is designed to protect the interests of people living around 200 metres from an installation only, while an installation nowadays may create negative effects, such as air or water pollution, that can reach miles away from its source.[19] The first concept may not face any resistance or objection from national and local bureaucrats because it does not remove their powers.

The second concept of an integrated licence would like to integrate or unify five of the existing licences. These are: (1) the nuisance licence under the

---

17 See Moestadji (2003).

18 See, for example, Posner (2003, pp. 10–16); Posner (2003, pp. 31–144); Chand (1994, pp. 225–38). For a discussion of the economic analysis of environmental law and policy, see, for example, Stewart and Krier (1978) and also Faure and Skogh (2003).

19 For discussion weaknesses of *Hinder Ordonnantie* of 1926, see Rangkuti (2000, pp. 148–9).

Hinder Ordonnantie of 1926, (2) the licence to engage in industry under the Industrial Act of 1984, (3) the licence to discharge liquid waste under the pollution control regulation, (4) the licence to operate hazardous waste under the regulation concerning hazardous waste and (5) the licence to dump waste in an environmental medium under the EMA of 1997.[20] Although the proponents of the second concept use the terminology of an integrated environmental licence, it only embraces licences related to pollution issues. The proponents also suggests that the Ministry of the Environment should be assigned to issue such an integrated pollution licence system and the status of the Ministry of the Environment should be changed from a ministry without department to being one with department.[21] The second concept may meet the criterion of an efficient licence regime, but it is inconsistent with the trends or notions of regional autonomy.

The third concept of an integrated licence would like to integrate four of the existing licences. These are: (1) the nuisance licence under the *Hinder Ordonnantie* of 1926, (2) the licence to discharge liquid waste under the pollution control regulation, (3) the licence to operate hazardous waste under the regulation concerning hazardous waste and (4) the licence to dump waste into the environmental medium under the EMA of 1997.[22] Thus, the third concept also embraces licences related to pollution issues only. According to the third idea, the status of the licence to engage in industry under the Industrial Act of 1984 should be changed to become an 'approval' only.[23] The proponents of the third concept suggest that the power to issue such an integrated licence should be assigned to both the national governmental agency and to the local government agency. The national agency, for instance, the Ministry of the Environment, is assigned with the power to issue an integrated licence for activities with very sophisticated technologies, while the district or municipal governments have the power to issue an integrated licence for activities with non-sophisticated technologies.[24] The third concept may also meet the criterion of an efficient licence regime and is also consistent with the notion of regional autonomy. The weakness is that it is concerned with pollution issues only.

The fourth concept could also be proposed here. It is the one that integrates or unifies the seven licences into one licence. The power to issue this could be distributed between the national and local government on the basis of activities with high and ordinary technologies as under the third concept. The

20 See Rangkuti (1999a); Rangkuti (1999b, pp. 3–11).
21 Ibid.
22 See Santosa (2001, pp. 250–2); and also Rahmadi and Santosa (1998).
23 Ibid.
24 Ibid.

national agency, for example, the Ministry of the Environment, could be assigned the power to issue licences for activities with high technologies, while the local governments could issue licences for activities with ordinary technologies. This idea may fully meet the criteria of an efficient licence regime and also of an integrated environmental licence because it deals not only with issues of pollution but also with issues of spatial planning. The fourth concept may be the ideal, but it may face strong opposition from the current licensing power holders because they would lose their powers.

3.3. Combination of Command and Control, Voluntary Approach and Market-based Instruments

The EMA of 1997 is a type of legislation that is heavily based on the command and control approach. It contains an instrument of the voluntary approach, that is, the environmental audit, but it lacks provisions related to market-based instruments. The only provision that can be related to economic instruments is Article 8 paragraph (2) e that states that the government shall develop an environmental fund. Some scholars have discussed various types of economic instruments.[25] Discourses upon the possibility of Indonesia adopting economic instruments in its environmental policy have taken place since the early 1990s. In 1994, BAPEDAL hired a foreign expert who examined the opportunities for Indonesia to apply economic incentives in its environmental policy.[26] It is unclear, however, why economic incentives have not been introduced in the EMA of 1997. Therefore, the idea of incorporating market-based instruments into the future EMA, as also suggested by Marjan Peeters,[27] should be seriously taken into account this time. Market-based instruments such as pollution fees, marketable permits and deposit and return systems need to be considered. The use of economic incentives as environmental policy instruments does not aim at completely abolishing the command and control approach. A combination of both command and control and the economic approaches is needed.[28]

---

[25] See, for example, Stewart (1981, pp. 1326–37); Stewart (1993, p. 85). See also Chapter 10 of this volume.

[26] See Anderson (1994).

[27] Chapter 5, this volume.

[28] Sagoff (1991, p. 267). He argues: 'that successful regulation must draw on each of these approaches. The failure to reconcile them, and the growing divergence between these two positions threatens to stall efforts both to improve environmental quality and to minimize risk to public safety health'.

4. CONCLUSIONS

In pursuance of integrated environmental law in Indonesia, the future EMA should be developed in the direction of creating an environmental code that is concerned with issues that are directly related to environmental management, such as spatial planning, environmental pollution control, conservation of natural resources and the environmental impact assessment procedure. The merger or fusion of existing licences into one integrated environmental licence should be established. The future EMA should moreover consist of a combination of command and control, voluntary and economic approaches.

REFERENCES

Anderson, G. (1994), 'Economic Incentives in Environmental Policy: Opportunities for Indonesia', unpublished paper, Bapedal: USAI-Indonesia.

Birnie, P. and A. Boyle (2002), *International Law and the Environment*, Oxford: Oxford University Press, second edition.

Chand, H. (1994), *Modern Jurisprudence*, Kuala Lumpur, Indonesia: International Law Book series.

Cribb, R. (2003), 'Environmentalism in Indonesian Politics', in Adriaan Bedner and Nicole Niessen, *Toward Integrated Environmental Law in Indonesia?*, Leiden, the Netherlands: School of Asian African and Amerindian Studies.

Danusaputro, M. (1982), *Hukum Lingkungan Buku V: Sectoral*, Jilid 1, Jakarta: Bina Ciptam.

Faure, M. and G. Skogh (2003), *The Economic Analysis of Environmental Policy and Law, An Introduction*, Cheltenham, UK and Northampton, MA, USA: Edward Elgar.

Koesnadi, H. (1986), *Hukum Tata Lingkungan*, Yogyakarta: Gadjah Mada University Press.

Moestadji, M. (2003), 'Perbandingan Undang-Undang Mo. 4 Tahun 1982 dan Undang-Undang No. 23 Tahun 1997', a paper presented at the Workshop of Effectiveness of the Implementation of the Act No. 23 of 1997, held by ICEL, Jakarta 28–9 April 2003.

Otto, J.-M. (2003), 'Co-ordination, Harmonisation and Integration', in Adriaan Bedner and Nicole Niessen, *Toward Integrated Environmental Law in Indonesia?*, Leiden, the Netherlands: School of Asian African and Amerindian Studies.

Posner, R.A. (2001), *Frontiers of Legal Theory*, Cambridge, MA: Harvard University.

Posner, R.A. (2003), *Economic Analysis of Law*, 6th edition, New York, USA: Aspen Law and Business.

Rahmadi, T. and M.A. Santosa (1998), 'Peta Perizinan Lingkungan di Indonesia', unpublished paper for CELA Course held by VROM, Van Vollenhoven Institute, the Indonesian Ministry of the Environment and ICEL, 24 August–25 September, in Leiden, the Netherlands.

Rangkuti, S.S. (1986), 'Hukum Lingkungan dan Kebijaksanaan Lingkungan Dalam Proses Pembangunan Hukum Nasional Indonesia', dissertation, University of Airlangga.

Rangkuti, S.S. (1992), 'Sistem Perizinan Lingkungan di Indonesia', paper presented at the Upgrading Courses, University of Airlangga, Surabaya.

Rangkuti, S.S. (1999a), 'Unifikasi Perizinan Lingkungan', *Suara Pembaruan.*

Rangkuti, S.S. (1999b), 'Penegakan Hukum Lingkungan Administrative di Indonesia', *Pro Justitia*, **1**, 3–11.

Rangkuti, S.S. (2000), *Hukum Lingkungan dan Kebijaksanaan Lingkungan Nasional*, Airlangga: University Press.

Sagoff, M. (1991), 'Here Ickes went Right or Reason and Rationality in Environmental Law', *Ecology Law Quarterly*, **14**, 267.

Santosa, M.A. (2001), *Good Governance & Hukum Lingkungan*, Jakarta, Indonesia: ICEL.

Stewart, R.B. (1981), 'The Regulation, Innovation and Administrative Law', *California Law Review*, **69**, 1326–37.

Stewart, R.B. (1993), 'Antidotes for the American Diseases', *Ecology Law Quarterly*, **20**, 85.

Stewart, R.B. and J.E. Krier (1978), *Environmental Law and Policy*, Indianapolis and New York: Bobbs-Merrill Co.

7. Decentralized environmental management

Nicole Niessen

1. INTRODUCTION

Indonesia's current Environmental Management Act dates from 1997,[1] which is shortly before the sudden end of Suharto's *Orde Baru* regime in May 1998. During the reformation process which started immediately thereafter, a main target of law reform has been the Law on Government in the Regions of 1974.[2] This Law 5 of 1974, which was imbued with centralism, was replaced in 1999 by the Regional Government Act (RGA).[3] Pursuant to the RGA 1999 the Indonesian government has embarked on a strong decentralization policy in almost every policy sector. To this end, a considerable amount of governance autonomy is granted to the Districts and Municipalities, which are the third level of government after the State and the Provinces.

This revolutionary change has been a mixed blessing for environmental management (and other policy sectors, for that matter). On the one hand, the devolution of government powers to the Districts and Municipalities was demanded time and again during Suharto's reign. In view of Indonesia's size as well as its cultural and geographical diversity, a substantial degree of regional autonomy is indeed essential.[4] On the other hand, an often-heard criticism is that today's scheme of regional autonomy has been too drastic and that it has come too quickly.[5] Article 133 RGA 1999 demands that the EMA 1997 is made consistent with the RGA 1999. It is debatable, however, whether today's approach to decentralization is conducive to a sustainable environment.

---

1 Undang-undang No. 23 Tahun 1997 tentang Pengelolaan Lingkungan Hidup.

2 Undang-undang No. 5 Tahun 1974 tentang Pokok-pokok Pemerintahan di Daerah.

3 Undang-undang No. 22 Tahun 1999 tentang Pemerintahan Daerah.

4 Niessen (1999, pp. 337–9).

5 Hofman et al. (2003). On p. 3 the authors refer to the RGA 1999 as the '*Big Bang* approach to decentralization'.

In subsequent order this chapter addresses the following issues. It starts with a short introduction on decentralization theory and a bird's eye view of environmental management systems worldwide (Section 2). Particular attention is paid to the Dutch system of environmental protection (Section 3). This is followed by an explanation of Indonesia's legal-institutional framework for the decentralization of environmental management, before and after the RGA 1999. Current constraints because the EMA 1997 fits ill with the RGA 1999 form the heart of this discussion (Section 4). On the basis of decentralization theory and comparative law some suggestions are formulated to change the EMA 1997 and the RGA 1999 (Section 5). In the final section the main conclusions and recommendations of this chapter are summarized (Section 6).

2. DECENTRALIZATION OF ENVIRONMENTAL MANAGEMENT: A COMPARATIVE ANALYSIS

2.1. Decentralization: Pros and Cons

Lately, in many (developing) countries decentralization strategies occupy a prominent place on the reform agenda.[6] Even though the empirical evidence is scarce and conflicting, still many people hold strong beliefs about the effectiveness of decentralization. The World Bank warns in its report *Rethinking Decentralization in Developing Countries*, that '[a] particular challenge is to understand how best to match fiscal, political, and administrative arrangements to achieve the potential benefits of decentralization for any given service in any given country'.[7]

What then are the potential benefits of decentralization, specifically with regard to environmental protection? The Food and Agriculture Organization (FAO) of the United Nations has listed the following in its paper *Environment in Decentralized Development: Economic and Institutional Issues*:[8]

> Local institutions and people have a better knowledge of the environmental and socio-economic problems of the area and therefore are best placed to enhance and protect the environment if they are given clear rights (and obligations) with regard to natural resources
> Higher responsibility in decision-making will be accompanied by higher motivation for a more efficient use of natural resources
> It is more likely to involve less favored groups and populations in the decision-making

6 Niessen (1999, p. 22).
7 Litvack et al. (1998, p. 7).
8 Cistulli (2002, chapter 2).

It facilitates local participation because of the higher homogeneity of common needs with lower sizes of population, higher transparency of the decision-making process; and
It allows the building of local capacities for the provision of services that are more consistent with the local requirements.

In that same paper, however, the FAO also mentions important countervailing forces to explain why decentralized environmental management often produces disappointing results:

Weak administrative or technical capacity at local levels may result in services being delivered less efficiently and effectively in some areas of the country;
Administrative responsibilities may be transferred to local levels without adequate financial resources, making equitable distribution or provision of services more difficult;
Decentralization can sometimes make coordination of national policies more complex and may allow functions to be captured by local elites;
Also, distrust between public and private sectors may undermine cooperation at the local level;
Decentralization may entail higher costs of enforcement of compliance with the regulations;
It may also lead to increasing conflicts among various areas sharing the same natural resources, and also between hierarchical levels if coordination is not effective;
Local organizations may lack the necessary scientific knowledge to complement their indigenous experience and knowledge; and
Finally, decentralization may have initial high costs, which, in a first stage, can increase government spending.

All pros and cons considered, the FAO-paper concludes that local governance is not necessarily better than higher level governance. It asserts: 'that decentralized decision-making is an important condition for addressing environmental problems properly, [but] this is not a sufficient reason to assume that all related decisions should be taken at the decentralized level'. The FAO therefore stresses that most frequently institutional arrangements must be developed 'at multiple levels to cope with the specificity of the environmental issues and to provide the correct incentives to the users at each level of the hierarchy'.

Young, too, points out that the capacity of environmental regimes to prevent and tackle environmental problems is determined in considerable measure by the degree to which they are compatible with the bio-geophysical systems with which they interact.[9] In his view we should resist the temptation to think that one size fits all when it comes to designing environmental protection regimes.

---

9 Young (2002, p. 55).

Simple generalizations to solve a variety of environmental problems across a wide range of bio-geophysical settings are prone to cause disturbances. An arrangement that works well for one particular environmental problem may prove disastrous when applied to other ecosystems. Existing jurisdictional boundaries, however, are generally not determined on the basis of ecological considerations. They are the product of a range of political, economic, and cultural forces. Even though the ecological consequences may be well understood, jurisdictional boundaries often cause mismatches between ecosystems and institutions.[10] The preceding analysis reveals that instead of being in favour of or against decentralization, the question is 'what functions of what sectors for what areas can most fruitfully be decentralized?'[11]

The provision of a service often requires the involvement of two or three levels of government. It is therefore crucial to determine how the different levels of government can cooperate in a multi-level governance scheme. The optimal mix is not easily determined and it shifts as social, economic, and political conditions change.[12]

2.2. Decentralized Environmental Management in Europe and the USA

It is not the purpose of these comparative sections to provide an in-depth analysis of all the possible similarities and differences in the field of state–region relations regarding environmental management. That would be practically impossible. In order to fully understand the environmental management system of a particular country it is of vital importance to have a full knowledge of its legal, historical, political, economic, and social context. This chapter, however, can only point to certain trends in a number of countries across the globe. As a preliminary remark, it can be said that in all countries there is some form of decentralized environmental management, although there are considerable differences in the amount of legislative and executive powers assigned to the regional authorities.

A first distinction can be made between federal states and unitary states. Within a federal system – for example, the USA, Germany, and Belgium – the states enjoy separate sovereign authority. At the same time, either explicitly or implicitly, certain matters belong to the exclusive domain of the federal government. In the USA, the mere existence of a federal environmental statute pre-empts state regulations on that same subject unless the latter pertains to

---

10 Ibid., pp. 70–1.

11 Prud'homme (1994, p. 31).

12 Niessen (1999, p. 21).

supplementary regulation.[13] In addition, the federal Environmental Protection Agency (EPA) plays an important regulatory role. On the basis of federal acts, the EPA is the primary regulator for pollution, waste disposal, and toxic substances.[14] In Germany, the federal level has exclusive powers in a number of regulatory matters, meaning that the States (*Länder*) bear responsibility only for the execution of federal environmental laws, whilst in other matters the Federation and States share regulatory powers.[15] In Belgium, on the other hand, the communities-regions below the federal level are endowed with the most important environmental powers, and moreover, community-region legislation is of the same level as federal legislation.[16]

Within a unitary state – like France or Spain – the sub-national authorities are not independent sovereigns, but they nevertheless enjoy a certain amount of governance autonomy. France is rightly classified as a rather centralized state, even though Article 72 of the French Constitution stipulates that local entities are freely administered by elected assemblies.[17] It is not unusual for the central government to retain substantial powers on issues entrusted to local entities, which of course restricts their autonomy. It often happens that on a particular issue (of environmental management) a local decision and a central government decision must be delivered jointly.[18] Decentralization in Spain, by contrast, almost approaches a federal system. The territory of the state is divided into Autonomous Communities that enjoy legislative, judiciary, and executive powers. Below this level are provinces and municipalities that merely perform administrative functions.[19] The autonomy of the municipalities is guaranteed directly by the Constitution, but concrete municipal competences are regulated by State Act. On the one hand, environmental protection is an irrevocable municipal competence, on the other hand, it is one of the municipal activities which according to that same act – the Local Government Act – is complementary to 'the same activities of other public administrations'.[20]

---

[13] Yang (2002, p. 528). On p. 520 a reference is made to Article VI of the US Constitution which provides that federal law supersedes all state law (supremacy clause). Federal law includes statutory enactments by Congress, federal court rulings, federal agencies' regulations, Presidential executive orders, and treaties conclude by the United States.

[14] Seerden et al. (2002, p. 565).

[15] Rodi (2002, p. 236).

[16] Seerden et al. (2002, p. 565).

[17] Auby (2002, p. 63).

[18] Auby and Jegouzo (2002, p. 174).

[19] Vaqués (2000, p. 397).

[20] Ibid., pp. 413–14. In Spanish the Regional Government Act is called *Ley 7/1985, de 2 de abril, reguladora de las bases del regimen local*, commonly abbreviated to LBRL.

In a unitary state, the central government is empowered to confine, control, and intervene in matters of the regional authorities. The same applies to state–region relations within the constituent states of a federal nation. These mechanisms are incorporated not only in the general legal-institutional framework for regional government but also in the laws on environmental protection (general environmental codes as well as sectional statutes). In a federal state, a constitutional court watches over the demarcation of federal and state powers. This does not mean that there is a strict delineation of competences everywhere.[21] The federal government of the United States, for example, delegates environmental management responsibility contingent on a state's performance. State environmental agencies must monitor and report to the federal Environmental Protection Agency (EPA) on the enforcement of national minimum standards. The EPA can withdraw the delegation of functions for poor performance, and one of its regional offices is then entitled to take over. In other countries, too, functional – and to some extent independent – administrative authorities play an important role in the regulation and enforcement of environmental law.[22]

An overall conclusion is that nowhere are centralization and decentralization treated as mutually exclusive or dichotomous arrangements for environmental management. There is, however, a trend towards centralism in the USA as well as in (the Member States of) the European Union (EU) under the influence of EU directives. This can be explained by the need for technical expertise in environmental regulation, the need to curb transboundary externalities, the need to economize on administrative costs, and the need to avoid economic disparities between the Member States. Where at first sight decentralized authorities play an important role – as in Italy, Finland, and the Netherlands – the real extent of their regulatory discretion is often relatively small. Within the EU the principle of 'subsidiarity' – meaning that the EU does not regulate matters that are best dealt with at the Member State level – serves as a yardstick against which the appropriate level for environmental regulation is assessed.[23] A similar approach can also be discerned in the national systems for environmental protection.

---

21 Koopmans (2003, pp. 169–72): The German Basic Law (*Grundgesetz*), for example, enumerates a list of relatively few 'exclusive' federal powers, but gives a long list of subjects for 'concurrent' state legislation. To give another example, at first sight the US Constitution seems very precise in its delimitation of federal powers. The wide interpretation of the 'interstate commerce clause' by the Supreme Court, however, has broadened the scope of federal powers. Summarizing, although the courts play an important role in delimiting the extent of federal powers, developments in the interpretation of relevant constitutional concepts nevertheless demonstrate an intimate link with the evolution of political opinion in American society.

22 Seerden et al. (2002, pp. 564–5).

23 Ibid., p. 565.

2.3. Decentralized Environmental Management in Developing Countries

In the previous section we have seen that in Europe and the United States there is a trend to (re)centralization of environmental management. Many developing countries, by contrast, have lately embarked on decentralization policies in this field.

According to a recent study of the World Resources Institute (WRI) on *Decentralization in Mainland Southeast Asia* – in Vietnam, Cambodia, Thailand, China, and Laos – the decentralization reforms in these countries are a reaction to the implementation failures of highly centralized systems that have characterized the post-colonial era. Decentralization is supposed to bring decision-making and implementation closer to the target population while at the same time reducing the central government's costs and improving efficiency by reducing the size of the central bureaucracy. Decentralization may also be motivated by a desire to empower citizens and increase their participation in the development planning and implementation process. Another impetus for reform is formed by donor conditions – for instance, the World Bank – requiring decentralization and central government downsizing.[24] A main question addressed by the WRI is '[u]nder what conditions does decentralization contribute to environmentally and socially sustainable development?'[25]

The five countries in the study have each experienced periods of devastation and turmoil, and consequently their successive governments have focused on strengthening national security and development from the centre. In the past 10–20 years, however, all these countries have enjoyed a period of relative peace and economic growth. These conditions proved favourable to decentralizing political, administrative, and fiscal government functions to the regions. Of the five countries, Thailand has embarked upon the most ambitious decentralization reform, namely a full-scale political decentralization to the sub-district level.[26]

An overall conclusion is that no simple governance model – centralized, decentralized, or privatized – alone holds the promise of sustainable environment.[27] Essentially the central government must create a legal and institutional framework that allows local governments to balance upward accountability to national standards and downward accountability to communities for locally appropriate environmental management choices.[28] But across the case studies

---

24 Dupar and Badenoch (2002, p. 9).

25 Ibid., p. 1.

26 Ibid., p. 13.

27 Ibid., p. 57.

28 Ibid., pp. 53–4: In this manner a web of accountability can be created.

such monitoring and evaluation mechanisms were largely missing.[29] In particular the study warns against the danger of the 'missing middle', meaning that decentralization reforms may lose sight of the ecosystem scale.[30] Regarding this, another vital condition is the willingness of neighbouring jurisdictions to cooperate.[31] Lastly, clear and independent mechanisms for conflict resolution are of overriding importance to make decentralization efforts successful. In the countries mentioned, however, the judicial system is – largely due to corruption – another weak point of the system.[32]

The decentralization of environmental management in Brazil – a Federal State – has been critically reviewed by ABDL (Leadership for Environment and Development). In Brazil, the Municipality is not subordinate to the State, and the State is not subordinate to the Federal Government. The 1988 Federal Constitution establishes the autonomy of the Municipalities (Art. 18). In addition, several Brazilian States have issued regulations concerning the decentralization of environmental management. On the whole, the Municipalities mainly perform licensing and inspection activities. In some States decentralization was carried out rashly, without a vision to strengthen the environment but only to decrease the burden of State institutions. In those States the lack of a detailed reflection about roles has resulted in the absence of interaction mechanisms between State and Municipality. Altogether, this has led to institutional chaos.

Although the ABDL stresses the absolute importance of the role of Municipalities because many environmental problems have a local source, it also points to the process's inherent risks. Most importantly, decentralization should not hinder the integration of environmental policies and their implementation. This demands much of the institutional set-up of environmental management systems at state and municipal levels. If not, the decentralization of environmental protection is prone to have negative impacts.[33]

3. THE DUTCH MODEL: A ROUGH SKETCH

3.1. A Decentralized Unitary State

The Netherlands is a decentralized unitary state. Chapter 7 of the Dutch Constitution contains the basic provisions on decentralization. The Dutch

---

29 Ibid., p. 63.
30 Ibid., p. 57.
31 Ibid., p. 67.
32 Ibid., pp. 67–8.
33 de Costa Novaes (2003, pp. 1–9).

territory is divided into 12 provinces, each divided into a number of municipalities (Art. 123).[34] Next to this, water boards within the provinces are responsible for water surface management (Art. 123).

The provinces and municipalities perform autonomous tasks as well as tasks of co-governance (Art. 124). The term 'co-governance' may give rise to the misleading thought that it entails a mechanical execution of central government's orders, but nothing is further from the truth. In fact, tasks of co-governance can entail considerable discretion regarding the content of decisions – for example, by-law, plan, concrete binding decision (*beschikking*) – that must be taken pursuant to the enabling act. The amount of discretionary power depends on the specific policy field and is laid down in particular administrative laws. Concerning environmental protection, for example, the amount of central government steering is relatively large. At the same time, the term 'autonomy' does not mean that the provinces and municipalities have full discretion in managing their 'own affairs' (*eigen huishouding*). The central government not only has powers of financial supervision, but it can also take autonomous matters in hand if considered necessary.[35]

The basic provisions of Chapter 7 of the Dutch Constitution are elaborated in the Provincial Act and the Municipality Act. These acts lay down the organization, tasks, and competences of the regional governments. Each level of government is entrusted with its own responsibilities – either on the basis of co-governance or autonomy – and has its own administration: a head of region named Commissioner of the Queen (province) or Mayor (municipality), a provincial or municipal executive board, and a provincial or municipal council of elected representatives (Art. 125). The distinction between autonomy and co-governance has no impact on the division of tasks between the provincial or municipal executive on the one hand, and the provincial or municipal council on the other hand. Generally, legislative (enactment of by-laws) and control functions are entrusted to the council of elected representatives, and matters of daily governance are assigned to the executive board (Art. 127).

There are various mechanisms for vertical coordination and accountability. For example, the central and provincial governments are authorized to supervise the municipal governments and take the necessary measures in case of (possible) wrongful practices. The legal basis for these high-handed measures is laid down in the Dutch Constitution, the Provincial Act, the Municipality Act, the General Administrative Law Act, and in particular administrative

[34] In the Netherlands there is no legal distinction between urban and rural communities.

[35] Bellekom et al. (2002, pp. 204–6).

laws.[36] Supervision can take various forms, such as prior approval (preventive supervision), suspension and annulment (repressive supervision) of decisions (to be) taken by the provincial or municipal government, and compulsory directives. The law spells out in which circumstances and under which conditions supervision can be exercised so as not to encroach too much on the independence of municipalities.

3.2. General Administrative Law

Regarding the performance of government functions, the General Administrative Law Act (GALA; in Dutch *Algemene wet bestuursrecht*) contains provisions on terminology, principles of proper administration, decision-making procedures, transfer of administrative authority and mandate, the exercise of supervision, and legal protection against the administration. The GALA is a typical build-on law that came into force in 1994. Every few years new chapters have been – and will be – added.[37]

A principal concept of the GALA is 'jointed regulation' (*gelede normstelling*) meaning that chapters on general provisions are followed by chapters on special provisions. The following examples illustrate how this functions. For instance, Chapter 3 of the GALA contains provisions concerning the 'administrative order' (*besluit*). A special type of administrative order is the 'decision in individual cases' (*beschikking*, for example, the licence), to which the GALA addresses special provisions in Chapter 4.[38] In order to find out how a decision should be made in individual cases, both Chapters 3 and 4 must be consulted. This jointed regulation is also reflected in the chapters on legal protection against the administration. Chapter 6 provides the general rules on objections against administrative decisions and judicial review, whereas Chapters 7 and 8 elaborate on objections and judicial review respectively.[39]

---

[36] Article 132 Dutch Constitution, Articles 110–21, 173, 207 Provincial Act, Articles 112–24, 203 Municipality Act, Title 10.2 GALA, (e.g.) Article 37 Spatial Planning Act.

[37] Thus far, three so-called *tranches* of the GALA have entered into force, respectively in January 1994 (Tranches 1 and 2) and in January 1998 (Tranche 3). The fourth tranche on attribution, administrative publicity, administrative financial claims, and administrative fines is at an advanced stage. From Schlössels and Stroink, in cooperation with Albers and Hillegers (2003, pp. 112–17).

[38] Article 1:3 GALA lays down the definitions of 'order' and 'decision in an individual case'.

[39] The term objection (*bezwaar*) I borrowed from the authorized English translation of the Dutch *Algemene wet bestuursrecht*. Article 1:5 (1) GALA gives the following definition: 'making an objection' means making use of a statutorily conferred power to seek redress against an order from the administrative authority

Hence to find out whether the court is competent to review a decision in an individual case, all three chapters are to be consulted.

The concept of jointed regulation also has an external component. It then means that the GALA provides a general framework of rules and principles applying to all administrative law. It must always be read in connection with the applicable particular administrative law, for example, on spatial planning, social security, or environmental protection. The particular administrative laws are generally congruous with the GALA but sometimes deviate from the GALA on specific issues. Whenever the particular administrative law differs from the GALA, then the provisions of the particular administrative law have priority.[40] By way of illustration, the provisions on legal protection against the decision to issue or to refuse an environmental licence are incorporated into both the GALA and the *Wet milieubeheer* (that is, the Environmental Management Act, abbr. Wm). In the first place, this type of decision is taken on the basis of an 'elaborate public preparation procedure' laid down in part 3.5 of the GALA, which differs from the regular decision-making procedure of parts 3.1 to 3.3 GALA.[41] Because of this, the legal protection scheme follows a somewhat different path, meaning that it deviates from the usual scheme of first lodging an objection with the administrative organ that took the decision, then addressing the administrative court for judicial review, and finally, appeal to the Council of State (that is, the highest administrative court).[42] Instead of this three-step scheme, the dissatisfied citizen must apply to the Judicial Department of the Council of State directly, and further judicial review is not possible (Articles 8.6 and 20.1 Wm juncto Article 7:1 and Part 3.5 GALA).

---

which made the order. The term 'appeal' applies to both administrative appeal to an administrative authority other than the one which made the order and judicial review (Art. 1:5 (2–3) GALA).

40 Ibid., p. 30.

41 This is the so-called *uitgebreide openbare voorbereidingsprocedure*. Interestingly, this special decision-making procedure used to be part of the Wm, and was later transferred to the GALA. In the near future the special preparation procedures of part 3.4 and part 3.5 will be integrated into one. As a result, it is not unlikely that the Wm will re-incorporate specific features of the decision-making procedure of part 3.5, in particular the *actio popularis*. From Verschuuren 2000, pp. 178–83).

42 In point of fact, next to the Judicial Department of the Council of State, i.e. the general administrative court of appeal, there are two more highest administrative courts, namely the Central Appellate Council (*Centrale Raad van Beroep*) hearing public service and social security cases, and the Corporations Tribunal (*College van Beroep voor het Bedrijfsleven*). From Seerden and Stroink (2002, pp. 178–9).

3.3. Environmental Protection Law

Environmental protection is laid down as a basic right in Article 21 of the Dutch Constitution:

> It shall be the concern of the authorities to keep the country habitable and to protect and improve the environment.

This does not mean that Dutch citizens are entitled to a clean environment. Article 21 obliges the Dutch government to develop environmental policy, yet in doing so the government is entitled to consider, and prioritize, other interests as well. Pursuant to Article 21, the Dutch government has produced numerous regulations to protect the environment. In point of fact, many achievements in this field have been prompted by international law. In particular, environmental regulations of the European Union (EU) increasingly impose a strait-jacket on Dutch environmental law and policy. Although the EU normally lays down goals by means of directives instead of concrete legal prescriptions for its Member States, this no doubt sets considerable limits on their regulatory discretion.[43]

Presently the Dutch legal framework for environmental law consists of sector legislation addressing specific environmental pollution as well as a general environmental management act. The enactment of the *Wet milieubeheer* (Wm) in 1993 has been a major step forward in the construction of integrated environmental management. Like the GALA, the Wm is a typical build-on law. Thus far it has fully absorbed the sector legislation on nuisance, waste, and small chemical waste. At the same time, other sector legislation has remained in place.[44] The Wm distinguishes between the following regulatory instruments: (a) environmental policy plans, (b) licences, (c) general rules, (d) environmental quality norms, and (e) financial instruments.[45] Below I discuss in further detail the categories (a) to (c).

(a) Environmental *policy* plans must be established by the central government and the provinces (Articles 4.3 and 4.9 Wm), whilst the municipal governments are not obliged to do so.[46] Environmental *operational* programmes, on the other hand, shall be made by all three levels of government

---

[43] Directive 96/61/EC of 24 September 1996 concerning Integrated Pollution Prevention and Control (IPPC), *Official Journal* L 257, 10.10.1996, pp. 26–40, for example, lays down the duty to coordinate environmental licensing. See Chapter by Marjan Peeters, Section 2.2.

[44] Michiels (2003, p. 19).

[45] Ibid., p. 4.

[46] Ibid., p. 27.

(Articles 4.7, 4.14, and 4.20 Wm). There is no hierarchical relationship between the environmental plans or programmes of state, provinces, and municipalities.[47] In addition, environmental plans and programmes have no direct legal force. Licensing authorities must nevertheless 'take into account' (*rekening houden met*) the provisions of environmental plans and programmes because of the general principle of 'careful preparation' (*zorgvuldige voorbereiding*).[48]

(b) The Wm licence is commonly referred to as the integrated environmental licence. This, however, is only partly correct because besides the Wm licence separate environmental licenses still exist, as enumerated in Article 22.1 Wm.[49] A Wm licence is required for polluting establishments (*inrichting*) not falling within the scope of general rules (Article 8.1 Wm). Next to the integrated environmental licence, the Wm contains special coordination mechanisms between the Wm licence and other (environmental) licences. Here it suffices to mention the coordination provisions concerning the Wm licence on the one hand and the Water Surface Pollution licence and the Building licence on the other hand.[50] On the basis of Article 8.2 Wm, the executive board of the municipality (rural as well as urban areas) in which the polluting establishment is located, entirely or primarily, is the competent authority to issue the Wm licence. In exceptional cases the provincial government or the central government is appointed as the licensing authority.

This does not mean that the municipal executive can freely decide to grant – on condition of specific instructions and restrictions – or to refuse the Wm licence. The Wm, in Articles 8.8. to 8.11, imposes an elaborate reference framework on the municipal executive when deciding on the application for a Wm licence. In essence this reference framework guarantees that due consideration is paid to national as well as to provincial environmental regulations and interests.[51] Naturally, the environmental quality standards as determined by general government order (*algemene maatregelen van bestuur*) on the basis of Chapter 5 Wm or Article 8.45 Wm must be observed (Article 8.8 (3) Wm).[52] Next to this, the loose concept of 'protection of the environment'

---

47 Ibid., p. 29.

48 Ibid., pp. 30–1. See Article 8.8 (2) Wm and Article 3:2 GALA.

49 Article 22.1 Wm stipulates that *inter alia* the Groundwater Act, the Manure Act, the Nuclear Energy Act, the Surface Water Pollution Act maintain their own licensing system next to the Wm licence.

50 Articles 8.28 to 8.34 Wm, Article 8.5 Wm *juncto* Articles 8 and 52 of the Housing Act, and Articles 7b to 7e of the Water Surface Pollution Act.

51 Michiels (2003, p. 52).

52 On the basis of Article 8.46 Wm, the provincial government is authorized to issue additional requirements next to those issued by the central government pursuant to Article 8.45 Wm.

(*bescherming van het milieu*), which Articles 8.8 and 8.10 Wm establish as the principal ground on which to refuse an environmental licence, is largely specified by a series of extra-legal instructions (*buitenwettelijke richtlijnen*). These instructions contain environmental expert information, and the court considers it very important that licensing authorities comply with these standards.[53]

(c) The instrument of general rules has become quite popular in the 1980s. General rules are established by government regulation (*algemene maatregelen van bestuur*), and they replace the environmental licence (Article 8.40 Wm).[54] Today approximately 75 per cent of polluting establishments fall within a category to which general rules apply.[55] There are several advantages to this system. First, a set of general rules applies to whole categories of polluting establishments, which relieves the (licensing) administration. Secondly, in principle the holders of polluting establishments that are regulated by means of general rules need not apply for an environmental licence. Thirdly, general rules contribute to legal certainty and equality.

But there are also some disadvantages to general rules. For example, general rules produce confection rather than tailor-made environmental standards, they complicate the adjustment of environmental standards to the prescriptions of other relevant licences in individual cases, and they reduce the participation of interested citizens in the decision-making process. Another issue is that general rules entail a re-centralization of environmental decision-making. This, however, is not necessarily a negative effect. Some of these disadvantages have been compensated for by giving municipalities the opportunity to issue supplementary requirements.[56]

On the basis of Article 8.12 Wm the licensing authority – equally the authority to which notice is given of the applicability of general rules ex Article 8.41 (2) Wm – is also responsible for administrative enforcement.[57]

---

[53] These instructions are normally issued by the central government, but sometimes also by private institutions. The court punishes non-compliance with these standards for neglect of the principles of careful preparation (Article 3:2 GALA) and motivation (Article 3:46 GALA) of administrative decisions. By the way, the licensing authority is entitled to deviate from the instructions 'in favor of the environment'. From: Michiels (2003, pp. 61–62, 105–108).

[54] Also on the basis of the Water Pollution Act (WPA), Articles 2a–2e, the government is authorized to promulgate general rules that replace the licence for water pollution. It is possible that a single set of general rules deals with Wm- and WPA-activities simultaneously. Marjan Peeters has written more extensively on this issue in Section 3.2.3 of her paper for this workshop.

[55] Michiels (2003, p. 85).

[56] Ibid., pp. 86–7.

[57] Ibid., p. 220: Before the enactment of the Wm it was difficult to identify the authority responsible for enforcement in a particular case due to scattered environmental legislation.

The provisions on administrative enforcement of environmental law are laid down in both the GALA (Chapter 5: basic provisions) and the Wm (Chapter 18: additional provisions). Taking care of enforcement includes responsibility for supervision as well as the imposition of sanctions. The enforcing authority holds final responsibility but does not need to perform all supervision activities itself. Next to the Wm authority a number of other agencies conduct supervision as well, such as the authority entrusted with the protection of water surface quality, the VROM inspectorate, the national General Inspectorate, the police, and the public prosecutor. In point of fact, *any* administrative body involved in the implementation of the Wm and other environmental legislation can appoint environmental inspectors.[58] Their supervision competences are spelled out in Article 18.4 Wm and in Article 5.11 GALA,[59] and Article 18.3 Wm warrants that in each Province their activities are coordinated. Finally, *any* citizen can request the Wm authority to take enforcement measures, and if such a request is refused, the citizen can start court proceedings (Article 18.4 (1) Wm).

3.4. Multi-level Environmental Management

The Dutch Wm illustrates how environmental protection law is embedded in the legal-institutional context of decentralization law and general administrative law. Within this setting, environmental protection law holds a twofold position: on the one hand it fits existing regulations and institutions, but on the other hand it deviates from the general system for reasons of environmental protection. The Dutch system is not presented here as an ideal model, but it is interesting for our analysis of decentralized environmental management because it neatly reveals a great many interactions between the three levels of government: state, provinces, and municipalities.

In the Netherlands, the municipalities perform certain environmental management tasks of which the issuing of the Wm licence is the most important. The banner under which the municipalities take charge of this task is co-governance. This means that the central government sets the boundaries within which the municipal government is accorded some discretion to decide. With regard to environmental protection, the amount of central government influence is relatively large compared to other policy sectors. For certain polluting activities a Wm licence granted by the municipal government is not required because general rules have been issued instead. Where the Wm accords the

---

58 The particular civil servant (of the central, provincial, or municipal government) is authorized insofar as the instructing administrative organ is empowered to act on the basis of the Wm or other environmental legislation.

59 Article 18.5 Wm juncto Articles 5:5 to 5:19 GALA.

municipal government discretion to refuse a Wm licence (Sect. 8.10 Wm), 'in the interest of the protection of the environment', at the same time the Wm in Articles 8.8 to 8.11 as well as on the basis of Article 8.45 largely defines which particular interests are relevant and how these interests are to be weighed by the licensing authority. In addition, environmental expert reports have to be taken into account.

The combined application of Wm, the Municipality Act, and GALA enables higher government levels, the provinces, and the state, to interfere with the decisions of the municipal government. This applies to all types of 'environmental' decisions: planning, licensing, and enforcement. The relevant laws specify when and how this shall be done. In this manner, municipal governance sides with a system of central steering and upward accountability. This does not mean, however, that environmental pollution never goes unchecked, or that 'the environment' always wins when decisions are taken. As elsewhere, the enforcement of environmental law is a permanent matter of concern, and instances of so-called 'intentional tolerance' (*gedogen*) of violations of environmental law are not unusual.[60] Essentially, it is of vital importance that politicians and administrators – at all levels of government – have a strong commitment to protect the environment.

4. DECENTRALIZATION OF ENVIRONMENTAL MANAGEMENT IN INDONESIA

4.1. The Legal-institutional Framework for Regional Government

Indonesia is a unitary decentralized state. Starting from colonial times it developed decentralization policy and law, but repeated attempts to secure some amount of regional autonomy were not very successful.[61] In order to understand

---

[60] According to Dutch law, the imposition of administrative sanctions is a discretionary measure requiring a careful weighing of interests. Nevertheless, the administrative courts increasingly restrict the amount of discretion involved, and nowadays one can rightly speak of an 'obligation in principle to enforce' (beginselplicht tot handhaving). This means that the intentional tolerance of violations of environmental law is allowed in the following instances only: in the short term legalization will be possible, in the short term the illegal activities will end, experiments, and *force majeure*. Intentional tolerance takes the form of an administrative decision that is to comply with the requirements of the GALA concerning preparation, motivation, and publication. From Michiels (2003, pp. 219, 244, and 248). See further on administrative enforcement Chapter 8 of this volume.

[61] Niessen (1999, p. 41) takes the colonial Decentralization Act of 1903 as the starting point for decentralization policies in Indonesia.

current issues of regional autonomy, it is important to pay attention to Indonesia's present decentralization act, Law 22 of 1999, and its predecessor, Law 5 of 1974.

Law 5 of 1974 was the product of *Orde Baru*. It took 'concrete and responsible' (*nyata dan bertanggungjawab*) as its leading notion of regional autonomy. This general notion was further specified by three sub-principles, each referring to a different type of regional government: decentralization (*desentralisasi*), co-governance (*tugas pembantuan*), and de-concentration (*dekonsentrasi*). On the basis of these principles a two-tier system of regional government had been established, each consisting of two parallel administrations. Under the banner of decentralization autonomous tasks had been entrusted to the Regions Level I and II (*Daerah Tingkat I/II*), which were also responsible for tasks of co-governance. Parallel to this, a great many deconcentrated agencies of the sector departments at national level operated within the Provinces (*Propinsi*) – level one – as well as within the Districts (*Kabupaten*) and Municipalities (*Kotamadya*) – level two. These parallel administrations were headed by one and the same person: the Governor Head of Region Level I, the District Head of Region Level II, and the Mayor Head of Region Level II.

These parallel administrations were not on equal footing. On the contrary, in terms of competences, funding, equipment, and qualified personnel, the deconcentrated pillar used to be very much superior to the decentralized one. This imbalance was also reflected in the assignment of important functions to the Governor, District Head, or Mayor, whilst some inferior leftovers remained for the Head of Region. Besides this, on the basis of Article 22 (1) Law 5 of 1974 the Regional Representative Council (*Dewan Perwakilan Rakyat Daerah*) could not bring the (Governor, District Head, or Mayor) Head of Region to account for his performance.[62] As a result, both in his capacity as Governor, District Head, or Mayor and in his capacity as Head of Region, his prime orientation was the central government in Jakarta.

On the basis of Law 5 of 1974, the central government possessed a vast array of instruments to instruct, interfere with, and control the regional governments. During the latter years of *Orde Baru* some half-hearted attempts were made to relax the strait-jacket within which the regional governments had to operate. The way in which the central government had steered the regions proved ineffective and created growing resentment against 'Jakarta'. At the same time, however, 'Jakarta' remained on the alert not to give in too much. Government Regulation 45 of 1992[63] – the long-awaited implementing

---

62 Ibid., pp. 178–9.

63 Peraturan Pemerintah nomor 45 tahun 1992 tentang Titik Berat Otonomi pada Daerah Tingkat II.

order of Article 11 (2) of Law 5 of 1974 which promised that the centre of gravity of regional autonomy should lie with the Regions Level II – seemed a perfect compromise. It contained a gradual process of decentralization in the sense that the regions first had to prove they were ready to take charge of new autonomous functions, and the central government was to assess their readiness. Part of this new strategy was an experiment with enlarged autonomy in 26 Districts. But still by the end of Suharto's reign mere lip-service had been paid to the *idea* of decentralization.[64]

The RGA 1999 has changed this dramatically.[65] Following the sudden demise of the Suharto regime in May 1998, many political reforms were quickly taken. Under the banner of *Reformasi* the Indonesian people claimed democracy, transparency, and regional autonomy. The enactment of a new law on regional government was considered a priority, for it was broadly agreed that three decades of *Orde Baru* had demonstrated many serious drawbacks of a strongly centralist government.[66] The RGA 1999 has maintained the existing two-tier system of regional government, but the parallel administrations for decentralization and de-concentration no longer exist. Autonomous government is the rule, although in general the Provinces are granted substantially less autonomy than the Districts and Municipalities.[67] The Governor, District Head, and Mayor now take their positions as the result of direct elections (Art. 2 RGA), whilst under Law 5 of 1974 they had been appointed by the President. Another novelty is that the Regional House of Representatives (RHoC) is authorized to control all institutions of the regional government, and for this purpose the RHoC has been endowed with many new competences (Art. 14, 49–50 RGA).

Although on various occasions the re-establishment of a federal state – as in the years 1949–50 – was seriously considered, the RGA 1999 has maintained the *concept* of a unitary state.[68] At the same time, however, Article 4 (2)

---

64 Niessen (1999, pp. 86–7, 337–40).

65 Undang-undang nomor 22 tahun 1999 tentang Pemerintahan Daerah, translated as Regional Government Act (RGA).

66 Hofman et al. (2003, p. 3): 'Regional autonomy was considered to be, and presented as, the natural complement to the emerging democracy at the central level'.

67 Ibid., pp. 3–4: In the new decentralization scheme the Provinces originally would not be granted autonomy but merely serve as outposts of the central government. The Indonesian government was fearful of powerful Provinces as they were the centre of regional unrest in the 1950s. New election laws, however, had already specified how the provincial parliament was to be elected. A provincial parliament without an autonomous provincial government would have been absurd, and therefore the Province was maintained as an autonomous region, too.

68 The short-lived United States of Indonesia, 1949–50, had been opposed from the outset. The Indonesian people felt as if the federation had been imposed by the

RGA 1999 firmly rejects the existence of hierarchical links between the three levels of government. Provisions concerning upward accountability used to be quite prominent in Law 5 of 1974,[69] but they are ostensibly lacking in the RGA 1999. Articles 70, 113, and 114 RGA 1999 nevertheless stipulate that lower legislation must comply with higher legislation, and to this end regional by-laws must be submitted to the central government for approval.[70] In line with the RGA 1999, Law 25 of 1999 on 'Fiscal Balance between Centre and Regions' and GR 25 of 2000 on 'the Authority of the Government and the Authority of the Provinces as Autonomous Regions' have further reinforced the idea of *self-sufficiency* of the Districts and Municipalities.

The new decentralization is given a basis in the 1945 Constitution as amended in the year 2000.[71] Article 18 (1) stipulates that 'the Unitary State of the Republic of Indonesia shall be divided into provinces and those provinces shall be divided into districts and municipalities, each of which shall have regional authorities which shall be regulated by law'. In Article 18 (5), furthermore, the Constitution states expressly that:

> The regional authorities shall exercise wide-ranging autonomy, except in matters specified by law to be the affairs of the central government.

4.2. The Legal-institutional Framework for Environmental Management

Since the 1970s Indonesia has actively pursued an environmental protection strategy. In 1978 a specialized State Ministry (non portfolio) for Development and the Environment was created. Several years later, in 1982, Indonesia

---

Dutch colonizer. Another argument against a federal structure is the urge to 'oneness' that is deeply embedded in the Javanese concept of power. From Niessen (1999, pp. 69–70, 337).

69 The Articles 68 to 71 Law 5 of 1974 dealt with various modalities of supervision by the central government.

70 This notwithstanding, by means of Government Regulation 20 of 2001 the Indonesian government has elaborated various provisions concerning development (*pembinaan*) and control (*pengawasan*) of the district and municipal governments by the central government. In this scheme, the Governor fulfils several tasks as an intermediary. Part of the control mechanism is the imposition of sanctions upon regional governments ignoring directions from central government (Article 16). The overall conclusion, however, is that this system of supervision is ineffective (2003 Report of the Indonesian Ministry of Home Affairs and the Deutsche Gesellschaft für Technische Zusammenarbeit (GTZ GmbH, *Decentralization in Indonesia since 1999 – An Overview*)).

71 Since the end of *Orde Baru*, the 1945 Constitution has been amended four times, in 1999, 2000, 2001, and 2002.

promulgated its first Environmental Management Act (EMA 1982).[72] The enactment of the EMA 1982 was seen as a milestone in Indonesian history, but its practical effects have been quite disappointing.[73] A large number of implementing regulations had to be issued pursuant to the parent act, but by the time of its replacement in 1997 follow-up regulations on many of the EMA's vital issues were lacking. Another obstacle to its effective implementation was the often ambiguous wording of the EMA 1982. The law's official elucidation, for that matter, provided little guidance. It meticulously clarified, and actually repeated, self-evident provisions of the EMA. Many of the EMA's vague provisions, by contrast, were often disposed of as 'self-explanatory' (*cukup jelas*) by the elucidation. Thus for various reasons the EMA 1982 left both implementing administrations and the public empty-handed.[74]

Considering these constraints, in 1997 a new EMA was enacted to strengthen the practical enforcement of environmental policies.[75] The EMA 1997 has taken 'integration' (*keterpaduan*) as the leading concept for environmental management. The aim of integration is most prominently reflected in Articles 15 and 18 (1) EMA 1997 which state that the applicant for a business licence – to start or continue with industrial operations or other activities causing considerable environmental impacts – shall conduct an environmental impact analysis (EIA) beforehand. When this EIA has been approved by the authority for environmental impact control,[76] it must be submitted to the licensing authority together with the application for the business licence. On the basis of Article 18 (3) EMA 1997, this business licence is to contain obligations regarding compliance with environmental regulations.[77] The business licence is issued by the relevant sector department, such as the Ministries for Forestry, Mining, and Industry. Article 20 EMA 1997, on the other hand, refers to separate environmental licences for waste disposal. The licensing authority

---

72 Undang-undang nomor 4 Tahun 1982 tentang Ketentuan-ketentuan Pokok Pengelolaan Lingkungan Hidup.

73 Niessen (2003, p. 67).

74 Ibid., p. 78.

75 Koesnadi (1996, p. 14).

76 Government Regulation 27/1999 concerning Environmental Impact Assessment (*Analisa Mengenai Dampak Lingkungan*) leaves aside which particular government institution is authorized for this purpose, but this is specified in Presidential Decree No. 10 of 2000 regarding the Agency Controlling Environmental Impacts.

77 The elucidation of Article 18 (3) EMA 1997 mentions *inter alia* the following examples: the obligation to treat waste, waste quality conditions for disposal to an environmental medium, the obligation to conduct self-monitoring, and the obligation to submit environmental performance reports to the responsible agency in the field of environmental impact control.

for waste disposal is the Minister for the Environment ex Article 20 (3) EMA 1997.[78] The supervision of compliance with environmental regulations is carried out under the responsibility of the Minister for the Environment ex Article 22 (1) EMA 1997, but he can also delegate this competence to the regional governments. Specialized environmental inspectors of the national and regional governments (Art. 22 (2–3) EMA 1997) possess various supervisory competences, such as the taking of samples and the inspection of an installation (Art. 24 EMA 1997). The party responsible for a business is obliged to provide an explanation when asked for by an environmental inspector (Art. 24 (2) EMA 1997). Enforcement powers are rather fragmented distributed between the sector departments responsible for the business licence and the regional government (Arts. 25 and 27 EMA 1997).

In order to achieve integrated environmental management, the elucidation of the EMA 1997 emphasizes that environmental legislation shall be clear, comprehensive, and provide legal certainty.[79] Regarding this, the EMA 1997 itself is not satisfactory. It has delegated the regulation of many vital topics to follow-up regulations. Insofar as follow-up regulations have been made available they often lack specificity or are inconsistent with other regulations on related topics. Notwithstanding some improvements, the overall picture very much resembles that of the EMA 1982.[80]

4.3. Discord between the EMA 1997 and the RGA 1999

Both the EMA 1997 and the RGA 1999 contain provisions regarding the decentralization of environmental management. Related to this topic, the key provisions of the EMA 1997 are the following:

> Article 12
> To create integration and harmony in the implementation of national policy regarding environmental management, the Government-based legislation can:
> Delegate certain environmental authority to central government offices in the regions;
> Give a role to regional government to assist the central government in the implementation of environmental management in the regions.
> Further stipulations as provided for in (1) above are regulated by laws and regulations.

---

[78] Waste is a very broad category. For some waste categories, the Minister for the Environment has delegated licensing authority to the Districts and Municipalities. More about this in Section 4d on the prospects for an integrated or coordinated business-environmental licence.

[79] Niessen (2003, pp. 70–1).

[80] Ibid., p. 79.

> Article 13
> In the scheme of the implementation of environmental management, the Government can transfer part of its affairs to regional government to become part of its general affairs.
> The transfer of affairs as provided for (1) above is determined by Government Regulation.

Article 12 (1) refers to de-concentration (a) and co-governance (b), whereas Article 13 refers to regional autonomy in the field of environmental management. This decentralization scheme is tailored to the provisions of Law 5 of 1974. It is also reflected in Articles 18 and 20 EMA 1997 regarding licensing authorities, and Articles 25 and 27 EMA 1997 regarding supervision and enforcement.

Summarizing, the EMA 1997 presumes that, in principle, environmental management is a task of the central government *unless* it transfers specific tasks to the regional governments. The RGA 1999, by contrast, takes a completely opposite point of departure. It stipulates that, in principle, all government tasks are to be performed by the regional governments, *unless* expressly excepted by law. Regarding this, Articles 7, 10, and 11 RGA 1999 are crucial.

> Article 7 (1)
> The Regional Authority covers the authority in all areas of government, except authority in the field of foreign policy, defense and security, judiciary, monetary and fiscal matters, religious matters, as well as authority in other fields.
>
> Article 10 (1)
> The Region shall be authorized to manage the national resources available in its territory and shall be responsible to maintain the environmental conservation in accordance with the legislative regulation.
>
> Article 11 (1)
> The authority of the District Region and the Municipal Region shall cover all administrative authority other than the authority excepted in Article 7 [quoted above] and the authority regulated in Article 9 [i.e. the authority of the Provinces as Autonomous Regions and Administrative Areas].

These provisions clearly refer to a shift of government authority – not only but also in environmental matters – from the centre to the regions, notably the Districts and the Municipalities. Government Regulation 25 of 2000 (abbr. GR 25/2000) gives an exhaustive enumeration of the tasks of the central government and the provincial government in those policy areas that have not been exempted in Article 7 of the RGA 1999. Regarding environmental management, the Articles 2 point 18 and 3 point 16 are relevant. Article 2 (3) point 18 lists the tasks of the *central government* in the field of environmental protection:

Establishing guidelines for the control of natural resources and preservation of the environment.
Regulating environmental management in the use of seabed resources beyond the 12-mile limit.
Evaluating the analysis concerning the environmental impacts of activities that could cause potential negative impacts on the public in general and/or that involve defense and security, which include more than one Province, activities located in conflict areas with other Countries, in the ocean below the 12-mile limit and area located at border crossings.
Establishing environmental quality standards and establishing guidelines on environmental pollution.
Establishing guidelines for the conservation of natural resources.

Article 3 (5) point 16 lists the tasks of the *provincial government* in the field of environmental protection:

Controlling environmental areas within Districts/Municipalities
Regulating the management of the environment in the use of ocean resources from 4-miles up to the 12-miles seabed.
Regulating the safety and preservation of water resources in Districts/Municipalities.
Evaluating the analysis of environmental impacts (AMDAL) of activities that would cause potential negative impacts to the public in areas located in more than one District/Municipality.
Supervising the conservation of the environment in Districts/Municipalities.
Establishing environmental quality standards based on the national environmental standards.

The preamble explains that no such enumeration is necessary to determine the competences of the *district* and *municipal governments* since for them all tasks remain that are not mentioned in the GR 25/2000. This of course conflicts with Articles 12 and 13 of the EMA 1997.

The new decentralization laws may give the impression that regional autonomy of the Districts and Municipalities is almost sacrosanct. The RGA 1999 and the GR 25/2000 nevertheless provide for several checks and balances to prevent or correct a misallocation of functions to the Districts and Municipalities. The practicality of these provisions is questionable, however.

On the basis of Article 9 (2) RGA 1999 and Article 4 GR 25/2000 the district and municipal governments can voluntarily *surrender* their authority to the provincial government when they prove incompetent to fulfil their autonomous tasks. According to Article 115 RGA 1999 a Regional Autonomy Advisory Council (RAAC) *advises* the President on the creation, merger, and discontinuance of a District or Municipality, the financial relations between centre and regions, and the ability of Districts and Municipalities to perform their autonomous tasks. To this end, the RAAC conducts research and it monitors the performance of the regional governments.[81] In addition, it follows from Article 87 RGA 1999 that the Districts and Municipalities can establish *inter-regional cooperation*, for example in the form of a joint agency. In the field of environmental management such cooperation has obvious advantages, not only because it will strengthen a single region's legal-technical capacity to tackle environmental problems, but also because both sources and effects of many environmental problems are of a cross-regional nature. Furthermore, on the basis of Article 65 RGA 1999 the central government can establish *technical institutes* in the Region (Province, District, or Municipality) in accordance with the particular requirements of that Region.[82] Because environmental management requires specific legal as well as technical knowledge, it seems reasonable to create technical institutes providing assistance to the regional governments.

At the same time, however, the Indonesian government has vowed to foster regional autonomy (Article 112 RGA 1999), the three levels of government are not hierarchically organized (Article 4 (2) RGA 1999), and ultimately the implementation of these mechanisms depends on the willingness of the malfunctioning District or Municipality to surrender or share government authority, or to accept assistance.

4.4. Constraints and Criticism

The RGA 1999 has increased environmental management problems in the Districts and Municipalities. Most district and municipal governments are not ready to deal with their new responsibilities to protect the environment. In general their administrations lack the necessary legal and technical expertise to take on this task. Furthermore it seems that many district and municipal governments mainly use their expanded autonomy to increase their regional incomes, with negative consequences for the environment within their territories. A common explanation for this is the double goal of regional autonomy as reflected in the RGA 1999 and the Law 25 of 1999 on Fiscal Balance between Centre and Regions. Whilst the RGA 1999 pushes for a political balance between the centre and the regional governments, at the same time Law 25 of 1999 gives the regional economies a fairer share in the revenues

---

[81] The criteria upon which a decision is based to create, split up, merge, or dissolve a certain District or Municipality are laid down in Government Regulation 129 of 2000. In all instances mentioned, the initiative lies with the District or Municipality concerned.

[82] The Elucidation of Article 65 RGA 1999 mentions the following examples of such technical institutes: Research and Development Agencies, Planning Agencies, Inspection Agencies, Education and Training Agencies, etc.

yielded by the exploitation of natural resources as well as taxation.[83] In order to meet the latter aims, in recent years many Districts and Municipalities have developed policies to boost their regional economies at the expense of environmental protection.[84]

The RGA 1999 nevertheless offers some good prospects for Indonesia's highly fragmented licensing structure. Prior to the RGA 1999, the sector ministries issued all business permits for large- or medium-scale establishments. Which ministry was competent depended on the type of business activity. The licensing authority for small-scale activities was usually assigned to the departmental branches in the regions. Pursuant to the RGA 1999, however, many business licences – with the exception of logging concessions and mining permits – are presently issued by the district or municipal government. Also important environmental licences – such as the waste water licence and the nuisance licence – are issued by the district or municipal government.[85] In the opinion of Bedner this should eventually lead to a combined business-environmental licence granted by the district/municipal government. This has two major advantages: a single licensing authority will reduce the administrative burden for government and industry, and it will also facilitate the supervision and enforcement of compliance with licence conditions.[86] A coordination mechanism with reciprocal effects can achieve similar advantages: in case (one of) the environmental licence(s) of Article 20 EMA 1997 is lacking, then the business licence of Articles 18–19 EMA either shall not be issued or shall be revoked.

Regarding the enforcement of environmental law, Article 25 EMA 1997 stipulates that the *Governor* is entitled to impose administrative coercion (*paksaan pemerintahan*) against the party that carries out business activities in violation of environmental law.[87] The Governor can *delegate* this competence to the District Head or Mayor. It is in contravention of the spirit of the RGA 1999 to assign enforcing authority to the provincial government when licensing authority rests with the district/municipal government. After all, the RGA 1999 has abolished any hierarchical links between the three levels of government. Furthermore, on the basis of Article 27 EMA 1997, the *Head of Region* – that is, the Governor, District Head, or Mayor in RGA 1999 terminology –

---

[83] Kleden (2004).

[84] Koesnadi (2003).

[85] Bedner (2003, pp. 82–3).

[86] Ibid., pp. 91–1.

[87] It *can* be induced from Article 25 EMA 1997 that administrative coercion applies to acting without a business/environmental licence as well as not complying with the business/environmental licence. The elucidation of Article 25 EMA 1997 considers the matter 'self-explanatory' (*cukup jelas*).

can propose the revocation of a business licence to the competent official (*pejabat yang berwenang*) in case of serious infringements of environmental law. Now that the RGA 1999 assigns important licensing powers to the Districts and Municipalities, the chances are that both licensing and revoking powers are vested in one and the same administration. If in the current situation licensing and revoking powers are distributed among different administrations, one administration can submit a non-binding proposal to revoke a business licence to another administration.[88] Altogether, the enforcement structure is complex and not very practical.

In 2002 the National Environmental Impact Management Agency (*Bapedal*) was merged with the Ministry for the Environment.[89] Previously, the tasks of Bapedal had been to assist the President in the management of environmental impacts, including licensing, prevention of and control over pollution and environmental damage, and rehabilitation of environment quality in accordance with prevailing legislation. It particularly made significant contributions to the enforcement of environmental laws in the regions. Its merger with the Ministry for the Environment was to give the latter powers not only to formulate policies, but also to enforce them. The merger was much criticized by environmental NGOs, however, who feared that it would terminate Bapedal's control function at a time when the enforcement of environmental policy should be more powerful.[90] Several years have passed since the merger, and there is widespread dissatisfaction with the new situation.[91]

Because of regional autonomy, there is no direct relationship between the Ministry for the Environment and the Environmental Agencies of the regional governments.[92] The Regional Environmental Agencies do not follow a particular model that is copied across Indonesia.[93] They perform planning, licensing, monitoring, and enforcement functions on behalf of the regional government, whereby generally the District/Municipal Environmental Agencies have a stronger operational role than the Provincial Environmental Agencies. In line with the obscure delineation of responsibilities between the

---

88 For a more detailed discussion of administrative enforcement of environmental law I refer to Chapter 8 of this volume.

89 Presidential Decree 2 of 2002.

90 Simanjuntak (2002a, 2002b, and 2002c).

91 Interviews with participants of the workshop 'Revision of EMA 1997', Bogor, 30–31 August 2004.

92 It should be noted that prior to the RGA 1999, the Ministry of the Environment did not have its own branches at the regional level since its status was non-portfolio.

93 Some are named *Bapedalda*, in line with Decree 98/1996 and Instruction 11/1997 of the Minister of the Interior, but this is not the case everywhere. The Regional Environmental Agencies are established by regional by-law.

three levels of government on the basis of the EMA 1997, the RGA 1999, and the GR 25/2000, the division of competences between the Environmental Agencies at national, provincial, and district/municipal levels is also very unclear and varies from region to region.[94]

To avoid many of today's problems it is of crucial importance to clearly allocate specific authority for specific functions. It is recommended that the Ministry for the Environment holds a strong grip on nationwide environmental protection. It should coordinate environmental decision-making between the different sectors of government as well as between the three levels of government. It should take the lead in the formulation of environmental standards that must be observed by the regional governments, as Articles 8–11 and 14–15 EMA 1997 already presume. The provincial and district/municipal governments can issue additional environmental requirements that are tailored to specific local conditions. Regarding this, Article 70 RGA 1999 indeed assumes that lower legislation complies with higher legislation.[95] Operational functions – such as licensing, monitoring, and enforcement – are best delegated to the regional governments. To some extent this is done in the GR 25/2000, but its loose provisions allow for contradictory interpretations and lead to messy environmental management.

Given the absence of a clear and comprehensive legal-institutional framework for environmental management, the RGA 1999 was prone to produce further distortions.[96] Ultimately the RGA 1999 has led to the unintended result that every District or Municipality has become more and more inward-looking. There is a widespread misconception that regional autonomy must be understood as a sort of regional self-sufficiency or political parochialism. This not only leads to an absence of collaboration between Districts/Municipalities where this would be necessary to tackle a problem, but it also makes Districts/Municipalities reluctant to obey to their 'superior' levels of government.[97] According to a 1998 World Bank study, policy-makers in developing countries may not sufficiently understand the specific problems they want to overcome through decentralization, or they may adopt an ineffective strategy to solve them.[98] This once again brings us to the principal question of whether

---

94 Unpublished Australian consultancy report.

95 Article 70 RGA 1999: The by-law shall not be contradictory to the public interest, another by-law and higher legislation.

96 Hofman et al. (2003, pp. 20–1): The delivery of some services has improved or remained the same since the RGA 1999, notably education and health services. In other policy areas, however, there has been a fair amount of friction in the first years of decentralization. Among these conflicts environmental issues feature prominently.

97 Kleden (2004).

98 Litvack et al. (1998).

environmental management in Indonesia should be decentralized, and if so, how?

5. TOWARDS A NEW PARADIGM FOR ENVIRONMENTAL MANAGEMENT IN INDONESIA?

5.1. Why Legal Reform?

On the basis of Article 133 of the RGA 1999, sector laws and regulations must be adjusted to conform with the new decentralization act. This forms an immediate order to change the EMA 1997.[99] At the same time, the Indonesian government intends to take the 'opportunity' to conduct a full review of the EMA, addressing subjects other than the division of responsibilities between the three levels of government as well.[100] A serious complication for the Indonesian government is that the experience thus far with the RGA 1999 has not been satisfactory in a number of respects. Some of its deficiencies have been discussed above, and it should be stressed that the problems mentioned are not unique to environmental management. It is therefore that the Indonesian government also intends to revise the RGA 1999.

This 'complication' compels us to consider various law reform strategies at the same time: either we concentrate on the EMA alone, or we deal with both the EMA and the RGA simultaneously. While doing so we must keep in mind the possibility that the enactment of a new RGA precedes the enactment of a new EMA, or the other way round. A number of legal conflicts caused by simultaneous or subsequent revisions of the EMA or the RGA can be avoided as follows: the RGA forms a general legal-institutional framework for regional government whilst the EMA forms a special legal-institutional framework for environmental management. The *lex specialis* (EMA) is to be as much as possible consistent with the provisions of the *lex generalis* (RGA). Nevertheless, it can always be upheld that for the sake of environmental protection, the EMA deviates from the general framework on various points. The legal facility for this deviation can either be included in the EMA or in the RGA, or in both acts.

---

[99] As a matter of fact, Article 132 of the RGA 1999 stipulates that it shall be implemented effectively within two years after its promulgation. Considering this, the revision of the EMA 1997 is about three years behind schedule.

[100] The other contributions to this workshop attest to the fact that indeed many other parts of the EMA 1997 are likely to be reviewed as well.

5.2. General Lawmaking Caveats

Both the EMA 1997 and the RGA 1999 are umbrella acts. Umbrella acts remove the tension between permanent and flexible legislation, for they provide the basic legal framework that is to be filled in by a range of implementing regulations. A major advantage of umbrella acts is that implementing measures can be easily adjusted to changing circumstances, new information, and technical developments. At the same time, however, the umbrella act must preclude any doubts about its objectives and terminology. This sets high demands on the structure and textual quality of the umbrella act itself, which is to be accompanied by an elaborate elucidation to provide additional information. In addition, the announced follow-up regulations are to be issued swiftly after and consistently with the parent act. Since the EMA 1997 and the RGA 1999 do not meet many of these vital criteria, their implementation and enforcement are fraught with difficulties.

At this point in time, environmental protection is of marginal political concern in Indonesia. When it comes to striking a balance between environmental and economic interests, then clearly the latter will prevail.[101] This does not offer good prospects for the drafting of a solid new EMA. There is a risk that contradictory opinions concerning the aims and effects of environmental management result in a new EMA that is even less satisfactory than the current one. After all, lawmaking takes place in a political arena in which environmentalists must compromise with other factions. Despite the good intentions of the Ministry for the Environment, the final outcome of this process is highly insecure.

To avoid some political loopholes, one may consider incremental legal reform instead of a full revision of the EMA 1997 (and the RGA 1999) all at once. This can be done in two ways. One possibility is to develop changes *within* the existing legal-institutional frameworks. Since both the EMA 1997 and the RGA 1999 are umbrella acts, many of their framework provisions need further sharpening by means of subordinate regulation. Another possibility is to develop new laws *in stages*, taking the EMA 1997 and the RGA 1999 as build-on laws to which changes are made in the form of separate amendments, tackling key issues first. Preferably, the suggested approaches take place side by side in a concerted effort. On the basis of such a step-by-step approach, environmental protection can improve while the law is under construction.

Several of the suggested changes in this chapter are inspired by comparative law. Legal drafters are faced with a major challenge to fit imported solutions into the Indonesian socio-legal context, for 'a law or a presumed

---

101 Moestadji (2003, p. 7).

"international standard", will induce in its new home the same behaviors as it did in its original one only if all the relevant factors in its addressees' social and physical surround, including the new country's implementing agency, closely resemble those in its place of origin. . . . Without empirical evidence that in the relevant ways a law's addressees live in substantially the same milieu in both countries, one country cannot safely copy another country's law.'[102]

5.3. Legal-institutional Design for Multilevel Environmental Management

The preceding analysis brings us to propose some suggestions of change to the EMA 1997. In particular on the basis of legal comparison (Sections 2.1–2.3) and the characteristics of Indonesia's current legal-institutional framework for environmental law (Sections 4.3–4.4), I have selected the following main topics:

Table 7.1 EMA 1997

	Subject	Elaboration
1.	Decentralization modalities for Districts and Municipalities	Delete Article 12 (1) sub a EMA 1997, for de-concentration is at odds with the RGA 1999.
2.	General rules	Introduce a new chapter on general rules.
3.	Simplify enforcement mechanisms	Rewrite Articles 25 and 27 EMA 1997 because they complicate the enforcement of environmental law.
4.	(Integrated/coordinated) decision-making procedures	A new EMA is to specify decision-making procedures for licensing, supervision, and enforcement.
5.	Allocation of authority for environmental protection	A new EMA is to be more specific on the division of responsibilities for environmental protection.

102 Seidman and Seidman (1999, pp. 261–2).

Explanation

(1) The RGA 1999 contains only two decentralization modalities, namely regional autonomy (Art. 7–12 EMA 1999) and co-governance (Art. 13). A separate central government administration running parallel to the regional government administration, as was imposed by Law 5 of 1974, is not only in conflict with the RGA 1999 but is also not necessary. If the central government desires to keep a close eye on the performance of certain government tasks, it will suffice to assign these tasks on the basis of co-governance. In the Netherlands, for example, environmental protection is a task of co-governance of the municipal government.

(2) A system of general rules has some important advantages. First, it reduces the administrative burden of the Districts and Municipalities. Redundant licensing personnel can be deployed in the supervision and enforcement departments instead. Secondly, environmental decisions are taken by the central government which must be considered most capable in terms of legal-technical environmental knowledge. Thirdly, a system of general rules warrants the uniform application of environmental standards across the country. And most important, the application of general rules reduces the risks of lobbying, corruption, and collusion in the licensing process. For this purpose, the Dutch system could serve as an example. The Dutch Wm contains a special chapter on general rules (8.2 Wm) which is placed directly after the chapter on licences (8.1 Wm), and there are several cross-references between these two chapters. For example, Article 8.1 (1), Chapter 8.1, stipulates that '[t]his prohibition [to set up, modify or operate an establishment] shall not apply to establishments included in a category designated by government regulation pursuant to Article 8.40 (1)'. Besides this, Article 8.40 (1), Chapter 8.2, contains the following provision: '[r]ules which are needed to protect the environment may be laid down by government regulation with respect to categories of establishments designated therein'. The remaining provisions of Chapter 8.2 deal with specific elements that must be taken into account when establishing general rules,[103] the obligation to give notice of the creation or modification of an establishment to which general rules apply,[104] and the competence of the provincial and municipal governments to lay down additional requirements.[105] For special categories of establishments, the Wm provides for a combination of environmental licence and general rules.[106] In such instances, general rules only partly replace the environmental licence.

---

103 Article 8.40 (2) Wm.

104 Article 8.41 Wm.

105 Article 8.42 Wm.

106 Articles 8.44 to 8.46 Wm.

(3) On the basis of Articles 25 and 27 EMA 1999 *in principle* it is not the licensing authority, that is, the district or municipal government, that is responsible for supervision and enforcement, because either the Governor is the competent authority to apply administrative coercion (Art. 25 EMA 1997), or the Governor addresses a proposal to the licensing authority to revoke the business licence in case of violations of environmental law. Articles 25 and 27 EMA can be rewritten so as to assign *in general* supervision and enforcement tasks to the District Head or Mayor.[107] In order to fulfil these responsibilities, the district and municipal governments can be assisted by *technical institutes*, for which a provision is made in Article 65 RGA 1999. Besides this, a new EMA is to contain provisions on *second-line* supervision and enforcement by higher levels of government, which can step in whenever the district or municipal government fails to perform its supervising or enforcing duties. In addition, special environmental law can assign licensing and enforcing powers to other government authorities depending on the scale, complexity, and polluting effects of the polluting activity.

(4) The EMA 1997 is almost free of specific obligations to give content to integrated environmental management. If the revised EMA is to maintain 'integration' as a principal goal, then this EMA shall specify the procedures for licensing, supervision, and enforcement. Minimal procedural elements to be addressed are: which parties are to be involved at which stage of the decision-making process, consultation processes, time frames, reciprocal integration and coordination mechanisms between licences as well as between enforcement decisions, consultation processes, and legal protection. These are vital issues that cannot be delegated to implementing regulations. In the Dutch Wm, for example, it is laid down that for issuing the Wm licence the 'elaborate public preparation procedure' of the GALA is imperative.

(5) On the whole, the EMA 1997 does not really specify 'who is responsible for what', which negatively affects its implementation. For example, Article 11 EMA 1997 stipulates that integrated environmental management is to be implemented by an 'institution' (*perangkat kelembagaan*) coordinated by the Minister for the Environment. This crucial item is best dealt with in precise words by the EMA itself. In addition, the EMA's official elucidation is to give clear directions for its interpretation and application. This may help to avoid the promulgation of implementing regulations that conflict with the EMA or sector legislation, or with

[107] Cf. Article 18.2 Wm.

one another. If the Indonesian government strives for the nationwide application of environmental (minimum) standards (Arts. 8–11 and 14–15 EMA 1997), then those standards are to be issued (and made public). Article 70 RGA 1999 warrants that regional by-laws and decisions conform to national law and regulations.

The above-mentioned changes to the EMA 1997 cannot be considered in isolation from the RGA 1999, for the parameters for decentralized environmental management are first set by the general legal-institutional framework for regional government.

Explanation

(1) It is recommended that regional administrations are *accountable* not only

Table 7.2 RGA 1999

	Subject	Elaboration
1.	Re-establish a hierarchical organization between State, Province, and District/Municipality	The 'no-hierarchy clause' of Article 4 (2) RGA 1999 should be rephrased so as to facilitate upward accountability.
2.	Strengthen the role of the Provinces	Rewrite Article 9 (2) RGA 1999.
3.	Strengthen the role of the RAAC	Reinforce current advisory functions of the RAAC by empowering it to *start* proceedings to take over district or municipal tasks by the Province (see 2) as well as to lift or merge a District or Municipality (Art. 6 RGA 1999), and to *advise* on the conditions for asymmetric decentralization (see 5).
4.	Allow sector legislation, e.g. the EMA, to deviate from the general framework for regional government	Specify the conditions under which sector legislation may deviate from the RGA.
5.	Asymmetric decentralization	Assign differentiated authority to (groups of) Districts and Municipalities on the basis of regional management capacity.

to democratically elected representative councils,[108] but also to higher government levels. This is quite common in a decentralized unitary state. Naturally, the specific conditions under which the provincial governments and the central government are allowed to interfere, preventive as well as repressive, in the governance autonomy of the Districts and Municipalities should be limited and spelled out in the RGA. Regarding this, Law 5 of 1974 had given too much discretion to the central government. Additional requirements for specific policy areas can be laid down in particular administrative laws, such as the Environmental Management Act. The courts should be enabled to test the use of supervisory powers by higher government levels.

(2) This builds on what is stated above. The RGA 1999 and the GR 25/2000 together have granted a weak position to the Provinces as *intermediate* governments. Only when a District or Municipality willingly surrenders its government responsibilities, is the Province allowed to take over (Art. 9 (2) RGA 1999). The law should however provide for a mechanism that enables the Province to take the initiative when necessary. Obviously that same law must define the conditions and process for such a take-over, which of course must be considered an extraordinary event.

(3) The RAAC (Regional Autonomy Advisory Council) is to perform a crucial role in assessing the management capacity of the regional governments. On the basis of these assessments, policies can be developed to *gradually* upload regional autonomy. See 'asymmetric decentralization', below.

(4) For the sake of environmental protection it is justified that an EMA contains provisions that deviate from the general framework. This can be illustrated by the Dutch Wm, which on various points 'differs' – for example, deviates, complements, refines – from the GALA and the Municipality Act. The legal facility for these 'differences' is included in the relevant laws.

(5) Asymmetric decentralization can also be pursued as a transitional phase, see 'RAAC' above. I quote from a 2001 World Bank report that '[a]ssigning differentiated authority to regional governments based on political commitment, technical capacity, revenues, population, and constituency strength can alleviate the pressure of having to implement a country-wide uniform decentralization program'.[109] This may prove difficult to realize, however, for in an earlier report the World Bank asserts that 'asymmetrical decentralization may raise a fundamental

---

108 Articles 18 (1) sub f, 19 (1), 20, 21, 31 (2) 32 (3), and 46 (3) RGA 1999.

109 The World Bank (2001, p. 115).

political problem: the perceived need to have a law that treats all units similarly, in the face of the reality that there are wide and relevant differences between them'.[110]

In the long term, it can be considered to issue an Indonesian *General Administrative Law Code* pertaining to general issues of administrative law. Then these issues no longer need to be included in the RGA, the EMA, or other particular administrative laws.

5.4. Non-legal Means to Strengthen Environmental Management Capacity

Having thus far emphasized the importance of law, I do of course acknowledge that the success of any environmental protection strategy to a large extent depends on other factors as well. Ideally, the development of environmental law goes hand-in-hand with changes outside the legal system. It requires the application of financial and human resources, a strong court system, and a growth in environmental awareness across Indonesian society. A serious problem is the lack of environmental information in Indonesia, technical as well as legal. To improve the dissemination of accurate and up-to-date environmental information, the Dutch government has launched the website '*Infomil*: linking environmental policy and implementation' (www.infomil.nl), which on a two-weekly basis provides updates of environmental regulations, environmental technology, enforcement targets and strategies, court decisions, implementation guidelines and checklists, tips, and FAQs.[111] This website is publicly accessible, but its target groups are the Dutch Provinces, Municipalities, and water boards. By means of *Infomil* there is a continuous flow of information from the central government to the regional governments, and vice versa. It may be useful for Indonesia to invest in a similar project for capacity building.

6. CONCLUSION

If one is to advise the Indonesian government on designing an infrastructure for environmental management, then decentralization should be one pillar besides others. A main reason is that environmental protection requires special knowledge of complex (and constantly changing) legal and technical matters,

110 Litvack et al. (1998, pp. 23–4).

111 In 1995 *Infomil* was launched by the Ministry for Housing, Spatial Planning and the Environment, the Dutch Association of Municipalities, the Inter-Provincial Consultation Board, and the Union of Water Boards.

which is often lacking at the district and municipal level. Another reason is that many environmental problems manifest themselves beyond the district/municipal borders, and should therefore be tackled by the higher administrations. It is not without reason that environmental issues take a prominent position on the agenda for international cooperation. As a matter of fact, increasingly national environmental legislation follows international environmental agreements, rather than the other way round. Considering this, a top-down approach is to remain a consistent feature of any environmental management system.

The RGA 1999 appears to be an over-reaction against Law 5 of 1974, which used to be a cornerstone of *Orde Baru*. It embraces the notion of wide-ranging regional autonomy instead of limited regional autonomy as advocated by Law 5 of 1974. Today there is much evidence that in many policy sectors, and in environmental management more than anywhere else, the RGA 1999 has worked out adversely. For the sake of environmental protection some re-centralization of government powers seems inevitable. For this purpose I have suggested re-establishing a hierarchical organization of State, Province, and District/Municipality, and strengthening the role of the Provinces as intermediate levels of governments. Ultimately the Indonesian government needs to steer a middle course between Law 5 of 1974 and the RGA 1999.

The EMA 1997 pursues a rather centralist approach for it is modelled on Law 5 of 1974. This is reflected in the provisions on environmental standard setting, licensing and enforcing authority. At the same time, however, these provisions are loosely worded and refer to follow-up regulations for their further elaboration and implementation. In particular procedural rules for licensing (including EIA), supervision, and enforcement are missing in the EMA 1997. Besides this, many of the announced follow-up regulations have not been issued or have failed to live up to expectations of legal specificity and cohesion. Altogether, this has resulted in environmental management that is ineffective and lacks transparency.

Since the enactment of the RGA 1999 this general picture has worsened. The RGA 1999 lays important environmental management tasks at the level of the district and municipal governments. Given the absence of an elaborate legal-institutional framework for environmental protection, many district and municipal governments operate at random. Because regional autonomy to a substantial degree also means financial self-sufficiency, many decisions of the district and municipal governments do not take into account environmental considerations. The RGA 1999 states that lower regulations must comply with higher regulations, but solid provisions concerning cooperation and upward accountability between the three levels of government are lacking.

In any case, a positive contribution of the RGA 1999 is the abolition of a parallel administration for central government functions at the regional level.

Now that these functions are performed by the regional government itself, many business licences as well as environmental licences are issued by the Districts and Municipalities. This certainly improves the chances for integrated and coordinated licensing. The next step would be to vest licensing as well as enforcing powers in one and the same authority. In view of these recommendations it is necessary to rewrite Articles 18 to 27 EMA 1997. At the same time, it is important to establish mechanisms for second-line supervision and enforcement by higher levels of government and/or Environmental Inspectorates. The legal facility for these arrangements can be laid down in an EMA, an RGA, or in both acts.

In order to reduce the administrative burden of Districts and Municipalities, Indonesia could follow the Dutch example by introducing so-called 'general rules' – which are in fact detailed technical prescriptions – for various categories of polluting activities. Whenever such general rules apply to a particular activity, they replace, fully or partly, the environmental licence. One could devise a system of general rules that allows for certain local-specific adjustments. In this manner, the regional governments can – but need not – tailor general rules to local circumstances, for example by means of regional by-laws. An additional important virtue of general rules is that one can steer around corruption pitfalls in the licensing process.

This chapter has identified some problems with the EMA 1997, the RGA 1999, and their interactions. On the basis of decentralization theory and comparative law some proposals are made to change the EMA 1997 and the RGA 1999, following a step-by-step approach. These changes must go hand-in-hand with capacity building at all levels of government. Regarding this, it is important that the competent authorities are provided with accurate and up-to-date environmental information. The Indonesian government may consider investing in a nationwide information network on environmental regulations and technology. For this purpose the Dutch *Infomil* may serve as a useful example.

REFERENCES

Auby, J.B. (2002), 'Administrative Law in France', in R. Seerden and F. Stroink, *Administrative Law of the European Union, its Member States and the United States. A Comparative Analysis*, Antwerpen-Groningen: Intersentia-Metro, pp. 59–89.

Auby, J.B. and Y. Jegouzo (2002), 'Public Environmental Law in France', in: R.J.G.H. Seerden, M.A. Heldeweg and K.R. Deketelaere, *Public Environmental Law in the European Union and the United States: A Comparative Analysis*, The Hague: Kluwer Law International, pp. 171–98.

Bedner, A. (2003), 'From the Old to the New EMA: Integration or Disintegration of the

Legal Potential for Enforcement?', in A. Bedner and N. Niessen (eds), *Towards Integrated Environmental Law in Indonesia?*, Leiden: Research School CNWS, pp. 1–20.

Bellekom, T.L., A.W. Heringa, J. van der Velde and L.F.M. Verhey (2002), *Koopmans' Compendium van het Staatsrecht*, ninth edition, Deventer: Kluwer.

Cistulli, V. (2002), *Environment in Decentralized Development. Economic and Institutional Issues*, Training materials for agricultural planning, Rome: FAO-UN.

da Costa Novaes, P. (2003), *Decentralization of the Environment Management in Brazil: Theory and Practice*, The Challenges of Social Environmental Governance, Joint Brazil-China-Mexico Session, LEAD-ABDL, Brasilia-Pirenópolis, November 21–7.

Dupar, M. and N. Badenoch (eds) (2002), *Environment, Livelihoods, and Local Institutions. Decentralization in Mainland Southeast Asia*, Washington DC: World Resources Institute.

Hofman, B., K. Kaiser, S. Goga and J. Chakeri (2003), *Decentralizing Indonesia. A Regional Public Expenditure Review Report*, Washington, DC: The World Bank.

Kleden, I. (2004), 'Regions Dishonor Spirit of Autonomy Law', Indonesia Outlook 2004, *The Jakarta Post*, 14 April.

Koesnadi, H. (1996), 'The History and Future Trends of Environmental Legislation', ICEL, *Indonesian Journal of Environmental Law*, Edition I, pp. 1–15.

Koesnadi, H. (2003), 'Kebijakan Pengelolaan Lingkungan Hidup di Era Otonomi Daerah', paper presented at the seminar 'Pemikiran Perubahan Undang-undang Nomor 23 Tahun 1997 tentang Pengelolaan Lingkungan Hidup', Jakarta, 15 December.

Koopmans, T. (2003), *Courts and Political Institutions. A Comparative View*, Cambridge: Cambridge University Press.

Litvack, J., J. Ahmad and R. Bird (1998), *Rethinking Decentralization in Developing Countries*, Sector Studies Series, Washington, DC: The World Bank.

Michiels, F.C.M.A. (2003), *De wet milieubeheer*, Studiepockets staats- en bestuursrecht, fourth edition, Deventer: Kluwer.

Moestadji, M. (2003), 'Pengembangan Penataan Kelembagaan Pengelolaan Lingkungan Hidup di Era Otonomi Daerah', paper presented at the seminar 'Pemikiran Perubahan Undang-undang Nomor 23 Tahun 1997 tentang Pengelolaan Lingkungan Hidup', Jakarta, 15 December.

Niessen, N. (1999), *Municipal Government in Indonesia. Policy, Law, and Practice of Decentralization and Urban Spatial Planning*, Leiden: Research School CNWS.

Niessen, N. (2003), 'Indonesia's Environmental Management Act of 1997: Comprehensive and Integrated?', in A. Bedner and N. Niessen (eds), *Towards Integrated Environmental Law in Indonesia?*, Leiden: Research School CNWS, pp. 66–79.

Prud'homme, R. (1994), *On the Dangers of Decentralization*, Policy Research Working Papers, Transportation, Water and Urban Development Department, Washington, DC: The World Bank.

Rodi, M. (2002), 'Public Environmental Law in Germany', in R.J.G.H. Seerden, M.A. Heldeweg and K.R. Deketelaere (eds), *Public Environmental Law in the European Union and the United States. A Comparative Analysis*, The Hague: Kluwer Law International, pp. 199–245.

Schlössels, R.J.N. and F.A.M. Stroink, in cooperation with C.L.G.F.H. Albers and S. Hillegers (2003), *Kern van het bestuursrecht*, Den Haag: Boom Juridische Uitgevers.

Seerden, R.J.G.H., M.A. Heldeweg and K.R. Deketelaere (2002), 'Comparative

Remarks', in R.J.G.H. Seerden, M.A. Heldeweg and K.R. Deketelaere (eds), *Public Environmental Law in the European Union and the United States. A Comparative Analysis*, The Hague: Kluwer Law International, pp. 563–83.

Seerden, R. and F. Stroink (2002), 'Administrative Law in the Netherlands', in R. Seerden and F. Stroink, *Administrative Law of the European Union, its Member States and the United States. A Comparative Analysis*, Antwerpen-Groningen: Intersentia-Metro, pp. 345–60.

Seidman, A. and R.B. Seidman (1999), 'Using Reason and Experience to Draft Country-Specific Laws', in A. Seidman, R.B. Seidman and T. Wälde, *Making Development Work: Legislative Reform for Institutional Transformation and Good Governance*, The Hague and London: Kluwer Law International, pp. 249–83.

Simanjuntak, T.Z.B. (2002a), 'Govt Defends Plan to Dissolve Bapedal', *Jakarta Post*, 5 January.

Simanjuntak, T.Z.B. (2002b), 'Environmentalists Oppose Scrapping of Bapedal', *Jakarta Post*, 10 January.

Simanjuntak, T.Z.B. (2002c), 'Bapedal Gone, Fears of Environment Abuse Up', *Jakarta Post*, 28 January.

The World Bank (2001), *Indonesia. Environment and Natural Resource Management in a Time of Transition*, Washington, DC: The World Bank, February.

Vaqués, M.A. (2002), 'Public Environmental Law in Spain', in R.J.G.H. Seerden, M.A. Heldeweg and K.R. Deketelaere (eds), *Public Environmental Law in the European Union and the United States. A Comparative Analysis*, The Hague: Kluwer Law International, pp. 395–436.

Verschuuren, J.M. (2000), 'De openbare voorbereidingsprocedure Awb en de actio popularis in het milieurecht', *Nederlands Tijdschrift voor Bestuursrecht*, pp. 178–83.

Yang, T. (2002), 'Public Environmental Law in the United States', in R.J.G.H. Seerden, M.A. Heldeweg and K.R. Deketelaere (eds), *Public Environmental Law in the European Union and the United States. A Comparative Analysis*, The Hague and London: Kluwer Law International, pp. 517–61.

Young, O.R. (2002), *The Institutional Dimensions of Environmental Change. Fit, Interplay, and Scale*, Cambridge, MA: MIT Press.

8. Supervision and enforcement in the Law Concerning Environmental Management, Law No. 23 of 1997

Frits Stroink

1. INTRODUCTION

In this chapter I will focus on my lecture on supervision and enforcement in the Indonesian Environmental Management Act (EMA), especially in the field of licences.

First, I will mention briefly the relevant articles in the EMA, next discuss some general starting points of constitutional and administrative law and finally compare the Indonesian law with these general starting points and some notions of Dutch environmental and administrative law.

Part II of the EMA (Arts. 22–4) deals with supervision. The Minister is the competent organ (Art. 22, s. 1). He can appoint officials with authority to carry out supervision (Art. 22, s. 2). I will elaborate later on the relationship with the Decentralization Act of 1999.

There is a possibility of delegation of supervisory powers to local government. In that case the Regional Head appoints the officials to carry out supervision (Art. 22, s. 3). Environmental impact control as a supervisory instrument is carried out by an institution formed especially for that purpose by the government (Art. 23).

The supervisory officials have the power to conduct monitoring, request an explanation, make copies of documents and/or make the notes they need, enter certain places, take samples, inspect equipment, inspect installations and/or transportation equipment, and request an explanation from the party responsible for a business and/or activity (Art. 24, s. 1). The party responsible for a business and/or activity must obey the request of the supervisory official in accordance with the stipulations of applicable laws and regulations.

The power to carry out administrative sanctions lies with the Governor of the Province (Level I Region). He has the authority to carry out administrative sanctions against the party responsible for a business and/or activity to prevent and end an infringement and to deal with the consequences caused by an infringement, carry out safeguarding, mitigating and/or remedial measures at the expense of the party responsible for a business and/or activity, except where otherwise stipulated based on law (Art. 25, s. 1). By Level I Region Regulation the powers can be delegated to the District Head of the Regency or the Mayor of the Municipality (Art. 25, s. 2).

A third party who has an interest has the right to submit an application to the authorized official to carry out an administrative sanction (Art. 25, s. 3). Administrative sanctions are preceded by an order from the authorized official (Art. 25, s. 4). Safeguarding, mitigating and/or remedial measures can be replaced by payment of a certain sum of money (Art. 25, s. 5). Withdrawal of a licence is possible in certain cases (Art. 27, s. 1). Both the Regional Head and an interested third party can ask for a withdrawal (Art. 27, ss. 2 and 3).

The Minister has the authority to order the party responsible for a business and/or activity to conduct an environmental audit if the party concerned indicates his non-compliance with the stipulations arranged in this law (Art. 29, s. 1).

Chapter IX (Art. 41–48) contains the criminal provisions.

2. SOME GENERAL STARTING POINTS OF CONSTITUTIONAL AND ADMINISTRATIVE LAW

There is a very close relation between (a) legislation, (b) administrative acts, (c) supervision and (d) enforcement.

In the field of administrative law the principle of legality implies among other things that the powers of the administration must be defined as clearly as possible (legal certainty; *lex certa*). Also, administrative acts must be circumscribed as clearly as possible. A licence holder, for example, must know exactly his rights and duties based on the licence. Clear legislation and clear administrative acts facilitate supervision and enforcement.

To ensure effective enforcement it is recommended that the administrative supervision and enforcement powers should be brought together,[1] or at least supervision and enforcement powers should be combined.[2] When supervision and enforcement powers are in different hands, miscommunication lies in wait. No need to say that supervisors must have the required technical knowledge. Furthermore supervisors need clear powers corresponding with clear duties of the supervised and powers to enforce their supervisory powers.

See for example afdeling 5.2 Algemene wet bestuursrecht (AWB), containing the powers of the supervisors. Article 184 Wetboek van Strafrecht contains

---

[1] Cf. Art. 18.2 Wet milieubeheer: the licensing authority is also the enforcement authority.

[2] This means that the supervisors are subordinate to the enforcement authority.

the penal provision for not obeying the supervisors' demands. Article 18.6 Wet Milieubeheer (the Dutch Environmental Management Act) attributes enforcement power (bestuursdwang) to the licensing authority in the case of non-compliance with the supervisors' demands.

When a licence holder does not act in accordance with a licence or a person acts without a licence, there are in theory three ways of enforcement. These are:

- administrative law;
- criminal law;
- civil law.

Administrative law

There are several administrative sanctions if a person acts without or not in accordance with a licence. The most important are:

(a) enforcement (bestuursdwang)[3] or, alternatively, imposing a coercive sum (dwangsom);
(b) imposing a penalty;
(c) withdrawing the licence.

(a) Enforcement

The power of enforcement is a very suitable instrument for enforcing the law. In this field there are very important developments in Dutch case law. In the past enforcement power was considered to be a discretionary power, that is, the administration has to weigh the different interests of the licence holder, third parties and the general interest. But for five or six years the Dutch administrative judge (de Afdeling bestuursrechtspraak van de Raad van State) has not spoken of a (discretionary) power to enforce but of a duty to enforce.[4] A duty with a few exceptions (for example, emergency situations, transition period). This means that when a third party asks for enforcement in principle the administrative authority has to issue an order.

According to Dutch law the order must provide the offender with the opportunity to repair the situation himself within a certain period of time (Art. 5:24 lid 4 AWB). Also according to Dutch law, the authority with the power of enforcement can, instead of using that power, impose a coercive sum

---

3 Art. 5:21 AWB.

4 *ABR* v *S* 2 February 1998, AB 1998, 181 with learned comment of Michiels. For the English situation, see Jones and Thompson (2002, p. 219): 'Although it is normally the express duty of the authority to enforce the standard in question, it is usually left to the authority to decide for itself what steps it should take, if any, to ascertain whether the standard has been complied with'.

(Art. 5:32 lid 1 AWB). In this case, too, the perpetrator must be given the opportunity to repair the situation himself (Art. 5:32 lid 5 AWB). Imposing a coercive sum is, in certain cases, more effective than exercising enforcement powers, for example in the case of continuing offences.

(b) Imposing a penalty

In recent years we have seen a shift in the Netherlands from criminal enforcement to administrative enforcement. An administrative approach is very often more efficient, faster and also cheaper to enforce than the criminal route. Administrative laws may confer the power to impose a penalty instead of a criminal prosecution.[5, 6]

(c) Withdrawing the licence

This instrument needs no further comment.

Criminal law

Under most administrative laws, acting without or not in accordance with a licence is penalized. Such action is a criminal offence. Criminal prosecution and administrative enforcement can coincide, because administrative enforcement is not a punitive sanction.[7] Criminal prosecution and a punitive administrative sanction such as a fine cannot coincide. This is called the principle of *una via*.

Civil law

Is it possible for the administration to sue a perpetrator for tort in a civil court? In the past that was possible. But in the Netherlands, since the power of enforcement has been connected to the power to impose a coercive sum, it is no longer possible.

In the opinion of the Dutch Supreme Court the administration can reach the same ends with public instruments as with private law actions. And also, because the public way gives more guarantees than the private way, the public way is exclusive.[8]

---

[5] A new tranche of the Awb will give general provisions concerning administrative penalties.

[6] Be aware that in the eyes of the European Court of Human Rights an administrative penalty is a criminal charge in the sense of Art. 6 of the treaty. So this means that the guarantees of the treaty are applicable.

[7] In Dutch literature administrative enforcement is called 'een *reparatoire* of *herstel* sanctie'.

[8] HR 7 October 1994, AB 1995, 47. In the past the Supreme Court accepted that the administration used private law to reach public ends. Since 1990 (HR 26 January 1990, AB 1990, 408, Windmill) the Supreme Court has limited the use of private law considerably.

3. THE INDONESIAN EMA REVISITED?

Is it necessary to change the Indonesian EMA? That question is difficult to answer, especially by a non-Indonesian. In the first place one has to distinguish between law in the books and law in action. A good law can be applied in a bad way and a bad law can be applied in a good way.

I was very surprised when I heard that in Indonesia a third party has never yet asked for an order for administrative enforcement. Of course one must first try to solve problems in a peaceful way. But if that does not succeed, the administration has to act either on its own behalf (ambtshalve, ex officio) or on the request of a citizen. If the administration does not comply with the request of the citizen such a refusal is a decision in the sense of the Law on Administrative Courts.[9] So the citizen can appeal to the administrative court and the administrative judge can test the administrative decision. Maybe the administration needs to give more information and guidance to the public.

But now back to the EMA.

First I want to say something about criminal provisions. I can imagine that the application of many articles causes a lot of evidence problems. One can prevent those problems by simply penalizing acting without a licence or not in accordance with a licence. Articles 41, section 2 and 42, section 2, are general provisions that belong in the General Criminal Code.[10]

I think it is highly recommended to bring at least the supervisory powers and the powers to impose administrative sanctions under one authority. That will stimulate more effective enforcement. Besides, the mere fact of regular inspection will usually ensure attention to the maintenance of standards.[11]

It is a principle of decentralization that powers should be conferred on the lowest possible scale. On the other hand it is necessary for the empowered authority to meet certain requirements such as sufficient knowledge of the technical and legal problems. These two principles can collide with each other.

If I am not mistaken these powers are already in one hand. These powers now lie with the Head of the Region II (regency, municipality) based on the Act No. 22 of 1999 (Decentralization Act). I think it is absolutely necessary to adapt the EMA in this respect, namely to attribute the powers to the administrative authorities according to the Decentralization Act. The present text can give rise to misunderstandings.

It is very important for the administration not only to have the power of enforcement but also the power to impose coercive sums. Especially in the

---

9 See Art. 3, s. 1 LAC. The refusal to issue an administrative decision (beschikking) is put on a par with an administrative decision.

10 Cf. Art. 173 a and b Wetboek van Strafrecht.

11 Cf. Jones and Thompson (2002, p. 215).

case of frequent offences, the power to impose coercive sums is more effective than enforcement by the administration itself. In both situations, however, the perpetrator must be given the opportunity to end the offences by himself and to restore the old situation.

The text of Article 25, s. 1, is not quite clear to me. What exactly are safeguarding, mitigating and/or remedial measures? Do they also include the power to close a factory? And why is there a possibility of buying off the offence (Art. 25, s. 5)? That is not in the interests of the environment. And what is the meaning of, for example, 'certain infringements' in Article 27, s.1?

According to the Elucidation, by certain infringements is meant infringement by a business and/or activity which is regarded as sufficiently serious that the business activity be stopped, for example where people from the community have had their health impaired as a result of environmental pollution and/or damage. However, this Elucidation is not clear enough.

Here I must leave it. Of course, a law contains general objectives (especially in the preamble), but, as I have already stated, the principle of legal certainty implies clear powers and clear administrative decisions. So the law, or regulations based on the law, has to circumscribe the powers of the administration as clearly as possible. But, of course, absolute clearness is very often not possible. Often the law contains vague terms. These terms need to be interpreted by the administration and the judge. Therefore the publication in journals of the most important case law together with learned comments of scholars is very important for the further development of law.

REFERENCE

Jones, B. and K. Thompson (2002), 'Administrative Law in the United Kingdom', in R. Seerden and F. Stroink (eds), *Administrative Law of the European Union, its Member States and the United States, A Comparative Analysis*, Antwerpen: Intersentia.

9. Towards a new model of criminalization of environmental pollution: the case of Indonesia

Michael Faure

1. INTRODUCTION

Applying the criminal law to environmental pollution has always been problematic, due to the structure of environmental legislation. The basic problem is that environmental interest and values do not enjoy an absolute protection in the law (such as is the case with traditional values protected by the criminal law). Instead most environmental statutes regulate the way in which through pollution environmental values may be endangered by industrial activities. One can understand the basic structure of environmental law for the simple reason that most polluting activities not only cause costs for society, but also generate substantial benefits. That is of course the basic difference with other crimes such as, for example, theft or murder. These activities may cause personal benefits to the criminal, but not for society at large. Thus most of environmental law in many countries is aiming at administrative control of environmental pollution, usually through licensing and permitting systems. Administrative agencies decide on the permitted degree of environmental pollution.

This basic structure of environmental law also has its importance for the structure of environmental criminal law. Indeed, there is a strong interweaving of administrative and criminal law since most environmental statutes reveal that authorities generally only punish the lack of a permit, or a violation of emission standards. This is referred to as the administrative dependence on environmental criminal law. However, although this administrative dependence on the criminal law may have been the general starting point of environmental criminal law when it originated in the second half of the last century, increasingly legal doctrine has pointed at serious weaknesses in this administrative dependence. Indeed, if the role of the criminal law is limited to punishing administrative disobedience, this may seriously limit the scope of criminal law and hence its practical value in protecting ecological values. This legal doctrine, criticizing the absolute dependence of the criminal law upon administrative law, has also had its effects in legislation and in international conventions. Therefore one can now increasingly observe an increasing use of other models of criminalization of environmental pollution, which are less dependent on administrative law.

The goal of this chapter is to explain not only the major weaknesses of too absolute a dependence of environmental criminal law upon administrative law, but also to show that an effective environmental criminal law needs a combination of various provisions in order to enable it to provide an adequate remedy against environmental pollution and thus to contribute to sustainable development. This chapter will moreover show that these new insights from legal doctrine and the trends in some international conventions can be very fruitful for the debate on the reform of environmental criminal law, more particularly in developing countries. Thus, this point will be shown by using the case of Indonesia as an example. The Indonesian Environmental Management Act of 1997 will therefore be studied in more detail, whereby attention will of course more particularly be given to the provisions with respect to material environmental criminal law. It will be shown that some of these provisions, which largely depart from an ideal model of criminalization of environmental pollution, are problematic in the sense that they cannot contribute to an effective remedy against environmental pollution. Hence, alternative formulations will be suggested.

The reader should, however, understand that the case of Indonesia is chosen only to provide a specific example of legislation and to make the recommendations of the theoretical model more lively and clear. Moreover, focusing on a specific case also has the advantage that one can clearly show the implications of the theoretical model for practical legislative work. The theoretical recommendations can in other words be implemented at the policy level as well. This chapter, however, by no means wishes to imply that the provisions in the Indonesian Environmental Management Act of 1997 in relation to criminal law are particularly problematic in comparison to other legislations. One could as easily have given examples from other environmental statutes in developing countries and also from developed countries. There too one might initially find too strong a dependence upon administrative law, with subsequent ineffectiveness as a consequence. Providing the specific example of Indonesia may have the advantage of on the one hand showing the Indonesian policy-maker how legislation may be improved, benefiting from some theoretical insights. On the other hand it may equally show lawyers and policy-makers in other (developing) countries how insights from the literature can be used to reform their legislation.

The chapter is set up as follows: after this introduction I will first briefly address the concept of the administrative dependence of environmental criminal law (Section 2) and then discuss the problems that may occur as a result of too absolute an administrative dependence of environmental criminal law (Section 3). Next a new model for the protection of the environment through criminal law will be presented, taking into account insights from legal doctrine (Section 4) and it will be shown that some of these new insights are already being applied in legislation and more particularly in a recent Convention of the Council of Europe on the Protection of the Environment through Criminal Law (Section 5). Then I will turn to the case of Indonesia and discuss the provisions concerning criminal law in the Environmental Management Act and compare them with the model (Section 6). A few suggestions for alternative provisions will be formulated (Section 7) as well as a few concluding remarks (Section 8).

2. ADMINISTRATIVE DEPENDENCE OF ENVIRONMENTAL CRIMINAL LAW

As was made clear in the introduction there is a strong relationship between administrative law and environmental criminal law. Indeed, it is usually pollution without a permit or the violation of permit conditions (or other obligations), which is criminalized. Therefore environmental criminal law in many countries was characterized as 'administratively dependent'.[1] Administrative law therefore largely provides the norms which individuals and corporations have to obey. Often the criminal law is limited to a disposition at the end of a particular administrative environmental law holding that he who violates the provisions of this statute shall be punished with a particular sanction.

One consequence of this structure of environmental criminal law is that ecological values are not directly protected through the criminal law. Indeed, (even grave) pollution of, for example, soil or water is not always punishable. This will only be the case if this act constitutes at the same time a violation of an administrative obligation. Administrative dependence therefore limits the scope to criminalize pollution directly. Moreover, this administrative dependence also has as the consequence that it will be the administrative authorities that receive large competences to determine the punishable nature of certain polluting acts. Indeed, administrative authorities define the conditions of a permit and with that they effectively also determine the conditions for crimi-

---

[1] This administrative dependence of the criminal law has especially been studied in German legal doctrine. It was there known under the notion 'Verwaltungsakzessorietät'. On this topic see more particularly the dissertation of Winkelbauer (1985).

nal liability. Therefore some have held that as a result of this administrative dependence the criminal law loses some of its autonomy since the intervention of the criminal law is only possible in case of a violation of administrative obligations.[2]

In that sense one can clearly notice that the structure of environmental criminal law is quite different from the structure of the traditional crimes which protect individual values like life, health or property. Violations or endangerments of these traditional individual interests and values are directly criminalized without an intervention of administrative authorities. Therefore some scholars have held that a consequence of the administrative dependence of environmental criminal law is that the legal interest protected by law in this case is not the environment as such. The environment is indeed only protected to the extent that administrative law actually provides it. Each case of environmental pollution will not automatically be criminalized; this will only be the case if a certain act equally constitutes a violation of an administrative obligation.[3]

3. PROBLEMS WITH THE ABSOLUTE ADMINISTRATIVE DEPENDENCE OF ENVIRONMENTAL CRIMINAL LAW

3.1. Too Limited Protection of the Environment

There has been some debate in the literature on whether or not this model is directed at protecting environmental values. To some extent one could indeed argue that the only value that is protected in case of administrative dependence, is the interest of the administrative authority in the proper enforcement of the environmental law.[4] However, it is now more widely accepted that these administrative statutes, especially as far as they lay down emission limit values, are also directed at the protection of the environment. Therefore a criminal provision punishing a violation of these administrative rules also aims at the protection of the environment, albeit in an indirect way. Therefore it is now usually held that, for example, the criminal provision punishing anyone who operates a chemical plant without a licence is also directed at

---

2 This was traditionally the case in many legal systems. For a good comparative overview in that respect see *inter alia* Prabhu (1994, pp. 699–728).

3 See for instance De Nauw (1994, p. 84).

4 Compare Hendriks and Wöretshofer (1995, pp. 29 and 31–2); Buiting (1993, pp. 32–4) as well as Waling.

protecting ecological values in an indirect way.[5] Indeed, operating such a plant without a licence might endanger the protected interest, being a clean environment. However, since the criminal law applies irrespective of any specific damage or threat of harm to the environment it is said that these provisions punish the abstract endangerment of the environment.[6] Although the goal of the criminal law provision can indirectly be the protection of the environment, this is not clear from the way these provisions are formulated and operate. Indeed, the criminal law applies as soon as the administrative provision (for instance, in the form of an emission limit value in a licence) has been violated, whether or not this causes harm to the environment.

In sum: if administrative provisions/obligations are fulfilled no protection will be granted through the criminal law. If on the other hand administrative obligations have not been determined at all the protection cannot be granted through the criminal law either. With this model of absolute administrative dependence of environmental criminal law one therefore has the impression that it is administrative interests rather than ecological values that are protected.

3.2. Example: Bayer-case

The provisions with an absolute administrative dependence of environmental criminal law can thus hardly be effective in providing an adequate protection of ecological values. Indeed, since they do not directly aim at the protection of the environment, they can be considered ineffective in the sense that on the one hand criminal liability will be applied even if no environmental damage has occurred (which is essential in a model of abstract endangerment), whereas on the other hand as long as no administrative rule has been violated no penalty will apply even if substantial environmental harm occurs.[7]

This disadvantage became apparent in a famous Antwerp case against Bayer. Some employees of Bayer were prosecuted before the Antwerp Criminal Court for having emitted waste water without a licence. It concerned emissions of titanium dioxide into the surface waters. There was no valid licence and therefore there was a prosecution for the violation of the prohibition to emit waste water without a licence. The court, however, held that Bayer was not to blame since there was no licence due to administrative error. Therefore the employees of Bayer were acquitted, without the question having ever been asked whether or not the Bayer's emissions as such had an illegal or polluting

---

5 Hendriks and Wöretshofer (1995, pp. 16–19).

6 Buiting (1993, pp. 1103–6) and Waling (1990, pp. 24 and 58).

7 See Faure and Visser (1995, p. 325).

character.[8] This court decision has been heavily critized in the literature, but it clearly shows a major disadvantage of a legal system that bases its environmental protection through the criminal law merely on the violation of administrative rules. If the system is only based on a violation of administrative rules there will be no environmental protection from the criminal law if, for no matter what reason, an administrative violation cannot be proven and environmental pollution nevertheless takes place.[9]

3.3. Farewell to Administrative Dependence of the Criminal Law?

From the above it follows that it is inevitably necessary to find other solutions than the absolute administrative dependence of environmental criminal law. However, this does not necessarily mean that one should immediately abandon any link between environmental criminal law and administrative law. Indeed, this link may even have certain advantages. First of all, administrative dependence has the advantage that it respects the *lex certa* principle which follows from the principle of legality in criminal law. This holds that the legislator should prescribe the criminalized behaviour as precisely as possible. In case the legislator punishes violation of administrative norms (for example, conditions in a permit) usually the criminalized behaviour will *ex ante* be relatively clear.[10] However, one should also realize that referring to a permit may not always be the ideal way of criminalizing pollution since permit conditions can be vague and ambiguous.

Secondly, one can hold that to some extent a link with administrative law is indispensable since the alternative of simply criminalizing 'pollution' would be too broad and vague. In that case (if such a broad definition were to be used) it would no longer be clear *ex ante* which behaviour is criminalized and which is not. The example is given that it would not be useful to criminalize for instance 'the one who would have contributed to climate change'. The impossibility of proving a causal link between certain behaviour and the criminalized result would render such a provision inapplicable in practice.[11]

Moreover, the formulation of obligation in administrative law may also contribute to making more precise the concept of unlawfulness in environmental criminal law. Indeed, one can hope that it is probably the administrative authority who is best situated to determine whether a specific form of pollution is lawful or not. Indeed, administrative authorities may be far better qualified (given their expertise and thus their information advantage) than the

8 Court of Appeals of Antwerp, 7th Chamber, 6 April 1989, unpublished.

9 Faure (1990, pp. 78–9).

10 See De Nauw (1994, p. 85).

11 In this respect, see more particularly the French scholar Robert (1994, pp. 954–5).

judge in a criminal court to determine which type of pollution should be considered unlawful and which not. And this information advantage of administrative authorities is thus a strong argument in favour of some link between administrative and environmental criminal law.

Fourthly, one can hold that retaining some relationship between administrative law and environmental criminal law is indispensable because of the principle of the 'unity of the legal order'. Taken literally this would mean that a judge in a criminal court could only consider a behaviour as unlawful when that behaviour has also been considered as unlawful by administrative law. This may take the principle too far. However, there is some truth in the fact that a complete abandonment of the link between administrative and environmental criminal law would have as a consequence that in theory a certain form of pollution could be authorized under an administrative permit whereas the judge could later nevertheless punish an individual for the same type of pollution which was first allowed by administrative authorities. This would violate the idea of the unity of the legal order. It means basically that the legal order should show one face towards the citizens and the public at large. It cannot be that when a certain behaviour is allowed by administrative authorities that another branch of government (the judge in a criminal court) would nevertheless prohibit the same behaviour.

3.4. Towards a more Limited Administrative Dependence of the Criminal Law?

A consequence of the previous ideas is that probably some link between environmental criminal law and administrative law should be retained. The primary decision on the admissibility of certain polluting acts should remain with administrative authorities, of course, within the limits set by law and respecting general principles of administrative law. There is, moreover, almost no legal system where the link between administrative law and environmental criminal law has been completely abandoned. From the citizen's perspective it would also be strange if the judge in a criminal court inflicted a sanction for a behaviour that was first allowed by the administrative authorities. The consequence of these ideas is that the administrative dependence of environmental criminal law is apparently unavoidable. It can, however, be amended and limited. Indeed, the Bayer case clearly showed the shortcomings of too absolute an administrative dependence of the criminal law.

One way of improving environmental criminal law would be to criminalize unlawful emissions instead of merely criminalizing the non-respect of administrative obligations. This system has the advantage that when administrative obligations are lacking (as in the Bayer case) the emission remains unlawful and remedy by the criminal law remains possible.

Moreover, one should also consider abandoning completely the administrative dependence of environmental criminal law in serious cases, more particularly when the pollution constitutes an endangerment of human life or health. In that case one can hold that pollution should be criminalized even though it might be covered by a permit. The reason is that administrative law also holds that a permit is never a blank cheque allowing endangerments of human life or health. Hence, limiting administrative dependence to specific situations (where human life or health is not endangered) is in conformity with administrative law. Thus, this more limited form of administrative dependence of environmental criminal law would lead us towards a new model for the protection of the environment through the criminal law whereby a variety of provisions would be introduced which have to be combined in order to reach an optimal protection of the environment through the criminal law.

4. TOWARDS A NEW MODEL FOR THE PROTECTION OF THE ENVIRONMENT THROUGH THE CRIMINAL LAW

Different types of criminal provisions seem necessary to protect the environment, all with a different goal. Hence, an adequate protection of the environment through criminal law requires a combination of different types of provisions. The ideas that will be developed here follow from a legal doctrine concerning environmental criminal law that has been developed in Germany especially in the 1980s.[12] According to this legal doctrine an effective environmental criminal law needs a combination of the penalizing of the abstract endangerment of the environment, the concrete endangerment of the environment as well as the independent crime for when pollution has serious consequences.

4.1. Abstract Endangerment

The notion of abstract endangerment refers to the fact that within this model the criminal provision usually does not punish environmental pollution directly. In this model the criminal law is an addition to a prior system of administrative decisions concerning the amount and quality of emissions into the environment. Indeed, most systems of administrative law are based on administrative statutes regulating the conditions under which the administrative authorities can allow environmental pollution. Crucial within these

12 For an overview see more particularly Heine (1994, pp. 731–59).

administrative statutes are the so-called emission standards or emission limit values that fix the amount of a certain compound that can be emitted into the environment. These emission limit values can be laid down in general legislation, which is widely applicable to the whole industry; they can also be specific for a certain branch of industry or, as is usually the case, they can be laid down in individual licences. A combination of the three systems can be found as well.[13] Within this system the role of criminal law usually limits itself to the enforcement of prior administrative decisions that are taken. A distinction may indeed be made between a dependency upon general administrative rules and principles (Verwaltungsrechtsakzessorietät) and the dependency upon individual decisions of administrative agencies (Verwaltungaktsakzessorietät).[14]

In these types of provisions, protection under criminal law is usually provided in one article at the end of an administrative statute. Such an article states generally that everyone who violates the provisions of the act, regulation or the licences issued pursuant thereto will be punished with a specific sanction. In some cases it is, in addition, specifically stated that anyone who operates without a licence or violates the conditions of a licence is criminally liable under the specific provision.

It is important to stress that environmental criminal law has usually started with these kinds of provisions, where the criminal law follows prior administrative decisions and punishes abstract endangerment of environmental values. Traditionally criminal law applies in these kinds of cases as soon as the administrative provision (for example, in the form of an emission limit value in a licence) has been violated, whether or not this causes harm to the environment. In some legal systems these abstract endangerments, for instance violations of permit conditions, are not even primarily punished under criminal law, but, for instance, by means of fines under administrative penal law.

In sum: the non-respect of administrative obligations certainly needs to be sanctioned. Some legal remedy needs to be used to guarantee the compliance with important administrative obligations, since these also aim at the avoidance of environmental pollution. However, since in this model the link between the provision and the environmental harm is rather remote, the sanction should not

---

13 For instance in the system of the 1971 Belgian Surface Water Protection Act a subsequent 1976 Royal Decree laid down general emission limit values; but specific Royal Decrees could set separate emission limit values for a certain branch of industry; in addition the administrative authority was empowered to set specific emission limit values within the individual licence; on this system, see Goethals (1991, pp. 87–92).

14 Heine (1990, pp. 2425–34); Heine (1989, pp. 728–32); Heine (1991, pp. 370–8) and Schall (1990, pp. 1265–6). Prabhu refers in this respect to the 'administrative accessoriness of penal law' (Prabhu (1994, p. 708)).

necessarily be very high and in some cases administrative penal law may suffice as a remedy. It is, however, clear that in addition to the penalizing of abstract endangerment an effective environmental criminal law should do something more than merely punishing the non-respect of administrative obligations.

4.2. Concrete Endangerment

Concrete endangerment refers to the fact that, in this case, some kind of an endangerment of environmental values by posing a concrete threat to the environment is a prerequisite for the criminal liability.[15] But in this case, a mere abstract danger that, for example, the illegal operation of a plant might cause danger to the environment is too abstract and therefore insufficient for criminal liability. Usually at least an emission is required. This can indeed lead to a concrete danger for the environment although usually the provisions falling under this model do not require that an actual harm needs to be proven as well. Usually a threat of harm is sufficient.

In addition to this requirement of causing a concrete danger to the environment usually these provisions only lead to criminal liability if a second condition is met, namely that this emission takes place illegally. In a model of absolute administrative dependence, all that needs to be shown is that the act violated administrative rules. In this case, in addition the emission or pollution that can cause a threat of harm needs to be proven. However, as long as the administrative rules are followed usually no criminal liability will follow since the act will not be considered unlawful. This is the major difference with the subsequent model, to be discussed below, in which criminal liability can occur even if administrative requirements were formally met. The major difference with a model of absolute administrative dependence is also that problems, as in the Bayer case discussed above, can be avoided by a criminal provision, aiming at concrete endangerment. Indeed, even if there is no administrative regulatory framework that has been violated, criminal liability can apply in this case since the emission can still be illegal. In such circumstances, no criminal liability would occur under a traditional model of abstract endangerment, merely aiming at the enforcement of prior administrative decisions.

Examples of this model can be found, for example, in the Dutch Article 173a and 173b of the 'Wetboek van Strafrecht' (Penal Code), the German § 324 of the 'Strafgesetzbuch' (StGB) (Criminal Code)[16] and Belgian case law

---

[15] Buiting (1993, pp. 28–9); Hendriks and Wöretshofer (1995) and Waling (1990).

[16] One could argue about the precise characterization of this provision. In its statutory form it has been shaped as an 'Erfolgsdelikt' since a certain consequence,

concerning Article 2 of the Surface Water Protection Act of 1971. Interestingly enough there has also been a historic evolution whereby the criminal law protection of the environment started with criminal law provisions at the end of administrative acts. A shift could be noted in the 1980s when, for example, Germany introduced a whole paragraph on environmental crimes in 1980 through its 18e 'Strafrechtsänderungsgesetz'[17] and the Netherlands substantially changed its environmental law provisions in the Penal Code in 1989.[18] Also the Belgian case law punishing emissions into surface waters, even in the absence of administrative violations, dates from the late 1980s. This new model can therefore in some way be seen as a reaction of legislators and judges wishing to provide more direct protection to environmental values.

This type of provision, in which simply the unlawful concrete endangerment of the environment (through emissions) is penalized has the major advantage that one does not merely focus on the non-respect of administrative obligations. This equally means that if administrative obligations are lacking (as in the Bayer case), criminal law can nevertheless intervene since an unlawful endangerment of the environment (through emission) might have taken place.

4.3. Independent Crime for Pollution with Serious Consequences

A third type of criminal provision directly punishes some cases of very serious pollution. In fact, this model also punishes emissions, but the consequences are of a more serious nature, namely, long-lasting pollution, serious consequences for the health of persons and/or a significant risk of injuries to the population. The main difference between this model and the others discussed so far is that the linkage between criminal law and prior administrative decisions can now be left aside totally. Under this type of provision, serious environmental pollution can be punished even if the defendant has complied with the conditions of his licence. The underlying notion is that the administrative regulation never allowed this specific risk or harm. These are therefore cases where the veil of the famous dependency of the administrative law is pierced.

---

water pollution, has to be reached. Through a broad interpretation of case law, the endangerment of water quality already leads to criminal liability. Heine therefore even classifies § 324 as an abstract endangerment provision (Heine 1987, p. 78). On this classification problem, see also Rogall (1988, pp. 518–20), who calls § 324 StGB a 'potential endangerment' crime.

17 See on the topic Faure (1991, pp. 320–3); see on the practical importance of this change Meinberg (1988, pp. 112–57) and Heine (1994, pp. 731–59).

18 Waling (1990).

Examples of this model are still relatively rare. A classic example is § 330a of the German Criminal Code that punishes the endangerment of human life or health through the emission of toxic substances. In addition, in some countries it has been advanced in the literature that in order to provide a truly autonomous protection of ecological values, serious attacks on the environment should be punishable even if these would be allowed under an administrative licence. Therefore, for example, in the Flemish region a proposal has been made by an Interuniversity Commission for the Reform of the Environmental Law in Flanders to introduce a new article within a Decree on environmental policy that would punish cases of serious pollution irrespective of administrative law. This proposed Article 7.3.4 punishes anyone who emits substances into the water, soil or air if he/she knew or should have known that these emissions pose a concrete danger to human health.[19] A similar tendency to criminalize serious environmental pollution even though the conditions of the licence were followed, can be found in international documents. For instance, in the Council of Europe Convention for the Protection of the Environment through Criminal Law the signatory States agree to adopt measures to criminalize the intentional discharge which causes or creates a significant risk of death or serious injury to any person.[20] It should thus be noted that there is an international tendency to limit the justificative effect of a licence if the defendant knowingly caused serious harm to the environment.[21]

Moreover, one could think of provisions totally unrelated to environmental law or to emissions into the environment that punish the one who causes bodily harm to another. Most Penal Codes have provisions punishing the one who negligently or intentionally caused injuries to another, unrelated to whether or not these injuries were caused through emissions into the environment. Again, in most legal systems these provisions still apply even if the defendant followed the conditions of a licence.[22]

In sum this independent crime for serious pollution, of which several examples also exist, focuses again on emissions, but in this case on emissions that may in addition concretely endanger human health. The major difference with the model previously discussed is that unlawfulness is no longer required.

---

19 See Art. 7.3.4 Voorontwerp Decreet Milieubeleid, Brugge, Die Keure, 1995, 82 and see Roef (1995, p. 505). We will discuss this provision further below in Section 7.4.

20 See Article 2a of the Convention, which will be further discussed in the next section.

21 See Resolution 10 of the XVth International Congress of Penal Law, *International Review of Penal Law*, 1995, p. 50.

22 Heine (1986, p. 83).

That is why one can understand that these provisions really focus on cases of serious pollution where a concrete danger to human health is caused. In that case it is clear that under administrative law the licence would not have granted protection either.

4.4. An Optimal Combination of Various Provisions

From a historic perspective it seems fair to state, in general, that there has been an evolution from the model of abstract endangerment to the punishment of concrete endangerments, and an increasing focus on serious pollution even independently of administrative law. The protection of the environment under criminal law began, in most cases, with criminal provisions that were annexed to environmental statutes of a highly administrative nature (abstract endangerment). The disadvantage of this type of criminal provision is that there is usually no direct protection of ecological values. As a result of increasing environmental awareness, one could therefore notice a shift in many legal systems in the 1980s and 1990s to the criminalization of the concrete endangerment of ecological values. To show the importance of environmental crimes some countries have, moreover, incorporated these provisions in criminal codes. These provisions aim at a more direct protection of ecological values, but still keep the relationship with administrative law to some extent intact. Indeed, it is not possible to obtain protection under criminal law if the defendant has complied with the conditions of administrative regulations. Precisely for that reason, one can observe a tendency in legal doctrine and (sometimes) legislation to punish, under criminal law, certain cases of serious pollution notwithstanding compliance with the conditions of a licence.

At the policy level the strength and weaknesses of the various models show that an effective environmental criminal law really needs a combination of these various types of provisions. The penalization of abstract endangerment, merely focusing on the non-respect of administrative obligations, is certainly important and necessary. However, the weakness of these provisions is that they apply even if no ecological harm or danger exists. Moreover, they cannot provide an adequate protection if there is no violation of existing administrative rules because of the too strong relationship with administrative law and the too high dependency on administrative decisions.[23] In that respect the provisions merely penalizing the non-respect of administrative obligations (which remain necessary) need to be complemented with provisions aiming at the concrete endangerment of the environment. This can be done by penalizing unlawful emissions. However, in this case, the conditions of an adminis-

[23] Faure and Visser (1995, p. 358).

trative licence will still have a justificative effect. But the protection granted to the environment by the judge is already far more autonomous since it is not limited to the penalization of non-respect of administrative obligations. Finally the system needs to be complemented with an independent crime applicable to serious pollution if a concrete danger to human life or health exists. Only in this case the interdependence of environmental criminal law and administrative law is entirely abandoned.

The choice of a specific model of criminalization obviously also has consequences for the way a violation can be proven and the possibilities of a countercheck. Usually the way samples are to be taken and counterchecked is only regulated in detail in provisions aiming at abstract endangerment. Judicial discretion is much larger when it comes, for example, to establishing whether or not there was concrete endangerment of the environment or human health. Once more the judge can to a large extent rely on expertise, but there is a much larger scope for the truly 'judging' function of the Criminal Court than in case of a violation of merely technical provisions.

Although one would therefore also expect that the guarantees of the defence and appropriate judicial protection would best be provided in models where judicial discretion is greatest, this need not necessarily be the case. In such circumstances, the methods of proving environmental pollution are not regulated and although the judge might aim at true protection of ecological values by restricting criminal liability to situations where these values have really been endangered, in legal practice one cannot be certain that it will turn out that way. In that respect the question arises whether, even if one shifts in the direction of models that aim more directly at the protection of ecological values by criminalizing concrete endangerment, this should not be accompanied by clear legal rules, for example, guaranteeing a right of countercheck.[24]

This characterization of the different roles of the judge in the various models does not necessarily mean on a normative level that this should lead to a preference for a specific model. Indeed, in the case of criminalization of abstract endangerment, there is control by the judiciary as well, but it plays a role at the procedural level, by controlling whether the procedural guarantees concerning, for instance, the way samples were taken, were met. In the other models there is – in theory – more room for independent consideration of the pollution problem. This might lead to more adequate protection of ecological values and a better balancing of the interests of the defendant.[25]

---

24 On the importance of procedural guarantees, see Heine (1995, pp. 63–71).

25 For further details see Faure and Visser (1995, pp. 360–1).

5. APPLICATION: COUNCIL OF EUROPE CONVENTION

5.1. Applying the New Model

We have just shown that there is an historical evolution in the legislation of many countries from provisions which merely aim at penalizing non-respect of administrative obligations to more ecological crimes, where penalization is also possible even if administrative obligations have not been violated. The legal doctrine which pursued the above-mentioned model consisting of a combination of various provisions apparently had influence at the international level. Indeed on 4 November 1998 the Council of Europe adopted a Convention on the Protection of the Environment through Criminal Law.[26] In this Convention, the various signatory states agreed to adopt specific provisions to protect the environment in their criminal law. It hence contains minimum provisions on environmental criminal law. Interestingly, many of the ideas presented above can be found in this convention, more particularly the three types of provisions mentioned above.

5.2. Concrete Endangerment

The core is – not surprisingly – a concrete endangerment crime which can be found in Article 2. This article lists a long list of behaviours that the signatory states will criminalize on the basis of their national law. Article 2(1b) refers to:

> The unlawful discharge, emission or introduction of a quantity of substances or ionising radiation into air, soil or water, which causes or is likely to cause their lasting deterioration or death or serious injury to any person or substantial damage to protected monuments, other protected objects, property, animals or plants.

Here one recognizes clearly the concrete endangerment crime. It is the unlawful emission which is penalized. This provision goes, as was mentioned above, much further than provisions which would merely aim at penalizing the non-respect of administrative obligations.

5.3. Independent Crime

However, the Convention also goes a step further and has in Article 2.1(a) also an independent crime aiming at serious pollution:

---

[26] The text has *inter alia* been published in Faure and Heine (2000, pp. 407–16) and is also available on the Internet at the following address: http://www.coe.fr/eng/legaltxt/172ehtm.

> The discharge, emission or introduction of a quantity of substances or ionising radiation into air, soil or water, which:
> causes death or serious injury to any person, or
> creates a significant risk of causing death or serious injury to any person

Note that in this particular case, when the emission has these serious consequences of creating death, serious injury or a significant risk of death or serious injury, the unlawfulness requirement is abandoned. This is hence a truly independent crime, in the sense that this provision applies irrespective of the violation of administrative obligations. The idea is apparently that emissions that cause death/serious injury or create a significant risk of such damage can never be justified under administrative law.

5.4. Abstract Endangerment

Finally the Council of Europe Convention also has the traditional abstract endangerment provisions, but they – logically – occupy a less important place in the Convention. More particularly Article 4 refers *inter alia* to:

> d The unlawful operation of a plant

Note, however, that in this particular case it holds:

> Each party shall adopt such appropriate measures as may be necessary to establish as criminal offences or administrative offences, liable to sanctions or other measures under its domestic law

The drafters of the conventions clearly recognize that in the case of abstract endangerment, ecologic values are not endangered in the same way as with a concrete endangerment. In this case Member States can rely on administrative offences.

Although this Council of Europe Convention has not yet entered into force, it is an instrument that truly demonstrates a new attitude towards environmental criminal law. If environmental criminal law really wants to play an important role in supporting sustainable development, it should not limit itself to sanctioning administrative obligations, but criminal law should grant more direct protection to ecological values. This has been realized in the Council of Europe Convention, which also refers to unlawful emissions and even recognizes truly independent crimes in the case of pollution which has serious consequences.

6. INDONESIAN ENVIRONMENTAL MANAGEMENT ACT

6.1. Chapter IX

Let us now address in more detail the provisions that can be found in the Indonesian Environmental Management Act,[27] in which many criminal provisions can be found in Chapter IX that deals with criminal provisions. The reason we want to address the criminal provisions in the Indonesian Environmental Management Act in further detail is, as we made clear in the Introduction, to show how the ideal model we have just developed in Section 4 above (with an application in Section 5) compares to the criminal provisions that can be found in the legislation of a particular country like Indonesia. Moreover, by making this comparison, we can also show that at least at a theoretical level, there can be some flaws or weaknesses in certain provisions, which might be remedied.

When one looks at Chapter IX of the Environmental Management Act one is struck by the large number of relatively detailed provisions and the high number of sanctions that are threatened. Moreover, Article 48 provides that all the criminal acts provided for in that chapter are crimes.

However, when the provisions, are examined in more detail, many of the problems that we have discussed above concerning the effectiveness of environmental criminal law become apparent. It is indeed to be feared that some of the provisions contain specific conditions or elements that may make them very hard to apply and therefore rather inadequate at providing good protection to ecological values and interests. Let us go over some of these provisions in further detail, looking at some weaknesses and address how they could be remedied, and if those provisions are necessary at all.

6.2. Article 41(1)

A first provision is Article 41(1) that stipulates that:

> Any person who in contravention of the law intentionally carries out an action which results in environmental pollution and/or damage, is criminally liable to. . . .

After that rather high imprisonment (of 10 years) and a fine of 500 million rupiah follows.

---

[27] Law of the Republic of Indonesia No. 23 of 1997 regarding environmental management.

A first problem with this provision is of course that intent is required. Experience in many countries has shown that as soon as the legislator requires intent as far as environmental pollution is concerned, the provision immediately becomes extremely difficult to apply. The question indeed arises what intent means in the specific context of environmental pollution. Of course one can argue that this is not such a problem since Article 42 refers to a situation where a person has acted with negligence. However, as we will show below, some of the same flaws apply to the situation of negligence as well.

A second issue is that the provision looks extremely severe, by threatening severe punishment, but in fact the provision can only be applied to 'any person who in contravention of the law' intentionally carries out an action which results in environmental pollution and/or damage. In other words, in this case there is total dependence on administrative law. As such, one could still understand, as we have explained above, that a relationship with administrative law remains in existence, which certainly can be defended in this case. The major weakness of this provision, however, lies in a third problem.

The provision will probably be totally inapplicable since it requires a certain result to be achieved, namely that the action 'results in environmental pollution and/or damage'. The literature has generally held that these kinds of provision are quite problematic since they require the public prosecutor to prove that a certain action or emission resulted in environmental pollution. To prove such a result will be a very difficult task for the prosecutor. Indeed, it requires that the prosecutor proves that there is a causal relationship between the action which has been carried out intentionally in contravention of the law and the pollution or damage. This means that the criminal law only intervenes at a very late stage and in other words only protects ecological values or interests when it is already too late, that is, when environmental pollution has occurred. It would be better, as we have explained above, to focus on the punishment of endangerment. This allows the criminal law to intervene at an earlier stage, when ecological values are merely endangered, without necessarily having resulted in environmental pollution. Moreover, if pollution and/or damage is required, the defendant can always argue that his illegal acts alone have not caused the pollution, but that others may have contributed to this result as well.

In sum, this provision may play some role, but it will be extremely difficult to apply. Given its focus on intent, unlawfulness and environmental pollution, it can effectively only be applied in exceptional cases where someone intentionally breaches the law and where it is clear that his or her action has resulted in environmental pollution and/or damage. These cases may be very rare and therefore this provision is certainly not capable of catching the major cases of environmental pollution where someone simply violates the conditions of a licence and therefore emits illegally into soil, water or air. We will therefore have to look whether a provision aiming at the punishment of unlawful emissions is also available.

6.3. Article 41(2)

Article 41(2) goes a lot further by providing that:

> If a criminal action as provided for in (1) above causes the death or serious injury of a person, the person who carried out the criminal action is criminally liable to a maximum imprisonment of 15 years and a maximum fine of 750 million rupiah.

Again one notices a seemingly extremely severe criminal provision with even higher sanctions for a case where the actions discussed above lead to the death or serious injury of a person. This looks at first sight like an independent crime aimed at pollution with serious consequences. The latter is definitely true, in that if the pollution has serious consequences (death or serious injury) more severe sanctions apply. However, it is unfortunately not at all an independent crime, since it will apply only if the person acted 'in contravention of the law'. Moreover, the other conditions discussed above, namely intent and that the action has to result in environmental pollution and/or damage, will also have to be fulfilled.

This is therefore rather strange. It means that even if one caused environmental pollution leading to death or serious injury, this will lead to criminal liability only in the case where one has acted 'in contravention of the law'. The truly independent crime, as we showed also in the example of the Council of Europe Convention, would mean that if an environmental crime (for instance, concrete endangerment) also brings about the risk of serious consequences it should apply independently of administrative law. Otherwise no autonomous protection is granted where environmental pollution has serious consequences. Therefore Article 41(2) is again very difficult to apply and surely no independent crime. If the legislator wished to introduce such an independent crime, a different provision could be chosen, more in line with the provisions of the Council of Europe Convention.

6.4. Article 42(1)

Article 42(1) of the Environmental Management Act refers to the situation where environmental pollution was caused not with intent but negligently. It should probably be a copy of Article 41(1) (although it is accidentally wrongly drafted), but then the negligent version of Article 41(1). Thus Article 42(1) reads:

> Any person who due to their negligence performs an action that causes environmental pollution and/or damage, is criminally liable to a maximum imprisonment of 3 years and a maximum fine of rp. 100 million.

It is good legislative practice to make a distinction between a situation where the actor acts negligently or with intent. Logically a higher sanction should threaten in the case of wilful polluting acts. In other legislations also, many examples can be advanced of such a model.

Since Article 42(1) is supposed to be a copy of Article 41(1) the same problems will arise with respect to the requirement that a certain action has caused environmental pollution and/or damage. There is, however, a more serious issue at stake, namely that the legislator apparently forgot to add an unlawfulness requirement in Article 42(1). The result is that when someone acts intentionally this intentional act is according to Article 41(1) only punishable when the person involved acted 'in contravention of the law', whereas this requirement is omitted in Article 42(1). That would mean that if the pollution is caused with negligence there would be an independent crime, whereas there would be administrative dependence in case of intent. It is apparently not a mistake in the English translation of the Environmental Management Act, since the same appears in the Indonesian text. Indonesian experts hold that it must have been a mistake of the legislator. It is surely one that needs urgent repair since the effect of course is that now the threshold for punishing negligent behaviour is lower than for punishing intentional behaviour, which is hardly logical.

Article 42(2) is a copy of Article 41(2) in that a more serious sanction applies if the act provided for in Article 42(1) causes the death or serious injury of a person. Hence we can refer to the discussion above of Article 41(2).

6.5. Article 43

Article 43 contains a variety of different provisions, the most important being Article 43(1) which specifies:

> Any person who in violation of applicable legislation, intentionally releases or disposes of substances, energy and/or other components which are toxic or hazardous on to or into land, into the atmosphere or the surface of water, imports, exports, trades in, transports, stores such materials, operates a dangerous installation, whereas knowing or with good reason to suppose that the action concerned can give rise to environmental pollution and/or damage or endanger public health or the life of another person, is criminally liable to a maximum of 6 years imprisonment and a maximum fine of rp. 300 million.

Again this provision suffers from the same flaws as the previous ones. There is again an unlawfulness requirement, since the person will only be criminally liable if he acted ‘in violation of applicable legislation’. Hence, there is full administrative dependence and the provision cannot be applied if there is no ‘applicable legislation’. Secondly, intent is again required, which seems odd. If someone violates applicable legislation by releasing toxic or hazardous substances, why should that only lead to criminal liability in case of intent?

Thirdly, what ‘toxic or hazardous’ substances are is not further defined in the Environmental Management Act. Usually a substance is only considered toxic when certain thresholds are passed. Hence, this provision may be hard to apply if no further definition of these issues is given. Moreover, the provision contains another condition which may make it very hard to apply, namely that the person should have acted knowingly or with good reason to suppose that the action concerned could give rise to environmental pollution and/or damage. This means that not only the release of the substance has to be intentional, but that it is in addition required that the person should know or should have known that the action could have had harmful consequences. That may of course make such a provision difficult to apply in practice.

The problem is also that when one looks carefully at this provision it is not very clear what the precise nature of the provision is. On the one hand, it seems to aim at preventing abstract endangerment, by requiring the violation of applicable legislation, but on the other hand, there are so many additional conditions that make it impossible to intervene when there is merely a threat of environmental pollution, for example, in case of the operation of a dangerous installation. Note that according to Article 43(1) the operation of a dangerous installation only leads to criminal liability when this is done in violation of applicable legislation and where the specific knowledge requirement is met as well. Thus the provision seems rather to aim at concrete endangerment of the environment, but then it is strange that it only intervenes if all of these additional strict conditions are met. Hence, this provision may not be a very adequate remedy against environmental pollution either.

In addition Article 43(2) renders someone criminally liable if intentionally false information is provided and Article 43(3) again provides for more severe punishments if the actions caused the death or serious injury of a person.

6.6. Articles 44–46

Moreover, Article 44(1) specifies that any person who ‘in violation of applicable legislative provisions, because of their carelessness performs an action as in article 42 is criminally liable to imprisonment for a maximum of 3 years and a maximum fine of rp. 100 million’.

The meaning of this article is totally unclear, since Article 42 itself already aims at the person who through his negligence would cause environmental pollution. There we exactly pointed at the weakness that this provision has no unlawfulness requirements. There is an unlawfulness requirement in Article 44(1), but it would be more logical to amalgamate the two.

The chapter on criminal provisions also contains articles on criminal responsibility of legal entities (Articles 45 and 46) and specific sanctions in case of environmental crime (Article 47) but these will not be discussed any further at this stage.

6.7. In sum

If we thus envisage the overview of available criminal sanctions in the Environmental Management Act in Indonesia, the problem is that there are on the one hand many provisions, but on the other hand they are so ill structured and contain so many heavy conditions that they can hardly be effectively applied in legal practice. For instance, a simple environmental endangerment crime, holding that anyone who generally violates administrative permits is criminally liable, is lacking. Also a simple concrete endangerment crime, holding anyone who unlawfully emits substances into air, soil or water liable, is lacking as well. There are provisions that are similar but these require the proof of environmental pollution and/or damage. That has the major disadvantage that the criminal law can only intervene when it is too late, namely when the pollution has already occurred. If the criminal law were to aim at emissions, it could intervene at a much earlier stage and thus protect the environment against concrete endangerments and not only intervene when concrete pollution has been caused. Moreover, it is not very likely that proof of pollution or damage could ever be brought by the public prosecutor, given causation problems.

Finally, there is no truly independent crime for pollution with serious consequences either. In every case there is an aggravated circumstance, namely causing death or serious injury, but that again only applies in case of 'violation of applicable legislative provisions'. Hence, it seems that although there are undoubtedly good intentions, the current way in which environmental criminal law is shaped in the Environmental Management Act can hardly provide adequate protection to the environment.

7. AN ALTERNATIVE FORMULATION

7.1. Goal

Having first presented a model of environmental criminal law (Section 4) and its application (Section 5) and having established that the current criminal provisions in the Indonesian Environmental Management Act do not correspond to this model (Section 6), we will now see in what way the provisions concerning material environmental criminal law could be revised in such a way that they could, on the one hand, correspond better to the model and thus, on the other hand, could provide better and more complete protection of the environment through criminal law. Of course the way in which provisions are drafted is also a matter of national culture and tradition. Hence, we do not claim that there is one ideal way of drafting these provisions. However, the analysis in Section 6 made clear that the more conditions one adds to provisions and the more complicated the legislator makes it, the more difficult it will be to apply these provisions. Hence, we will start from the basic framework of the model, holding that an ideal environmental criminal law should contain three types of provisions (abstract endangerment, concrete endangerment and independent crime for pollution with serious consequences). The precise way in which these are shaped can of course depend upon national tradition and culture. However, in order to make the proposals a bit more concrete I will use the example of the Interuniversity Commission for the Reform of Environmental Law in the Flemish Region.[28] This Commission drafted on the request of the Minister of the Environment a new environmental code which also contained proposals on environmental criminal law. These neatly follow the model we have developed in Chapter 4 and also correspond to the provisions of the Convention of the Council of Europe. We will therefore for each category of crimes examine what this Flemish Interuniversity Commission proposed and then see whether we can use the current language of the Indonesian Environmental Management Act to come up with a proposal for the Indonesian case. The reason we present the exercise in this way is that it can hopefully also serve as a model for other countries in search of a new environmental criminal law.

7.2. Concrete Endangerment

The core provisions in the Flemish Draft Environmental Code are, understandably, the ones aiming at concrete endangerment.

As far concrete endangerment is concerned, the Flemish Commission makes a distinction between the case of intent and the case of negligence. The provision referring to intent is formulated as follow:

> Anyone who voluntarily introduces or discharges, either directly or indirectly – in violation of the applicable regulatory provisions or contrary to a license awarded in

[28] See Interuniversity Commission for the Revision of Environmental Law in the Flemish Region, *Draft Decree on Environmental Policy*, pp. 90–5; these provisions are also published in Faure and Heine (2000, pp. 53–74).

> accordance with this decree – substances, micro-organisms, noise and other vibrations or radiations on or into the water, soil or atmosphere, shall be punished. . . .

For the case of negligence the provision is similar, but then refers to 'anyone who, through carelessness or lack of foresight'.

The basic model is again that an emission is punished (aiming at protecting ecological values against concrete endangerment), but only when the emission happens in an unlawful manner. The distinction can thus be made between the case of negligence and intent, but further conditions or requirements should be omitted. In that respect, it should be remembered that any further condition or requirement which is added also has to be proven by the public ministry and thus limits the scope of the provision.

Of course it is a matter of taste what particular language one uses since the language in the Flemish draft differs a bit from the language used in the Environmental Management Act in Indonesia today, but that is more a matter of taste than of principle. If one were to take this Flemish model and combine it with the Indonesian language, a provision aiming at protecting the environment against concrete endangerment might read:

> Any person who intentionally introduces or discharges, either directly or indirectly in contravention of the law substances, micro-organisms, noise and other vibrations or radiations on or into the water, soil or atmosphere, shall be punished. . . .

In case of negligence, using the language from the Indonesian Environmental Management Act the provision might read:

> Any person who through his negligence introduces or discharges either directly or indirectly in contravention of the law substances, micro organisms, noise and other vibrations or radiations on or into the water, soil or atmosphere, shall be punished. . . .

Of course the sanction should be higher in the case of intent than with mere negligence.

This simple provision effectively replaces Articles 41(1), 42(1) and 44 of the current Environmental Management Act, makes it much more practicable and thus provides better protection of the environment. The rights of the citizens are still sufficiently protected as well, since they only risk criminal liability if they have acted 'in contravention of the law'. This, however, is of course broader than the mere violation of administrative provisions or a licence.

7.3. Abstract Endangerment

In addition there should of course also be a provision protecting the environment against abstract endangerment. The Flemish Interuniversity Commission had a very simple solution in that respect and suggested punishing:

> Anyone who infringes the provisions of this decree or of its implementing decisions or infringes the provisions of a license issued in accordance with this decree.

Translated to the situation of Indonesia (more particularly the current language of Article 43 of the Indonesian Environmental Management Act) this would read:

> Any person who infringes the provisions of this act or of its implementing decisions or infringes the provisions of a permit issued in accordance with this act shall be punished by a fine of. . . .

This is a purely administrative dependent provision, whereby the non-respect of administrative obligations is punished. Since no concrete danger for the environment is caused, but a mere abstract danger, a fine would normally be a sufficient deterrent. Moreover, since only a fine is necessary, this would be a provision which could also be handled by administrative fines and where an intervention of the criminal law is not absolutely necessary. The material contents of this provision (the prohibitions) are of course given in administrative law. The addressees of this norm hence know precisely what to do and what not to do on the basis of administrative law.

Of course one could argue that there are some cases where administrative provisions are violated that are so serious that a more stringent sanction should apply, even though there is no concrete endangerment yet. This may be the case when one, for example, trades or transports hazardous or toxic products or waste without a licence or in violation of applicable legislation. If it is considered necessary at the policy level, a specific provision could be made for those cases as well where a sanction slightly higher than the general fine would apply, but less than in the case of concrete endangerment of the environment. One could think of provisions such as:

> Any person who in violation of applicable legislation operates a licensed installation or activity without a license or in violation of the conditions of that license will be punished with. . . .

> Anyone who in violation of applicable legislation or in violation of a license releases waste will be punished with. . . .

> Anyone who:
>
> - violates administrative sanctions or measures imposed by the Court or administrative authorities; and

- who violates the control as organized by this act
  will be punished with. . . .

These provisions would then effectively have replaced Article 43 of the current Environmental Management Act.

7.4. Independent Crime with Serious Consequences

Finally, the closing provision should be an independent crime aimed at pollution with serious consequences. Here one can debate what serious consequences are. The Indonesian legislator has chosen (although with a different legal technique) the situation where pollution causes the death of or serious injury to a person. The disadvantage is that this again requires proof of a causal link between a certain action (pollution) and a consequence (death or injury). The Flemish Interuniversity Commission made the following proposal:

> Anyone who, directly or indirectly, introduces or discharges on or into the water, soil or atmosphere, substances, micro-organisms, noise and other vibrations, or radiations, and is aware, or should have been aware, that to do so constituted a real danger to human health, shall be punished by an imprisonment. . . .

Here one notices that the Flemish Commission does not require proof of pollution (given problems with the causal link), but again simply an emission, as defined above. However, if the consequences are serious, the unlawfulness requirement is left out. The serious consequences are defined as 'a real danger to human health'. The advantage of focusing on 'danger' instead of on 'death or serious injury of a person' is that it is of course much easier to prove that a certain polluting act caused danger to human health than that it actually caused death or injury. Moreover, requiring the proof of death or injury again has the disadvantage that the criminal law only intervenes when it is very late, namely when these consequences have already occurred. Given the fact that this is a very stringent provision (it applies even if the conditions of a permit were respected), the Flemish draft required an additional condition, namely that the person was aware or should have been aware that his act constituted a real danger to human health.

Again, combining the Flemish proposal with the language in the Indonesian Environmental Management Act a proposal might read:

> Any person who directly or indirectly, introduces or discharges on or into the water, soil or atmosphere, substances, micro-organisms, noise and other vibrations, or radiations, while knowing or with good reasons to suppose that the action concerned can constitute a real danger to human health, shall be punished by an imprisonment. . . .

This provision would then effectively replace Articles 41(2), 42(2), 43(3) and 44 (2).

8. CONCLUDING REMARKS

Originally the role of the criminal law in protecting the environment was a rather limited one. Its role was restricted to sanctioning the non-respect of administrative violations. With the increasing role of the criminal law in the fight against environmental pollution, it became clear that this legislative technique provided too narrow a protection of the environment. Thus legal doctrine has been developing alternative models for protecting ecological interests in a more direct and more adequate manner. The way to do so is still to stick principally to the administrative dependence of environmental criminal law, but not to limit the criminal law to the sanctioning of administrative decisions. By focusing on unlawful emissions, a more adequate protection of the environment can be provided. Moreover, in cases where emissions constitute a real danger to human health, the intervention of the criminal law should be necessary even if the conditions of a licence are respected.

Apparently these ideas of (mainly German) legal doctrine have had an influence not only on various (European) legislators, but also on the Council of Europe. Indeed, the recent Council of Europe Convention on the Protection of the Environment through Criminal Law shows again that an adequate environmental criminal law needs a combination of different types of provisions, aiming at different goals and with differing sanctions. Although for Europe this Council of Europe Convention may be a real challenge and one can only wholeheartedly endorse a speedy ratification of it, the question of course arises to what extent this Convention could also play a role in a developing country like Indonesia. We tried to show that it is quite possible to use the basic model, such as it has *inter alia* also been laid down in the draft environmental code presented by the Interuniversity Commission for the Revision of Environmental Law in the Flemish Region, on condition that the language is adapted to national tradition and cultures. Thus we have presented a very basic draft that could perhaps serve as a discussion document for the revision of environmental criminal law in Indonesia.

The basic idea behind this model is that different provisions are used, aiming at different goals (abstract endangerment, concrete endangerment and an independent crime for pollution with serious consequences), whereby the sanction of course increases when ecological values (or human life) are more concretely endangered or violated. This complies with the proportionality requirement. The example also made clear that a model law for environmental criminal law can be relatively simple and should not contain too many conditions. Of course, depending upon national taste and political priorities, some specific provisions may be added for issues of particular importance for a specific country. For instance, one could well imagine that in the case of Indonesia a specific provision would be introduced aiming at anyone who endangers specific habitats or biodiversity, although it may be difficult to formulate such a provision in compliance with the *lex certa* requirement of criminal law.

Moreover, in this chapter we merely focused on the basic environmental criminal law. But other provisions may be needed as well, for instance with respect to sanctions and corporate criminal responsibility. That may be the subject of further collaborative research.

I hope that this chapter has demonstrated that some of the theoretical insights gained from the literature can be applied in a useful manner in the legislative process in developing countries. That is why at the end of this contribution the draft is added in an appendix. Of course I do realize that this will and must be subject to much criticism, since it should better be adapted to national needs. But at least the existence of such a draft may have the advantage that it can further debate on the type of criminal law a developing country like Indonesia needs in order to provide adequate protection of its environment.

REFERENCES

Buiting, T.J.B. (1993), *Strafrecht en Milieu*, Arnhem: Gouda Quint.

De Nauw, A. (1994), *Les métamorphoses administratives du droit pénal de l'entreprise*, Ghent, Belgium: Mys & Breesch.

Faure, M. (1990), *Preadvies Milieustrafrecht*, Antwerp: Maklu.

Faure, M. (1991), 'Het milieustrafrecht in rechtsvergelijkend perspectief', *Panopticon*, 310–29.

Faure, M. and G. Heine (2000), *Environmental Criminal Law in the European Union, Documentation of the Main Provisions with Introductions*, Freiburg in Breisgau: Max-Planck Institute for Foreign and International Criminal Law.

Faure, M. and M. Visser (1995), 'How to Punish Environmental Pollution? Some Reflections on Various Models of Criminalization of Environmental Harm', *European Journal of Crime, Criminal Law and Criminal Justice*, **4**, 316–68.

Goethals, E. (1991), *Handhavingsproblemen in het milieurecht. Rechtspraktijk en Milieubescherming*, Antwerp: Kluwer.

Heine, G. (1986), 'Aspekte des Umweltstrafrechts im internationalen Vergleich', *Goltdammer's Archiv für Strafrecht*, 67–88.

Heine, G. (1987), 'Umweltstrafrecht in der Bundesrepublik Deutschland: Entwicklung und gegenwärtiger Stand, Grundprobleme und Alternativen', in A. Eser and G. Kaiser (eds), *Dritter deutsch-sowjetischer Kolloquium über Strafrecht und Kriminologie*, Baden-Baden: Nomos.

Heine, G. (1989), 'Zur Rolle des Strafrechtlichen Umweltschutzes', *Zeitschrift für die gesamte Strafechtswissenschaften*, 722–55.

Heine, G. (1990), 'Verwaltungsakzessorietät des Umweltstrafrechts', *Neue Juristische Wochenschrift*, 2425–34.

Heine, G. (1991), 'Die Verwaltungsakzessorietät im deutschen Umweltstrafrecht unter Berücksichtigung des österreichischen Rechts. Aktuelle Probleme und Reformüberregungen', *Österreichische Juristen Zeitung*, 370–78.

Heine, G. (1994), 'Allemagne. Crimes against the Environment', *Revue Internationale de Droit Pénal*, **65**, 731–59.

Heine, G. (1995), 'Umweltstrafrecht im Rechtsstaat', *Neue Zeitschrift für Strafecht*, 63–71.

Hendriks, L.E.M. and J. Wöretshofer (1995), *Milieustrafrecht*, Zwolle: W.E.J. Tjeenk Willink.

Meinberg, V. (1988), 'Empirische Erkenntnisse zum Vollzug des Umweltstrafrechts', *Zeitschrift für die gesamte Strafrechtswissenschaften*, 112–57.

Prabhu, M. (1994), 'General Report. English Version', *International Review of Penal Law*, 699–728.

Robert, J.H. (1994), 'Le problème de la responsabilité et des sanctions pénales en matière d'environnement', *Revue Internationale de Droit Pénal*, **65**, 954–5.

Roef, D. (1995), 'Zoektocht naar een meer zinnige betekenis van het strafrecht voor het leefmilieu', *Recht en Kritiek*, 480–510.

Rogall, K. (1988), 'Gegenwartsprobleme des Umweltstrafrechts', *Festschrift der Rechtswissenschaftlichen Fakultät zur 600-Jahr-Feier der Universität zu Köln*, 518–20.

Schall, H. (1990), 'Umweltschutz durch Strafrecht: Anspruch und Wirklichkeit', *Neue Juristische Wochenschrift*, 1265–6.

Tonnaer, F.P.C.L (1994), *Handboek van het Nederlandse Milieurecht*, Utrecht: Lemma.

Waling, C. (1990), *Het materiële milieustrafrecht*, Arnhem: Gouda Quint.

Winkelbauer, W. (1985), *Zur Verwaltungsakzessorietät des Umweltstrafrechts*, Berlin, Germany: Duncker & Humblot.

APPENDIX

1. Any person who intentionally introduces or discharges, either directly or indirectly in contravention of the law substances, micro-organisms, noise and other vibrations or radiations on or into the water, soil or atmosphere, shall be punished . . .
2. Any person who through his negligence introduces or discharges either directly or indirectly in contravention of the law substances, micro-organisms, noise and other vibrations or radiations on or into the water, soil or atmosphere, shall be punished . . .
3. Any person who infringes the provisions of this act or of its implementing decisions or infringes the provisions of a permit issued in accordance with this act shall be punished by a fine of . . .
4. Any person who in violation of applicable legislation operates a licensed installation or activity without a licence or in violation of the conditions of that licence will be punished with . . .
   Anyone who in violation of applicable legislation or in violation of a licence releases waste will be punished with . . .
   Anyone who:
   - violates administrative sanctions or measures imposed by the Court or administrative authorities; and
   - who violates the control as organized by this act

   will be punished with. . . .
5. Any person who directly or indirectly, introduces or discharges on or into the water, soil or atmosphere, substances, micro-organisms, noise and other vibrations, or radiations, while knowing or with good reasons to suppose that the action concerned can constitute a real danger to human health, shall be punished by an imprisonment . . .

10. Economic instruments: suited to developing countries?

Michael Faure, Marjan Peeters and Andri G. Wibisana

1. INTRODUCTION

Economics has been expanding its scope for many years. It has long left the traditional areas of markets and is increasingly applied to many aspects of human behaviour, including environmental policy. Economists thus have for many decades paid attention in an abundant literature to the way in which environmental pollution could be remedied from an economic perspective. In the chapter concerning the principles of environmental law, attention was paid to the way in which economists generally address environmental issues.[1] In that chapter it was shown that economists traditionally view pollution problems as externalities. Hence they see the role of law as an instrument to internalize these externalities. In Wibisana's chapter it was explained that economists traditionally distinguish between on the one hand liability rules and on the other hand regulation as an instrument to achieve this optimal internalization of the externality caused by the pollution problem. The literature indicating under what circumstances regulation may be better suited than liability rules to internalizing this externality was extensively discussed in Wibisana's contribution to this volume.

However, although in practice environmental law consists to a large extent of regulation, economists have increasingly pointed out that this traditional approach of imposing pollution standards via government regulation may have several disadvantages as well. Thus, in recent years they have picked up on Pigou's classic message of the 1920s that taxation could be a perfect instrument to internalize externalities. Moreover, since the 1960s Dales has also pointed out that social welfare could be increased if pollution rights were allocated to those parties who could reduce pollution at the lowest costs. In order to make this idea effective trading in pollution rights should be made possible.

[1] See Chapter 3 of this volume.

These ideas are now referred to in the literature as the use of so-called economic instruments, sometimes also referred to as market-based instruments. Many policy analysts interested in environmental policy have for a number of years now advanced the increasing use of these economic or market-based instruments, more particularly as a reaction to regulation. Regulation is in that respect often referred to as a 'command and control' approach. Economic instruments are today, at least in the literature, but increasingly also at the policy level, very popular. The use of market instruments rather than relying on regulation sounds modern and flexible and hence politicians also increasingly argue that environmental policy should be market oriented instead of merely relying on top-down regulation by government.

This being said, one has to notice that many talk about economic or market-based instruments, without clearly defining what precisely is meant by those instruments. Indeed, one could, from an economic perspective, argue that all legal and policy instruments can be considered as 'economic' as long as they give appropriate incentives to polluters for an efficient reduction of the externality caused by the pollution. Hence, to an important extent liability rules too can be considered as 'economic' instruments in the sense that the foresight of being held liable will also give incentives to polluters to prevent environmental harm. Nevertheless, liability rules are traditionally not referred to in the literature when 'economic' instruments are discussed. By this concept one usually refers to instruments where only environmental targets are defined, but where it is largely left to the polluters to find the optimal instruments to reach the particular targets. Hence, key notions in the use of so-called economic instruments are on the one hand the fact that they are incentive driven and on the other hand that they allow for more flexibility than the traditional command and control approach under regulation.

Many instruments within that broad definition might qualify as 'economic'. Thus one could for instance also argue that environmental management systems (EMAS) and the promotion of environmental care systems or environmental audits are surely also 'economic'. However, within this contribution to the volume we are going to focus more particularly on two examples of economic instruments, namely environmental taxes on the one hand and emission trading on the other hand.

The goal of this exercise is in the first place to sketch the usefulness of economic instruments according to the literature and to provide some information on their use and effectiveness in practice. Secondly, we will of course also pay attention to the crucial question of whether the increasing popularity of these economic instruments in the developed countries of the north should also be followed by developing countries. Is the amount of flexibility inherent in economic instruments also a good idea for environmental legal systems that are still in the course of development, as is the case in Indonesia but also in many other developing countries? Indeed, economic instruments also urge strict government action: the emissions must be motivated and sanctions need to be imposed in case of unlawful emissions. Hence, the question arises what type of government action is needed in order to use economic instruments and whether developing countries can guarantee effective monitoring. In particular, can developing countries deal with the specific institutional tasks such instruments seem to demand?

The method we will use to present the economic instruments within this chapter is the economic analysis of law. Given the fact that economic instruments will be discussed, it seems useful to use this particular methodology. Moreover, we will to some extent use comparative analysis as well, by pointing out the way in which economic instruments have been introduced in particular countries.

Our contribution is structured as follows: after this introduction (Section 1) we will first sketch why economic instruments are presented as a remedy for the shortcomings of traditional command and control regulation (Section 2). Next, we will briefly set out the economic theory and ideas behind environmental taxation (Section 3) as well as emission trading (Section 4). Then we will provide a brief comparison of both instruments (Section 5) and address briefly some empirical evidence with respect to both taxes and emission trading (Section 6). We will then add a private interest group analysis to explain why environmental taxes in particular are not used in the way that economic textbooks prescribe (Section 7) finishing with a few concluding remarks (Section 8).

2. SHORTCOMINGS OF COMMAND AND CONTROL

Oates defines economic incentives as a system through which the authority creates economic inducements for abatement activity but leaves polluters free to determine their own responses to these incentives. In contrast, under command and control, the authority will specify how polluters are to behave.[2] As stated by Kolstad, the basic concept of command and control is that it is

[2] Oates (1996, p. 29). However, the same author has warned that a sharp distinction, especially related to cost efficiency, between the two approaches might be misleading. First, the command and control approach also includes a wide variety of measures, where some are quite crude but other measures that have taken into account cost-effectiveness can produce results as efficient as economic incentives. Secondly, most empirical studies that compare the performance of command and control with economic incentives programmes contain significant bias towards finding in favour of the superiority of economic incentives over the command and control approach. See Oates (1990, pp. 292–3).

the task of the regulator to collect the information necessary to decide upon actions to control pollution, and then to command potential polluters to take specified actions.[3] Therefore, the difference between the two approaches is mostly defined on the basis of the amount of government intervention with respect to the specific behaviour of polluters.

With respect to government intervention, Anthony Ogus has categorized several regulatory instruments according to the degree of intervention.[4] The least interventionistic instruments are information provision and economic instruments, while the most interventionistic instrument is prior approval. Between these two extreme instruments lie environmental standards. The information instrument requires the industry to disclose certain facts or information about the industry's activities or products, but does not impose behavioural control upon the industry. Under an economic instrument, the authority does not impose any legal constraints on the industry's behaviour. Instead, the instrument functions to provide economic incentives that confer financial advantages for compliance and disadvantages in case of non-compliance. The classification of the economic incentives approach usually embraces the use of pollution taxes and subsidies, marketable emissions permits,[5] deposit-refund systems,[6] and liability rules.[7]

After discussing the various types of command and control instruments, let us now cursorily summarize the advantages and disadvantages of the instruments that have been addressed by authors such as Kolstad, Oates, and Baumol.[8] First, measures arguably create more flexibility in regulating

3 Kolstad et al. (1990, pp. 888–901).

4 Ogus (1994, pp. 26–8).

5 Under the marketable emissions permit, the authority first determines the level of emission by issuing emission permits. Trading of such permits among polluters is then allowed, resulting in a price to be paid for these permits. Thus pollution will be seen as an expensive activity: more emitting means that more costs are required and less emitting means that more revenues are gained (through the selling of permits). For more discussion on this system, see Oates (1990, pp. 290–3). See also Barde (1995, pp. 218–20).

6 A deposit refund system can be defined as a refundable product charge that is charged to consumers when they buy a product and refunded to consumers when they return the used product to a certain place. It is commonly used to induce consumers to dispose of certain wastes, such as used batteries, bottles and other packaging, in a proper way and to an appropriate destination. See Barde (1995, p. 221).

7 Kolstad has considered the use of a liability rule as part of an economic incentives approach. See Kolstad (2000, pp. 144–5). Nevertheless we have already indicated that many do not immediately think of liability rules when one refers to 'economic instruments'.

8 See Kolstad (2000, pp. 141–2). Also Oates and Baumol (1996, pp. 105–7). See also Oates et al. (1989, pp. 1240–2).

complex environmental processes, and thus provide much greater certainty concerning how much pollution will result from regulation. Hence, if enforcement is effective, command and control could lead to expected alterations in pollution activities with greater certainty than the economic-incentives approach. Secondly, another implication is that command and control could generate more certain polluters' responses compared to, say, a pollution tax. Some authors argue that the uncertainty of polluters' responses to a Pigouvian tax will be even greater when industries are dominated by a few large firms whose market power enables them to pass on the tax to consumers without much incentive to undertake major adjustments with respect to pollution reduction. In addition, although command and control may involve high costs, it may guarantee substantial reductions of damage to the environment, especially under a situation where threats to the environment are severe and time is limited. Finally, if a regulation requires that particular equipment be installed, thus a specification is set forth; the costs of monitoring will decrease, since monitoring focuses only on the question of whether that equipment has been installed.

However, as we have already indicated, the regulatory approach of the command and control instrument has been subject to several criticisms, which can be summarized as follows:

First, a traditional command and control system indeed focuses on a permit or licensing system. Within this system, permits traditionally set emission standards, but these often disregard the effect of the aggregate level of emissions on the environmental quality of the receiving environmental medium. This was a criticism that was formulated especially in the 1970s when the approach focused heavily on emission systems. Whereas environmental policy had indeed been focusing on the control of emissions, the total effect of the emissions on environmental quality was disregarded. As a result of that, the effect was that notwithstanding severe emission controls total environmental quality was seriously reduced. It is indeed striking that within the US context emission trading could more particularly develop within the context of the Clean Air Act which had set target standards referred to as National Ambient Air Quality Standards (NAAQS).[9] Hence, the focus should of course be on target standards or environmental quality standards. However, this criticism of the use of emission standards is not necessarily a criticism of the use of command and control as such. Indeed, even within a system that focused largely on target standards one could still either have command and control or economic instruments. However, there are several other criticisms that can be formulated.[10]

---

9 See Hahn and Hester (1989, pp. 109–53).

10 For a summary of these criticisms see also Faure and Ubachs (2003, pp. 29–31).

A second criticism on command and control is that it requires high levels of information and enforcement costs. Indeed, each industry must be scrutinized in detail to determine the appropriate level of emission control. Hence, the government needs to set optimal standards and moreover the traditional regulatory approach only works optimally if there is also optimal enforcement. In many cases polluters will balance the possibility of being fined (when they have breached a regulation) against a marginal profit that can be realized with additional pollution. However, enforcement costs are often very considerable. If controls are too strict, social enforcement costs will be too high. If on the other hand the level of control is too low, the damage costs for society as a result of environmental pollution will be too high.[11] Of course one could argue that the authorities may reduce enforcement (and information) costs by relying on information provided by industry. However, the private interest theory of regulation teaches that it is still likely that industry will distort the information in favour of its own interests.

Thirdly, it has often been argued that the command and control approach has in many cases failed to generate sufficient incentives for polluters to reduce their pollution levels. The problem is that a command and control type regulation indeed only requires a polluter to follow the regulatory standard, as this is for instance incorporated in a permit. However, as soon as the polluting firm corresponds with the regulatory standard there is no additional incentive to invest, for example in research and development towards innovative environmental technologies.

Fourthly, the command and control approach has the disadvantage that it cannot equalize the marginal pollution costs of pollution control among different polluters that produce the same pollution. This has to do with the fact that a command and control approach is often too general and too unspecific. Indeed, with regulation, the standard set by the regulatory agency will often be similar for each polluter and will therefore not take into account the fact that for example an efficient pollution reducer could reduce pollution at much lower cost. This constitutes a major shortcoming of a command and control system. This failure to equalize marginal pollution costs will increase the costs of pollution control excessively. This of course also has to do with the difficulty that administrative agencies will in many cases not be able to determine what the efficient emission for each individual polluter is. Indeed, efficient pollution will of course vary from case to case. Ideally, authorities should be able to identify the polluters and should also determine the efficient pollution for that specific polluter. For certain factories, efficient pollution will probably be higher than the imposed standard; for other

---

11 See Tietenberg (2000).

factories, it may be lower. If the authorities are not able to acquire the correct information about the actual pollution of certain polluters, they may demand that all polluters reduce their emissions by the same percentage. This will inevitably lead to inefficiency and thus to welfare losses because the scope for pollution abatement will of course be different for each polluter.[12] The essential problem with the command and control approach is indeed that those polluters that have the possibility to abate pollution above the regulatory standard do not, under a command and control system, have any financial incentive to do so.

Fifthly, under a command and control approach polluters will only pay the prevention costs required to comply with the regulatory standard. However, polluters under command and control will not necessarily be required to pay for the costs of residual damages associated with the pollution that they have produced in conformity with the standard.

This shows that there are considerable disadvantages in the traditional command and control approach, which can be summarized by the fact that the regulatory standard is often too general and not flexible or differentiated enough. An optimal environmental policy would require flexible (and hence often referred to as market-based) instruments which on the one hand provide more flexibility (taking into account the individual prospects for optimal pollution abatement by each polluter) and on the other hand provide optimal incentives towards environmental technological innovation and not merely compliance with a regulatory standard.

An environmental technological difficulty in this respect is also that traditional regulatory standards of the command and control type only aim at 'end-of-pipe' solutions by merely controlling emissions. In fact environmental policy should also look for instruments that drive polluters towards the use of cleaner production technologies instead of merely imposing end-of-pipe solutions.

Bearing in mind the advantages and disadvantages of various instruments, we could say that there is no single instrument that can be used for all environmental cases. More importantly, it might even be more efficient to use a hybrid system that combines more than one instrument. In this regard, one may refer to Oates and Baumol who have concluded that the protection of the environment can be best pursued by using a combination of various regulatory instruments, namely the combination between command and control and economic incentives measures. They argue that the use of a pollution tax should not preclude the use of direct control, given the possibility of the tax rate being insufficiently low to induce the reduction of pollution levels. They

---

12 This point has also been made by Rosen (1999).

observe that whatever the level of emission taxes, environmental officials could still introduce various direct controls to ensure that the level of environmental quality associated with an environmental tax will not be less than what the authority defines as the 'accepted danger standard'. Hence, the higher the emission tax, the less frequently the environmental quality will threaten to fall below the danger standard, and thus the less often the use of direct controls will be required.[13]

Hence, we should bear in mind that although there are considerable disadvantages of the traditional command and control approach, in practice environmental policy may be based on a combination of economic instruments (like environmental taxes) with regulatory solutions (like emission standards in permits).[14] After having addressed the disadvantages of the traditional command and control approach we thus better understand why environmental policy analysts are increasingly interested in so-called economic instruments. Let us now focus on two of these economic instruments, namely on the one hand taxes (Section 3) and on the other hand emission trading (Section 4).

3. ECONOMIC PRINCIPLES OF ENVIRONMENTAL TAXATION

3.1. The Pigouvian Tax

The Pigouvian tax for environmental pollution is a concept of pollution tax first developed by the British economist, Arthur C. Pigou. This concept states that in order to reduce the output of goods or the pollution level to its social optimum level, the government may impose a tax which equals the damage cost of pollution, namely the level where the marginal private benefit (MB) is equal to the marginal social cost (pollution damage cost resulting from an extra unit of the private polluting activity – MSC). Theoretically, we could argue that the marginal benefit (MB) of the firm will decrease as its activity continues, while the marginal social cost (MSC) will increase as the activity continues, since we assume that more pollution will be produced. Hence, without tax, the firm will not have an incentive to reduce its activity level to the socially optimal level. In this case, the firm will continue its activity as long as its marginal benefit is larger than zero. Consequently, the optimal pollution

---

13 Oates and Baumol (1996, pp. 111–15).

14 On instrument mixes in environmental policy, see Gunningham and Grabosky (1998, pp. 422–53).

tax should be set at a point where MB is equal to MSC. This will induce the firm to reduce its activity to the socially optimal level of activity.[15]

Why will the firm be induced to carry out his activity up to the optimal level? Apparently, whenever the marginal benefit MB is greater than the tax, the firm will prefer carrying out his activity and paying the tax to reduce its activity. However, for any activity level higher than the optimal level, the marginal benefit MB is less than the amount of tax that the firm should pay to the government. Therefore in the latter case, the firm will be better off if it reduces its activity to the optimal level.

Compared to emission standards, a pollution tax may have several advantages, as follow:[16]

- First, a pollution tax entails fewer total abatement costs than the emissions standard does.
- Secondly, since pollution taxes could be administered by the government's existing tax framework, they have a lower risk of evasion compared to fixed emission standards that are controlled via irregular on-site inspections.[17]
- Thirdly, pollution taxes will provide an incentive for further emissions abatement, as reducing the amount of emissions means a reduction in the amount of tax and abatement cost.
- This leads to the fourth advantage of pollution taxes, namely that they may induce the firm to invest in research and development to search for new pollution abatement technologies or lower pollution production methods.
- Fifthly, taxes upon some pollutants may induce the reduction of some other related pollutants, for example a carbon tax may induce producers to use non-fossil fuel, which means reducing sulphur dioxide emissions that are also associated with the fossil fuel.

---

[15] See Turner et al. (1994, pp. 166–7). Other authors suggest that sometimes it is more useful to illustrate the figure in terms of abatement cost for the firm. Instead of showing the benefit of polluting, it would be better to show the cost of pollution abatement. Here, MB will be replaced by MCA (marginal cost of pollution abatement for the firm). See Pindyck and Rubenfield (2001, pp. 625–7). See also Perman et al. (2003, pp. 217–18).

[16] Turner et al. (1994, pp. 168–70). Taxes are also compared to tradable emission rights in Section 5.

[17] This particularly applies to taxes that have employed input substances rather than output emissions as their tax bases. One could argue that the opposite result, namely a higher risk of evasion, seems to be more likely where emissions are used as tax bases. In this case, the effectiveness of some emission taxes can be guaranteed only if we have sufficient control and monitoring from the authority. Unfortunately, such control and monitoring are not cheaper and less demanding than control and monitoring under regulatory standards.

Some economists have argued that subsidies will also generate as efficient results as pollution taxes. Intuitively, it does not matter whether the polluter is paid for its emission abatement or is taxed for its emissions. A closer look at this issue, however, shows that the allocative effects of a subsidy would not be the same as those of a tax. Karl-Gustaf Löfgren argues that a subsidy, contrary to a tax, improves the profit condition for individual firms within an industry. Hence, although emissions from individual firms would decline, as a result of incentives generated from subsidies, the level of emissions of the whole industry will not necessarily decrease. In principle, firms will enter the market as long as profits are higher than normal, and if the government employs a pollution subsidy, such profits will remain higher than normal. Therefore, the subsidy will attract more firms to enter the industry, which would mean that the industry's emission level would not be reduced.[18]

Several issues need to be considered when applying the Pigouvian tax, among which are:[19]

(a) The tax rate should be set a level that appropriately expresses environmental objectives to be achieved. This means that the function of marginal benefit and marginal cost should be defined accurately. Briefly, if the tax rate is set at a level that is less than the optimal one, too much pollution might be produced. Therefore, we could argue the failure to set an appropriate tax rate would undermine the effectiveness of the tax as a means to achieve environmental objectives.

(b) The assessment basis of environmental taxes must reflect emissions as closely as possible. Emissions are not always easy to monitor or may comprise a complex combination of different substances. To avoid such a difficulty, an approach called 'proxy variables' could be employed. In this case, the basis of the tax will be linked as closely as possible to emissions. The closer the linkage between the tax rate and emissions, the greater the effectiveness of the tax will be.[20] If it is impossible to link the

---

18 Löfgren (1995, p. 26).

19 Barde (1995, pp. 214–15). See also Turner et al. (1994, pp. 173–5).

20 However, one could argue that when consistently applied, the 'proxy variables' could end up in a situation where a firm finds itself amidst 'piles of taxes'. For example, if the government sets several taxes in relation to different assessment bases such as BOD level, used water, and several toxic wastes, then a company, say a mining company, will have to face different environmental taxes for its waste water. This could also significantly increase administrative costs, especially in terms of monitoring costs, which would undermine the efficiency of tax. Therefore, we often find taxes that combine several assessment bases, such as combined industrial water emissions taxes as applied in Germany, France, and the Netherlands, or combined industrial air emissions taxes in Latvia and China. See Stavins (2003, pp. 362–72).

assessment basis with pollution emissions, indirect indicators or a flat rate is usually used as basis.[21]

(c) It is often argued that taxes have regressive effects on some income categories. In some cases, for example in energy tax, taxes will have stronger effects on poorer households. Although it is highly debatable, the effects of taxes on distribution need to be considered appropriately.

(d) The effectiveness of pollution taxes will heavily depend on the shape of demand and supply functions of goods produced. When the demand curve of a good is so steep, indicating the inelasticity of the demand for that good, a substantial increase in the price of that good can only slightly reduce the consumption of that good. We may refer this situation to a tax imposed upon cigarettes. On the other hand, the availability of alternatives or substitutes will change the demand curve to be more elastic (flatter), indicating that a small increase in the price will reduce the consumption substantially. The illustration above explains that pollution tax will be more effective if the demand for polluting good is elastic.

The basic idea of the Pigouvian tax is therefore simple: economists claim that pollution should be taxed and the tax will reflect the true social costs of the pollution. The effect of that will be that the correct price is charged for the pollution. The idea behind this is, as we just mentioned, that in this way an incentive-based mechanism will be used which will drive the polluter towards alternative technologies. However, as we mentioned, the application of an efficient tax also requires optimal information on the part of the government in order to fix the correct tax rate.

3.2. In Practice: Regulatory Charges

Let us now address how these basic ideas, summarized above, of Pigouvian taxes might work in an environmental tax policy. To cope with the basic idea of the Pigouvian tax the policy-maker could install a regulatory charge with the aim of influencing the behaviour of potential polluters. The regulatory environmental charge is in other words a practical translation of the Pigouvian

---

21 The use of indirect measurement refers to indirect effects that are expected when assigning a tax for a particular basis. For example, by using carbon as an assessment basis for fuel tax, we might expect that it would also indirectly influence the reduction of sulphur emissions. However, using indirect measurement as an assessment basis is more likely to create errors, and hence it becomes a burden for the authority to minimize these errors. See de Kock (1980, pp. 64 and 67). One could also argue that the use of flat rate is not consistent with the idea of Pigouvian tax, since different people have different marginal cost functions and therefore, more importantly, a flat rate will not create appropriate incentives for further emissions reductions.

tax. The way this usually works is that at the policy level a certain environmental goal is identified after which a certain target for the regulatory charge is chosen. Ideally the target for the charge is chosen in such a way that alternative (less polluting) solutions are offered to the polluter. This means that if one were to consider, for example, a regulatory charge on consumption, this would only make sense if the charge is applied to so-called elastic goods. If the consumer had, notwithstanding the charge, no alternative consumption possibilities he might have no other option but to continue with the consumption of the polluting product, assuming that it is not possible to reduce demand.[22] Hence, the effectiveness of such a regulatory charge is very much related to the possibility of having less polluting alternatives available or the possibility of reducing demand. It depends, as we have just indicated, on the elasticity of the demand for the product.

As soon as the target for the charge has been defined (taking into account alternatives), the optimal amount of the charge should then be fixed. The amount of the charge will be dependent upon the environmental target chosen. Indeed, environmental policy usually starts with the setting of target standards.[23]

This target will determine the optimal quality of a certain environmental component. One could for example, within the framework of the discussion on climate change, agree that a country has to reduce CO_2 emissions to, say, X megaton. Then economists would argue that on the basis of trial and error an environmental tax rate could be fixed which best corresponds to the environmental target chosen.[24] The disadvantage of this approach, whereby the regulatory charge is linked to a certain target, is that some polluters may not be reached by the tax (for example, because the charge is linked and limited to specific products, services or production methods) although they do contribute to the externality.

These charges with a primarily regulatory nature have as their main goal the attainment of a specific environmental target. When, in common language, people discuss 'environmental taxes' they usually refer to these regulatory charges. It is important to stress that with these regulatory charges budgetary effects or goals play only a minor role. In its purest form one might argue that the regulatory charge should even be budget neutral. If the charge on a certain product, production method or service is a success, the logical consequence

---

22 This may be the case if the good is one of the 'bare necessities' of life.

23 Also referred to as ambiant quality standards (in the American terminology) or environmental quality standards (in the terminology of the European directive on integrated pollution prevention and control – IPPC Directive of 24 September 1996).

24 This approach has been proposed by Baumol and Oates. See Baumol and Oates (1971, pp. 42–54).

should be (given alternatives – see above) that the demand for the products or services to which the charge is targeted should reduce. Ideally the demand for the product on which the charge applies should become zero, whereas the demand for alternative (less polluting) products will increase. The end result of such a regulatory charge would be that the demand for a certain product, service or production method would be so low that in the end no income at all is generated as a result of this regulatory charge.[25] Hence, one can argue that the fact that a regulatory charge does not lead to great benefits for the treasury should not be considered as a problem at all. Quite the contrary, this could exactly prove that the charge has been quite successful since it has led to decreased demand for the polluting activity to which the regulatory charge was applied.[26]

3.3. Regulatory versus Budgetary Charges

It is well known that there is a fundamental difference between on the one hand regulatory charges, just discussed and charges with a primarily budgetary goal. Charges with such a budgetary character are more comparable to traditional taxes. Indeed, these budgetary charges have, just like traditional taxes, revenue raising as their main goal. Environmental effects are just a secondary goal or play no role at all. Although in common language these charges are sometimes also referred to as 'environmental taxes' one could argue that this may be somewhat misleading, since a budgetary charge does not primarily have environmental goals.[27] Charges with such a budgetary character are in fact an indirect tax on a certain good or product (often energy related, such as oil or electricity) or on a certain service (for example, a flight by aeroplane). As far as their nature is concerned, these budgetary charges (even though they apply to environmental polluting activities or the consumption of energy) can be compared with value added tax or with excise duties.

---

25 This, by the way, leads to the interesting question whether in such a scenario the policy-maker should continue to leave the environmental charge in existence. If the regulatory charge were to be abrogated, one would indeed run the risk that the polluting product would become attractive again and that its demand would again increase. Therefore, even in this scenario where demand for such a product has been reduced to zero as a result of the charge, in the long run the charge should remain in existence even though the revenue it brings is zero.

26 See further on these issues Faure and Ubachs (2002, pp. 301–29).

27 Obviously it does not make any difference from a legal perspective whether one qualifies a tax as a regulatory or a budgetary charge. From an economic perspective this difference is, however, important. Moreover, this difference is also important if one comes to ask whether environmental taxes can reach the goals set by policy-makers (the effectiveness test).

There are also charges which take a somewhat middle position between the regulatory charges on the one hand and budgetary charges on the other hand. These are referred to as charges with a 'double dividend' character.[28] These double dividend charges have on the one hand the goal of reducing environmental pollution, whereas on the other hand they nevertheless try to realize a certain tax revenue. Although we have just made a clear distinction between regulatory and budgetary charges, in practice with environmental policy it is difficult to draw a clear dividing line between the two. In practice many environmental charges will have this 'double dividend' character. Obviously one may note that with one charge the reduction of environmental pollution may be the primary goal (thus resembling more closely the regulatory charge), whereas with another charge the policy goal which is primarily stressed will relate more to the raising of revenue (thus making this charge look more like a budgetary charge). However, there will always remain ambiguity and tension between the regulatory and revenue-raising functions of taxes.[29]

4. EMISSIONS TRADING

4.1. Economic Principles

We have already mentioned that in particular the lack of flexibility and incentives was often considered a disadvantage of the traditional command and control approach. Some firms could abate pollution at relatively low costs or would innovate and invest in cleaner technologies whereas others would not. The problem is that the traditional command and control approach in the form of standards is too general and does not allow for a differentiation between polluting firms. And, in addition, fine-tuned regulation, like permit schemes, asks for a lot of (expensive and burdensome) bureaucratic work. The problems just mentioned could probably be solved by using marketable permits as a policy instrument. This instrument was introduced in the 1960s by Dales[30] and has become increasingly popular, especially at first in the United States.[31, 32]

---

28 For an extensive exposé on the difference between on the one hand environmental charges with a double dividend character and environmental charges with merely ecological goals, see Paulus (1995).

29 So Ogus (1999, pp. 245–66).

30 Dales (1968).

31 One can think of the National Sulfur Dioxide Trading Program and Regional Nox Trading Programs; see Nash and Revesz (2001).

32 For more discussion on the instrument, see Oates (1990, pp. 290–3). See also Barde (1995, pp. 218–20).

In this system, marketable permits that for instance allow the emission of a certain quantity of CO_2 during a certain period in a certain area are issued to polluters, for instance factories. Again the authorities will have to set a certain environmental target, for instance the limitation of carbon dioxide emissions to quantity X. The government will subsequently issue permits until quantity X is reached. The issuing of these permits takes places according to a certain distribution formula. Many different distribution schemes are possible; if the permits are issued for free, companies that pollute less than is allowed by their permit, can sell their remaining quota to companies that wish to pollute more than their assigned quota. If government chooses to auction the permits, factories simply buy units of pollution at the equilibrium price, depending on the total amount of their pollution.

According to the Coase Theorem, polluters have a mutual interest in trading permits; a polluter who pollutes less will have the chance to receive money by trading his remaining pollution rights, while the polluter who would like to pollute more is willing to pay for extra pollution rights.[33] This way, a possible loss of welfare – which arises if regulation is used as the instrument of environmental policy – can be reduced. If the government introduces such a system in which permits are sold to the polluters, the government acts like a broker and should in any case be able to control the functioning of the system.

Marketable emission permits have several major advantages, namely: first, they give the environmental regulator a direct control over the quantity of emissions; secondly, contrary to the tax system, marketable permits enable an automatic adjustment for inflation; thirdly, marketable permits may gain more acceptance simply due to the factor of familiarity, namely that trading originates from permit, of which the regulators have experience and thus are more comfortable with. Marketable permits may also have a number of disadvantages, such as: first, there is a disadvantage with respect to the initial allocation of the permit. In practice, permits are usually granted via grandfathering (thus free of charge) according to past emissions records, hence it can be assumed that initial rights to use the environment are assigned to the polluters; secondly, there are public concerns that the system will cause pollution to be transferred to another region; thirdly, marketable permits are also criticized in relation to revenue. It is argued that under marketable permit schemes, the industry's profit will increase while the pollution level remains the same, while in contrast the tax system will not only improve the level of pollution but also raise revenue for the government.

An important advantage of a system of marketable permits is that polluters have to reveal their willingness to pay for pollution rights, while in a system

---

33 Provided that transaction costs are low.

of command and control they will not reveal their willingness to pay. In a system of command and control, polluters will in many cases even try to mislead the authorities as far as their willingness to pay for pollution rights is concerned, in order to create a favourable system of regulation.

Marketable permits could also create another advantage, namely that in this system the government does not have to find the correct price of each pollutant when setting certain environmental targets.[34] In this case, once the government has set a certain target to be achieved, the market will automatically set the price. Hence, trading will take place because firms with high abatement costs will find it cheaper to buy a permit from other firms rather than to reduce their emissions, and firms with low abatement costs will be willing to sell their permit. In this way, the price will finally express the supply and demand of permits.[35] This will lead to another advantage as observed by Pearce and Turner, namely that by allowing emission permits to be traded, total abatement costs will eventually be minimized compared to direct regulatory standards.[36]

An important disadvantage of a system of marketable permits is, according to some authors, however, that these permits have a negative influence on the moral behaviour of polluters. In fact, polluters are able to buy off their undesired behaviour; it is questionable if it is desirable to offer such an opportunity.[37]

One should also note that a system of marketable permits only functions if emissions without permits are forbidden, and that this prohibition is actually enforced. If not, polluters are likely to emit anyway and not 'waste' their money on permits.

Moreover, if the government initially distributed the permits according to a certain distribution formula, one could argue whether this is desirable on grounds of distribution of wealth. This way, polluters receive free permits, which – if they wish – they can sell to other polluters. From the point of view of economic efficiency it does not matter how permits are distributed amongst polluters; it is even possible that the government grants all pollution rights to one single polluter. The functioning of the free market will automatically create a situation which is efficient from an economic point of view.[38]

---

[34] We could compare this advantage with environmental taxes which requires the tax rate to be set at a level that appropriately expresses the environmental objectives to be achieved. This advantage has already been mentioned by Dales (1968, p. 93). See discussion on environmental taxes.

[35] See Siebert (1995, p. 136).

[36] See Pearce and Turner (1990, p. 112). Perman and others compare the minimization of abatement costs resulting from marketable permits and environmental taxes. They conclude that the result is identical, namely that the environmental target will be achieved at the least cost. See Perman et al. (2003, p. 224).

[37] See Frey (1999, pp. 395–417) and Frey (1997, pp. 56–79).

[38] See further on these issues Faure and Ubachs (2003, pp. 27–49).

4.2. A Closer Look at some Potential Problems with Implementing Emissions Trading

Although on paper the system of emission trading sounds wonderful – it will create additional incentives and flexibility through trade whereby the government can act as broker – there are also several potential problems with developing the system for practical use that cannot be neglected. We will look more closely now at two of them.

First of all there is the issue of the choice of allocation method. Ideally (at least from an economic perspective) auctioning would be chosen. However, in practice grandfathering often is chosen whereby *de facto* a reward for (old) polluters takes place. Grandfathering has been criticized as a way for incumbent firms to prevent new firms from entering a competitive market.[39] Another objection is that grandfathering runs counter to the basic meaning of the polluter-pays principle. Indeed, with grandfathering, the bigger firms who polluted the most would be 'rewarded' with tradable emissions rights corresponding to their historic emissions. In this sense, it seems that not a 'polluter-pays', but a 'polluter-earns' principle would be applied.[40] New, cleaner companies might encounter the situation that they have to buy emissions rights from existing firms that have polluted more. Companies that have already started environmentally friendly activities before the market started (the 'early actors') would occupy a disadvantageous position. To avoid these negative effects, alternative criteria for the initial allocation of rights must be considered. But here it should be recognized that the government must respect to a certain extent the legitimate expectations firms may have in continuing activities allowed by a traditional permit. The (partial) revocation of such a permit must therefore fulfil legal criteria, like taking into account a reasonable transition period. Choosing to correct the undesirable outcome of grandfathering in the context of the polluter-pays principle can also probably be done through an additional financial instrument. It could, for instance, be examined whether setting a maximum price on tradable rights should be recommended.[41]

---

39 See Ogus (1999, p. 169). However Turner et al. argue that marketable permits, whether the initial allocation is auctioned or grandfathered, are already vulnerable to being used as an entry barrier. This could occur if existing firms retain as many ERCs as possible and then refuse to sell them to newcomers or are willing to sell only at a high price. See Turner et al. (1994, p. 186). The relationship between interest-group lobbies and the emission trading system in the US has been discussed by Svendsen (1998, pp. 133–44).

40 Peeters (2003).

41 Victor (2001, pp. 102 ff.).

In sum, the method of allocation needs to be fair, consistent, clear and feasible, and should not cause too many legal procedures over the decisions concerning the initial allocation.[42]

In addition to the basic methods of allocation already mentioned (auctioning and free allocation based on administrative criteria), another method of allocation of transferable rights is possible: this is the so-called baseline and credit trading programme. With this form of emissions trading, transferable rights will be derived from relative production or process standards. These performance standards, or baselines, will be set for a category of industry, and the individual firms may choose whether they will follow the standard, or will emit above or below this line. When a firm has caused fewer emissions compared to the baseline, it gains transferable pollution rights. A firm that exceeds the baseline needs – in order to compensate for this – to buy emission rights. One remarkable aspect is that this baseline and credit method does not have an absolute cap on total emissions in a certain period during a certain time as is the case with the more traditional concept of emissions trading, as described by J.H. Dales in 1968. The lack of a cap requires additional governmental action when the total quantity of emissions is too high. When there is (at the time of setting the baseline unexpected) economic growth, the government will have to take additional measurers in order to reduce the total amount of pollution.

It may be noted that in the baseline and credit system new entrants can easily enter the market since they do not have to buy the rights as long as they adhere to the baseline (however, when the baseline is set at a very tough level, that could also operate as a barrier to entry into the market).

Secondly, a system of marketable permits also requires effective control – which places strong demands on governmental institutions. Indeed, an emission without surrendering a corresponding emission right must of course be prohibited and this prohibition must be controlled and enforced. Much of the debate on emissions trading concerns the first steps that have to be taken on introducing and applying the instrument: how will it fit into the existing legal system, especially the existing permit procedures or other policy instruments, and how will the allocation of permits be done? Apparently, the focus on the enforcement of an emissions trading scheme has been less compared to the other topics mentioned. Even Dales didn't pay much attention to the enforcement aspects of

---

42 For instance in the Netherlands, 50 out of 200 industries went to court to challenge the allocation of tradable greenhouse gas emissions. The court partially agreed with the objections of 17 industries. *AB R* v *S* 8 April 2005, no. 20040926/1 and following numbers, Jurisprudentie Bestuursrecht 2005, no. 129, with comment by Peeters. See for the final court decision: *AB R* v *S* 9 September 2005, JB 2005 nr. 291, with comment by Peeters.

emissions trading, but nowadays we know that environmental legislation often has an enforcement deficit. However, policy-makers should be very alert to the enforcement task that belongs to emissions trading. It can be assumed that through introducing a financial incentive for reducing emissions, simultaneously an incentive for not following the rules is included. One should note the fact that it might be attractive for firms to camouflage their real emissions data in order to arrange for fewer rights to be surrendered to the government. We may assume that firms to a large extent will make decisions with a focus on minimizing expected costs, among which are emissions control costs, receipts or expenditures from permit market transactions, and expected penalties from reporting and emissions violations.[43]

4.3. Practice in the US: Emissions Trading for Stationary Sources under the Clean Air Act

One of the emission trading system practices in the US since the 1970s is the well-known emission reduction credit (ERC) system. Under this system, a source of emission that emits less than the standard is entitled to some amount of emission reduction credits which can be sold to other sources whose emissions exceed the standard.[44] There are several types of emissions trading that have developed within the ERC system, namely netting, offsets, bubble and banking.[45] The netting system is provided for sources undergoing modifica-

---

43 Stranlund et al. (2002, pp. 343–61).

44 Perman et. al. (2003, p. 228).

45 These four types of emission trading have a great deal to do with the US standard setting on air pollution that consists of the National Ambient Air Quality Standards (NAAQS) and technology-based standards. There are three subsets of technology-based standards that could be applied to a source of pollution, namely the Lowest Achievable Emission Reduction (LAER) standard as the most stringent standard, the Best Available Control Technology (BACT) standard which is less stringent than the LAER standard, and the Reasonable Available Control Technology (RACT) standard as the least stringent standard. Before determining which of these technology-based standards will be applied, the authority needs to know whether the NAAQS has been exceeded or not. An area will be considered a 'non-attainment' area if emissions in that area have exceeded the NAAQS and as an 'attainment' area if emissions are below the NAAQS. New or modified sources that are located in a 'non-attainment' area are subject to the most stringent standard, LAER. If they are located in an 'attainment' area, they are subject to the BACT standard, which is less stringent than the LAER standard.

In this arrangement, sources which existed when the trade rule was established, enjoy a more favourable situation, since they only face the RACT standard if they are located in a 'non-attainment' area, and face even no standard or only the obligation to maintain the existing air quality if they are located in an 'attainment' area. See Svendsen (1998, pp. 73–4).

tion (referred to as modified sources) which are willing to avoid being considered as new sources and, hence, subject to a strict standard (LAER if they are located in a 'non-attainment' area or BACT if they are in an 'attainment' area). In this system, the modified sources can avoid the stringent standard so long as there is a substantial decrease in emissions from other sources within the same plant. This system thus allows internal trading in order to maintain the same level of emissions from the plant.

The offsets system, in contrast, is applicable for new sources located either in an 'attainment' or 'non-attainment' area. New sources, including new plants, are welcomed so long as their emissions correspond to a substantial decrease in emissions from the existing sources. In this system, emission trading could occur internally, namely among sources within a plant, or externally, namely among independent plants.

The most famous emission trading from the US emission trading system is probably the bubble system. A 'bubble' is an aggregate limit for existing pollution sources. In this way, the aggregate emissions of firms within one area are treated as one source of emissions (a bubble). In this system, it does not matter whether the emissions of an individual firm exceed the specified standard for this firm, so long as the overall bubble in the area is able to meet the specified emissions limit. In this system, emissions permits could be traded among different plants.

Finally, under the emissions banking system, firms are allowed to store their ERCs in order to anticipate an increase of their emissions or simply to sell them to other firms in the future.

4.4. Practice in the US: The Acid Rain Allowance Trading Programme

The ERC system in fact emerged bottom-up, as a flexible way to comply with the ambient air standards. Very interesting is another practice within the US, namely the acid rain allowance trading system. This programme was established by the 1990 Clean Air Act amendments, and introduced a cap and trade emissions trading programme in order to combat SO_2 emissions from fossil-fuel burning power plants. This emissions trading programme focused on the non-local effects of SO_2 emissions; local effects are still covered by a traditional command and control regime. A cap on national SO_2 emissions was set, and tradable allowances were issued, representing the right to emit 1 ton of SO_2 emissions. The allocation of rights is mainly done by legislation, the other governmental tasks required within the programme are executed by the federal

Explanation and discussion about the four emission trading system can be found in: ibid., pp. 76–7. See also Turner et al. (1994, pp. 182–6); Perman et al. (2003, p. 228); and Pearce and Turner (1990, pp. 117–19).

Environmental Protection Agency. The rights are allocated free of charge (for 30 years), and may be banked for the future.[46] A small percentage of the allocated allowances is withheld for sale, in order to ensure for instance that new units may enter the market. The acid rain allowance trading system provides for opt-in possibilities for units and industries not covered by the programme. The programme has strong monitoring and enforcement provisions, like the obligation for covered units to install a 'Continuous Emissions Monitoring System'. As its title indicates, this monitoring system must be in continuous operation, and must be able to sample, analyse and record data at least every 15 minutes and then reduce the data to 1-hour averages.[47] It is stated that this system is capable of 'providing a nearly continuous and very accurate account of the volume of emissions leaving a facility', which is, as can be assumed, not a cheap approach.[48] There are provisions to make sure that the monitoring systems work properly, like initial equipment certification procedures, periodic quality assurance and quality control procedures, and procedures for filling in missing data. When monitoring equipment is not working properly, the amount of emissions will be estimated, whereby an over-estimation takes place, in order to include an incentive for industry to uphold a proper monitoring system.[49]

In Section 411(a) of the Clean Air Act it has been stated that an excess emissions penalty of $2,000 per tonne of excess emissions will be imposed. The rate of this fixed penalty is indexed to inflation. In addition, offenders are required to deduct the allowance allocation in the year following the excess emissions.

Already in the first years of its entry into force, almost all units succeeded in their reporting requirements based on the Continuous Emissions Monitoring System.[50] Only one utility has been fined for failing to complete a timely certification testing of its CEMS. And, very remarkably, during these two years all utilities have complied with their emissions cap.[51] Later publications also state that a 100 per cent compliance rate has been achieved.[52] Overall, the administrative costs (monitoring and enforcement) are significantly less (and of a

46 The description of the acid rain allowance trading programme is based on Ellerman (2004).

47 Stranlund et al. (2003, p. 14).

48 Stranlund et al. (2003, p. 14).

49 Stranlund et al. (2003, p. 15).

50 This provision is prescribed in Section 412 Clean Air Act.

51 Environmental Law Institute Research Report, Implementing an Emissions Cap and Allowance Trading System for Greenhouse Gases: Lessons from the Acid Rain Program, September 1997, p. 59.

52 Tietenberg (2000, p. 218).

different nature) compared to a traditional regulatory intervention.[53] Overall, the programme is judged to be an example of an emissions trading system that can reduce emissions as effectively as command and control regulations. In addition, the costs are considerably less than conventional regulatory approaches.[54]

4.5. Practice in Europe: EU Directive of 13 October 2003 on CO_2 Emissions (2003/87/EC)

The EU greenhouse gas emissions trading market resembles the acid rain allowance trading programme, as it intends to combat a non-local pollutant through a cap-and-trade emissions trading scheme based on a (mainly) free distribution of rights. The European greenhouse gas trading scheme commenced on 1 January 2005, and covers the main sources that emit CO_2.[55] In fact, it covers some 12,000 installations representing close to half of Europe's emissions of CO_2.[56] The programme focuses on greenhouse gas allowances, but it now only considers CO_2 emissions. The restriction of the emissions trading scheme to CO_2 is the result mainly of problems in monitoring other greenhouse gases. In the future, the scope of emissions trading may be broadened to other greenhouse gases.

The European framework for emissions trading needs to be filled in by the Member States. In the explanatory memorandum of the proposal for the directive, the European Commission expressed the basic idea that a common European emissions trading system should be preferred above a collection of national emissions trading systems.[57] One of the main tasks of the Member States is to allocate the greenhouse gas allowances through a National Allocation Plan, which needs to be approved by the European Commission. Other main tasks of the Member States are: the issuance of greenhouse gas permits (as distinct from the greenhouse gas allowances); to execute control and enforcement duties, and the registration of the transactions.

The greenhouse gas *permit* is to be issued to a particular installation, regulating some specific conditions under which it may operate. One of the permit conditions is that the operator shall surrender enough greenhouse gas

---

53 Ellerman (2004, p. 92).

54 Stated by Ellerman (2004, p. 94).

55 For a more extended prescription of the scheme, see Dornau (2005).

56 European Commission website, Questions and Answers on Emissions Trading and National Allocation Plans, posted at http://europa.eu.int/comm/environment/climat/emission.htm (entered on 19 April 2005).

57 Draft Directive (proposal presented by the Commission), Explanatory Memorandum, § 1.1.

allowances to cover its greenhouse gas emissions in one year.[58] The significance of the greenhouse gas permit scheme lies mainly in the fact that it contains specific demands as far as measurements, reports and verification are concerned. The greenhouse gas allowances are meant to be transferable rights. An allowance is defined in the Council agreement on the draft directive as:

> 'allowance' means an allowance to emit one tonne of carbon dioxide equivalent during a specified period valid only for the purposes of meeting the requirements of this Directive and which is transferable in accordance with the provisions of this Directive.[59]

The transferable allowances will exist only in electronic form, and can be transferred among firms and other persons. In fact, anyone within the European Community may hold and transfer the allowances.

Some coordination provisions are established in order to fine-tune the emissions trading instrument with the integrated permit approach as included in the so-called IPPC Directive. Member States need for instance to coordinate the conditions and procedures for permits under both schemes.[60] The IPPC permit may no longer include an emission limit value for direct emissions of a gas covered by the emissions trading scheme, unless it is necessary to ensure that no significant local pollution is caused. In addition, the Member States may choose not to impose requirements relating to energy efficiency for units emitting carbon dioxide on the site.[61]

Furthermore, provisions are laid down which relate to monitoring and enforcement.[62] Member States are expected to impose a financial penalty at a fixed price on any operator which does not surrender sufficient allowances to cover its emissions (40 euro during the three-year period beginning 1 January 2005; 100 euro thereafter).[63] The operator of an installation that acted against the law will be obliged to surrender enough allowances for the illegal emissions. In addition, a 'naming and shaming' provision has been introduced, meaning that Member States shall ensure publication of the names of operators who are in breach of requirements to surrender sufficient allowances.[64]

---

58 Art. 6 of the directive.

59 Art. 3(a) of the directive.

60 Art. 8 of the directive.

61 Art. 25 of the directive.

62 See also Commission Decision of 29/01/2004 establishing guidelines for the monitoring and reporting of greenhouse gas emissions pursuant to Directive 2003/87/EC of the European Parliament and of the Committee, *OJ* 29/01/2004 C(2004)130 final.

63 Art. 16 of the directive.

64 Art. 16(2) of the directive.

The Directive includes the choice of free allocation based on administrative criteria. It was feared by the Commission that if allowances were allocated on the basis of auctioning in one Member State but allocated free in another, competition might be distorted.[65] In Annex III of the directive criteria have been given which should be taken into account within the National Allocation Plan (NAP). Some of those criteria are rather vague, which leaves room for discretion for the authorities concerned.[66] Meanwhile, the European Commission has published a guidance document for interpreting these criteria.[67] A National Allocation Plan must be submitted to the Commission for approval. After approval, the allocation of allowances can take place. The National Allocation Plan must state the total quantity of allowances to be allocated, and must equally state how they will be allocated.

In 2004, decisions were taken by the Member States and the European Commission for the first phase of the greenhouse gas emissions trading scheme, running from 2005 till 2008. Subsequently, a new initial allocation needs to be made for the next period running from 2008 till 2013. The Member States are obliged to send in the NAPs for this second round before 1 July 2006.

Meanwhile, the emissions trading directive has been amended by the so-called linking directive, which provides industry with the opportunity to use credits gained by the flexible mechanisms of the Kyoto Protocol in order to offset their emissions.[68] This is an interesting experiment which might be an incentive for the development and use of the Joint Implementation and Clean Development Mechanisms included in the Kyoto Protocol.[69]

5. REGULATION, MARKETABLE PERMITS AND TAXES COMPARED

The central question in this chapter is through what kind of legal or policy

---

65 Draft Directive (proposal presented by the Commission), Explanatory Memorandum, § 13.

66 Peeters (2003, p. 90).

67 Communication from the Commission of 07/01/2004 on guidance to assist Member States in the implementation of the criteria listed in Annex III to Directive 2003/87/EC establishing a scheme for greenhouse gas emission allowance trading within the Community and amending Council Directive 96/61/EC, and on the circumstances under which force majeure is demonstrated, COM(2003) 830.

68 Directive of the European Parliament and of the Council amending Directive 2003/87/EC establishing a scheme for greenhouse gas emission allowance trading within the Community, in respect of the Kyoto Protocol's project mechanisms, *OJ* L 338 13.11.2004, pp. 18–23.

69 For more detailed information, see Lefevere (2005).

instruments a 'pricing' of environmental pollution can take place. This is the important question of the search for the optimal instruments to give incentives to a potential polluter to prevent environmental harm. Indeed, the issues of cost–benefit analysis and environmental standard setting give indications at what level the pollution should be internalized; they do not explain through what kind of instruments these optimal standards should be implemented.

Traditionally there were roughly three possible instruments which were addressed. First of all, as we indicated in the previous section, it is possible to tax the pollution and thus to use a system of levies or charges, which will give the potential polluter an incentive to reduce environmental harm. Secondly, it is possible to use the liability system, assuming that the potential polluter will be deterred by the foresight of having to pay compensation to a victim for the environmental harm he has caused. Thirdly, it is possible to fix pollution standards (notably emission standards) *ex ante* in regulation and more specifically in environmental licences. Now, in addition to these, a whole new set of policy instruments has been developed. Economists increasingly advocate the use of market-oriented policy instruments, such as systems of emission trading and marketable permits. In addition, attention is given to voluntary compliance mechanisms, such as environmental agreements.

It is obviously not possible to discuss the whole set of possible environmental policy instruments within the scope of this chapter.[70] Hence we have briefly discussed the literature concerning two types of instruments which have traditionally been very popular with economists, probably because they best represent the idea of 'pricing' environmental pollution. These concern marketable permits and taxes.

There is an abundant literature concerning the choice of a particular instrument to control a specific externality problem. This literature discusses the comparative benefits of various instruments in a given situation. Polinsky builds on the Calabresi/Melamed model, which discusses the optimal use of property rights and liability rules, by adding a tax-subsidy approach to this classic comparison between property rights and liability rules. Polinsky argues that when the government has full information about the externality problem, only the tax-subsidy approach can both control the externality efficiently and protect both parties' entitlements. This remains the case, also in a positive transaction costs world. Polinsky also addresses the more realistic setting in which the government has limited information. In that case, the approaches can be ranked to some extent.[71] He claims that

---

70 An excellent overview of these instruments is presented by Gunningham and Grabosky (1998).

71 Polinsky (1979, pp. 1–48). A comparison of Pegouvian taxes and the liability rule approach is also provided by Brown and Holahan (1980, pp. 165–78).

the tax approach will be inferior to the liability approach in a wide range of circumstances, but that in terms of entitlement protection there is a clear preference for the property rights approach. Hence, a distinction is made between on the one hand common law remedies such as property rights and liability rules and on the other hand incentive-based mechanisms such as taxes and charges.

Some attention has also been paid to the problem of combining tort recovery and effluent fees or tradable rights. Rose-Ackerman has argued that incentive schemes require a fundamental rethinking of the relationship between tort law and statutory law. She argued that incentive-based regulatory statutes should pre-empt tort actions: if fee schedules have been set to reflect social costs, tort actions would be redundant or even counterproductive.[72] This relates to the fundamental point mentioned above, namely that a combined use of instruments is useful when there are complementary benefits of both instruments. If, on the other hand, both instruments in fact reach the same goal, applying two instruments may only lead to increased administrative costs or to overdeterrence.

Economists have obviously tried to show that incentive-based mechanisms are superior to traditional command and control mechanisms. The theoretical literature pointing out the advantages of incentive-based mechanisms is overwhelming.[73] However, Oates and other co-authors indicate that incentive-based policies are not necessarily superior to command and control approaches. According to them, this is more particularly the case when command and control approaches are designed with at least one eye on cost savings.[74]

Frey also pointed to the importance of intrinsic motivation of citizens in the form of environmental morality. He argued that some instruments might encourage intrinsic motivation, whereas others rather undermine it. Frey argues that an environmental policy which is solely based on controls and commands undermines environmental morality, because it reduces the self-determination of people. Moreover, complex and abstract regulations are unlikely to improve environmental morality. The same is, however, true according to Frey for tradable emission rights. Being able to pay to undertake an undesired activity – the pollution of the environment – can be compared with the indulgences sold in the Middle Ages: the sense of punishment induced by sinning is lost as a result of the 'licence to pollute'. Emission rights of course tend to reduce pollution because they make violation costly, but on

---

72 See Rose-Ackerman (1992, p. 128).

73 See for example Ackerman and Stewart (1988, pp. 171–99) and Tietenberg (1990, pp. 17–33).

74 Oates et al. (1989, pp. 1233–42).

the other hand they destroy the intrinsic motivation to safeguard the environment.

The best way to promote environmental morality in the short term is by appeals and participation procedure and in the long run by education. Moreover, when legal regulations have an expressive function, this supports environmental morality. This is the case with easily comprehensible regulations whose punishments fit exactly the damage done to nature.

Because market-oriented policy instruments such as tradable licences do not always support environmental morality, Frey suggests using complementary environmental policies. However, a complementary policy should not be identified with a 'system's approach' in the sense that everything should be done at the same time. The aim must be to exploit the strong points of each instrument while at the same time compensating for the approach's negative aspects.[75]

Finally, concerning the choice of various instruments we should point to the law and economics literature where a combined use of a variety of instruments such as property rights, liability rules, emission and target standards has been advocated. Once more, we should stress that such a combined use of instruments does not mean that all instruments should be used at the same time, but that the comparative benefits of every instrument should be used in a complementary approach.[76]

6. PRACTICE

After having discussed the theoretical differences between both approaches and having compared the two systems, let us now look briefly at the experience with both marketable permits and taxes in practice, at least as far as this experience has been reported in the literature.

6.1. Marketable Permits

The starting point for most of the literature on tradable systems is the pioneering work of Dales.[77] Dales proposed that a market of marketable permits would be organized by the government whereby tradable pollution rights would be granted for a certain period. The government would act as broker for

---

75 Frey (1999, pp. 395–417) and Frey (1997, pp. 56–79).

76 See Hansson and Skogh (1987, pp. 132–44); Skogh (1982, pp. 67–80); Skogh (1989, pp. 87–101); Gravelle (1987, pp. 115–31) and more particularly see Gunningham and Grabosky (1998).

77 Dales (1968).

the trade and would monitor the system. Building on Dales' proposal other authors have formulated more specific proposals with respect to the shape of this market in pollution rights. Montgomery[78] suggested that the pollution right should also indicate which part of the concentration of a specific compound in a particular environmental component could be emitted from a particular source. Further proposals concerning the implementation of such a model have for example been formulated by Ackerman et al.,[79] Rose-Ackerman,[80] Noll[81] and Tietenberg.[82] Hahn and Hester[83] pointed to the importance of monitoring and enforcement in the framework of a market for pollution rights.

In addition to these papers sketching the theoretical benefits and the possible legal framework of a market for pollution rights, many subsequent contributions have analysed how some of these ideas have been implemented in environmental policy. Although most of the success stories in that respect come from the US, there is also a (modest) European experience with (some forms of) tradable pollution rights. For instance in the Netherlands, Peeters[84] discusses in her dissertation Dutch manure legislation, which allows for trade in the right to produce manure. As far as the US is concerned, the empirical material relating to the experience with transferable permits is overwhelming. Making an arbitrary selection, we can, for example, refer to the work of Oates[85] who discussed the emissions trading system for air pollutants and reports that trading has made real headway in certain regions. With equal enthusiasm, he reports on the success of a system of transferable discharge permits in Wisconsin, noting that even several European countries are closely following the US experience with transferable emissions entitlements.[86] His enthusiasm is supported by other sources. Hahn and Hester[87] claim that the trading programmes concerning the Clean Air Act have led to considerable cost savings, albeit that they had been less than anticipated. However, they also claim that it is hard to demonstrate major environmental improvements as a consequence of these market policies. Indeed, trading may have increased

78 Montgomery (1972, pp. 395–418).
79 Ackerman et al. (1974).
80 Rose-Ackerman (1977, pp. 383–406).
81 Noll (1982, pp. 116–28).
82 Tietenberg (1985).
83 Hahn and Hester (1989, pp. 109–53).
84 Peeters (1992).
85 Oates (1986, pp. 251–67).
86 See also Oates and Collinge (1982, pp. 346–54); Oates et al. (1983, pp. 233–47); Oates and McGartland (1985b, pp. 207–28) and Oates and McGartland (1985a, pp. 668–75).
87 Hahn and Hester (1989, pp. 109–53).

emissions in some cases where the pollution rights that were sold were previously not being fully utilized by the owner.[88]

Nash and Revesz have researched the functioning of some existing US tradable pollution permit regimes.[89] The National Sulfur Dioxide Trading Program aims at controlling acid rain and functions on a nationwide level, with no geographic restrictions on trading. According to Nash and Revesz, this programme is poorly designed, because it pays no attention to the location of the sulphur dioxide emissions. It is, for example, allowed to sell emission rights from regions that cause limited harm to the environment to regions that contribute most to the acid rain (the upwind states) problem. The programme does not therefore prevent the development of acid rain hotspots, although in 2000, the State of New York enacted a law to prevent the sale of sulphur dioxide permits to factories in upwind states. On the other hand, Ellerman is positive on the environmental effectiveness (and other aspects) of the scheme. He explains that the local effects of SO_2 emissions are covered by traditional regulatory interventions – which influences to a certain extent the freedom to trade. Nevertheless, important cost savings are made compared to traditional regulatory approaches. Moreover, he states that the fear that emissions in the Midwest would not be reduced has proved to be unfounded, and that hotspots did not occur (in a significant manner).[90]

Of course, one has to be realistic: on the one hand the system of emission trading is now extremely popular as one can see for instance in Europe where an EU Directive of 13 October 2003 introduced a system of emission trading for CO_2 emission rights. Notwithstanding this increasing popularity of emission trading with the policy-maker, one has to remain realistic, and to carefully consider under what conditions, and for what environmental problems, marketable permits should be recommended. Important information can be derived from *ex post* evaluations of emissions trading schemes, as has recently been done by the OECD. The impressive OECD report examines how marketable permits have been applied in a variety of different contexts, covering a variety of geographic locations. One of the main findings is that existing tradable permit systems, even with design shortages, have resulted in significant gains from trade.[91] Another important finding is that administrative costs are not excessive and may be considerably less than under alternative forms of regulation.[92]

---

88 See also Dewees et al. (1996, p. 267).

89 Nash and Revesz (2001).

90 Ellerman (2004, p. 86).

91 Tietenberg and Johnstone (2004).

92 Here Tietenberg and Johnstone make a distinction between cap and trade, and baseline and credit mechanisms (2004, p. 34).

The overwhelming arguments in economic theory in favour of the superiority of emission trading and the positive outcome of the *ex post* evaluation of several emissions trading schemes provide sufficient support for other experiments with this instrument. However, the key question is whether developing countries can cope with the specific institutional demands of emissions trading. The OECD report only reviewed emissions trading programmes established in developed countries. In another project, where a case study approach has been taken to assess the opportunities to implement economic instruments in developing countries, it has been concluded that emissions trading may be too burdensome for most but not necessarily all developing countries, due to the monitoring aspect.[93] In particular a CEMs system (continuous emissions monitoring system) is expected to be beyond the capacity of all but the wealthiest developing countries. It might be that an emission trading programme would place much higher burdens upon weak developing country institutions than a technology-based command and control system. The report states that it perhaps is to be recommended that developing countries with weak institutions should start with less institutional command and control regulations, and could move towards more complex but more economically efficient regulatory interventions, like taxes. Russell and Vaughan recommend as well a path, moving from general rules to specific industrial activities, which could be developed to a more market-based approach.[94] Nevertheless, one should bear in mind that the transition to emissions trading would often demand an explicit, new regulatory intervention, establishing an allocation of rights – taking into account the legitimate expectations of the existing polluters. Simply transforming existing traditional permits into tradable rights does raise some objections (like the fact that this will establish a barrier to new entrants, and that this grandfathering method might come into conflict with the idea of the polluter-pays principle).

6.2. Environmental Taxes

Finally we can briefly refer to the findings in some of the literature on environmental taxes. We mentioned above that the case for pollution taxes has been made since the early work of Pigou. Instead of focusing on the known literature that defends the importance of taxes from an economic point of view, it is more interesting to turn now to empirical results. As far as theoretical papers advocating that environmental policy be based on a tax system are concerned, we can refer to the papers mentioned above. The classical

93 Hruza et al. (2004, p. 237).
94 Russell and Vaughan (2003, pp. 331–70).

economic literature on environmental taxes in the Pigouvian tradition has been taken one step further by Paulus who examined the feasibility of ecological taxation, examining how the whole taxation system could be ecologically reshaped.[95]

As far as empirical material relating to experiences with taxes is concerned, it is remarkable that much more evidence seems to come from Europe than from the US. The situation was typically reversed for marketable pollution permits, which were apparently more popular in the American experience than in Europe. Dewees et al.[96] note that charges are rarely introduced 'in the text book form'. Hahn[97] moreover claims that most emission charges or fees are used as a revenue-generating device for public services rather than as instruments of environmental policy, as prescribed by economists. The reason why taxes are relatively rarely used in the US is also discussed in a report drafted by Oates[98] for the OECD. Most empirical evidence concerning the effectiveness of environmental taxes and charges does indeed come from Europe. Dewees et al.[99] argued that in the Netherlands water pollution by 14 industries responsible for 90 per cent of total water pollution decreased by 50 per cent between 1969 and 1975 and by another 20 per cent by 1980, whereby half of this reduction was due to the effluent charge. Similar success stories come from Germany[100] that due to water effluent charges there were significant increases in water treatment leading most firms to comply with the existing emission standards. Since Germany (like most European countries) still has a combination of effluent charges and emission standards, it is, however, hard to argue that the significant investments in water treatment plans were mainly due to the charges system and not for example to the threat of administrative and/or criminal sanctions in case of violation of emission standards. These findings concerning the success of effluent charges in Germany comply with reports by Frey, who argues that environmental taxes lead to a considerable reduction of emissions both into the aqua system and into the air.[101] We can finally point at a study by Bongaerts and Kraemer[102] comparing water pollution charges in France, the Netherlands and the Federal Republic of Germany, which comes to the same conclusion that effluent charges provide a strong incentive to invest in water pollution abatement equipment, but that it is

---

95 Paulus (1995).
96 Dewees et al. (1996).
97 Hahn (1989a, pp. 95–114).
98 Oates (1994).
99 Dewees et al. (1996).
100 Brown and Johnson (1984, pp. 929 ff.).
101 Frey (1992).
102 Bongaerts and Kraemer (1987, pp. 12–19).

impossible to disentangle the separate effects of charges and emission standards. The latter effect is especially strong in Germany where charges are halved for emitters who meet the effluent standards.

There are, however, also clear examples of regulatory failure as far as environmental taxation is concerned. For instance in the Netherlands in 1996 a regulatory energy tax was introduced in the Act concerning taxes on an environmental basis. It is a regulatory charge, being a charge that has as its primary goal the realization of certain ecological goals. However, this energy tax is only targeted at small consumers since it imposes a system of digressive taxes. This simply means that the larger the energy use, the lower the tax will be. This curious model hence seems to give incentives to increase the use of energy rather than decreasing it.[103]

7. INTEREST GROUP ANALYSIS

7.1. Lobby for Barriers to Entry or Lenient Standards

Up to now we have assumed that governmental regulation is always made 'in the public interest'. Thus, the government always makes regulations to increase social welfare and to raise efficiency. This implies that the government would pass a regulation only if it was considered to be efficient. Reality is often different. Looking at legislation one can often see regulation of activities for which such a method of control seems inefficient; in other cases there is a proper argument for regulation, but the formulation of the regulation is inefficient.

Economists of the 'public choice' school have studied the phenomenon of regulation and have examined the reasons why some are inefficient.[104] In this public choice approach, microeconomic models are used to explain processes of regulation. A starting point is the assumption that the politician himself is also a *homo economicus*, who will have a preference for the introduction of regulations which will benefit those interest groups which support him. From this point of view, the politician is no longer someone who is serving the public interest, but a utility maximizer serving his own interests.

The starting point of public choice analysis is that regulation is considered as the product of supply and demand in a political market. On the demand side we find the various interest groups who demand favourable regulation and on

---

[103] For a critical analysis, see Faure and Ubachs (2002, pp. 321–22) and Faure and Ubachs (2005, pp. 521–32).

[104] See in general Buchanan and Tullock (1962); Buchanan et al. (1962).

the supply side, the wealth-maximizing politicians who wish to favour interest groups which provide them with political support. The product is environmental legislation protecting an interest group in exchange for political support. Thus a wealth transfer (a so-called rent) can be transferred to the interest group protected. According to the literature, this rent-seeking behaviour will be especially successful if the transactions costs for the group of bringing together individuals to defend a common interest are relatively small and if the information costs incurred by the public at large in discovering the rent-seeking behaviour are relatively high. These conditions for rent-seeking may often be met in case of environmental regulation. The fact that a transfer to an interest group has taken place will often be disguised by arguing that environmental protection or victim protection is provided by the particular piece of legislation. Transactions costs are often low if only a few firms come together to defend a common interest.

Indeed, the reason why this wealth transfer to interest groups can take place may be found in these two well-known economic phenomena of information costs and transaction costs.

The *information* costs are those incurred by the public at large in finding out the effect of the regulation. Because the wealth transferred to an interest group is derived from the general public, one individual will usually not realize that such a transfer to an interest group has taken place. Moreover, it is claimed most interest group legislation protects the general public. This is often the case with regulation which is supposed to protect consumers (and which often only protects the retail trade)[105] or regulation which is supposed to protect victims (and which often only protects the interests of insurers of certain industries).[106]

Transaction costs are those incurred by a group in bringing individuals together to defend a common interest. Only a group which is relatively small, well organized and single issue oriented, will have low transaction costs and will be able to benefit from wealth transfers through regulation.[107]

There is a lot of literature providing theoretical support for the rent-seeking argument in the case of environmental regulation, as well as empirical evidence. The starting point for environmental regulation is often the political will to provide some action on environmental protection. Keenan and Rubin

---

105 This has been proven with respect to Sunday closing regulation and 'unfair trade practices' statutes. See Van den Bergh (1986, pp. 185–205). See also the article of Jaffer and Kay (1986, pp. 169–83).

106 This has been proven with respect to legislation concerning liability for nuclear accidents. See Faure and Van den Bergh (1990, pp. 241–54).

107 See Olson (1982, pp. 26–7); Posner (1974, p. 345); McCormick and Tollison (1982, p. 17).

would argue that this demand for regulation, which is not represented by a well-defined and active particular interest group, may be initiated by a so-called shadow interest group.[108] This is a group that would have members and come into being if an accident occurred. Potential victims of environmental pollution can thus be seen as members of this latent group. If a shadow interest group ceases to be a shadow group and becomes active, it will have all the characteristics of a normal interest group. Knowing that shadow interest groups have the potential to become an effective lobby, rational politicians will, under certain circumstances, respond to these groups in the same way that they respond to normal interest groups, even though the shadow groups have not yet organized.

If under these circumstances legislative intervention seems unavoidable, the theory of regulation suggests that the interest groups involved will accept a general principle of regulation, but may strive to change its scope.[109] The industrial interest groups to whom an environmental regulation is to be applied may realize that regulation may enhance producer wealth while it simultaneously corrects, or at least reduces, an externality problem. This outcome has been stressed by Maloney and McCormick with respect to environmental quality regulation. They argue that the industry, realizing that environmental regulation is unavoidable, will cooperate in the development of the regulation and try to change its contents to their advantage. A classic example is the introduction of so-called 'grandfather clauses' which stipulate that the regulation will not be applicable to firms or products which are already in existence. Hence, the regulation can create a new barrier against market entry and so protect existing industrial practices and products.[110] In other cases, for example as far as standard setting is concerned, industry may lobby for lenient environmental standards to increase their own profits.

As indicated above, the efforts of industry may go in various directions: sometimes regulation will be used in order to establish grandfather clauses to limit market entry;[111] in other cases there will be lobbying for more lenient environmental standards. With respect to the first type of lobbying we can refer also to the function of licences, which are considered a central instrument of environmental policy. Moore[112] has pointed out the anti-competitive effects of licensing.[113]

---

108 Keenan and Rubin (1988, pp. 21–36).

109 Pelzman (1976, pp. 211–40).

110 Dewees (1983, pp. 53–71).

111 Maloney and McCormick (1982, pp. 99–123).

112 Moore (1961, pp. 93–117).

113 On the use of standards to seek competitive advantages, see also Ogus (1994, pp. 23–37); Hahn (1990a, pp. 149–75); Hahn (1990b, pp. 21–47) and Huber (1983, p. 1025).

Evidence of rent-seeking behaviour in environmental regulation in the US was recently reported by Adler[114] and similar stories can be found in Europe as well.[115]

Lobbying for lenient standards may be directed at the legislator. But since legislators usually give standard-setting power to administrative agencies, this type of lobbying, for example to get lenient emission standards for an individual firm, will usually target the administrative agency. The behaviour of bureaucracies in response to this capture by industry is analysed in different papers, for example by Downing.[116] Rent-seeking will obviously not only affect the standard-setting process, but can also play a role in the case of zoning.[117]

Remarkably, a recent OECD report showed that marketable permit schemes reduce the potential benefits associated with rent-seeking behaviour, especially with respect to the cap-and-trade model. The baseline-and-credit form however seems to come close to command and control interventions with respect to rent-seeking behaviour.[118]

7.2. Influence of Private Interest on Instrument Choice

The influence of private interest in environmental law has been addressed specifically in the literature with respect to the issue of instrument choice. Above, we indicated the variety of instruments that can be used to control environmental pollution, indicating that the literature suggests under what kind of circumstances a particular type of policy instrument would be optimal. In practice these 'economic prescriptions'[119] are not always followed. One reason why for example in the US emission taxes are seldom used and policy still relies to a large extent on the command and control approach is that firms will prefer emission standards to taxes, because standards serve as a barrier to the entry of new firms, thus raising the profits of existing firms. Charges on the other hand do not preclude entry by new firms and represent an additional cost to the existing firms in the market.[120] This basic point made by Buchanan and Tullock has been extended by other scholars, examining the implication of

---

114 Adler (1996, pp. 26–34).

115 Faure and Van den Bergh (1989a, pp. 308–30) or Faure and Van den Bergh (1989b).

116 Downing (1989, pp. 255–71).

117 Ault and Ekelund (1988, pp. 69–76); Fischel (1980, pp. 37–43) and Fischel (1985).

118 Tietenberg and Johnstone (2004, p. 34).

119 Hahn (1989a, pp. 195–211) and Hahn (1989c, p. 135).

120 Buchanan and Tullock (1975, pp. 139–147) and see the comments by Coelho (1976, pp. 976–978) and Yohe (1976, pp. 981–82).

rent-seeking for pollution taxation.[121] The influence of lobbying on instrument choice has also been analysed in the many papers by Hahn,[122] Hahn and Noll,[123] Körber[124] and by De Grauwe.[125] Hahn points out that policy instruments are almost never used in the way that is suggested by economic theory. Emission charges are for example used as a revenue-raising device with few direct effects on polluters and many marketable permit approaches are not really designed to create markets. Through grandfathering the rights of existing firms are often protected. In addition, even where economic prescriptions (marketable pollution rights) were followed, there is some evidence that emissions trading systems were used as a loophole by which industry could forestall compliance.[126] Hahn also argues that the varying interest group attitudes in for example the US and Europe may account for the fact that European countries tend to rely more on the use of fees, whereas marketable permits have been introduced on a relatively important scale only in the US.[127] Hence, the selection of an appropriate mix of policy instruments will to a large extent be determined by the way political choices are actually made in different countries.

Indeed, one can therefore often notice that the mix of policy instruments will also be determined by political choices and by interest groups politics. Hence, the fact that a certain (command and control) instrument is introduced rather than another (market oriented) instrument can, as the various examples showed, be due to the result of effective lobbying by interest groups. But also in the way in which even market oriented instruments such as emission trading are organized one can notice the influence of interest groups. Notice in this respect the fact that when an emission trading system is introduced the legislator will often prefer a grandfathering of emission rights to existing polluters rather than allocating the new emission rights through auctioning. Grandfathering is of course in the interest of the existing firms and it grants them a right to pollute, protects in fact the (old) polluters and may again create barriers to entry.

7.3. Example: The Dutch Energy Tax

We have already provided above the example of the regulatory energy tax in

---

121 Lee (1985, pp. 731–44) and Brooks and Heijdra (1987, pp. 335–42).

122 Hahn (1989b, pp. 95–114); Hahn (1989a, pp. 195–211); Hahn (1989c, p. 135).

123 Hahn and Noll (1983, pp. 63–91).

124 Körber (1995, pp. 161–91).

125 De Grauwe (1995, pp. 111–68).

126 Hahn (1989c, pp. 109–53).

127 Hahn (1989b, p. 111).

the Netherlands, which largely seems to protect large energy consumers instead of achieving ecological goals. The Dutch tax reform which took place was apparently not primarily concerned with ecological goals, but rather with improving the competitiveness of Dutch industry.

To some extent the changes in the Dutch tax system in 2001 can be explained by the above-mentioned public choice framework.[128] Indeed, as mentioned, a greening of the tax system may have been the result of demand from the public at large. However, if one addresses the way this has been shaped and who actually benefits and loses as a result of the change, one can come to a few striking conclusions. Apparently it is the small, average households who pay the increased energy taxes and a large part of the benefit feeds back on the one hand into a reduction of income and wage taxes, but on the other hand also as subsidies to industry. These two measures obviously benefit industry. Indeed, the reduction of taxes on wages and income decreases production costs for Dutch industry, hence strengthening their international competitiveness. That environmental subsidies to industry benefit them directly needs no further explanation. Therefore one has the impression that the whole tax reform led to a redistribution from smaller taxpayers (who will have to pay a higher electricity bill) to Dutch industry, which may have seen their competitive position in the international market improve as a result of these measures. This shows once more that taxation, even if it is called environmental taxation, has redistribution as its main goal and much less so behavioural change. Moreover, the redistribution resulting from the Dutch tax reform seems to a large extent to be a negative redistribution. It will be precisely the lower income groups who will suffer most as a result of increased energy prices.

The fact that tax reform in the Netherlands probably did not have primarily ecological goals in mind, but was mostly concerned with improving the competitiveness of Dutch industry becomes quite clear if, once more, one considers the increased energy tax. If this energy tax were to have a regulatory character, it should obviously primarily be targeted at the largest energy consumers, namely industry. But strikingly enough this regulatory energy tax decreases the more one consumes and larger consumers are actually totally exempt from the tax. This makes clear that the tax, even though it is called 'regulatory', can hardly be seen as serving ecological goals. Here the government has quite bluntly defended the exemption of large consumers with reference to the competitiveness of Dutch industry in the international market.

---

[128] For a public choice analysis of the Dutch Tax reform see Faure and Ubachs (2002, pp. 323–4).

8. CONCLUDING REMARKS

In this chapter we have presented so-called economic instruments as tools of environmental policy. Economists, since the early work of Pigou in the 1920s, have advanced taxation as the perfect way to internalize externalities. We noticed that, at least theoretically, environmental charges can indeed have substantial benefits as environmental policy tools. This is especially the case if one compares financial instruments like taxes to the traditional command and control approach under regulation. Taxes would provide additional incentives for pollution reduction, and thus incentives for investments in innovative environmental technology and would moreover be more flexible. The overall environmental effectiveness of environmental taxes would thus – at least on paper – be a lot higher than traditional regulation. Nevertheless we also noticed that, notwithstanding the theoretical advantages of this instrument, environmental taxes are apparently not often used in practice (especially in the US).

In addition we showed on the basis of the literature that the two economic instruments that we discussed in this contribution, namely both environmental taxes and emission trading have comparable benefits to the command and control approach, although there are some disadvantages as well. As a result, the more recent economic literature argues that an environmental policy should seek an optimal use of a variety of instruments and not opt just for one policy tool. This is also what one can see in the regulatory practice of many countries. Environmental policy usually relies on emission standards, combined with regulatory charges and – in cases where it is possible – emission trading as well.

One can understand the popularity of particular economic instruments, like environmental taxes. Nevertheless Bruno Frey provides a powerful argument on why environmental taxes might not be the optimal instrument to control externalities. Frey argues that they may have a negative effect on environmental morality. However, Frey argues that the same may be true of tradable emission rights. Both are instruments that would not have a positive effect on the intrinsic motivation to safeguard the environment. This theory, therefore, may explain why policy-makers still rely more heavily on traditional command and control instruments than on the so-called economic instruments. Moreover, we also noticed, while discussing the example of emission trading, that the theoretical benefits of economic instruments should not be overstated. Economic instruments too require a lot of information and enforcement costs in order to be applied in an effective manner.

In addition we noticed that private interest theory explains why some economic instruments, like environmental taxes, are not introduced in textbook form. This theory relies on the classic argument presented by Buchanan and Tullock that industry will probably prefer command and control regulation since this type of regulation (especially licences) can be used to create barriers to entry. Indeed, a result of licensing is that it will be more difficult for new entrants to enter the market, thus profits for existing firms may be raised. Taxes, on the other hand, will only increase costs for industry without the capacity to create barriers to new entrants. Tradable emission rights may have this advantage, depending on what allocation mechanism is chosen. If grandfathering is chosen to allocate tradable emission rights, one can again understand that firms that were already in the market would be more enthusiastic about tradable emission rights than about taxes. The situation would of course be different if another allocation mechanism for marketable permits were to be used, such as auctioning.

All of this also raises the question to what extent the use of economic instruments presented in this contribution (in particular taxes and emission trading) would be useful in environmental policy in a developing country like Indonesia. In fact our analysis established that the application of so-called economic instruments also requires a great deal of regulation. Indeed, in order to apply taxes efficiently, information is needed by public authorities to establish the marginal tax rate and taxes need to be collected by reliable officials. Also a market-oriented instrument like emission trading still requires a great deal of regulatory intervention, for instance to control the trade in emissions and also to guarantee that no more is emitted than is allocated in emission rights. In sum, developing countries should be wary of embracing the market-oriented instruments presented in this contribution in the belief that they would require less information and enforcement costs.

Nevertheless, some careful guided experiments might be considered, like using emissions trading for non-local pollutants. The acid rain allowance trading programme and European greenhouse gas emissions trading are important experiments from which much can be learned. Those systems might serve as useful examples for developing countries, provided that they can deal with the distribution of rights and the control and enforcement tasks. In future, it might even be the case that international negotiations and agreements on climate change measures will include (some) emission reduction commitments for (the most developed) developing countries, which might be a reason or an incentive for the establishment of emissions trading for greenhouse gases within those countries.

Moreover, some may argue that the risk of collusion may be larger when a greater deal of flexibility is introduced in legal instruments. Some authors like Ogus have therefore argued that if a particular developing country feared a great deal of collusion or corruption, the best remedy is probably not merely to fight the corruption problem, but to choose those types of instrument that limit the margin of discretion of the administrative authorities. In that way the scope for collusion and corruption will be reduced simply by choosing instruments that are less vulnerable to those practices.[129] One conclusion of that literature might be that a developing country like Indonesia should probably be very cautious about the introduction of economic instruments given the collusion risk, and that scholars from the developed world should indeed be careful not to oversell economic instruments to developing countries.[130]

If one wishes to limit the margin of discretion of administrative authorities, the best remedy is probably for the legislator to set very precise rules and standards which leave little scope for interpretation. Of course the disadvantage of this would be that the system might be too rigid, too unbalanced and not flexible enough. In such cases a trade-off would have to be made, between, on the one hand, choosing more efficient and flexible economic instruments but realizing that the introduction of flexibility increases the collusion risk and, on the other hand, reducing the collusion risk by choosing more rigid rules and standards of the command and control type. It will of course depend very much on the individual situation of any given country what the optimal combination of various instruments may be. A lesson from the literature is at least that in those cases where there is a high risk of collusion one should be very careful in general over embracing flexible economic instruments. The traditional more rigid command and control instruments – like general rules – might in those cases precisely be more suitable on condition that they can be structured in such a way that standards are set in the public interest and that the scope for collusive practices can be reduced as much as possible.

REFERENCES

Ackerman, B.A., S. Rose-Ackerman, J. Sawyer Jr. and D.R. Henderson (1974), *The Uncertain Search for Environmental Quality*, New York, USA: Free Press.

Ackerman, B.A. and R.B. Stewart (1988), 'Reforming Environmental Law: The Democratic Case for Market Incentives', *Columbia Journal of Environmental Law*, **13**, 171–99.

Adler, J.H (1996), 'Rent Seeking Behind the Green Curtain', *Regulation*, 26–34.

Ault, R.W. and R.B. Ekelund (1988), 'Rent Seeking in A Static Model of Zoning', *American Real Estate and Urban Economics Association Journal*, **16**, 69–76.

Barde, J.-P. (1995), 'Environmental Policy and Policy Instruments', in H. Folmer, H.L. Gabel and H. Opschoor (eds), *Principles of Environmental and Resource Economics: A Guide for Students and Decision-Makers*, Aldershot, UK and Brookfield, US: Edward Elgar, pp. 218–20.

Baumol, W.J. and W.E. Oates (1971), 'The Use of Standards and Prices for Protection of the Environment', *Swedish Journal of Economics*, **71**, 42–54.

---

129 See Ogus (2004, pp. 229–46).

130 We agree with this statement made by Russell and Vaughan (2003).

Bongaerts, J.C. and R.A. Kraemer (1987), 'Water Pollution Charges in Three Countries. Control through Incentives', *European Environment Review*, **1** (4), 12–19.

Britt, G. (2001), 'Pollution Tax', in Boudewijn Bouckaert and Gerrit de Geest (eds), *Encyclopedia of Law and Economics Volume II: Civil Law and Economics*, Cheltenham, UK and Northampton, MA, USA: Edward Elgar, pp. 541–5.

Brooks, M.A. and B.J. Heijdra (1987), 'Rent-Seeking and Pollution Taxation: An Extension', *Southern Economic Journal*, 335–42.

Brown, G. and R. Johnson (1984), 'Pollution Control by Effluent Charges: It Works in the Federal Republic of Germany, Why Not in the US?', *Natural Resources Journal*, 929–66.

Brown, J.P. and W.L. Holahan (1980), 'Taxes and Legal Rules for the Control of Externalities When There are Strategic Responses', *Journal of Legal Studies*, **9**, 165–78.

Buchanan, J., R. Tollison and G. Tullock (eds) (1962), *Toward a Theory of the Rent Seeking Society*, Michigan: University of Michigan Press.

Buchanan, J. and G. Tullock (1962), *The Calculus of Consent*, Michigan: University of Michigan Press.

Buchanan, J. and G. Tullock (1975), 'Polluters' Profits and Political Response: Direct Controls versus Taxes', *American Economic Review*, **65**, 139–47.

Coelho, P.R.P. (1976), 'Polluters' Profits and Political Response: Direct Control versus Taxes: Comment', *American Economic Review*, **66**, 976–8.

Dales, J. (1968), *Pollution, Property and Prices: An Essay in Policy*, Toronto: University of Toronto Press.

De Grauwe, P. (1995), 'Political Economy of the Choice of Environmental Policy Instruments in the EC', in F. Abraham, K. Deketelaere and J. Stuyck (eds), *Recent Economic Legal Developments in European Environmental Policy*, Leuven: Leuven University Press, pp. 111–68.

de Kock, S. (1980) 'Government Financial Incentive for the Protection of the Environment', in M. Bothe (ed.), *Trends in Environmental Policy and Law*, Gland: IUCN, pp. 64–7.

Dewees, D.N. (1983), 'Instrument Choice in Environmental Policy', *Economic Inquiry*, **21**, 53–71.

Dewees, D, D. Duff and M. Trebilcock (1996), *Exploring the Domain of Accident Law: Taking the Facts Seriously*, New York and Oxford: Oxford University Press.

Dornau, R. (2005), 'The Emissions Trading Scheme of the European Union', in David Freestone and Charlotte Streck (eds), *Legal Aspects of Implementing the Kyoto Protocol Mechanisms*, Oxford: Oxford University Press, chapter 23.

Downing, P.B. (1989), 'A Political Economy Model of Implementing Pollution Laws', *Journal of Environmental Economics and Management*, **8**, 255–71.

Ellerman, D. (2004), The US SO2 Cap-and-Trade Programme, OECD Report: Marketable Permits, Policy Evaluation, Design and Reform, Paris: OECD.

Faure, M. and S. Ubachs (2002), 'Environmental Taxation in the Netherlands: A Dutch treat?', in L.A. Kreiser (ed.), *Critical Issues in International Environmental Taxation. Insights and Analysis for Achieving Environmental Policy Goals through Tax Policy*, Chicago: CCH, pp. 301–29.

Faure, M. and S. Ubachs (2003), 'Comparative Benefits and Optimal Use of Environmental Taxes', in J. Milne, K. Deketelaere, L. Kreiser and H. Ashiabor (eds), *Critical Issues in Environmental Taxation. Vol. I: International and Comparative Perspectives,* Richmond: Richmond Law and Tax, pp. 29–49.

Faure, M. and S. Ubachs (2005), 'Harmful Tax Measures and Greying of Taxation in the Netherlands; What Went Wrong?', in H. Ashiabor, K. Deketelaere, L. Kreiser and J. Milne (eds), *Critical Issues in Environmental Taxation: International and Comparative Perspectives Volume II,* Richmond: Richmond Law and Tax, pp. 521–32.

Faure, M. and R. Van den Bergh (1989a), 'Compulsory Insurance for Professional Liability', *The Geneva Papers on Risk and Insurance*, 308–30.

Faure, M. and R. Van den Bergh (1989b), *Objectieve Aansprakelijkheid, Verplichte Verzekering en Veiligheidsregulering*, Antwerpen: MAKLU.

Faure, M. and R. Van den Bergh (1990), 'Liability for Nuclear Accidents in Belgium from an Interest Group Perspective', *International Review of Law and Economics*, **10**, 241–54.

Fischel, W.A. (1980), 'Externalities and Zoning', *Public Choice*, **35**, 37–43.

Fischel, W.A. (1985), *The Economics of Zoning Laws: A Property Rights Approach to American Land Use Controls*, Baltimore and London: The Johns Hopkins University Press.

Frey, B.S. (1992), *Umweltökonomie*, third edition, Göttingen: VandenHoeck & Ruprecht.

Frey, B.S. (1997), *Not Just For the Money: An Economic Theory of Personal Motivation*, Cheltenham, UK and Northampton, MA, USA: Edward Elgar.

Frey, B.S. (1999), 'Morality and Rationality in Environmental Policy', *Journal of Consumer Policy*, **22**, 395–417.

Gravelle, H.S.E. (1987), 'Accidents, Taxes, Liability Rules and Insurances', *Geneva Papers on Risk and Insurance*, **12**, 115–31.

Gunningham, M. and P. Grabosky (1998), *Smart Regulation. Designing Environmental Policy,* Oxford: Clarendon Press.

Hahn, R.W. (1989a), 'A New Approach to the Design of Regulation in the Presence of Multiple Objectives', *Journal of Environmental Economics and Management*, **17**, 195–211.

Hahn, R.W. (1989b), 'Economic Prescriptions for Environmental Problems: How the Patient Followed the Doctor's Orders', *Journal of Economic Perspectives*, **3**, 95–114.

Hahn, R.W. (1989c), *A Primer on Environmental Policy Design*, New York: Harwood Academic.

Hahn, R.W. (1990a), 'Regulatory Constraints on Environmental Markets', *Journal of Public Economics*, **42**, 49–175.

Hahn, R.W. (1990b), 'The Political Economy of Environmental Regulation: Towards a Unifying Framework', *Public Choice*, **65**, 21–47.

Hahn, R.W. and G.L. Hester (1989), 'Where Did All the Markets Go? An Analysis of EPA's Emissions Trading Programme', *Yale Journal on Regulation*, **6**, 109–53.

Hahn, R.W. and R. Noll (1983), 'Barriers to Implementing Tradeable Air Pollution Permits: Problems of Regulatory Interaction', *Yale Journal on Regulation*, **1**, 63–91.

Hansson, I. and G. Skogh (1987), 'Moral Hazard and Safety Regulation', *The Geneva Papers on Risk and Insurance*, **12**, 132–44.

Hruza, J., S. Logan, E. Martin and N. Sahni (2004), 'Opportunities and Challenges to Implementing MBIs in Industrializing and Developing Countries: A Case Study Approach', *Yale University Environmental Protection Clinic*, 12 May 2004, 237.

Huber, P. (1983), 'The Old–New Division in Risk Regulation', *Virginia Law Review*, **63**, 1025.

Jaffer, S. and J. Kay (1986), 'The Regulation of Shop Opening Hours in the United Kingdom', in Graf J.M. von den Schulenburg and G. Skogh (eds), *Law and Economics and the Economics of Legal Regulation*, Dordrecht: Nijhoff, pp. 169–83.

Keenan, D. and P. Rubin (1988), 'Shadow Interest Groups and Safety Regulation', *International Review of Law and Economics*, 21–36.

Kolstad, C.D. (2000), *Environmental Economics,* New York: Oxford University Press.

Kolstad, C.D., T.S. Ulen and G.V. Johnson (1990), 'Ex Post Liability for Harm vs. Ex Ante Safety Regulation: Substitutes of Complements?', *The American Economic Review*, **80** (4), 888–901.

Körber, A. (1995), 'Standards and Taxes in Environmental Law from a Public Choice Perspective', in B. Bouckaert and G. De Geest (eds), *Essays in Law and Economics II*, Antwerp: MAKLU, pp. 161–91.

Lee, D.R. (1985), 'Rent-seeking and its Implications for Pollution Taxation', *Southern Economic Journal*, 731–44.

Lefevere, J. (2005) 'Linking Emissions Trading Schemes: The EU ETS and the Linking Directive', in D. Freestone and C. Streck (eds), *Legal Aspects of Implementing the Kyoto Protocol Mechanisms,* Oxford: Oxford University Press.

Löfgren, K.-G. (1995), 'Market and Externalities', in H. Folmer, H. Landis Gabel and H. Opschoor (eds), *Principles of Environmental and Resource Economics: A Guide for Students and Decision-Makers*, Aldershot, UK and Brookfield, US: Edward Elgar.

Maloney, M.T. and R.E. McCormick (1982), 'A Positive Theory of Environmental Quality Regulation', *Journal of Law and Economics*, 99–123.

McCormick, R. and R. Tollison (1982), *Politicians, Legislation and the Economy: An Inquiry into the Interest Group Theory of Governments*, Boston: Martinus Nijhoff.

Montgomery, D.W. (1972), 'Markets in Licenses and Efficient Pollution Control', *Journal of Economic Theory*, **5**, 395–418.

Moore, T.P. (1961), 'The Purpose of Licensing', *Journal of Law and Economics*, 93–117.

Nash, J.R. and R.L. Revesz (2001), 'The Design of Marketable Permit Schemes to Control Local and Regional Pollutants', *Ecology Law Quarterly,* **28**.

Noll, R. (1982), 'The Feasibility of Marketable Emissions Permits in the United States', in R.B. Stewart and J.B. Krier (eds), *Environmental Law and Policy*, Virginia: Charlottesville, pp. 116–28.

Oates, W.E. (1986), 'Market Incentives for Environmental Protection: A Survey of Some Recent Developments', in M. Peston and R. Quandt (eds), *Prices, Competition, and Equilibrium,* London: Philip Allen, pp. 251–67.

Oates, W.E. (1990), 'Economics, Economists, and Environmental Policy', *Eastern Economic Journal,* **XVI** (4), 292–3.

Oates, W.E. (1994), 'Environment and Taxation: The Case of the United States', *OECD Documents, Environment and Taxation: The Cases of the Netherlands, Sweden and the United States*, Paris: OECD.

Oates, W.E. (1996), 'The Environment and the Economy: Environmental Policy at the Crossroads', in W.E. Oates (ed.), *The Economics of Environmental Regulation,* Cheltenham, UK and Northampton, MA, USA: Edward Elgar, p. 29.

Oates, W.E. and W. Baumol (1996), 'Instrument for Environmental Policy', in W.E. Oates (ed.), *The Economics of Environmental Regulation,* Cheltenham, UK and Northampton, MA, USA: Edward Elgar, pp. 105–7.

Oates, W.E. and R.A. Collinge (1982), 'Efficiency in Pollution Control in the Short and

Long Run: A System of Rental Emission Permits', *Canadian Journal of Economics*, **15** (2), 346–54.

Oates, W.E., A.J. Crupnik and E. Van de Verg (1983), 'On Marketable Air Pollution Permits: The Case for a System of Pollution Offsets', *Journal of Environmental Economics and Management*, **10** (3), 233–47.

Oates, W.E. and A.M. McGartland (1985a), 'Marketable Pollution Permits and Acid Rain Externalities: A Comment and Some Further Evidence', *Canadian Journal of Economics*, **18** (3), 668–75.

Oates, W.E. and A.M. McGartland (1985b), 'Marketable Permits for the Prevention of Environmental Deterioration', *Journal of Environmental Economics and Management*, **12** (3), 207–28.

Oates, W.E., P.R. Portney and A.M. McGartland (1989), 'The Net Benefits on Incentive-Based Regulation: A Case Study of Environmental Standard Setting', *The American Economic Review*, **79** (5), 1233–42.

Ogus, A. (1994), 'Standard Setting for Environmental Protection: Principles and Processes', in M. Faure, J. Vervaele and A. Weale (eds), *Environmental Standard in the European Union in an Interdisciplinary Framework*, Antwerp: MAKLU, pp. 23–37.

Ogus, A. (1999), 'Nudging and Rectifying: The Use of Fiscal Instruments for Regulatory Purposes', *Legal Studies*, **19**, 245–66.

Ogus, A. (2004), 'Corruption and Regulatory Structures', *Law and Policy*, 229–46.

Olson, M. (1982), *The Rise and Decline of Nations*, New Haven and London: Yale University Press.

Paulus, A. (1995), *The Feasibility of Ecological Taxation*, Antwerp: Maklu Uitgevers.

Pearce, D.W. and R.K. Turner (1990), *Economics of Natural Resources and the Environment*, Baltimore: Johns Hopkins University Press

Peeters, M. (1992), *Marktconform Milieurecht? Een Rechtsvergelijkende Studie naar de Verhandelbaarheid van Vervuilingsrechten (Market Oriented Environmental Law? A Comparative Legal Study into the Tradeability of Pollution Rights)*, Zwolle: Tjeenk Willink.

Peeters, M. (2003), 'Emissions Trading as a New Dimension to European Environmental Law: The Political Agreement of the European Council on Greenhouse Gas Allowance Trading', *European Environmental Law Review*, **12**, 82–92.

Pelzman, S. (1976), 'Toward a more General Theory of Regulation', *Journal of Law and Economics*, **19**, 211–40.

Perman, R., Y. Ma, J. McGilvray and M. Common (2003), *Natural Resources and Environmental Economics*, third edition: Essex: Longman.

Pindyck, R.S. and D.L. Rubenfield (2001), *Microeconomics*, New Jersey: Prentice Hall.

Polinsky, A.M. (1979), 'Controlling Externalities and Protecting Entitlements: Property Right, Liability Rule and the Tax-subsidy Approaches', *Journal of Legal Studies*, **8**, 1–48.

Posner, R. (1974), 'Theories of Economic Regulation', *Bell Journal of Economics*, 345.

Rose-Ackerman, S. (1977), 'Market Models for Water Pollution Control: Their Strength and Weaknesses', *Public Policy*, **25**, 383–406.

Rose-Ackerman, S. (1992), *Rethinking the Progressive Agenda, the Reform of the American Regulatory State*, New York: Free Press.

Rosen, H.S. (1999), *Public Finance*, Chicago: Irwin.

Russell, C.S. and J.W. Vaughan (2003), 'The Choice of Pollution Control Policy Instruments in Developing Countries: Argumens, Evidence and Suggestions', in H. Folmer and T. Tietenberg, *The International Yearbook of Environmental and Resource Economics 2003/2004*, Cheltenham, UK and Northampton, Ma, USA: Edward Elgar, pp. 331–70.

Siebert, H. (1995), *Economics of the Environment: Theory and Policy*, fourth edition, Berlin: Springer-Verlag.

Skogh, G. (1982), 'Public Insurance and Accident Prevention', *International Review of Law and Economics*, **2**, 67–80.

Skogh, G. (1989), 'The Combination of Private and Public Regulation of Safety', in M. Faure and R. Van den Bergh (eds), *Essays in Law and Economics. Corporations, Accident Prevention and Compensation for Losses*, Antwerp: Maklu, pp. 87–101.

Stavins, R.N. (2003), 'Experience with Market-based Environmental Policy Instruments', in K.-G. Mäler and J.R. Vincent (eds), *Handbook of Environmental Economics Volume I: Environmental Degradation and Institutional Responses*, Amsterdam: Elsevier, pp. 362–72.

Stranlund, J.K., A.C. Chavez and B.C. Field (2002), 'Enforcing Emissions Trading Programs: Theory, Practice and Performance', *Policy Studies Journal,* **30** (3), 343–61.

Svendsen, G.T. (1998), *Public Choice and Environmental Regulation: Tradable Permit Systems in the United States and CO_2 Taxation in Europe,* Cheltenham, UK and Northampton, MA, USA: Edward Elgar.

Tietenberg, T. (1985), *Emissions Trading: An Exercise in Reforming Pollution Policy*, Washington, DC: Resources for the Future.

Tietenberg, T. (1990) 'Economic Instruments for Environmental Regulation', *Oxford Review of Economic Policy*, 17–33.

Tietenberg, T. (2000), *Environmental and National Resource Economics*, Reading: Addison-Wesley.

Tietenberg, T. and N. Johnstone (2004), 'Ex Post Evaluation of Marketable Permits: Methodological Issues and Literature Review' in *Tradable Permits: Policy Evaluation, Design and Reform*, Paris: Organisation for Economic Co-operation and Development, pp. 9–44

Turner, R.K., D. Pearce and I. Bateman (1994), *Environmental Economics: An Elementary Introduction,* New York: Harvester Wheatsheaf.

Van den Bergh, R. (1986), 'Belgian Public Policy towards the Retailing Trade', in J.M. Graf von den Schulenburg and G. Skogh (eds), *Law and Economics and the Economics of Legal Regulation*, Dordrecht: Nijhoff, pp. 185–205.

Victor, D.G. (2001), *The Collapse of the Kyoto Protocol and the Struggle to Slow Global Warming,* New Jersey: Princeton University Press.

Yohe, G. (1976), 'Pollutors' Profits and Political Response: Direct Control versus Taxes: Comment', *American Economic Review*, **66**, 981–2.

11. Towards effective environmental legislation in Indonesia?

Michael Faure and Nicole Niessen

1. INTRODUCTION

The preceding chapters each dealt with distinct aspects of environmental law reform in developing countries, focusing on Indonesia. In this final chapter we draw some general conclusions and formulate some general recommendations. To that end, our final analysis also builds on general theories about law reform in developing countries and which obstacles law reformers must anticipate.

The direct cause for the revision of the Environmental Management Act 1997 (EMA 1997) has been the enactment of the Regional Government Act 1999 (RGA). But the ambitions of the Indonesian Ministry for the Environment, supported by environmental non-government organizations – go beyond merely adjusting the EMA 1997 to the RGA 1999. Presently, a full revision of the EMA 1997 will be under way due to dissatisfaction with various elements of its environmental protection regime. For this purpose a research team of Maastricht University was asked to give legal advice. An analysis of the EMA 1997 has indeed revealed a number of problems that can be healed, or avoided, by drafting new legal provisions. To that end all the chapters in this book contain concrete recommendations. At the same time, however, the authors emphasize that law does not provide answers to all the shortcomings in the environmental protection scheme, but instead profound cultural and institutional changes are demanded.

In these conclusions we briefly refer back to the major issues that have been raised in the various chapters. As we made clear in the Introduction, on the one hand, we wish to present contributions which at a general level discuss how environmental law and policy could be shaped in developing countries if an effective environmental protection is to be achieved; on the other hand, we do not wish to examine this question just in the abstract but by focusing on the concrete example of Indonesia. That is why the reform of Indonesia's EMA 1997 was taken as the specific starting point for many contributions in this book. In this concluding chapter we analyse which general conclusions can be derived from the specific Indonesian situation. We indeed believe that some of the shortcomings that were discussed in the various contributions are not unique to Indonesia (although of course many features are country-specific) but occur in other developing countries as well. One can therefore draw lessons from the Indonesian experience for the design of environmental law and policy in developing countries. To that end we first address the development of environmental law within the context of law reform in developing countries (Sections 2–3), then focus on the choice of instruments (Section 4) and enforcement techniques (Section 5). Subsequently, we discuss a few implementation constraints that may play a role in designing and enforcing an effective environmental law in developing countries (Section 6). A few words with regard to future prospects conclude the book (Section 7).

Although this book covers many aspects of the development of environmental law, there are of course a few issues that could not be examined in greater detail. For instance, the issue of civil liability could only be briefly touched upon in the contribution by Wibisana. Furthermore, although criminal law was discussed in the contribution by Faure, the issue of criminal procedure was not dealt with in much detail. These limitations notwithstanding, we do believe that all the contributions together contain sufficient material to draw some general conclusions.

2. LAW AND DEVELOPMENT

2.1. Law Reform in Developing Countries

Fairly recently law has become an essential component of the development agenda.[1] Law is a complex and contradictory instrument, however. First of all, there is no single model for legal reform. It should be recognized that a legal model, derived from an ideal type of market and legal system, cannot be made to work in every country, regardless of local circumstances. Also, legal reform is slow and difficult to achieve. It requires careful preparation, meticulous planning, effective execution, elaborate coordination between government and disparate institutions, and ultimately the consent of those directly responsible for its implementation. As Faundez[2] argues, '[s]uccess in carrying out legal reform requires considerable commitment, patience and a certain amount of good luck'. In addition, legal reformers must anticipate that the reform process may have unintended (adverse) consequences and that unexpected events may become serious obstacles to the process.

1 Faundez (2000, p. 1).
2 Faundez (2000, p. 2).

Certainly, the number of new laws drafted and enacted is not a success indicator. For example, developing countries have enacted a large number of new laws over the past two decades, but legal reform amounts to much more than drafting and enacting new rules. To ensure that new legislation is successfully implemented, legal reformers are required to consider the compatibility of the new rules and institutions with the existing legal and political system.[3]

2.2. Drafting Country-specific Laws

Faundez[4] asserts that knowledge of the local context is a *conditio sine qua non*. It is important to understand local conditions before deciding whether legal reform is necessary, and if so, how to implement it. In practice, however, a thorough analysis of the local context is often lacking. Foreign legal experts generally tend to underestimate the fragility of institutional frameworks in developing countries, and how this impacts negatively on the outcome of the reform process. Considering this, it is interesting to note that in our project it was the foreign experts who emphasized the importance of a thorough *ex ante* problem analysis, the relativity of legal solutions, and a gradual approach. The receiving party, by contrast, was very keen to solve the problems of environmental protection management in Indonesia by means of a full revision of the EMA 1997 all at once.

In the context of law reform, it is common practice to model institutions on the experience of another country or on a general model. This is not necessarily negative for it may enrich and add diversity to local legal cultures, provided that it takes into account the specificities of the receiving country.[5] The drafting of the Dutch General Administrative Law Act (GALA), for example, was much inspired by the German Laws on Administrative Procedure and Administrative Courts. The GALA is not, however, a copy of the German model. Notwithstanding some evident foreign influence, the GALA still very much builds on typically Dutch legal-historical traditions and experiences.[6]

While the stated aim of legal reform is to strengthen the institutional capacity of recipient countries, paradoxically the process itself may undermine this when a profound knowledge of the existing legal institutional framework and culture is absent. Especially when a large number of reforms have to be implemented over a relatively short period of time, there is a serious danger that the institutional framework of a state deteriorates instead of improves.

---

3 Faundez (2000, p. 4).
4 Faundez (2000, p. 7).
5 Faundez (2000, p. 11).
6 For further information, see Faundez (1997); Seidman and Seidman (1999); Seidman et al. (1999).

2.3. Legislative Quality Indicators

In point of fact, quite often the enactment of new legislation is not the answer to the problems identified.[7] Veerman[8] stresses that an important preliminary question concerns the *necessity* of drafting a law: is the problem identified best solved by means of new legislation? And if so, what type or level of regulation is most suitable?

Concerning the EMA 1997, to a considerable extent non-legal factors – such as the limited dissemination of environmental information (legal as well as technical), the lack of qualified personnel working at institutions responsible for the implementation of environmental regulations, a generally low priority accorded to matters of environmental protection, etc. – have impacted in a negative manner on its effectiveness. Having said this, some legal changes are indeed necessary. Peeters and Niessen, however, argue that a gradual adjustment of the EMA 1997, by means of successive amendments, would be the most fruitful approach to securing the desired improvements. After all, the EMA 1997 is a framework law and it offers abundant opportunities to realize vital changes by means of secondary legislation, such as government regulations and ministerial decrees. To this day, quite a few provisions of the EMA 1997 have still not been elaborated upon by means of secondary legislation, although the law itself expressly states that this should be done. In other words, some flexibility is already incorporated in the EMA 1997 itself, and prudent use of this flexibility should be made, if only to circumvent the tardiness and political uncertainty that are inherent in the drafting of a completely new law.

Legislative quality indicators, whether these are of Dutch or European origin, or launched by an international organization such as the OECD, in essence boil down to the following elements:[9]

(a) legality
(b) effectiveness
(c) efficiency
(d) practicability
(e) enforceability
(f) subsidiarity and proportionality
(g) attunement
(h) simplicity, clarity and accessibility

---

7 Faundez (2000, p. 4).
8 Veerman (2004, p. 1).
9 Veerman (2004, p. 4).

Taken separately, these quality indicators are sufficiently clear, but their practical application often runs into problems. The element of accessibility, for example, means that a regulation should be clear and accessible to the people addressed by it, for example children, pharmacists, farmers. Most commonly, however, a law is interpreted and applied by legal specialists. A minimum requirement, therefore, is that the law should be accessible for legally trained professionals. The above scheme also requires flexible application because several quality indications interfere with one another. Therefore, the essential value of these quality indicators is that they insert a certain amount of legal-technical rationality into the lawmaking process, which is basically a political process. The outcome of that process is a law, which is presented to the public as the best solution to solve the problem. Veerman,[10] however, emphasizes that lawmaking to a considerable degree means 'governing in the mist'. In the drafting process some problems of implementation can be discerned at an early stage by means of an impact analysis. But *ex ante* studies cannot offer absolute guarantees about the actual effects of new legislation. It is therefore necessary to accompany the introduction of any new law with publicity, and the investment of the money, time, personnel and skills necessary to implement it. Finally, it should be recognized that no law is perfect. Legal drafters simply cannot expect that their product will deliver all of the intended results because people work with it, and against it.[11]

The EMA 1997 is a framework law. A main advantage of this legal technique is that implementing measures – in the form of secondary legislation – can be easily adjusted to changing circumstances, new information and technical developments. A major problem of Indonesian law – not only with regard to environmental protection – is the poor legislative quality of framework laws and their secondary legislation since they meet hardly any of the above-mentioned criteria. This largely explains why their implementation and enforcement are fraught with difficulties.[12]

3. DEVELOPING ENVIRONMENTAL LAW

3.1. Definition of the Environment

A recurring theme in our project has been the scope of environmental legislation in Indonesia. To put this precisely, the question was whether a new

10 Veerman (2004).
11 Veerman (2004, pp. 5–6).
12 Niessen (2003).

environmental management act must pertain to brown issues (pollution) only, or should include green issues (natural resources management) as well. The Indonesian counterpart, for that matter, supported the drafting of an all-encompassing – brown and green – environmental management act. However, in 2004 draft legislation concerning natural resources management was already at an advanced stage,[13] hence the enactment of distinct laws for brown and green issues is the most likely outcome. In our opinion, there are no compelling reasons to treat brown and green issues in a single law. In the Netherlands, for that matter, environmental pollution and natural resources management are treated separately, a distinction that is taken for granted. In other countries, like Belgium for instance and more particularly in the Flemish region, similar issues arise. For instance a draft decree on environmental policy was presented in 1995.[14] This document in fact mainly contains proposals for provisions with respect to brown issues. Nature protection, forestry and related issues are dealt with in separate legislation. It is important, though, to put in place effective coordination mechanisms regarding planning, licensing and enforcement between those two domains of the environment.

A related question is whether all brown issues should be dealt with by a single environmental code. In the Netherlands, Peeters argues, the predominant aim of integration has fuelled many discussions about improving the structure of environmental legislation, thereby taking a single fully integrated Environmental Code as the ideal situation.[15] But although the Dutch EMA of 1993 has incorporated a number of separate environmental laws, some important specific environmental laws have remained in place, such as the Surface Water Pollution Act, the Soil Protection Act and the Hazardous Substances Act. A comparative survey among six Member States of the European Union, furthermore, has revealed that in none of these countries has a single Environmental Code been accomplished. Interestingly, in countries like Denmark and the United Kingdom, the integration of national environmental legislation is hardly discussed at all. In other countries, such as Sweden, there has been a tremendous effort to enact a single Environmental Code, but an overall substantive integration has still not been achieved.[16]

---

[13] When we held our first seminar in Maastricht, January 2004, the draft was presented by the Indonesian counterpart. At that time it incorporated the results of an intensive public participation process undertaken in 159 localities as well as inputs from relevant sectors/departments.

[14] See Bocken and Ryckbost (1996).

[15] For the various notions of integrating environmental law, see Faure (2000, pp. 174–82).

[16] Peeters (2003a). A summary of this research is presented by Peeters in her contribution to this book.

Indonesia's EMA 1997, for that matter, is not an all-encompassing environmental code containing all the provisions – and the basis for secondary legislation – for the entire environmental field. Medium-specific regulations, for example, are still contained in separate laws. In addition, most provisions of the EMA 1997 are formulated in loose terms, and secondary legislation is necessary to further specify them.

3.2. Integration, Harmonization and Coordination

There are quite a few compelling reasons to improve the Indonesian legal-institutional framework for environmental protection, but Peeters argues that the enactment of a single Environmental Code will not solve current problems in this field. On the contrary, rather than proposing the radical transformation and adjustment of the environmental law system she opts for a pragmatic step-by-step approach to improving the existing legislation. Such an approach first of all demands the identification of priorities. Although the legislative framework should strive as much as possible for coherence, sometimes there are strong arguments in favour of tackling pollution problems in a rather isolated manner.

What then is the optimal structure for an environmental code? In order to answer this question, Peeters has analysed the above-mentioned Flemish draft decree on environmental policy. This scheme is modelled on legislative developments in Sweden, Belgium and Germany. A main feature of this scheme is a division into horizontal layers and vertical columns. The horizontal layers contain common provisions pertaining to every environmental policy field, such as environmental principles, environmental quality standards, environmental planning, environmental impact assessment and licensing. The vertical columns deal with medium-specific regulations for distinct pollution sources, such as air pollution, soil pollution, etc. The clear and simple structure of this scheme is indeed attractive, but Peeters cautions that the filling-in of the scheme runs into a number of serious dogmatic questions and pitfalls. In her opinion, the fundamental question should be whether the enactment of a single Environmental Code does indeed contribute to the transparency, effectiveness, and efficiency of environmental law? After all, it is not the form but the substance of environmental law that should take priority.

Not only in Indonesia and other developing countries, but also in most developed countries, environmental law has emerged in a non-integrated manner. This means that sectoral legislation was first promoted and only after years of disappointing experiences did the need for integration take priority, because sectoral differences regarding procedures and standards proved to hamper the effectiveness of environmental management. This notwithstanding, as Peeters indicates, a full integration of all environmental legislation may prove to be too difficult to accomplish. Still, Peeters demonstrates that there are a few other techniques that enable the legislator to deal with differences in legislation without necessarily requiring a solution by means of full integration. A typical problem is that of a water board that is not aware of relevant decisions taken by other agencies in the same field, for example, on spatial planning. Such incongruities can of course be prevented if at least coordination takes place as an alternative to full integration. The least one can expect in that respect is that various decision-making authorities take each other's decisions into account and that hence also procedures are structured in such a way that they not only enable, but also compel administrative agencies to do so. Without such coordination, one can expect that a shifting of emissions from one medium to another one would take place.[17] It is precisely in order to prevent this shifting of emissions that Europe in 1996 promulgated the Directive on Integrated Pollution Prevention and Control (IPPC Directive). This directive indeed promotes integration as an instrument to prevent the said shifting of emissions.[18]

Takdir Rahmadi makes clear in his chapter that in Indonesia too the need for an integrated approach is strongly felt, but in practice proves hard to introduce. With regard to pollution control, some integration has been achieved in the sense that Indonesia has enacted the EMA 1997. But Rahmadi immediately makes clear that the EMA 1997 merely provides a 'paper integration'. The basic problem in his view is that the powers of the Ministry of the Environment are too weak, so that many issues related to environmental problems (like, for example, licensing for mining and timbering activities) fall within the competence of other ministries.

Rahmadi clearly shows the shortcomings of a non-integrated approach to environmental law. One consequence is that today companies are confronted with a series of at least seven licences, all relevant to pollution control. Not surprisingly, the power to issue these licences is also assigned to different governmental agencies, whereby effective coordination is lacking. Rahmadi demonstrates that in practice this leads to many difficulties and inconsistencies and – ultimately – weak environmental management. In any case, although there have been various proposals to integrate at least some of the existing seven licences, so far a definitive solution has not been reached.

Remarkably, Rahmadi combines the discussion of integration with the choice of instruments (see also Section 4). Hence, he criticizes the Indonesian EMA 1997 because it fails to meet the requirements of an integrated environmental act and also because it relies too heavily on the command-and-control

---

17 See Faure and Lefevere (1996, pp. 112–22).

18 See Directive 96/61/EC concerning Integrated Pollution Prevention and Control, *Official Journal*, 1996 L 257/27.

approach. Regarding the latter, Rahmadi suggests that more use should be made of either market-based instruments or even voluntary approaches as alternatives to the traditional command-and-control approach.

3.3. Multi-level Approach

Like many developing countries, Indonesia endorses a strong decentralization strategy after several decades of post-colonial centralism. Decentralization is a prominent feature of the *Reformasi* movement, which started when Suharto stepped down as President of the Republic in 1998. The new decentralization strategy is contained in a number of legislative documents. In particular, the Regional Government Act (RGA) 1999 has prepared the ground for the devolution of government powers from the central government to the districts and municipalities. In the field of environmental management also, autonomous regional government has become the norm, which is at odds with the EMA 1997. As a matter of fact, the new decentralization laws serve as immediate incentives to change the EMA 1997. An often-heard criticism, however, is that Indonesia's recent scheme of regional autonomy has been too drastic and that it has come too quickly.

Some amount of decentralization is indeed important in addressing environmental problems properly. At the same time, however, decentralizing of all environmental decisions should be avoided.[19] Rather than using a simple governance model – be it centralized or decentralized – legal-institutional arrangements must be developed 'at multiple levels to cope with the specificity of the environmental issues and to provide the correct incentives to the users at each level of the hierarchy'.[20] The Dutch model of environmental management indeed reveals that there are a great many interactions between the three levels of government – state, provinces and municipalities – regarding all types of environmental decisions: planning, licensing and enforcement. In this manner, environmental management by the municipal government goes alongside a system of central steering and upward accountability. Naturally, the Dutch model is not presented here as an ideal situation, but it does demonstrate some important advantages of a multi-level approach. Such a multi-level approach, although with a stronger emphasis on central steering and supervision, is also contained in the EMA 1997.

Niessen argues that the RGA 1999 has been harmful to environmental management in Indonesia. Most districts and municipalities cannot deal with their new responsibilities for lack of necessary legal and technical expertise.

---

19 Young (2002, p. 55).
20 Cistulli (2002).

In addition, many districts and municipalities have used their government autonomy to boost their regional economies at the expense of measures to secure environmental protection. She therefore recommends the re-establishment of a hierarchical organization of state, province and district/municipality, and the strengthening of the role of the provinces as intermediate governments. Ultimately, Indonesia is to steer a middle course between the old decentralization of Law 5 of 1974 and the new decentralization of Law 22 of 1999. At the same time, the introduction of asymmetric decentralization – as was cautiously embarked upon in the early 1990s – should be reconsidered as well. This would allow for the assignment of differentiated government authority to (groups of) districts and municipalities on the basis of objective performance standards. This approach would be realistic since the performance of regional government units throughout the Indonesian archipelago is highly uneven.

The question whether environmental policy should be centralized or whether decisions can be left to decentralized authorities is an issue that often reappears in environmental legal discourse. The advantage of granting powers to decentralized authorities is, from a public interest perspective, of course that these decentralized authorities usually possess better information on local conditions and thus are able to adapt environmental standards to the local situation.[21] A central government agency may not be in a position to know exactly what the optimal standard should be on an island thousands of kilometres away from the capital city. On the other hand, an adverse consequence of decentralization may be that interest groups work too closely with local government, which may well lead to the so-called 'capture' of agencies by the industry. Especially where a particular industry contributes substantially to employment in a particular area, the local government may be inclined to set less optimal environmental standards so as to reduce the costs for the industry involved. Moreover, as the Indonesian example shows, too far-reaching a decentralization is risky when emissions have polluting effects across the boundaries of particular regions (province, district or municipality).[22] The authorities of that region may be inclined to set lenient standards when pollutants have effects in other regions. Traditionally, the transboundary effects of pollutants have always been a strong argument in favour of centralized standard setting.[23]

The decentralization of environmental policy-making and regulation is to be handled with great caution. The Indonesian message that too far-reaching a decentralization may conflict with environmental policy goals bears importance

---

21 See Oates and Schwab (1988, pp. 333–54).

22 For a critical approach, see Revesz (1996, pp. 2341–416).

23 Faure (1998, pp. 169–75).

for other developing countries as well. Especially in the case of transboundary polluting effects, the setting of environmental standards should be assigned to a level of government with jurisdiction over a sufficiently large territory. With regard to particular emissions, this may justify centralized standard setting.[24] Also, when there are no transboundary effects, there is a strong case for centralized standard setting when the above-mentioned influence of interest groups on local authorities may play a substantial role in environmental decision-making. In those cases, one could argue that emission standards and other environmental parameters should be determined by central government. This does not necessarily mean that all standards are to be harmonized and thus apply equally throughout the country. Concerning Indonesia, obviously the local conditions on, for example, Sumatra are different than those on Java. However, a national environmental protection agency in Jakarta can still obtain information and advice on location-specific conditions from the decentralized authorities. In this manner, environmental standards can be adapted to location-specific circumstances, whilst at the same time the 'capturing risk' is kept to a minimum.

3.4. International Environmental Law

Two Indonesian authors, Andri Wibisana and Daud Silalahi, discuss another aspect of multi-level governance in environmental policy, more particularly the fact that the revision of environmental legislation in a developing country like Indonesia can never be discussed in an isolated manner. Indeed, Indonesia is party to many international environmental agreements which are relevant to the design of national environmental legislation.

It may be clear that when a revision of the EMA 1997 is considered, this should be taken as an opportunity to translate international treaty obligations into national legislation. Silalahi demonstrates that in many respects Indonesia's EMA 1997 is not in compliance with international obligations. He moreover indicates that the implementation of international treaty obligations should be taken as an opportunity for Indonesia to improve the quality of its national legislation. Again, the example is provided of environmental instruments. Many international documents employ a variety of environmental instruments to realize policy goals. The implementation of these international conventions might therefore be an excellent opportunity for Indonesia to improve the quality of its environmental legislation. Silalahi also points to the importance of environmental legal principles, like the polluter-pays principle, the prevention principle, and the precautionary principle. The importance of

24 Faure (2001, pp. 263–86).

these principles is further discussed by Andri Wibisana in this volume. He explains their legal origins and shows that the general principles of environmental law give guidance to the national legislator when drafting environmental legislation.

Wibisana uses the economic approach to law to discover the precise meaning of the principles mentioned and to demonstrate the importance of a cost–benefit analysis for environmental policy-making and regulation. The polluter-pays principle is probably the oldest and best known of the environmental principles. When polluters are forced to pay the environmental costs resulting from their activities, the prices of their products and services will reflect the true social costs of these activities. However, Wibisana equally shows that the polluter-pays principle does not require polluters to reduce pollution to zero because from an economic perspective that would only be possible at very high costs.[25]

Closely related is the prevention principle, which basically means that pollution should be prevented at source and before it occurs. The difference with the precautionary principle lies in the fact that the prevention principle assumes that sufficient scientific evidence is available of both the possible negative environmental effects of a certain activity and the measures that could be taken to avoid the risk. The precautionary principle, on the other hand, comes into play when no scientific information is available, or when there is still much uncertainty about the potential risks. Again, Wibisana argues that in order to provide an adequate interpretation of the precautionary principle, economic analysis has to be used. If this is not the case, the danger would be that using the precautionary principle would stifle industrial innovation and thus lead to great socio-economic losses.

Clearly, the lessons of these chapters are of great importance, also in the context of other developing countries. Silalahi and Wibisana show that it is indeed useful to incorporate (international) principles of environmental law in legislation. These can guide policy-makers and legislators when setting environmental standards.[26] For example, the precautionary principle can, when correctly interpreted, assist policy-makers and administrative agencies when deciding on certain economic activities and the measures to control them, even if their possible polluting effects are still uncertain.

---

25 See more generally Ogus (1994) and Richardson et al. (1982).

26 See more generally Faure et al. (1994) and Vig and Kraft (1997).

4. CHOICE OF INSTRUMENTS

4.1. Command and Control

The traditional approach to control environmental pollution is the so-called command-and-control approach. Indeed, looking at the origins of environmental law in most countries, one sees that, already in the nineteenth century, the polluting effects of industries were being controlled through permits and licences. The licensees of specific activities were obliged to obtain a permit before an activity was started, and environmental control was exercised by means of imposing conditions in these permits. To a large extent, this approach, whereby the permit is the central instrument, still dominates in most environmental legal systems in both developed and developing countries, as Faure, Peeters and Wibisana show in their joint contribution to this volume and Takdir Rahmadi shows in his chapter on Indonesia. However, again as a result of economic analysis, over the years this approach has been criticized, as Faure et al. demonstrate. A major criticism is that an environmental policy based on permit conditions lacks the necessary flexibility: the industry is required to meet the licence conditions, but no further incentives are provided to invest in new production techniques to achieve a further reduction in pollution. This is precisely why economists refer to this traditional method as 'command and control': the government basically decides (and 'commands') the parameters with which industry must comply, and in case of non-compliance, public sanctions ('control') are applied. A traditional command and control system does not provide industry with adequate incentives to invest in profitable further reductions in environmental pollution. That is why, as Faure et al. show, there has been an increasing interest – first in the economic literature, but later also at the policy level – in the development of more flexible instruments.[27]

However, as their contribution also reveals, although the use of economic instruments undoubtedly has some benefits, there are also a number of shortcomings. The countries that have experimented with more flexible (usually referred to as 'economic') instruments have never fully relied on them. For example, the introduction of environmental taxes or an emission-trading system usually coincided with the traditional command and control approach. In this regard, various contributions in this volume pay attention to the question of how the functioning of the command-and-control approach can be improved. One obvious way to increase the quality of command and control consists, as already advanced by Peeters and Rahmadi, of the integration of

---

27 See Hahn (1990, pp. 21–47).

environmental permits (see above). Furthermore, the permit system will become more flexible if permit conditions can be easily adapted to new circumstances and technologies. Next to this, the application of general principles of environmental law (discussed by Wibisana), for example the prevention and polluter-pays principles, can compel polluters to introduce best-available technologies not entailing excessive costs, going beyond the standards required in a permit. Also the introduction of periodic reviews of environmental permits may be considered, with the possibility that the authorities adapt permit conditions to changes either in ecological circumstances (for example the fact that quality standards cannot be reached) or in available technologies (for example taking into account that as a result of new technologies, environmental standards can be changed). Thus, even a command-and-control system can be made more dynamic than is often the case today.

The traditional command-and-control system can also be reshaped in the sense that for certain activities environmental standards are not laid down in permit conditions. For certain categories of enterprises, *general rules* (for example, an executive order or decree) can be used that are to be complied with by a whole sector of industry. A major advantage of such general rules is a substantial reduction in administrative procedures. Peeters discusses the application and experience with general rules in the Netherlands, and Niessen analyses the possible advantages of such a system in the Indonesian context. General rules may indeed be suitable to overcome a few of the problems we mentioned above, in particular the capture problems – that is, the susceptibility of government agencies to lobbying enterprises – that result from decentralized standard setting. The capture of decentralized authorities is no longer an issue when all sectors of a particular industry are subject to one and the same set of general rules. An effective system of general rules, however, must meet various conditions. One is of course that the capture problem will not emerge when general rules are set. This means that an independent environmental protection agency is to set the general rules in the public interest, free from any influence or lobbying by interest groups. Furthermore, general rules can be a solution for categories of industry that are relatively simple, such as bakeries and butchers, and where location-specific circumstances are relevant. For major and complex industries (for example, a petrochemical plant), however, it will still be necessary to define specific environmental standards in a permit, at least to an important extent. General rules may still play a role, but will then have to be complemented by individualized conditions in a permit. Lastly, the enforcement of general rules requires special attention, in particular the susceptibility of enforcement agencies to corrupt practices should be avoided.

4.2. Economic Instruments

As several chapters have made clear, the traditional command-and-control approach has important restrictions, most importantly a lack of flexibility. An optimal environmental policy requires instruments which provide legal certainty next to considerable flexibility, as well as optimal incentives for technological innovation. Faure et al. discuss the economic literature where some of these instruments have been advanced. In particular, they discuss two examples of these so-called 'economic' instruments, namely environmental taxes and emission trading.

On paper the advantages of environmental taxes are that they provide important incentives for the industry to reduce pollution and, moreover, to invest in pollution-abatement technologies. However, Faure et al.'s contribution equally makes clear that there is relatively little actual experience with environmental taxes thus far.[28] One reason is that determining the marginal tax rate (necessary for the tax to function optimally) requires high information costs. Moreover, for the tax to function effectively, there should be control on emissions and enforcement, as is the case with the traditional command-and-control approach. In point of fact, enforcement costs will most probably be substantial. The principal reason why environmental taxes are still not very popular is that industry has strongly lobbied against it. For industry, an important advantage of the permit system is that permits serve as barriers to entry (for the system allows the industry to exclude competitors from the market). Taxes have the disadvantage that they raise costs for all firms in the market and do not function as barriers to entry.[29] Because of this, scholars pointing at the influence of interest groups on legislation have argued that industry will always strongly lobby against environmental taxes and in favour of regulation. This may well be the reason why, for example in the US, environmental taxes are hardly ever used. Considering that there will be lobbying problems in a developing country like Indonesia, too, one can envisage that the introduction of environmental taxes will meet with strong opposition.

Faure et al. showed that another economic instrument, emission trading, has quite some potential for environmental policy. This can be concluded from the modest experience with the CO_2 emission trading scheme, as introduced in Europe in 2004 to implement the Kyoto Protocol.[30] However, Faure et al. equally make clear that a market-oriented instrument such as emission trading still requires considerable regulatory intervention, for instance to control the

---

[28] In the words of Hahn (1989, pp. 95–114) and see Hahn and Hester (1989, pp. 109–53).

[29] This is the classic point made by Buchanan and Tullock (1975, pp. 139–47).

[30] See Peeters (2003b).

trade in emissions and to guarantee that more is not emitted than is allocated by means of emission rights. At the same time, they argue that in Indonesia some carefully guided experiments might be considered, in particular for non-local pollutants.

Overall, an important drawback of economic instruments is that they leave a large margin of discretion to the administrative authorities. Indeed, the larger the margin of discretion for the administrative authorities, the larger also is the scope for collusion and corruption. One should thus probably advise a developing country to choose an instrument that is less vulnerable to these practices. Therefore, on balance, command-and-control approaches are more appropriate provided that these are reasonably flexible and shaped in such a manner that collusive practices can be reduced as much as possible.

4.3. Instrument Mix

A lesson from the literature[31] is that there is no 'single' environmental instrument that can provide a miracle solution to all environmental problems. Since this is not the case for developed countries, naturally neither is it the case for developing countries. The starting point is the command-and-control approach, notwithstanding its shortcomings. Environmental permits, permit conditions and general rules, provided that they can be created in an open and transparent procedure, do warrant that standards are set in the public interest. Next to these 'traditional' control mechanisms there can be room for flexible 'new' instruments like environmental taxes. In those countries where environmental taxes have been introduced on a larger scale (as for example in the Netherlands) they have always been combined with environmental permits, and the same is true for emissions trading. There is certainly scope for some experiments with tradable permits even in developing countries, although this may be on a relatively limited scale. Probably one could start at a relatively simple level, for example with a market for manure rights, and only after successful experiments have been completed, could more complex emission rights markets (such as for example for CO_2 emissions) be set up.

Furthermore, environmental liability rules (briefly touched upon by Wibisana) can provide an additional deterrent, especially for those cases where regulation fails. Liability rules can also provide an important counterweight against lobbying by industry. Where regulatory standards are low or where the enforcement of regulatory standards is weak, the foresight that polluters can still be held liable for the damage caused could provide an additional incentive

---

[31] In particular, from the well-known book by Gunningham and Grabosky (1998, pp. 422–53).

for pollution abatement. However, it is well known that a liability rule functions only when there is a victim that has an incentive to bring a suit against the polluter. This may be a problem in the case of widespread and diffuse pollution. In those cases, liability rules could still be used if standing were granted to NGOs, who could use liability rules to ask for an injunction to stop the continuation of the pollution. The EMA 1997 provides formally for a strict liability rule in Article 35 for particular types of environmental harm and for the possibility of out-of-court settlements (Articles 31–3). However, a provision on compulsory insurance or an environmental guarantee fund is lacking. Moreover, due to corruption problems, it often proves difficult to make effective use of environmental liability rules as a remedy. Once again, for environmental liability to be an effective instrument, not only is legislative design important (for instance by including financial instruments as a guarantee against insolvency) but also effective enforcement by an independent judiciary.

Finally, instruments would have to be devised to guarantee that polluters can indeed pay for the pollution they have caused and that funds are available to pay for the clean-up of polluted sites.[32] Currently, there are many legal systems that have introduced compulsory insurance for environmental harm. This is for instance the case under the German Environmental Liability Act of 1990 and the Swedish Environmental Code of 1998.[33] Moreover, in many legal systems a duty to seek financial coverage is included as a condition in an environmental permit. The necessity to create an environmental guarantee fund is stressed in the contribution by Silalahi. Given potential insolvency problems, a condition may well be inserted into environmental permits that potential polluters show financial security, for example in the form of insurance. This may be particularly important for developing countries, but it may be very difficult to put into practice. In many developing countries, financial and insurance markets are still relatively underdeveloped, especially as far as providing coverage for environmental harm is concerned.

In sum, a mix of various instruments should be in place to guarantee both optimal prevention and compensation for environmental harm.

5. ENFORCEMENT

The difference between civil liability, as discussed above, and regulation is that civil liability is enforced through private enforcement, namely through a

32 See Faure (2003, pp. 180–93).

33 See Faure (2003, p. 189).

liability suit that will in principle be brought by the victim. Regulation, in particular, of the command-and-control type such as in the EMA 1997 of Indonesia, requires public enforcement and public sanctions. They can also be found in the EMA 1997 and are discussed in the contributions of Faure and Stroink.

5.1. Administrative Sanctions

The contribution by Stroink makes clear that in many cases it is not necessary to use the heavy instrument of the criminal law. Stroink discusses Dutch experience with administrative sanctions. Indeed, lately the Netherlands has experienced a shift from criminal enforcement to administrative enforcement of environmental law. An important reason for this is that the administrative authorities often have more expertise than the public prosecutor concerning environmental law. Moreover, administrative procedures are often faster and less costly than the criminal procedure. In the Netherlands, the administrative authorities can impose a penalty instead of a criminal prosecution. Stroink discusses this model and compares it with the EMA 1997. He also formulates various recommendations to adapt the EMA 1997. In this respect, he advises giving supervisory and enforcement powers on the basis of the principle of decentralization, meaning that supervision and enforcement should in principle be undertaken by the authority at the lowest possible scale. At the same time Stroink is aware of the fact that environmental problems may be so complex that local authorities lack sufficient knowledge of the technical and legal problems involved. Moreover, as we mentioned earlier, local authorities may suffer severely from the capturing risk. A solution to these problems may be to differentiate between types of environmental damage and scale of industry regarding the allocation of supervisory powers.

In addition Stroink formulates various suggestions to improve the quality of current administrative sanctions in the EMA 1997. In this respect he argues especially that – following the Dutch example – administrative authorities should be granted the right to impose coercive sums. These are considerable payments to be made by the offender each time he does not comply with environmental legislation (for example the conditions of his environmental permit).

5.2. Criminal Law

Faure provides a new model for the protection of the environment through criminal law and argues that an effective criminal law requires a combination of various provisions. On the one hand, there should be criminal liability for those who violate administrative provisions which merely focus on the endangerment of the environment in an abstract way, for example operating a plant without a licence (in that case there should not necessarily be a concrete environmental danger). On the other hand, there should be (more severe) criminal penalties where the environment is endangered in a concrete way, for example by an illegal emission into the environment. It is argued that provisions punishing this illegal emission are necessary, since merely punishing a violation of administrative law would provide too shallow a protection of the environment. Focusing on the emission has, so it is argued, moreover the advantage that the criminal prosecution can start as soon as an illegal emission takes place. It is therefore not necessary to prove a 'pollution', as the Indonesian EMA 1997 requires (Articles 41 and 42). A major disadvantage of this requirement is that the public prosecutor must prove a negative change in the receiving environmental medium, which is often impossible.

Finally, it is argued that for pollution with very serious consequences an independent crime should be introduced. This means that the criminal law intervenes even if the provisions of an administrative permit are followed. Thus the so-called administrative dependence of the criminal law would be pierced when pollution has very serious consequences, in particular, when an emission endangers human health.

It is shown in Faure's contribution that this new model for the protection of the environment through criminal law has already been incorporated into a convention of the Council of Europe.[34] Faure compares his model for the optimal protection of the environment through criminal law with the current provisions of the EMA 1997 in Indonesia. He shows that these provisions are ill-structured and contain too many onerous conditions to be effective in practice. Thus he suggests redrafting the provisions of the EMA 1997 on the basis of his model. Faure therefore presents an example of how the environmental criminal law of a country like Indonesia might be re-shaped in such a way that it provides better protection to the environment. Of course, this example can equally serve as a model for other countries in search of a new environmental criminal law.

5.3. Mix of Enforcement Instruments

Not only regarding environmental standard setting, but also concerning enforcement instruments, the optimal method appears to be a mix of instruments. Both Faure and Stroink argue that for relatively simple violations, for example non-compliance with permit conditions where no environmental

---

[34] Council of Europe Convention on the Protection of the Environment through Criminal Law, Strasbourg, 4 November 1998, published in Faure and Heine (2000, pp. 397–406).

harm has been caused, administrative sanctions suffice. Of course they should be imposed by an objective authority after supervision and inspection by qualified inspectors who are independent of the polluting firms they are supposed to control. Administrative sanctions should moreover be imposed as a result of a procedure which is fast and effective but at the same time allows the offender to advance his arguments of defence.

However, for more serious violations, more particularly illegal emissions resulting in serious pollution, an administrative sanction will certainly not suffice. For those cases, severe criminal sanctions imposed by an independent judge after a fair trial are needed. We therefore recommend a combination of administrative and criminal sanctions to construct an effective enforcement policy of environmental law.

6. IMPLEMENTATION CONSTRAINTS

6.1. Conflicting Interests

Environmental protection is of marginal concern in Indonesia today. The country is slowly recovering from a period of political turmoil, national bankruptcy and the tsunami disaster. This condition does not offer favourable prospects for the drafting of a solid new EMA. Lawmaking is a political process and there is a risk that good environmental intentions get crushed by economic and other interests. Some of these lawmaking loopholes, we argue, can be avoided by incremental reform of the EMA 1997. This entails two different, but related, approaches: (1) giving concrete meaning to vague framework provisions by means of secondary legislation, and (2) completing the EMA 1997 by means of successive amendments, tackling key issues first. In this manner, the environmental protection scheme will improve while the law is under construction. The Civil Code, the General Administrative Law Act and the EMA 1997 are typical examples of Dutch build-on laws.

Examples of conflicting interest are noted by many contributors to this volume when discussing the case of the EMA 1997 and the decentralization scheme of the RGA 1999. Niessen for instance shows that after the implementation of the RGA 1999 the National Environmental Impact Management Agency (BAPEDAL) was merged with the Ministry for the Environment. It was feared by many (and unfortunately confirmed in practice) that this would terminate BAPEDAL's control function precisely at a time when the enforcement of environmental policy needed to be more powerful. One can indeed often note that conflicts of interests – for example at the subnational level between various sectors, but also between different ministries – jeopardize the implementation of an environmental policy. In this respect, we need only recall the brief history of environmental legislation in Indonesia as mentioned in the Introduction to this book: the 'first' Environmental Management Act 1982 had barely been put into practice before its successor was promulgated in 1997. The provisions of both acts required substantial implementing regulations which were, *inter alia* as a result of conflicting interests, never promulgated. The current debate concerns, as we have mentioned, how to revise this EMA 1997. One can, however, fear that as long as the underlying conflicts of interests have not been resolved, the result will again be a mere 'paper document'. Indeed, the EMA 1997 is evidence of the fact that when serious conflicts of interest cannot be resolved at the policy level, the legal provisions are kept vague and ambiguous (for example, the provisions concerning criminal law), and demand considerable refinement by means of executive orders (for example, environmental standards and the allocation of concrete tasks to administrative authorities). It seems however naïve to hope that a conflict of interest that apparently could not be resolved at the legislative level will then be satisfactorily resolved through executive orders.[35]

6.2. Capacity Building

After legislative reform, serious efforts should be made to improve the capacities of the agencies entrusted with environmental management tasks. However, as Esman rightly asserts, quite often the management dimension is not attended to in the shaping of policies, or is merely attached as an afterthought.[36] Unfortunately such practices increase the risk that new legislation goes astray. Any legal drafter should take this to heart because when the announced reforms do not yield the intended results, new legislative programmes lose credibility in the eyes of the public at large. This is particularly relevant with regard to environmental legislation since the failures of environmental management cannot go unnoticed. National, regional and international environmental organizations are prepared to raise the alarm in case of environmental pollution and degradation. After all, the continued existence of life on earth is at stake.

It is therefore important that the introduction of new environmental legislation is well timed and accompanied by a series of measures to increase the management capacities of those agencies to which particular roles have been assigned under the new legislative scheme. As Veerman puts it, 'the most important aspect of the quality of a law in fact exists outside that law: the

[35] See further Asmeron et al. (1992); Esman (1991).
[36] Esman (1991, p. 22).

implementation of the law and the policy formulated therein'.[37] This means that the introduction of a new law goes together with the allocation of extra money to make the necessary institutional adjustments and to train personnel. In fact, all addressees of a new environmental law – government agencies, the private sector, and the general public – need to be informed about the consequences of that new law for their own behaviour. It is of great significance that practical experiences with the new environmental law are regularly evaluated. The outcomes of such assessments are to constitute the basis for further refinements of the legal scheme.

A lack of environmental information, legal as well as technical, seriously hampers the execution of environmental protection policies and law. To improve the dissemination of accurate and up-to-date environmental information, the Dutch government has launched the website 'Infomil: linking environmental policy and implementation' (www.infomil.nl), which on a two-weekly basis provides updates of environmental regulations, environmental technology, enforcement targets and strategies, court decisions, implementation guidelines and checklists, tips, and FAQs. This website is publicly accessible, but its target groups are the Dutch provinces, municipalities, and water boards. By means of Infomil there is a continuous flow of information from central government to the regional governments, and vice versa. It may be useful for Indonesia to invest in a similar project for capacity building of its subnational authorities that are charged with various important tasks in the field of environmental protection.

6.3. Corruption, Collusion, Nepotism

The corruption problem in Indonesia was widespread under the Suharto regime. Immediately after Suharto stepped down, the so-called KKN movement (Korupsi, Kolusi, Nepotisme) started and many reforms in the fight against corruption were announced. Public opinion was largely opposed to the corruption problems that existed during the New Order period. Today, more than seven years after Suharto stepped down, critics argue that the results of the so-called Reformasi are disappointing, in particular as far as the fight against corruption is concerned. The problems of KKN that the Reformasi movement was supposed to fight have unfortunately not been reduced. To some extent it is obvious that the problems the contributors to this book have discovered with the implementation and enforcement of environmental policy are due to corruption. Corruption is a serious problem not only in Indonesia and the issue is studied extensively in the literature. This book clearly could

---

37 Veerman (2004, p. 6).

not deal extensively with the complicated question of how to fight corruption and collusion in Indonesia. Still, many contributions have dealt with these issues by indicating that when a developing country like Indonesia suffers severely from corruptive practices, instruments should be devised that limit the possibilities of corruption. Indeed, various contributions to this book make concrete suggestions for instruments that are less vulnerable to collusion and corruption, and thus increase the likelihood of effective environmental management.

One such instrument is the introduction of general rules. General rules that apply without the need for local standard setting may thus reduce the likelihood that local authorities become captured by the regulated industry. It is furthermore argued that Indonesia should be very cautious about embracing flexible economic instruments on a large scale. On balance, for a country like Indonesia, the traditional more rigid command-and-control instruments – like general rules – are more suitable. This leads to an altogether relatively optimistic conclusion: even though corruption and collusion will undoubtedly affect the effectiveness of environmental policy, this should not lead to the pessimistic view that it is impossible to formulate an effective environmental policy. Instead, one should search for those instruments that are, in the context of the particular developing country, less vulnerable to corruption and collusion practices.

7. THE WAY FORWARD

The purpose of this book has been to examine to what extent developed countries' experiences with environmental policy instruments can assist in designing effective environmental legislation for a developing country. We used the case of Indonesia to illustrate some of these points, but we equally indicated that Indonesia is not an isolated case. Other developing countries struggle with similar questions and thus the results may be useful in those countries as well. In our opinion, experiences in developed countries do indeed entail some important consequences and lessons for the formulation of environmental legislation in developing countries, even though in various respects the contexts differ. This sometimes means that an instrument that works well in a developed country (like emission trading or environmental taxes) may still be too risky in the context of a concrete developing country.

This book has been an attempt to go further than the existing literature, which either deals with environmental policy instruments at an abstract level or with general problems of law and development. Taking the concrete context of Indonesia as an example, we have indicated how environmental legislation for a developing country can be made. Since this is only a first step, further academic research into various issues is necessary. For instance, many contributions have pointed at the relationship between the choice of (enforcement) instruments and decentralization issues. This is an issue that undoubtedly merits further research. The Indonesian case has shown some clear conflicts between the decentralization objective and the objectives of an effective environmental policy (which often requires more centralization).

An issue which equally requires more attention, also in combination with the decentralization issue, is how environmental policy instruments and enforcement mechanisms can be developed that are less vulnerable to collusion and corruption. Various contributions to this book have already made careful suggestions in that respect, but further research into this particular problem is surely needed. Indeed, scholars interested in environmental policy cannot merely stop with the finding that collusion and corruption render the implementation of an environmental policy difficult and at times even impossible. The next step should be to devise instruments that are less vulnerable to those practices and that should therefore be preferred within the context of a developing country.

Another issue requiring more attention concerns our general finding that widely used environmental policy and enforcement instruments may not be suitable in developing countries. In this book various examples have been presented of instruments that work well in the context of a developed country, but surely need adaptation in the context of a developing country. For example, it is not appropriate to impose compulsory environmental insurance on an industry in a country where environmental insurance markets have not yet been developed. Further research, therefore, should go into the question of whether alternative (financial) mechanisms can be developed to guarantee compensation for environmental harm, even in the absence of well-functioning insurance markets.

Therefore, as far as 'the way forward' is concerned, there is a challenging and interesting research agenda, probably also for combined research by environmental lawyers and scholars specializing in law and development studies. Far more difficult to predict is the future of the Indonesian Environmental Management Act. Although this book contains several pessimistic observations, the overall conclusion is modestly optimistic. The mere fact that the Ministry for the Environment of a developing country like Indonesia seeks cooperation with scholars in other countries is to be judged as positive. In this manner, a developing country can learn from foreign experiences and assess which experiences are useful within its own context. Whether and how the revision of the EMA 1997 will actually take place is difficult to predict. Besides, no less important than the question of how a new Environmental Management Act is to be formulated is the question of how it will work in practice. The way forward in environmental policy indeed requires not only a sound normative framework, but also effective implementation tools.

This book has provided some indications on how a normative framework for environmental management could be developed. The next step will be the development of an administrative structure guaranteeing the setting of standards, inspection, control and enforcement activities. If the next phases of academic partnership focus on these issues, there can be some modest grounds for optimism. However, the bottom line will probably be whether a developing country like Indonesia is serious about investing in environmental protection, for it unavoidably requires financial efforts from all social actors involved: industry, the government and the public at large. A broadly shared willingness to upgrade environmental protection, even in a period of economic decline, is a *conditio sine qua non* for any environmental policy and law to work effectively. If not, environmental policy and law will remain of marginal importance, no matter how beautifully they have been formulated.

REFERENCES

Asmeron, H.K., R. Hoppe and R.B. Jain (1992), *Bureaucracy and Developmental Policies in the Third World*, Amsterdam: VU University Press.

Bocken, H. and D. Ryckbost (eds) (1996), *Codification of Environmental Law. Draft Decree on Environmental Policy*, London: Kluwer Law International.

Buchanan, J.M. and G. Tullock (1975), 'Polluter's Profits and Political Response: Direct Control versus Taxes', American Economic Review, **65**, 139–47.

Cistulli, V. (2002), *Environment in Decentralized Development. Economic and Institutional Issues, Training Materials for Agricultural Planning*, Rome: FAO-UN, chapter 2.

Esman, M.J. (1991), *Management Dimensions of Development, Perspectives and Strategies*, West Hartford: Kunarian Press.

Faundez, J. (ed.) (1997), *Good Government and Law: Legal and Institutional Reform in Developing Countries*, London: Macmillan Press Ltd.

Faundez, J. (2000), 'Legal Reform in Developing and Transition Countries – Making Haste Slowly', paper presented at the Global Conference on Comprehensive Legal & Judicial Development, Washington, DC.

Faure, M. (1998), 'Harmonization of Environmental Law and Market Integration: Harmonizing for the Wrong Reasons?', European Environmental Law Review, 169–75.

Faure, M. (2000), 'Harmonisation, Codification and Integration of Environmental Law: A Search for Definition', European Environmental Law Review, 174–82.

Faure, M. (2001), 'Regulatory Competition versus Harmonization in EU Environmental Law', in D. Esty and D. Geradin (eds), *Regulatory Competition and Economic Integration*, Oxford: Oxford University Press, pp. 263–86.

Faure, M. (ed.) (2003), *Deterrence, Insurability and Compensation in Environmental Liability. Future Developments in the European Union*, Vienna: Springer.

Faure, M. and G. Heine (2000), *Environmental Criminal Law in the European Union, Documentation of the Main Provisions with Introductions*, Freiburg im Breisgau: Max Planck Institute for Foreign and International Criminal Law.

Faure, M. and J.G.J. Lefevere (1996), 'The Draft Directive on Integrated Pollution

Prevention and Control: An Economic Perspective', *European Environmental Law Review*, 112–22.

Faure, M., J. Vervaele and A. Weale (eds) (1994), *Environmental Standards in the European Union in an Interdisciplinary Framework*, Antwerp: Maklu.

Gunningham, N. and P. Grabosky (1998), *Smart Regulation. Designing Environmental Policy*, Oxford: Clarendon Press.

Hahn, R.W. (1989), 'Economic Prescriptions for Environmental Problems: How the Patient Followed the Doctor's Orders', *Journal of Economic Perspective*, **3**, 95–114.

Hahn, R.W. (1990), 'The Political Economy of Environmental Regulation: Towards a Unifying Framework', *Public Choice*, **65**, 21–47.

Hahn, R.W. and G.L. Hester (1989), 'Where Did All the Markets Go? An Analysis of EPA's Emission Trading Programme', Yale Journal on Regulation, **6**, 109–53.

Niessen, N. (2003), 'Indonesia's Environmental Management act of 1997: Comprehensive and Integrated?', in A. Bedner and N. Niessen (eds), *Towards Integrated Environmental Law in Indonesia?*, Leiden: (NWS Publications, pp. 66–79.

Oates, W.E. and R. Schwab (1988), 'Economic Competition among Jurisdictions: Efficiency Enhancing or Distortion Inducing?', *Journal of Public Economics,* **35**, 333–54.

Ogus, A. (1994), *Regulation. Legal Form and Economic Theory*, Oxford: Clarendon Press.

Peeters, M. (2003a), *Buitenlandse wetgeving als mogelijke inspiratie voor de verdere ontwikkeling van de wet milieubeheer*, report for the Evaluatiecommissie Wet Milieubeheer, Zwolle: Tjeenk Willink.

Peeters, M. (2003b), 'Emissions Trading as a New Dimension to European Environmental Law: The Political Agreement of the European Council on Greenhouse Gas Allowance Trading', *European Environmental Law Review*, **12** (3), 82–92.

Revesz, R. (1996), 'Federalism and Interstate Environmental Externalities', *University of Pennsylvania Law Review*, **144**, 2341–416.

Richardson, G., A. Ogus and P. Burrows (1982), *Policing Pollution: A Study of Regulation and Enforcement*, Oxford: Clarendon Press.

Seidman, A. and R.B. Seidman (1999), 'Using Reason and Experience to Draft Country-specific Laws', in A. Seidman, R.B. Seidman and T. Wälde, *Making Development Work: Legislative Reform for Institutional Transformation and Good Governance*, The Hague and London: Kluwer Law International, pp. 249–83.

Seidman, A., R.B. Seidman and T. Wälde (1999), *Making Development Work: Legislative Reform for Institutional Transformation and Good Governance*, The Hague and London: Kluwer Law International.

Veerman, G.J. (2004), 'A Conceptual Framework for the Quality of Legislation', Lecture for the delegation of the Indonesian Ministry of Environmental Affairs, 12 January 2004, Maastricht University.

Vig, N.J. and N.E. Kraft (eds) (1997), *Environmental Policy in the 1990s, Reform or Reaction*, third edition, Washington, DC: CQ Press.

Young, O.R. (2002), *The Institutional Dimensions of Environmental Change. Fit, Interplay, and Scale*, Cambridge, MA: MIT Press.

12. Appendix: Law Concerning Environmental Management Law No. 23 of 1997

WITH THE BLESSING OF ALMIGHTY GOD
PRESIDENT OF THE REPUBLIC OF INDONESIA

Considering:

a. that Indonesian environment as a gift and blessing of the Almighty God given to the Indonesian people and nation constitutes a space for life in all its aspects and dimensions in accordance with the Archipelagic Concept;

b. that in utilising natural resources to enhance public welfare as stipulated in the 1945 Constitution and to achieve happiness of life based on the Pancasila, it is necessary to implement environmentally sustainable development guided by an integrated and comprehensive national policy which takes into account the needs of present as well as future generations;
c. that there is a need to implement environmental management to preserve and develop environmental capacity in a harmonious, coordinated and balanced manner to support the implementation of environmentally sustainable development;
d. that the implementation of environmental management in the scheme of environmentally sustainable development should be based on legal norms taking into account the level of community awareness and global environmental developments as well as international law instruments related to the environment;
e. that the awareness and life of the community in relation to environmental management has developed to such an extent that the substance of Law No. 4 of 1982 regarding Principles of Environmental Management (State Gazette 1982 Number 3215) needs to be perfected to achieve environmentally sustainable development;
f. that in relation to the above points a, b, c, d, and e, it is necessary to enact a Law regarding Environmental Management.

Recalling:
Article 5(1), Article 20(1), and Article 33(3) of the 1945 Constitution.

WITH AGREEMENT THE HOUSE OF REPRESENTATIVES OF THE REPUBLIC OF INDONESIA DECIDES TO ENACT:

The Law Regarding Environmental Management

CHAPTER I GENERAL PROVISIONS

Article 1

In this Law what is meant by:

1. The **environment** is the spatial unity of all materials, forces, situations, and living creatures, including humans and their behavior, which influences the continuance of the life and welfare of humans and other living creatures;
2. **Environmental management** is an integrated effort to preserve environmental functions which covers planning policy, exploitation, development, maintenance, reparation, supervision and control of the environment;
3. **Environmentally sustainable development** is a conscious and planned effort, which integrates the environment, including resources, into the development

process to ensure capability, welfare, and quality of life of present and future generations;

4. An **ecosystem** is an ordering of an element of the environment which constitutes a whole and complete unit which interacts to produce environmental balance, stability, and productivity;
5. **Preservation of environmental functions** is a set of efforts to maintain the continued supportive and carrying capacities of the environment;
6. **Environmental supportive capacity** is the capacity of the environment to support humans and other living creatures;
7. **Preservation of environmental support capacity** is a set of efforts to protect environmental viability against pressures for change and/or negative impacts that arise because of an activity, so that it can continue to support the life of humans and other living creatures;
8. **Environmental carrying capacity** is the capability of the environment to absorb substances, energy, and/or other components that enter or are discharged into it;
9. **Preservation of environmental carrying capacity** is a set of efforts to protect the capability of the environment to absorb substances, energy, and/or other components which are discharged into it;
10. **Resources** are environmental elements that consist of human resources, natural resources, biological as well as non-biological, and artificial resources;
11. **Environmental quality standards** are the threshold limits or levels of living creatures, substances, energy, or components that exist or must exist and/or polluting elements the existence of which in a certain resource as an element of the environment is set at a certain level;
12. **Environmental pollution** is the entry or the entering into of living creatures, substances, energy, and/or other components into the environment by human activities with the result that its quality decreases to a certain level which causes the environment not to be able to function in accordance with its allocation;
13. **Standard environmental damage criteria** are threshold limits of physical and/or biological changes in the environment which can be measured;
14. **Environmental damage** is an action which gives rise to direct or indirect changes in the physical and/or biological characteristics of the environment which causes the environment to no longer be able to function to support sustainable development;
15. **Conservation of natural resources** is the management of non-renewable natural resources to ensure their prudent utilisation, and renewable resources to ensure their continued availability through maintaining and improving quality levels and diversity;
16. **Waste** is the residue of a business and/or activity;
17. **Hazardous and toxic material** is every matter which due to its nature or concentration, both directly and indirectly, can pollute and/or damage the environment, health, the continuation of human life and of other living creatures;
18. **Hazardous and toxic waste** is the residue of a business and/or activity that contains hazardous and/or toxic material which due to its nature and/or concentration and/or amount, directly as well as indirectly, can pollute and/or damage the environment, and/or endanger the environment, health, the continuation of human life and of other living creatures;
19. An e**nvironmental dispute** is a disagreement between two or more parties which arises as a result of the existence of or suspected existence of environmental pollution and/or damage;

20. **Environmental impact** is the influence for change on the environment which is caused by a business and/or an activity;
21. **Environmental impact analysis** is a study of large and significant impacts of a planned business and/or activity which is needed in the decision making process regarding business and/or activity implementation;
22. An **environmental organisation** is a group of persons formed of their own volition and desire in the midst of the community, with its objectives and activities in the environmental field;
23. An **environmental audit** is an evaluation process performed by those responsible for a business and/or activity to assess the level of compliance with applicable legal conditions and/or policy and standard set by the party responsible for the business and/or activity concerned;
24. A **person** is an individual person, and/or a group of people, and/or legal body;
25. **Minister** is the Minister who has been given the task of managing the environment.

Article 2

The scope of the Indonesian environment covers space, the location of the United Indonesian State with an Archipelagic Outlook in performing its sovereignty, sovereign rights, and jurisdiction.

CHAPTER II
BASIS, OBJECTIVE, AND TARGET

Article 3

Environmental management which is performed with a principle of national responsibility, a principle of sustainability, and a principle of exploitation, aims to create environmentally sustainable development in the framework of the holistic development of the Indonesian human and the development of an Indonesian community in its entirety which is faithful and devoted to God the Almighty.

Article 4

The targets of environmental management are:

a. achievement of harmony and balance between humans and the environment;
b. formation of the Indonesian person as an environmental being disposed toward and acting to protect and foster the environment;
c. guaranteeing the interests of present generations and future generations;

d. achievement of preservation of environmental functions;
e. prudent control of the exploitation of resources;
f. protection of the Unitary Indonesia Republic against impacts of business and/or activity outside the national region which causes environmental pollution and/or damage.

CHAPTER III
COMMUNITY RIGHTS, OBLIGATIONS AND ROLE

Article 5

1. Every person has the same right to an environment which is good and healthy.
2. Every person has the right to environmental information which is related to environmental management roles.
3. Every person has the right to play a role in the scheme of environmental management in accordance with applicable laws and regulations.

Article 6

1. Every person is obliged to preserve the continuity of environmental functions and protect and combat environmental pollution and damage.
2. Every person who carrying out a business or other activity must provide true and accurate information regarding environmental management.

Article 7

1. The community has the same and the broadest possible opportunity to play a role in environmental management.
2. Implementation of the stipulation in (1) above, is carried out by:

a. increasing independence, community empowerment, and partnership
b. giving growth to community capability and initiative;
c. increasing community responsiveness in carrying out social supervision;
d. providing suggestions;
e. conveying information and/or conveying reports.

CHAPTER IV
ENVIRONMENTAL MANAGEMENT AUTHORITY

Article 8

1. Natural resources are controlled by the state and are utilised for the greatest possible public welfare, and the arrangements thereof are determined by the Government.
2. To implement the stipulation provided for in (1) above the Government:

a. regulates and develops policy in the scheme of environmental management;
b. regulates the supply, allocation, use, [and] management of the environment, and the reuse of natural resources, including genetic resources;
c. regulates legal actions and legal relations between persons and/or other legal subjects as well as legal actions regarding natural resources and artificial resources, including genetic resources;
d. controls activities which have social impact;
e. develops a funding system for efforts to preserve environmental functions.

3. The stipulations provided for in (2) above are further regulated by Government Regulation.

Article 9

1. The Government determines national policies on environmental management and spatial management whilst always taking into account religious values, culture and traditions and the living norms of the community.
2. Environmental management is performed in an integrated manner by government institutions in accordance with their respective fields of tasks and responsibilities, the public, and other agents of development while taking into account the integratedness of planning and implementation of the environmental management policy.
3. Environmental management must be performed in an integrated manner with spatial management, protection of non-biological natural resources, protection of artificial resources, conservation of biological natural resources and their ecosystems, cultural preservation, bio-diversity and climate change.
4. The integratedness of planning and implementation of national environmental management policy, as provided for in (2) above, is coordinated by the Minister.

Article 10

In the scheme of environmental management the Government must:

a. form, give growth to, develop and increase awareness and responsibility of decision makers' environmental management;
b. form, give growth to, develop and increase awareness of community rights and responsibilities in environmental management;
c. form, give growth to, develop and increase partnership between the community, business and the Government in the effort to preserve environmental supportive capacity and carrying capacity;
d. develop and apply environmental management policy which ensures the maintaining of environmental supportive and carrying capacity;
e. develop and apply instruments of a pre-emptive, preventive and proactive nature in the effort to prevent decreases in environmental supportive and carrying capacity;
f. exploit and develop environmentally sound technology;
g. carry out research and development in the environmental field;
h. provide environmental information and disseminate it to the community;
i. give awards to meritorious people or foundations in the environmental field.

Article 11

1. Environmental management at the national level is implemented integratedly by an institutional instrument which is coordinated by the Minister.
2. Stipulations on task, function, authority, and organisational arrangement as well as institutional working procedures as provided for in (1) above are regulated further by Presidential Decision.

Article 12

1. To create integratedness and harmony in the implementation of national policy regarding environmental management, the Government based on legislation can:

a. delegate certain environmental management authority to local Central Government offices;
b. give a role to Local Government to assist the Central Government in the implementation of environmental management in the regions.

2. Further stipulations as provided for in (1) above are regulated by laws and regulations.

Article 13

1. In the scheme of the implementation of environmental management, the Government can transfer part of its affairs to Local Government to become part of its general affairs.
2. Transferring of affairs as provided for (1) above is determined by Government Regulation.

CHAPTER V
PRESERVATION OF ENVIRONMENTAL FUNCTIONS

Article 14

1. To guarantee the preservation of environmental functions, every business and/or activity is prohibited from breaching quality standards and standard criteria of environmental damage.
2. Stipulations on environmental quality standards, prevention of and coping with pollution and restoration of its carrying capacity are regulated by Government Regulation.
3. Stipulations on standard criteria of environmental damage, prevention and coping with damage along with restoration of its supportive capacity are regulated by Government Regulation.

Article 15

1. Every plan of a business and/or activity with the possibility that it can give rise to a large and important impact on the environment, must possess an environmental impact analysis.
2. Stipulations concerning business and/or activity plans that give rise to a large and important impact on the environment, as is meant in (1) above, and the method for arrangement and evaluation of environmental impact analysis are determined by Government Regulation.

Article 16

1. Every party responsible for a business and/or activity must carry out management of wastes produced by their business and/or activity.
2. The responsible party for a business and/or activity as provided for in (1) above can transfer such waste management to another party.
3. Stipulations on the implementation of this article are regulated further by Government Regulation.

Article 17

1. Every party responsible for a business and/or activity must carry out management of the hazardous and toxic materials.
2. Management of hazardous and toxic materials covers: producing, transporting, distributing, storing, using and/or disposing.
3. Stipulations concerning management of hazardous and toxic materials are regulated further by Government Regulation.

CHAPTER VI
ENVIRONMENTAL COMPLIANCE REQUIREMENTS

Part I
Licensing

Article 18

1. Every business and/or activity which gives rise to a large and important impact on the environment must possess an environmental impact analysis to obtain the license to conduct a business and/or activity.
2. The license to conduct a business and/or activity as provided for in (1) above is conferred by the official who has authority in accordance with laws and regulations.
3. In the license provided for in (1) above is included conditions and obligations to carry out environmental impact control efforts.

Article 19

1. In issuing a license to carry out a business and/or activity it is compulsory to take into account:

a. spatial management plans;
b. public opinion;
c. considerations and recommendations of authorised officials who are involved with such business and/or activity.

2. The license to conduct a business and/or activity decision must be made public.

Article 20

1. Without a licensing decision, every person is prohibited from disposing of waste to an environmental medium.
2. Every person is prohibited from disposing of waste which originates from outside Indonesian territory to an Indonesian environmental medium.
3. The authority to issue or refuse a licensing application as provided for in (1) above lies with the Minister.
4. Waste disposal to an environmental medium as provided for in (1) above may only be carried out at a disposal site which is determined by the Minister.
5. Implementing provisions for this Article are regulated further by government regulation.

Article 21

Every person is prohibited from importing hazardous and toxic wastes.

Part II
Supervision

Article 22

1. The Minister carries out supervision of the compliance with those responsible for a business and/or activity to stipulations which have already been applied in the laws and regulations in the environmental field.
2. To carry out the supervision provided for in (1) above, the Minister can appoint officials with authority to carry out supervision.
3. Where supervisory authority is transferred to Local Government, the Regional Head appoints officials authorised to carry out supervision.

Article 23

Environmental impact control as a supervisory instrument is carried out by an institution formed especially for that purpose by the Government.

Article 24

1. To implement its task, the supervisor provided for in *Article 22* has authority to conduct monitoring, request an explanation, make copies of documents and/or make notes which are needed, enter certain places, take samples, inspect equipment, inspect installations and/or transportation equipment, and request an explanation from the party responsible for a business and/or activity.
2. The party responsible for a business and/or activity which has been requested to provide an explanation as provided for in (1) above, must fulfill the request of the supervisor official in accordance with stipulations of applicable laws and regulations.
3. Each supervisor must show a letter of instruction and/or proof of identity and must be attentive to the situation and conditions prevailing at such place of supervision.

Part III
Administrative Sanctions

Article 25

1. The Governor/Head of the Level I Region has the authority to carry out

administrative sanctions against the party responsible for a business and/or activity to prevent and end occurrence of an infringement, and to deal with the consequences given rise to by an infringement, carry out safeguarding, mitigating and/or remedial measures at the expense of the party responsible for a business and/or activity, except where otherwise stipulated based on Law.
2. Authority as provided by (1) above, can be transferred to the District Head/Major/Head of the Level II Region by Level I Region Regulation.
3. A third party who has an interest has the right to submit an application to the authorised official to carry out an administrative sanction, as provided for in (1) and (2) above.
4. Administrative sanctions as provided for in (1) and (2) above, are preceded by an order from the authorised official.
5. Safeguarding, mitigating and/or remedial measures as provided for in (1) above can be replaced with the payment of a certain sum of money.

Article 26

1. The procedure for determining expenses as provided for in *Article 25(1) and (5)* above and their retribution is determined by laws and regulations.
2. Where laws and regulations as provided for in (1) above are not yet formed, its implementation uses legal efforts according to applicable laws and regulations.

Article 27

1. Sanctions in the form of revocation of business and/or activity licenses can be imposed upon certain infringements.
2. The Regional Head can submit a proposal for the revoking of a business and/or activity license to an authorised official.
3. A party which has an interest can submit an application to the authorised official to revoke a business and/or other activity license because their interests are adversely affected.

Part IV
Environmental Audits

Article 28

In the scheme of improving business and/or activity performance, the Government encourages the party responsible for a business and/or activity to conduct an environmental audit.

Article 29

1. The Minister has the authority to order the party responsible for a business and/or activity to conduct an environmental audit if the party concerned indicates their non-compliance with stipulations arranged in this law.
2. The party responsible for a business and/or activity which is ordered to conduct an environmental audit must execute the order as provided for in (1) above.
3. If the person responsible for a business and/or activity does not execute the order as provided for in (1) above, the Minister can execute or instruct a third party to execute an environmental audit as provided for in (1) above, at the expense of the party responsible for the business and/or activity concerned.
4. The total expense as provided for in (3) above is determined by the Minister.
5. The Minister publicises the results of an environmental audit provided for in (1).

CHAPTER VII
ENVIRONMENTAL DISPUTE SETTLEMENT

Part I
General

Article 30

1. Environmental dispute settlement can be reached through the court or out of court based on the voluntary choice of the parties in dispute.
2. Out of court dispute settlement as provided for in (1) above does not apply to criminal environmental actions as regulated in this law.
3. If an out of court dispute settlement has already been chosen, legal action through the court can only be undertaken if such effort is declared to have not succeeded by one or several of the parties in dispute.

Part II
Out of Court Environmental Dispute Settlement

Article 31

Out of court environmental dispute settlement is held to reach agreement on the form and size of compensation and/or on certain actions to ensure that negative impacts on the environment will not occur or be repeated.

Article 32

In out of court environmental dispute settlement as provided for in *Article 31* the services of the third party can be used, both which do not possess decision making authority and which possess decision making authority, to help resolve an environmental dispute.

Article 33

1. The Government and/or community can form environmental dispute settlement service providing agency which has a free and impartial disposition.
2. Stipulations on an environmental dispute settlement service provider are regulated further by Government Regulation.

Part III
Environmental Dispute Settlement Through the Court

Paragraph I Compensation

Article 34

1. Every action which infringes the law in the form of environmental pollution and/or damage which gives rise to adverse impacts on other people or the environment, obliges the party responsible for the business and/or activity to pay compensation and/or to carry out certain actions.
2. As well as the burden of carrying out certain participatory actions provided for in (1) above, the judge can determine compulsory monetary payment to be made for every day of lateness in completion of such certain actions.

Paragraph II Strict Liability

Article 35

1. The party responsible for a business and/or activity which gives rise to a large impact on the environment, which uses hazardous and toxic materials, and/or produces hazardous and toxic waste, is strictly liable for losses which are given rise to, with the obligation to pay compensation directly and immediately upon occurrence of environmental pollution and/or damage.
2. The party responsible for a business and/or activity can be released from the obligation to pay compensation provided for in (1) above if those concerned can prove that environmental pollution and/or damage was caused by one of the following reasons:

a. the existence of a natural disaster or war; or
b. the existence of a situation of coercion outside of human capabilities; or
c. the existence of actions of a third party which caused the occurrence of environmental pollution and/or damage.

3. Where losses occur which have been caused by a third party as provided for in (2)(c) above, the third party is responsible for paying compensation.

Paragraph III Time Limits for Bringing Legal Actions

Article 36

1. The limitation period for bringing legal actions to court follows the periods set out in the applicable Civil Procedures Law, and is calculated from the moment the victim knows of the existence of environmental pollution and/or damage.
2. Stipulations on the limitation period for bringing legal actions as provided for in (1) above do not apply to environmental pollution and/or damage which is caused by a business and/or activity which uses hazardous and toxic materials and/or produces hazardous and toxic waste.

Paragraph IV Right of the Community and Environmental Organisation to Bring Legal Actions

Article 37

1. The community has the right to bring a class action to court and/or report to law enforcers concerning various environmental problems which inflict losses on the life of the community.
2. If it is known that the community suffers as a result of environmental pollution and/or damage to such an extent that it influences the basic life of the community, the governmental agency which is responsible in the environmental field can act in the community's interest.
3. Further stipulations as to what is intended by (2) above are regulated by Government Regulation.

Article 38

1. In the scheme of implementing responsibility for environmental management consistent with a partnership principle, environmental organisations have the right to bring a legal action in the interest of environmental functions.
2. The right to bring a legal action as provided for in (1) above is limited to a

demand for a right to carry out particular measures without the presence of a demand for compensation, except for expenses or real outlays.
3. Environmental organisations have the right to bring a legal action as provided in (1) above if they meet the following conditions:

a. they have the form of a legal body or foundation;
b. in the articles of association of the environmental organisation it is stated clearly that the goal of the founding of the organisation concerned was in the interests of the preservation of environmental functions;
c. activities consistent with its articles of association have already been carried out.

Article 39

Procedures for the submission of legal actions in environmental problems by individuals, the community, and/or environmental organisations refers to the applicable Civil Procedures Law.

CHAPTER VIII
INVESTIGATION

Article 40

1. Next to the National Police Investigators of the Republic of Indonesia, also particular Civil Government Officials of the government agencies with functions and responsibilities in the field of environmental management, are endowed with special authority as investigators as provided for in the Law on Criminal Procedure.
2. Civil Investigator Officers as provided for in (1) above have the authority to:

a. carry out examination of the correctness of a report or explanation in relation to a criminal action in the environmental area;
b. carry out examination of people or legal bodies who are suspected of criminal actions in the environmental field;
c. request an explanation and evidence from individuals or legal bodies in relation to a criminal incident in the environmental field;
d. carry out examination of account-keeping, notes and other documents which are relevant to a criminal action in the environmental field;
e. carry out examination at certain places which are suspected of containing evidence, accounts, notes, and other documents along with carrying out confiscation of materials resulting from infringements which can be used as evidence in criminal cases in the environmental field;
f. request expert assistance in the scheme of the implementation of the function of investigation of criminal actions in the environmental field.

3. Civil Investigator Officers provided for in (1) above inform the Republic of Indonesia National Police Investigators of the commencement and the results of their investigation.
4. Civil Investigator Officers provided for in (1) above convey the findings of investigation to the Public Prosecutor through Republic of Indonesia National Police Investigators.
5. Investigation of environmental crimes in Indonesian waters and the Exclusive Economic Zone is carried out by investigators according to applicable laws and regulations.

CHAPTER IX
CRIMINAL PROVISIONS

Article 41

1. Any person who in contravention of the law intentionally carries out an action which results in environmental pollution and/or damage, is criminally liable to a maximum imprisonment of 10 (ten) years and a maximum fine of Rp.500,000,000 (five hundred million rupiah).
2. If a criminal action as provided for in (1) above causes the death or serious injury of a person, the person who carried out the criminal action is criminally liable to a maximum imprisonment of 15 (fifteen) years and a maximum fine of Rp.750,000,000 (seven hundred and fifty million rupiah).

Article 42

1. Any person who due to their negligence performs an action that causes environmental pollution and/or damage, is criminally liable to a maximum imprisonment of three years and a maximum fine of Rp.100,000,000 (one hundred million rupiah).
2. If a criminal action as provided for in (1) above causes the death or serious injury of a person, the person who carried out the criminal action is criminally liable to a maximum imprisonment of five years and a maximum fine of Rp.150,000,000 (one hundred and fifty million rupiah).

Article 43

1. Any person who in violation of applicable legislation, intentionally releases or disposes of substances, energy and/or other components which are toxic or hazardous onto or into land, into the atmosphere or the surface of water, imports, exports, trades in, transports, stores such materials, operates a

dangerous installation, whereas knowing or with good reason to suppose that the action concerned can give rise to environmental pollution and/or damage or endanger public health or the life of another person, is criminally liable to a maximum of six years imprisonment and a maximum fine of Rp.300,000,000 (three hundred million rupiah).
2. Criminally liable in the same way as provided for in (1) above, is any person who intentionally provides false information or destroys or conceals or damages information which is needed in its connection with an action as is meant in (1) above, whereas knowing or with good reason to suppose that the action concerned can give rise to environmental pollution and/or damage or endanger public health or other people's lives.
3. If the criminal action as provided for in (1) and (2) above causes the death or serious injury of a person, the person who carried out the criminal action is criminally liable to imprisonment for a maximum of nine years and a maximum fine of Rp.450,000,000 (four hundred and fifty thousand rupiah).

Article 44

1. Any person who in violation of applicable legislative provisions of the effective legislation, because of their carelessness performs an action as in *Article 43* is criminally liable to imprisonment for a maximum of three years and a maximum fine of Rp.100,000,000 (one hundred million rupiah).
2. If the criminal action provided for in (1) above causes the death or serious injury of a person, the person who carried out the criminal action is criminally liable to a maximum of five years and a maximum fine of Rp.150,000,000 (one hundred and fifty million rupiah).

Article 45

If a criminal action as is provided for in this Chapter is done by or in the name of a legal body, company, association, foundation, or other organisation, criminal liability to a fine is increased by a third.

Article 46

1. If a criminal action as is provided for in this Chapter is done by or in the name of a legal body, company, association, foundation or other organisation, criminal charges are made and criminal sanctions along with procedural measures as provided for in *Article 47* are imposed both against the legal body, company, association foundation or other organisation concerned and against those who give the order to carry out the criminal action concerned or who act as leaders in the carrying out of it and against the two of them.

2. If a criminal action as is provided for in this Chapter is done by or in the name of a legal body, company, association, foundation or other organisation, and is done by persons, both based on work relations and based on other relations, who act in the sphere of a legal body, company, association, foundation or other organisation, criminal charges are made and criminal sanctions imposed against those who give orders or act as leaders regardless whether the people concerned, both based on work relations and based on other relations, carry out the criminal action individually or with others.
3. If charges are made against a legal body, company, association, foundation or other organisation, the summons to face court and submission of the warrants is directed to the management at their place of residence, or at the fixed place of work of the management.
4. If charges are made against a legal body, company, association, foundation or other organisation, which at the time of the bringing of the legal action is represented by someone who is not a manager, the judge can make an order so that the management face the court in person.

Article 47

Apart from criminal stipulations provided for in the Criminal Code and this Law, against those who carry out an environmental crime can also be imposed procedural measures in the form of:

a. seizure of profits which were received through the criminal action; and/or
b. closure of all or part of a business; and/or
c. reparation of the consequences of a criminal action; and/or
d. requiring that what was without right neglected be carried out; and/or
e. destroying what was without right neglected; and/or
f. placing the business under administration for a maximum of three years.

Article 48

Criminal acts as provided for in this Chapter are crimes.

CHAPTER X
TRANSITIONAL PROVISIONS

Article 49

1. At the latest 5 (five) years from the promulgation of this Law every business and/or activity which already possesses a license, must have complied with the conditions based on this Law.

2. From the enactment of this Law it is prohibited to issue a license for a business and/or activity which uses imported hazardous and toxic waste.

CHAPTER XI
CLOSING PROVISIONS

Article 50

Upon enactment of this Law all existing laws and regulations which are involved with environmental management shall continue to apply to the extent that they do not conflict with and are not replaced based on this Law.

Article 51

With the coming into effect of this Law, Law No. 4 of 1982 regarding Main Principles of Environmental Management (State Gazette of 1982 Number 12, State Supplement Number 3215) is declared no longer to be in force.

Article 52

This Law comes into force on the date it is promulgated.
In order that every person knows of it, the promulgation of this Law is ordered with its placement in the State Gazette of the Republic of Indonesia.

Authorized in Jakarta on 19 September 1997
President of the Republic of Indonesia
(signed) Soeharto
Promulgated in Jakarta on 19 September 1997
Minister of State Secretary of State, Republic of Indonesia
(signed) Moerdiono

State Gazette of the Republic of Indonesia Year 1997 Number 68
Cabinet Secretariat Republic of Indonesia
Head of Bureau of Law and Legislation
(signed) Lambock V. Nahattands

Elucidation
Law Regarding Environmental Management
Law No. 23 of 1997

A. GENERAL

1. The Indonesian environment which was bestowed by the Almighty God upon the Indonesian community and people constitutes God's gift and blessing the capacity of which must be preserved and developed so that it continues to be a resource and life support for the community and people along with living creatures in Indonesia for the continuation and increase of the quality of that life itself.

Pancasila, as the basis and philosophy of the nation, constitutes a whole and complete unity which gives the conviction to the Indonesian community and people that contentedness will be attained if it is based on harmony and balance both in the relationship of humans with the Almighty God and humans with humans, humans with nature, and humans privately, in the scheme of achieving external progress and spiritual happiness. There are reciprocal relations between humans, the community and the environment, which must always be fostered and developed so that a dynamic harmony, proportion and balance is maintained.

The 1945 Constitution as the constitutional basis makes it mandatory that natural resources are used for the greatest possible prosperity of the community. This prosperity must be enjoyed sustainably by current and future generations.

Development is a conscious effort in processing and exploiting natural resources for increasing community prosperity, both for achieving external prosperity as well as spiritual satisfaction. Therefore, the use of natural resources must be harmonious and balanced with environmental functions.

2. The environment in ecological terms recognises neither national region nor administrative region borders. However, the environment which is involved with management must have clear regional demarcation for the management authority. The environment which is meant is the Indonesian environment.

Legally, the Indonesian environment covers the space in which the nation of the Republic of Indonesia carries out sovereignty and the right to sovereignty along with its jurisdiction. In this respect the Indonesian environment is none other than the region, which occupies a cross position between two continents and two oceans with a tropical climate and weather and seasons which confer natural conditions and a position with a highly valuable strategic role as the place the Indonesian community and people carry out community life, be a nation and be a state in all its aspects. In this way, the concept in carrying out Indonesian environmental management is the Archipelagic Concept.

3. The Indonesian environment as an ecosystem consists of various subsystems, which have social, cultural, economic and geographic aspects with differing features which cause a varying supportive and carrying capacity of the environment. Such a condition requires the building and developing of the environment based on the fact that the presence of supportive and carrying capacity of the environment increases harmony and balance of subsystems, which also means an increase in the endurance of the substance of that very subsystem. In this way, the building and development of one subsystem will influence other subsystems, which finally will influence the endurance ecosystems in their entirety. Therefore, environmental management demands the development of a system with integratedness as its primary feature. Needed, then, is a national environmental management policy which must be implemented in strict accordance with principles and consequences from the centre to the regions.

4. Development continuously exploits natural resources for increasing community prosperity and quality of life. Meanwhile, the supply of natural resources is limited and uneven, both in quantity and quality, while requests for such resources accelerate as a result of the increase in development activities to satisfy accelerating and increasingly diverse needs of the population. On the other hand, the environmental supportive capacity can be interfered with and the environmental carrying capacity can decline.

Accelerating development activities carry environmental pollution and damage risks with the result that the structure and function of the ecosystem which acts as a support to life can be damaged. This environmental pollution and damage will become a social burden, the cost of reparation of which will ultimately be borne by the community and the government.

The maintenance of the sustainability of environmental functions constitutes a community interest, so that it demands responsibility, openness, and a role for members of the community, which can be channelled by people individually, environmental organisations, such as non-government organisations, traditional community groups, and others, for maintaining and increasing environmental supportive and carrying capacity which becomes a mainstay of sustainable development. Development which incorporates the environment, including natural resources, is a medium for attaining sustainable development which is a guarantee of prosperity and quality of life of present and future generations. Therefore, Indonesian environment must be managed by a principle of preserving environmental functions which are harmonious and balanced for supporting environmentally sustainable development for the increase in prosperity and quality of life of present generations and future generations.

5. The long range direction of Indonesian development is toward economic development based on industrial development, which among other things uses various types of chemical materials and radioactive substances. As well as producing products which benefit the community, industrialisation also gives rise to excesses, among others the production of hazardous and toxic waste, which if disposed of to an environmental medium can threaten the environment, health, and the continuation of human and other forms of life.

Globally, knowledge and technology has increased the quality of human life. In reality, lifestyles of industrial society marked by the use of products based on chemicals have increased the production of hazardous and toxic wastes. This matter constitutes a large challenge to a method of disposal which has a small risk toward the environment, health, and the continuation of human and other forms of life.

Conscious of this matter, hazardous and toxic materials need to be well-managed. What needs to be given attention is that the area of the Unitary Republic of Indonesia must be free of disposal of hazardous and toxic wastes materials from outside the Indonesian area.

6. The acceleration of development efforts causes an accelerating impact on the environment. This situation boosts an increasing need for efforts to control environmental impacts, such that the risk to the environment is held down as much as possible.

Efforts to control environmental impacts are inseparable from supervisory measures to ensure compliance with stipulations of laws and regulations in the environmental field. A legal instrument of a preventive nature is a license to carry out a business and/or other activity. Therefore, a license must explicitly contain conditions and obligations which must be complied with and implemented by the party responsible for a business and/or other activity. What has been put forward above implies the participation of various agencies in environmental management such that there is a need to clarify the limits of authority for every agency which participates in the environmental management field.

7. Appropriate with the essence of the Unitary Republic of Indonesia as a legal state, the development of a system of environmental management as a part of environmentally sustainable development must be given a legal basis which is clear, explicit and comprehensive to ensure legal certainty for environmental management efforts. This legal basis is underlaid by a basis of environmental law and the compliance of every person to the norms of environmental law which is in its entirety based on Pancasila and the 1945 Constitution.

Law Number 4 of 1982 regarding Basic Principles of Environmental

Management (Number 12 of the State Gazette of 1982, Supplement to State Gazette Number 3215) was an early sign of the development of legal instruments as a basis of Indonesian environmental management efforts as an integral part of the effort of environmentally sustainable development. In the more than one decade since the promulgation of this Law, environmental awareness of the community has rapidly increased, as indicated among other things by the increasingly many types of community organisations other than non-government organisations which are active in the environmental field. Also evident is the increasing community initiative in preservation of environmental functions such that the community does not merely participate, but is also able substantially to play a role. Meanwhile, the set of problems of environmental law which have emerged and developed in the community require regulation in the form of law for the guarantee of legal certainty. On the other hand, global environmental development and international aspirations will increasingly influence Indonesian environmental management efforts. In reflecting this situation, it is regarded as necessary to perfect Law Number 4 of 1982 regarding Basic Principles of Environmental Management.

This Law contains the norms of environmental law. Apart from this, this Law will be a foundation for evaluating and adapting all laws and regulations which contain stipulations on the environment, that is laws and regulations regarding irrigation, mining and energy, forestry, biological and ecosystem resource conservation, industry, human settlement, spatial ordering, land use, and others.

Increase in the effectiveness of various legal stipulations, including administrative law, civil law and criminal law, and efforts to give effect to alternative methods of dispute settlement, namely out of court dispute settlement to achieve agreement amongst the parties in dispute [*sic*]. Apart from this, there is also a need to open the opportunity for the bringing of class actions. With such a method of settlement of environmental dispute settlement it is hoped that the compliance of the community to the system of values regarding the importance of preservation and development of environmental capacity in present and future human life will be increased.

As a support to administrative law, application of criminal law continues to attend to subsidiary principles, namely that criminal law should be used if sanctions in other fields of law, such as civil and administrative sanctions, and alternative environmental dispute settlement are not effective and/or the level of blameworthiness of the party concerned is relatively serious and/or the results of the activity are relatively large and/or the action gives rise to uneasiness in the community. In anticipation of the possibility of increasing emergence of criminal actions carried out by a corporation, this Law also regulates the responsibility of corporations.

In this way, all such laws and regulations mentioned above can be included in one system of Indonesian environmental law.

B. PARAGRAPH BY PARAGRAPH

Article 1

Number 1: Sufficiently clear
Number 2: Sufficiently clear
Number 3: Sufficiently clear
Number 4: Sufficiently clear
Number 5: Sufficiently clear
Number 6: Sufficiently clear
Number 7: Sufficiently clear
Number 8: Sufficiently clear
Number 9: Sufficiently clear
Number 10: Sufficiently clear
Number 11: Sufficiently clear
Number 12: Sufficiently clear
Number 13: Sufficiently clear
Number 14: Sufficiently clear
Number 15: Sufficiently clear
Number 16: Sufficiently clear
Number 17: Sufficiently clear
Number 18: Sufficiently clear
Number 19: Sufficiently clear
Number 20: Sufficiently clear
Number 21: Sufficiently clear
Number 22: Sufficiently clear
Number 23: Sufficiently clear
Number 24: Sufficiently clear
Number 25: Sufficiently clear

Article 2

Sufficiently clear

Article 3

Based on a principle of state responsibility, on the one hand, and state guarantees that the use of natural resources will provide the largest possible benefit for the prosperity and quality of life of the community, both present generations and future generations. On the other hand, the state prevents the carrying out of natural resource exploiting activities in its jurisdiction which gives rise to adverse impacts on the jurisdictions of other nations, and protects the state from the impacts of activities outside its area. The sustainability principle contains the meaning that every person bears an obligation and responsibility to coming generations, and to others in the same generation. For the implementation of such obligation and responsibility, environmental capability must, then, be preserved. The preservation of environmental capacity becomes a prop for the continuity of development.

Article 4

Sufficiently clear

Article 5

Subsection (1): Sufficiently clear

Subsection (2): The right to environmental information is a logical consequence of the right to play a role in environmental management based on the principle of openness. The right to environmental information will increase the value and effectiveness of participation in environmental management, as well as opening an opportunity for the community to actualise their right to a good and healthy environment.

Environmental information as provided for in this subsection can be in the form of data, explanation, or other information involved with environmental management which according to its nature and goal is such that it is indeed open to be known by the community, such as environmental impact analysis documents, reports and evaluations on results of environmental monitoring, both monitoring of compliance and monitoring of environmental quality changes, and spatial arrangement ordering plans.

Subsection (3): The role as provided for in this Article covers the role in the decision making process, both by lodging objections, and by hearings or other methods which may be stipulated in laws and regulations. Such role is carried out among other areas in the process of evaluation of environmental impact analyses or environmental policy formation. Its implementation is based on the principle of openness. With openness the possibility is allowed for that the community joins in thinking about and providing views and considerations in decision making in the environmental field.

Article 6

Subsection (1): The obligation of every person as provided for in this section is not free of their position as members of the community which reflects human value as individual and social beings. This obligation implies that every person joins in playing a role in efforts to maintain the environment. For example, participation in developing a culture of a clean environment, in explanation and in leadership in the environmental field.

Subsection (2): This information which is correct and accurate is intended for evaluating compliance of those responsible for a business and/or activity to stipulations of laws and regulations.

Article 7

Subsection (1): Sufficiently clear
Subsection (2):

Letter a: Community independence and empowerment is a pre-condition for the growth of community capacity as an agent in environmental management together with government and other agents of development.
Letter b: The increase in community capacity and initiative will increase the effectiveness of the community role in environmental management.
Letter c: The increase in community responsiveness will increasingly decrease the possibility of occurrence of negative impacts.
Letter d: Sufficiently clear
Letter e: By the increase of the quick perception will increase the speed of information transfer regarding environmental problem, so it can be tackled immediately.

Article 8

Subsection (1): Sufficiently clear
Subsection (2): Sufficiently clear

Letter a: Sufficiently clear
Letter b: Sufficiently clear
Letter c: Sufficiently clear
Letter d: The activity that has social impact is activity that gives effect to general interest, either culturally or structurally.
Letter e: Sufficiently clear

Subsection (3): Sufficiently clear

Article 9

Subsection (1): In the scheme of arrangement of national environmental management policy and spatial management ordering rational and proportional attention must be given to the potential, aspirations, and needs along with values which emerge and develop in the community. For example, attention toward living traditional communities the life of which is supported by natural resources located in the immediate area.
Subsection (2): Sufficiently clear

Subsection (3): Sufficiently clear
Subsection (4): Sufficiently clear

Article 10

Letter a: What is meant in this stipulation by decision makers is the authorised parties, namely the Government, the community and other agents of development.
Letter b: This activity is carried out through explanation, leadership, and education and training in the scheme of increasing the quality and quantity of human resources.
Letter c: Community participation in this Article covers participation, both in efforts and in the decision making process concerning preservation of environmental supportive and carrying capacity. In the scheme of a community role partnership between agents of environmental management is developed, namely between the government, business world, and community including among others non-government organisations and professional/academic associations.
Letter d: Sufficiently clear
Letter e: In this stipulation what is meant by pre-emptive instruments is action which is undertaken at the decision making and planning level, such as spatial management ordering and environmental impact analysis. Preventive action is at the level of implementation through compliance with waste quality standards and/or economic instruments. Proactive action is action at the level of production with application of environmental standards, such as ISO 14000.
Examples of pre-emptive, preventive and proactive environmental management instruments are the development and application of environmentally sound technology, and the application of environmental insurance and environmental audits which are carried out voluntarily by those responsible for a business and/or activity to increase effectiveness.
Letter f: Sufficiently clear
Letter g: Sufficiently clear
Letter h: Sufficiently clear
Letter i: Sufficiently clear

Article 11

Subsection (1): The scope of implementation of environmental management in principle covers various sectors which are the responsibility of various departments and government agencies. To avoid overlap of authority and clashed of interest there is a need for coordination, integration, synchronisation and simplification through institutional devices which are coordinated by the Minister.
Subsection (2): Sufficiently clear

Article 12

Subsection (1):

Letter a: The Unitary State of the Republic of Indonesia has a rich variety of potential biological and non-biological natural resources, characteristic cultural diversity, and aspiration which can become the primary capital in national development. For this, and in order to achieve integration and unity in patterns of thinking, and in actions taken which guarantee the formation of useful and effective environmental management which is based on the Archipelagic Concept, the Central Government can confer certain authority while paying attention to the regional situation and conditions in terms of both natural potential and regional capability, to central agencies located in the regions in the scheme of the implementation of the principle of deconcentration.

Letter b: The Central Government or the Level I Local Government can entrust the Level II Local Government with playing a role in the implementation of environmental management policy as a co-administration task. Through this co-administration, authority, funding, instruments, and responsibility remain with the government which has given such task.

Subsection (2): Sufficiently clear

Article 13

Subsection (1): While attending to the regional capability, situation and conditions, the Central Government can transfer matters in the environmental field to the regions to become part of the authority, task, and responsibility of Local Government based on a principle of decentralisation.
Subsection (2): Sufficiently clear

Article 14

Subsection (1): Sufficiently clear
Subsection (2): Sufficiently clear
Subsection (3): Sufficiently clear

Article 15

Subsection (1): Environmental impact analysis on the one hand is a part of a feasibility study for implementing a plan for a business and/or activity, and on the other hand is a condition which must be fulfilled to receive a license to carry out a business and/or an activity. Based on this analysis, important and large impacts on the environment can be known in more detail, both positive impacts and negative impacts, which arise from an business and/or activity such that steps can be prepared to cope with negative impacts and maximise positive impacts.

To measure or clarify such large and important impacts among others criteria are used concerning:

a. the number of people who will be affected by the impact of the business and/or activity plan;

b. the extent of the area affected;
c. the intensity and duration of the impact;
d. the amount of other environmental components which will be affected;
e. the cumulative nature of the impact;
f. reversibility or non-reversibility of the impact.

Subsection (2): Sufficiently clear

Article 16

Subsection (1): Waste treatment is a set of activities which covers storage, collection, transport, use, and processing of waste including the stockpiling of the results of such processing.
Subsection (2): Sufficiently clear
Subsection (3): Sufficiently clear

Article 17

Subsection (1): The obligation to conduct waste management intended is effort to reduce the occurrence of the possibility of risk to the environment in the form of the occurrence of environmental pollution and/or damage, recalling that hazardous and chemical materials have a fairly large potential to cause negative effects.
Subsection (2): Sufficiently clear
Subsection (3): Sufficiently clear

Article 18

Subsection (1): Examples of the license intended includes the mining license for business in the mining field, and the industry business license for business in the industrial field.
Subsection (2): Sufficiently clear
Subsection (3): The license to carry out a business and/or activity must assert the obligations associated with compliance to stipulations in the environmental management field which must be implemented by the party responsible for a business and/or activity in carrying out their business and/or activity. For a business and/or activity which is obliged to make or implement an environmental impact analysis, the environmental management plan and monitoring plan which must be implemented by the person responsible for the business and/or activity must be included and clearly formulated in the license to carry out the business and/or activity. For example the obligation to treat waste, waste quality conditions for disposal to an environmental medium, and obligations associated with waste disposal, such as the obligation to perform self-

monitoring and the obligation to report the results of such self-monitoring to the responsible agency in the field of environmental impact control. If a business and/or activity plan according to applicable laws and regulations is obligated to carry out environmental impact analysis, approval of this environmental impact analysis must be submitted together with the application for a license to carry out a business and/or activity.

Article 19

Subsection (1): Sufficiently clear
Subsection (2): Publication of the license to carry out a business and/or activity constitutes the realisation of the principle of administrative openness [or good governance]. This public release of the license to carry out a business and/or activity allows public participation, in particular for those who have not used the opportunities available in the objections procedure, hearing, and other aspects of the licensing decision making process.

Article 20

Subsection (1): Sufficiently clear
Subsection (2): Sufficiently clear
Subsection (3): Sufficiently clear
Subsection (4): A business and/or activity will produce waste. In general this must be treated before it is disposed of to an environmental medium such that it does not give rise to environmental pollution and/or damage. In certain cases, waste which is produced by one business and/or activity can be exploited as raw materials for a product. However this process of exploitation will produce waste, as a residue which cannot be reused, which will be disposed of to an environmental medium. Waste disposal as intended in this Article is disposal of waste which is the residue of a business and/or activity and/or other unused materials or which have expired to an environmental medium, including land, water or air. This disposal of waste and/or materials to an environmental medium will give rise to an impact on ecosystems. With the stipulations of this Article, then, it is provided that in principle disposal of waste to an environmental medium is prohibited, with the exception of certain environmental media which have been allocated by the Government.
Subsection (5): Sufficiently clear

Article 21

Sufficiently clear

Article 22

Subsection (1): Sufficiently clear
Subsection (2): In the case where an official who has authority from another government agency is appointed to carry out supervision, the Minister carries out coordination with the leadership of the agency concerned.
Subsection (3): This stipulation in this subsection constitutes the implementation of Article 13(1).

Article 23

Sufficiently clear

Article 24

Subsection (1): Sufficiently clear
Subsection (2): Sufficiently clear
Subsection (3): Being attentive to the situation and conditions at the place of supervision is intended to mean respecting prevailing values and norms both written and unwritten.

Article 25

Subsection (1): Sufficiently clear
Subsection (2): Sufficiently clear
Subsection (3): Sufficiently clear
Subsection (4): Sufficiently clear
Subsection (5): Sufficiently clear

Article 26

Subsection (1): Sufficiently clear
Subsection (2): Sufficiently clear

Article 27

Subsection (1): The seriousness of infringements of environmental regulations can vary, beginning from infringement of administrative conditions and ranging up to infringements that give rise to victims.
What is intended by certain infringements is infringement by a business and/or activity which is regarded as sufficiently serious that the business's activity be stopped, for example where people from the community have had their health impaired as a result of environmental pollution and/or damage.

Subsection (2): Sufficiently clear
Subsection (3): Sufficiently clear

Article 28

An environmental audit is an important instrument for the party responsible for a business and/or activity to increase their activity efficiency and performance in complying with environmental conditions which have been stipulated by laws and regulations. In this sense, an environmental audit is conducted voluntarily to verify compliance with applicable environmental laws and regulations, and with policy and standards which have been applied internally by party responsible for the business and/or activity concerned.

Article 29

Subsection (1): Sufficiently clear
Subsection (2): Sufficiently clear
Subsection (3): Sufficiently clear
Subsection (4): Sufficiently clear
Subsection (5): The results of the environmental audit as intended in this subsection constitutes a document which has the characteristic of being open to the public. It must be publicly available because it is an effort to protect the public.

Article 30

Subsection (1): The stipulation in this subsection is intended to protect the civil process rights of the parties in dispute.
Subsection (2): Sufficiently clear
Subsection (3): The stipulation in this subsection is intended to prevent occurrence of varying decisions in one environmental case, to ensure legal certainty.

Article 31

Settlement of environmental cases through out of court discussions is carried out voluntarily by the parties which have an interest, namely the parties which have experienced losses and have caused losses, government agencies with an involvement with the subject in dispute, and also allowing for involvement parties which have a concern for environmental management.
Certain actions here are intended as an effort to restore environmental functions while being attentive to values which live in the local community.

Article 32

To facilitate the course of out of court discussion, the parties which have an interest can request the services of a neutral third party which can be in the form of:

a. a neutral third party which does not have decision making authority. This neutral third party functions as a party which facilitates the parties which have an interest such that agreement can be reached.
   The neutral third party must:
   1. be agreed to by the parties in dispute;
   2. not have familial relations and/or work relations with one of the parties in dispute;
   3. possess skill to carry out discussion or mediation;
   4. not have an interest in the process of discussion or its outcome.
b. a neutral third party which has decision making authority functions as arbitrator, and all such arbitration decisions are of a fixed and binding nature on the parties in dispute.

Article 33

Subsection (1): This environmental dispute settlement service providing agency is meant as an agency which is able to facilitate the implementation of the dispute settlement choice mechanism based on principles of impartiality and professionalism.

The service providing agency which is formed by the Government is intended as a public service.

Subsection (2): Sufficiently clear

Article 34

Subsection (1): This subsection constitutes the realisation of the environmental law principle that the polluter pays. As well as being obligated to pay compensation, the environmental polluter and/or damager can be burdened by the judge with an order to take certain legal measures, for example orders to:

- install or repair a waste treatment facility such that the waste complies with environmental quality standards which have been applied;
- restore environmental functions;
- remove or destroy the cause of the arising of environmental pollution and/or damage.

Subsection (2): The inflicting of compulsory payments for each day of lateness of executing court orders to carry out certain actions for the preservation of environmental functions.

Article 35

Subsection (1): Strict liability means that the element of fault need not be proved by a person bringing an action as the basis for payment of compensation. The stipulation of this subsection is a *lex specialis* in legal actions regarding actions which infringe the law in general. The size of compensation which can be imposed upon a polluter or damager of the environment according to this Article is constrained within certain limits.
Subsection (2):

Letter a: Sufficiently clear
Letter b: Sufficiently clear
Letter c: Sufficiently clear

Subsection (3): What is meant by action of a third party in this subsection is an action of unfair competition or a Government fault.

Article 36

Subsection (1): Sufficiently clear
Subsection (2): Sufficiently clear

Article 37

Subsection (1): What is meant by the right to bring a class action in this subsection is the right of small groups of the community to act in representing the community in a large number which has had losses inflicted on it according to a basis of sameness of problems, legal facts, and demands which have been given rise to because of environmental pollution and/or damage.
Subsection (2): Sufficiently clear
Subsection (3): Sufficiently clear

Article 38

Subsection (1): Sufficiently clear
Subsection (2): Legal action taken by an environmental organisation cannot be in the form of a demand for compensation, but rather is limited to other legal action, namely:

a. application to the Court for a person to be ordered to undertake certain legal actions which are involved with the goal of preservation of environmental functions;
b. asserting that a person has carried out an action in infringement of the law because of their polluting or damaging the environment;

c. ordering a person which carries out business and/or activity to install or repair a waste treatment unit.

What is meant by expenses or real outlays are expenses of an environmental organisation which it can be proved have actually been outlaid.

Subsection (3): Not every environmental organisation can act in the name of the environment; rather they must fulfill certain conditions. With the existence of the conditions as provided for above, environmental organisations are selectively acknowledged to possess *ius standi* to bring a legal action in the name of the environment to court, both in general courts and in administrative courts, depending upon the competency of the court which is involved with investigating and trying the case in question.

Article 39 up to Article 52: Sufficiently clear

Supplement to State Gazette Republic of Indonesia Number 3699

Index